Distance education: new perspectives

The wonders of technology have brought to the world the benefits of education at a distance. But the best research and analaysis of distance education is notoriously difficult to track down. *Distance Education: New Perspectives* chronicles the final chapter to date of the major writing in this fast-moving field. Bringing together into one volume the best writings of the leading authorities in distance education from the late 1980s and the early 1990s, the book may be seen as a companion volume to the much-cited *Distance Education: International Perspectives* (Croom Helm 1983; Routledge 1986 second impression). A number of the best authorities from outside the English-speaking world are translated and appear in English for the first time.

Distance Education: New Perspectives offers a comprehensive survey of the entire field: from the theory behind this special mode of teaching and learning to international case studies of distance education in practice. The book considers the introduction of electronic communication technologies to distance education, including one- and two-way video virtual classrooms. The final section discusses for the first time in the literature the growing number of professional degrees and awards in the field of distance education from universities around the world.

Keith Harry is Director of the International Centre for Distance Learning at the Open University of the United Kingdom; **Magnus John** is on the staff of the Open University Library and the International Centre for Distance Learning; **Desmond Keegan** is Manager of the European Virtual Classroom for Vocational Training Project at the Audio Visual Centre, University College Dublin and the editor of the *Routledge Studies in Distance Education* series.

Routledge studies in distance education
Series editor: Desmond Keegan

Theoretical Principles of Distance Education
Edited by Desmond Keegan

Collaboration in Distance Education
Edited by Louise Moran and Ian Mugridge

Distance education: new perspectives

Edited by Keith Harry, Magnus John
and Desmond Keegan

First published 1993
by Routledge
11 New Fetter Lane, London EC4P 4EE

Simultaneously published in the USA and Canada
by Routledge
29 West 35th Street, New York, NY 10001

Reprinted 1999, 2001

Reprinted 2001
by RoutledgeFalmer
11 New Fetter Lane, London EC4P 4EE

RoutledgeFalmer is an imprint of the Taylor & Francis Group

© 1993 Keith Harry, Magnus John and Desmond Keegan

Typeset in Times by Michael Mepham, Frome, Somerset
Printed and bound in Great Britain by
TJI Digital, Padstow, Cornwall

British Library Cataloguing in Publication Data
A catalogue record for this book is available from the British Library.

Library of Congress Cataloging in Publication Data
Distance education: new perspectives / [edited by] Keith Harry, Magnus
   John, and Desmond Keegan.
     p.   cm.
Includes bibliographical references and index.
ISBN 0–415–08941–7
1. Distance education—United States. 2. Educational
technology—United States. I. Harry, Keith.
II. John, Magnus, 1937– . III. Keegan, Desmond.
LC5805.D57   1993
378'.03—dc20   93-10555
                                                              CIP

Contents

Figures

Tables

Contributors

Bruce O. Barker is Professor and Chair of the Department of Media and Educational Technology in the College of Education, Western Illinois University, United States of America. He has previously taught at Brigham Young University-Hawaii Campus and Texas Technical University, Lubbock, Texas.

Anthony Bates is Executive Director, Research and Strategic Planning, Open Learning Agency, Vancouver, BC, Canada. Prior to moving to the Open Learning Agency in 1990, he was Professor of Educational Media Research at the British Open University.

John Daniel was appointed Vice-Chancellor of the Open University in 1990 after a twenty-five year academic career in France and Canada. The Open University is now offering its courses in Hungary, Czechoslovakia and Russia.

Becky S. Duning is currently the manager for sponsored programmes in the College of Continuing Education at the University of Northern Colorado, and is co-author of a forthcoming book with M. J. van Kekerix and L. M. Zaborowski (1993) *Reaching Learners Through Telecommunications: Management and Leadership for Higher Education*, San Francisco: Jossey-Bass Publishers.

D. R. Garrison is Professor and Associate Dean in the Faculty of Continuing Education at the University of Calgary. Previously he served as Director of Distance Education at the University of Calgary. His research interests are in the areas of adult and distance education. More specifically, he is exploring the teaching–learning transaction in adult and higher education.

France Henri is an educational technologist working for Télé-université, a branch of l'Université du Québec, since 1981. She specialized in course design and in the use of educational media. She is involved in research projects, operating under internal as well as external fundings, to develop computer-mediated communication in distance education.

Börje Holmberg is Emeritus Professor of the FernUniversität in Hagen, Germany. After his doctorate at Lund University and thereafter appointments in adult education, in school and as a university lecturer, he became Educational Director and later Director General of Hermods in Sweden. After twenty years as a practitioner and writer on distance education, he held a chair in distance education methodology at the FernUniversität and was Director of its Institute for Distance Education Research from 1976 to 1990. His latest book is (1989) *Theory and Practice of Distance Education* London: Routledge.

Solomon Inquai was Dean of Extension at the University of Addis Ababa from 1967 to 1973. During that time, he was a founder committee member of both the East African (and later African) Adult Education Association in the late 1960s and of the African Association for Correspondence Education in the early 1970s. After a short spell as Education Attaché at the Ethiopian Embassy in Moscow, Dr Inquai became the Director of the Botswana Extension College from 1975 to 1979. Since then he has been a Director of the International Extension College, based in Cambridge, and involved both in its training and consultancy activities.

Janet Jenkins is currently the Director of Programmes at the Open Learning Foundation (formerly the Open Polytechnic). Prior to that, she was a senior programme officer at the Commonwealth of Learning, with special responsibility for training. She has worked in the field of distance education and open learning since 1966, much of the time with the National Extension College and then with the International Extension College.

Anthony Kaye is a Senior Lecturer in Educational Technology at the British Open University. His current interests lie mainly in the use of information technology and computer networking for promoting collaborative learning in the distance education environment.

Desmond Keegan was Head of Distance Training for the Government of South Australia's Open College from 1976 to 1984 and then Director General of the Italian Distance University Consortium. He is currently an educational consultant and editor on Routledge's *Studies in Distance Education* series.

Erling Ljoså became interim President of the European Distance Education Network (EDEN) in May 1991. Until his retirement from the post at the end of 1992, he spent twelve years as Managing Director of NKS Foundation, Norway, where he now serves as Senior Adviser.

The challenge of writing distance education materials that engage students in deep approaches to learning continues to arouse interest and excitement in **Percy Marland** who has recently taken up a position in the Faculty of Education at the University of Southern Queensland, one of the major distance education providers in Australia.

Ian Mitchell, Executive Editor of *Distance Education*, works from the University of Southern Queensland as a full-time distance education consultant to university clients. He draws on twenty years experience as an academic, administrator and international consultant.

Michael Moore is Associate Professor of Adult Education at The Pennsylvania State University and Director of The American Center for Study of Distance Education. He has specialized in the practice, study and teaching of distance education for adults for more than 25 years, including seven years in Africa, three in Canada and nine in Great Britain. He is the editor of *The American Journal of Distance Education* and has served on the editorial boards of similar journals in Great Britain, Canada and Australia.

Ross Paul is currently President of Laurentian University and was formerly Vice-President (Academic) and Acting President at Athabasca University. He is a regular contributor to writing in open learning and distance education, including the book (1990) *Open Learning and Open Management: Leadership and Integrity in Distance Education*, London: Kogan Page.

Hilary Perraton works in the Education Programme of the Commonwealth Secretariat. He previously worked for the National and International Extension Colleges and set up the Botswana Extension College for the Botswana Ministry of Education.

Otto Peters is Professor Emeritus at the FernUniversität in Hagen, Germany. He was born in 1926 in Berlin. He studied Education, Psychology and Philosophy at the Humboldt University and Free University in Berlin and later earned his doctorate at the University of Tübingen. He has been active in the field of distance education since 1965 and has worked at the Deutsches Institut für Fernstudium in Tübingen and at the FernUniversität in Hagen.

Professor G. Ram Reddy is currently Chairman, University Grants Commission, New Delhi, India. Earlier, he was Vice-President, Commonwealth of Learning, Canada. Professor Reddy is a pioneer in distance education in India. He is the founder Vice-Chancellor of two open universities in India – The Andhra Pradesh Open University (now Dr B.R. Ambedkar Open University) and Indira Gandhi National Open University. He has published a number of papers on education, in particular on distance education. Professor Reddy was also Vice-Chancellor of one of the largest universities in India – Osmania University – where he was previously Professor of Science.

Bernadette Robinson joined the International Extension College on a two-year secondment from the UK Open University in December 1992, having formerly worked in the Open University East Midlands regional office as a staff tutor in education. She has extensive international experience, most recently in Africa, Asia and Central America.

Greville Rumble has worked for the Open University since 1970, holding posts as head of the Planning Office 1973–8 and 1985–9, and Regional Director, East Anglia 1990–2. He has published widely on the management, planning, costs and economics of distance education.

Louise Sauvé has been Professor at Télé-université, Québec, Canada, since 1981. She writes distance education courses, particularly in the Graduate Degree Diploma in Distance Education programme. Her research deals with drop-out in distance education, games and simulations, educational design and media in distance education.

Barry Scott has a Ph.D in Nuclear Physics and has been involved in distance learning developments in universities, Distance Education Centres and IBM. He is currently a consultant in IBM UK's Multimedia Solution Centre.

Ronald Store is a senior librarian at James Cook University of North Queensland in Australia. For several years his career has spanned an involvement in distance education and library services. He has published extensively in the fields of distance education. He was formerly a member of the editorial board of *Distance Education* and established the Special Interest Group in Distance Education of the Australian Library and Information Association.

Professor Jim Taylor is Head of the Distance Education Centre at the University of Southern Queensland, Toowoomba, Australia. He is an instructional designer, with particular expertise in cognitive science and knowledge engineering. Professor Taylor has been involved with distance education for several years, and is a member of the International Council for Distance Education (ICDE) and the Australian and South Pacific External Studies Association (ASPESA).

Benedetto Vertecchi is Professor of Education, University of Rome 'La Sapienza', as well as Director of postgraduate distance education courses in 'Methods of School Evaluation', 'Foundations of Dialectics' and 'Educational Psychology'. He is also the editor of *IAD – Istruzione a distanza*.

Vicki Vivian has been a primary classroom teacher, curriculum consultant and university lecturer. She spent four years as Senior Deputy Principal of the New South Wales Department of Education's Correspondence School.

Zhao Yuhui is Dean of Studies at the Central Radio and Television University of China in Beijing, China.

Preface

In 1971, Ossian MacKenzie and Edward L. Christensen published *The Changing World of Correspondence Study: International Readings* through the Pennsylvania State University Press. It presented a comprehensive overview of education at a distance up to the end of the 1960s.

In 1983, David Sewart of the Open University, Börje Holmberg of the FernUniversität and Desmond Keegan, produced a volume which gave an overview of distance education in the 1970s and early 1980s: *Distance Education: International Perspectives*.

The book brought together the best writing on distance education of the period. It was planned to provide a touchstone for decisions on the theory and practice of distance education for scholars and administrators in the field. For educators in other fields it was to be used as an authoritative introduction to distance education. It gives an introduction to the serious study of distance education and acts as a reader for the first taught university-level award in distance education.

The Sewart, Holmberg, Keegan book successfully filled the role for which it was planned. It was extensively cited. Few major publications on distance education in the last decade do not list it amongst their list of references. Published by Croom Helm in 1983, it was reprinted by Routledge in 1988.

It is now a decade since the original date of publication of the final contribution to that book. Taught degrees in distance education, both face-to-face and at a distance, have emerged in the 1990s as a major feature of the study of distance education. An up-to-date collection of the best writing on the subject is now needed for professors, Ph.D researchers and all who are seeking professional qualifications in this field.

Researchers in other areas of education are showing much greater interest in distance education and its methods, as are corporate trainers and administrators of international agencies. *Distance Education: New Perspectives* has been designed to give them an authoritative picture of this field in the early to mid-1990s.

Those who work in distance education still find it hard to locate information of the best analysis and discussion on this form of education. Library collections are poor. Conference proceedings are difficult to obtain and there are no copies of even the major texts on distance education in some countries where English is widely spoken. For these readers we have tried to put together a balanced selection of the best writing of the decade, with the proviso that each piece should have something of value for the practitioner in addition to its quality as a contribution to the literature of the field.

The progress of the last decade is reflected in the structure of this new book and its differences from the 1983 volume. There are no longer sections on the concept of distance education, course development, student support services or economics. This indicates that the concept of distance education and its relationship to cognate but discrete fields like educational technology, open/flexible learning and adult education has been clarified. Excellent work in the late 1970s and early 1980s has made it possible for course development, economics and student support services to be represented by a single chapter.

New sections deal with distance education as an international phenomenon and as a field of teaching or study. The aim of *Distance Education: New Perspectives* is to give an international overview of the successes, the problems, the institutions and the structures that characterize the millions of students throughout the world who study at a distance in the 1990s.

The problems confronting the editors have changed little in the last decade. Much of the best writing is in journals that are held by few universities and public libraries: *Distance Education, Open Learning, Epistolodidaktika, The American Journal of Distance Education* and *The Journal of Distance Education*. Other important contributions are in conference papers or local publications which may not appear on computerized databases; neither are they available to the individual reader or researcher. Every effort has been made to reflect the international nature of distance education with chapters which were first drafted or published in German, French, Italian, and Chinese. A number of these have been translated specifically for inclusion in this volume and appear in English for the first time.

The work of compilation of this volume was greatly facilitated by the availability of the excellent resources of the International Centre for Distance Learning at the Open University in Milton Keynes, United Kingdom. This is the world's most extensive collection of books, articles, courses and documents on distance education in many languages, and the world-wide network built up by the Centre greatly helped in the identification and selection of the articles in this volume.

K. Harry, M. John, D. Keegan

Acknowledgements

Peters, Otto, 'Understanding distance education', text of an address to the International ZIFF Symposium at the FernUniversität, Hagen, on 28 September 1990, first published in this volume. An edited version of this address was published as 'Towards a better understanding of distance education: analysing designations and catchwords', pp. 48–57 of Holmberg, Börje & Ortner, Gerhard E., (eds), *Research into Distance Education/Fernlehre und Fernlehrforschung*, Frankfurt-am-Main; Bern; New York; Paris: Verlag Peter Lang GmbH, 1991. Reprinted by permission.

Moore, Michael G., 'Three types of interaction', *The American Journal of Distance Education*, 3, 2 (1989): 1–6. Reprinted by permission.

Henri, France and Kaye, Anthony, 'Problems of distance education/Enseignement à distance – apprentissage autonome?', pp. 117–26 of Henri, France & Kaye, Anthony, (eds), *Le Savoir à Domicile: Pédagogie et Problématique de la Formatione à Distance*, Québec: Presses de l'Université du Québec/Télé-université, 1985. Extract translated by Josephine Kaye. English translation first published in this volume. Published with permission.

Ljoså, Erling, 'Distance education in the society of the future: from partial understanding to conceptual frameworks', pp. 84–91 of Holmberg, Börje and Ortner, Gerhard E., (eds), *Research into Distance Education/Fernlehre und Fernlehrforschung*, Frankfurt-am-Main; Bern; New York; Paris; Verlag Peter Lang GmbH, 1991. Reprinted by permission

Barker, Bruce O., Frisbie, Anthony G. and Patrick, Kenneth R., 'Broadening the definition of distance education in light of the new telecommunications technologies', *The American Journal of Distance Education*, 3, 1 (1989): 20–9. Reprinted by permission.

Daniel, John S., 'A duty for distance education in the 1990s', *Higher Education in Europe*, XVI, 1 (1991): 38–45. Reprinted by permission.

Keegan, Desmond, 'A typology of distance teaching systems'. An edited version of the text originally published as pp. 116–39 of Keegan, Desmond,

Foundations of Distance Education, London: Croom Helm, 1986. Reprinted by permission.

Taylor, James C. *et al.*, 'Student persistence in distance education: a cross-cultural multi-institutional perspective', *Distance Education: An International Journal*, 7, 1 (March 1986): 68–91. Reprinted by permission.

Rumble, Greville, 'Economics of mass distance education', in *Prospects: Quarterly Review of Education*, XVIII, 1 (65) (1986): 91–102. Reprinted by permission.

Paul, Ross H., 'Open universities – the test of all models', pp. 40–54 of Paul, Ross H., *Open Learning and Open Management: Leadership and Integrity in Distance Education*, London: Kogan Page/New York: Nichols Publishing, 1990. Reprinted by permission.

Vertecchi, Benedetto, 'A two-level strategy for mastery learning in distance education'. This translation of *'Un doppio* mastery learning *per l'istruzione a distanza'*, in *l'Istruzione a Distanza*, 3, 2, 1–10 (1991) was authorised by Professor Vertecchi and is published in English for the first time. Published with permission.

Marland, P. W. and Store, R. E., 'Some instructional strategies for improved learning from distance teaching materials', in *Distance Education: an International Journal*, 3, 1 (1982): 72–106. Reprinted by permission.

Vivian, Vicki, 'Electronic mail in a children's distance course: trial and evaluation'. An edited version of the text originally published as in *Distance Education: an International Journal*, 7, 2 (1986): 237–60. Reprinted by permission.

Bates, Anthony, 'Technology for distance education: a ten-year prospective'. An edited version of the text originally published in *Open Learning*, 3, 3 (1988): 3–12. Reprinted by permission.

Robinson, Bernadette, 'Telephone teaching and audio-conferencing at the British Open University', pp. 105–10 of Bates, A. W. (ed.) (1990) *Media and Technology in European Distance Education. Proceedings of the EADTU Workshop on Media, Methods and Technology*, Heerlen: European Association of Distance Teaching Universities. Reprinted by permission.

Garrison, D. R., 'Multifunction microcomputer enhanced audio teleconferencing: moving into the third generation of distance education', in *International Journal of Innovative Higher Education: the Official Journal of the University Without Walls International Council*, 3, 1 (1986): 26–9. Reprinted by permission.

Duning, Becky, 'The coming of the new distance educators in the United States: the telecommunications generation takes off', an edited version of the text originally published in *Distance Education: an International Journal*, 11, 1 (1990): 24–49. Reprinted by permission.

Scott, Barry, 'IBM distance learning developments using videoconferencing', pp. 15–20 of Lefevre, S., Nagtegall, C. and Peper, G. (eds) (1991) *European Training Technology Event 1991: Emerging Applications*, Amsterdam: Novep. Reprinted by permission.

Reddy, G. Ram, 'Open universities: the new temples of learning', pp. 1–18 of Reddy, G. Ram (ed.) (1988) *Open Universities: the Ivory Towers Thrown Open*, London: Oriental University Press. Reprinted by permission.

Perraton, Hilary, *National Developments and International Cooperation in Distance Education in Commonwealth Africa*, paper prepared by the Commonwealth Secretariat for the UNESCO Distance Education Seminar held in Arusha, Tanzania, 24–8 September 1990, Paris: UNESCO. Reprinted by permission.

Zhao, Yuhui, 'China: its distance higher-education system'. An edited version of the text originally published in *Prospects: Quarterly Review of Education*, XVIII, 2 (66) 1988: 217–28. Reprinted by permission.

Inquai, Solomon, 'Refugees and distance education', in *Convergence*, XXIII, 3 1990: 37–46. Reprinted by permission.

Mitchell, Ian, 'Academic education of distance educators', is published in English for the first time. An Italian version was published as 'La formazione universitaria per gli operatori dell' istruzione a distanza: la struttura internazionale creata in Australia', in *Istruzione a Distanza*, 3, 2 1991: 47–54. Published with permission.

Sauvé, Louise, 'Media and distance education: Course description' is published in English for the first time. It is a translation of the course unit EDU6012, *Médias en formation à distance* of the Diplôme de deuxiéme cycle en formation à distance (Diploma in Distance Education) of the Téléuniversité, Québec, Canada. Published with permission.

Jenkins, Janet, 'Strategies for collaborative staff training in distance education', pp. 57–66 in The Commonwealth of Learning (1990) *Perspectives on Distance Education: Report on a Round Table on Training Distance Educators*, Vancouver: The Commonwealth of Learning. Reprinted by permission. The Commonwealth of Learning is an international organization established by Commonwealth Governments in September 1988, following the Heads of Government meeting held in Vancouver in 1987. Its headquarters are in Vancouver and it is the only Commonwealth inter-governmental organization located outside of Britain.

COL has a mandate to create and widen opportunities for learning, through Commonwealth cooperation, with a particular emphasis on utilizing the potential of distance education and the application of communication technologies to education. The overall aim of the organization is to help strengthen the capacities of Commonwealth member countries to develop the human resources required for their economic and social development.

The Chairman of the Board of Governors is the Rt Hon. Lord Briggs of

Lewes and COL's President and Chief Executive Officer is Professor James A. Maraj.

Holmberg, Börje, 'Key issues in distance education: an academic viewpoint', in *European Journal of Education*, 24, 1 1989: 11–23. Reprinted by permission.

Our sincere thanks are also due to the following staff members, past and present, of the International Centre for Distance Learning, who have contributed in a variety of ways to the production of this volume: Brenda Barr, Stephanie Butters, Jonathan Cook, Barbara Humphreys, Nazira Ismail and Laury Melton. We are also indebted to Sabine Phillips, who has dealt patiently and efficiently with all the demands arising from our editing of the text, and to Josephine Kaye, who translated the piece written by France Henri and Anthony Kaye.

General introduction

Since the dawn of the Industrial Revolution in the nineteenth century, advances in technology have provided people with the means for a new form of education, known today as distance education. In recent decades the wondrous array of electronic communications technology has given distance education new status. It seems to have something to offer almost everyone. It is now a normal form of education for those in employment, for homemakers and for those who choose not to go to schools or universities for the purpose of learning.

In response to this interest, institutions of distance education attempt to provide for their students a complete education system from enrolment to examination that is equal in quality, in quantity and in status to that offered to ordinary students in schools, colleges and universities around the world. In the 1990s more than ten million students, most of them adults, study at a distance – many with notable success. Glamorous new technologies ranging from desktop publishing to satellites and hypermedia point the way to an exciting future.

The success and popularity of distance education presents the educational theorist, whether he or she works in conventional or distance education, with a series of problems. Two of these are considered in this introduction. The first is the location of the students. Conventional students attend the schools, colleges and universities of the world. Distance students do not. They stay at home or study at work as in the Chinese system. By claiming that the same quality of education can be achieved at home, distance educators could be seen to challenge the ethos of two of society's most venerable institutions: the school and the university.

The second concern is with the communication between teacher and student, student and student, and student and teacher. Distance education replaces, either totally or substantially, the face-to-face communication and interaction of ordinary education with its own media-based forms of communication. The breaking up of the interpersonal communication process of education challenges a structure which had been considered a cultural imperative for educating in most cultures for hundreds of years.

These thoretical issues have been particularly acute in the award of university degrees at a distance. Distance training, on the other hand, has generally been regarded as posing fewer theoretical problems, particularly at the lower levels of training. But university degrees which are won fully or partially at a distance still receive a reluctant welcome in certain countries in the 1990s. The idea of the university of scholars coming together in the pursuit of knowledge as enunciated by John Henry Newman in the middle of the nineteenth century and reiterated by Karl Jaspers a century later, has raised barriers to bachelors, masters and doctorate degrees at a distance.

Distance education theorists have been slow to provide grounded theoretical positions to justify these challenges. When distance education emerged in the 1990s as a field of teaching for university credit, it was generally conceded that the theoretical underpinnings of the field were far from solid. One was faced with the unsettling prospect of students studying for masters degrees and doctorates in a field of study in which the work of the theorist was flawed.

The present volume covers the period from mid-1982 to mid-1992 during which the importance of grounding distance education theory within general education theory was frequently advocated. Ljoså's view that distance education should be conceived as part of education but continue to be both a distinct and meaningful term and a particular field of study and practice provides a balanced position in this debate.

During the decade under review a constant theme has been the effort of grappling with a kaleidoscope of constantly changing telecommunications possibilities. Barker and his colleagues provide a useful introduction to the impact of these technologies on the perception of the field in their attempt to differentiate between correspondence-based and telecommunications-based distance education (see Chapter 5).

Researchers whose work is included in later sections of this volume have made major contributions too to distance education theory in the period under review. In particular, the insistence upon and the analysis of the concept of interdependence by Garrison (Chapter 16) has been especially fruitful. Garrison sees this interdependence as a bringing together of the teacher and the student through the process of communication in distance education and the effect that the message has on both the partners in the communication relationship.

The work of Vertecchi (Chapter 11) in Italy has shown how distance education research can impact on general theory. Vertecchi sees the world of distance education as a privileged forum for educational research because it is so much easier to isolate the research variables. His addressing of the age-old and ever-present problem of streaming in a classroom or a lecture group because of the differing abilities of students studying the same material has been instructive. His work indicates that the problem of streaming can be solved in distance education by establishing a student database of sufficient complexity that, when this is merged with a file containing the course, an individualized text for each student's requirements is printed.

The most incisive contribution to the development of distance education in the decade under review may prove to be the emergence of taught university degrees in the field as reported by Mitchell (Chapter 23). This represents a coming of age for the field of study. It may lead to the abandonment of over-ambitious claims for this form of education which, on examination, may prove to be only hopes which do not correspond to the concrete realities of the types of courses on offer from the institutions. This should lead to a needed maturity with the faults and failings of distance education, as well as its successes and glamour, revealed.

Part I
Theory of distance education

Introduction

Distance education theory, like the theory of any other field of educational study, has as its focus what is characteristic of the field. This is what Sparkes in 1983 called the general acceptance in the academic community of the emergence of a new set of problems. The new set of problems with which distance education theory deals focus on the concept of distance. As distance education is a field within the discipline 'education', it is educational distance that is in question here: distance from the schools, colleges, universities and other educational institutions around the world.

Distance education theorists can, and do, discuss what exactly are the characteristics of distance education, but the criterion of distance from schools and universities is clear: conventional students attend the schools, colleges and universities of the world; distance education students do not. They study at home, or at work as in the Chinese system; they choose not to go to school.

Working from UNESCO statistics for the period covered by this book, Dieuzeide showed that there were six hundred million students in the world, of whom ten million study at a distance. Dieuzeide's global figures, however, give a skewed picture. One would not want to underestimate the importance for the distance education theorist of the children who study at a distance (mainly in France, Canada, Australia and New Zealand), but it is necessary to underline that Dieuzeide's ten million distance students are nearly all adults; most of his six hundred million are children.

Thus distance education theory deals with a statistically important and little-studied grouping of students worldwide, reaching towards 10 per cent of adult enrolments in some countries.

The situation of the students at home (or at work) of necessity separates them from their teachers, and this creates problems for the theorist. These problems may seem to be insurmountable for those who insist that face-to-face interpersonal communication in the learning group at a school is a cultural imperative for education in both east and west, and has been so for at least 2,000 years. For those who try to set out grounded theory for distance education, the task has proved difficult, as the fragile underpinnings of this form of education so far provided testify all too clearly.

Theorists were slow to tackle the challenge presented by the new form of education created by industrial technology. For over one hundred years there was little theoretical development. One of the main reasons for this was that up to the 1970s much of the world of distance education was proprietary. The major development of the 1970s was the foundation of the open universities and the sudden swing from proprietary to government provision. Universities which differed so radically from the traditions that started at Salerno, Bologna, Paris and Oxford nearly one thousand years ago clearly needed a thorough theoretical explanation. In the 1990s the widespread offering of university degrees at a distance makes the provision of theory more urgent.

In the 1990s, also, there has been a rapid development of distance training. Working from American data in the early 1990s Devlin (1993) has claimed that distance training is now a preferred option for many multinational and transnational corporations (see also chapter 17). If training at a distance is, in fact, to become a preferred option then the onus on providing a proper scientific grounding for such a provision is increased.

Another dramatic new feature of the early 1990s is the provision of funding for research and development of distance and flexible education by government agencies. Van den Brande (1993) provides a detailed analysis of the funding by one agency: the European Commission structures in Brussels for advanced technological investigations.

The present volume covers the period mid-1982 to mid-1992. Peters, the founding Vice-Chancellor (*Rektor*) of the German FernUniversität who has written extensively on distance education since 1965, discusses various ways of understanding distance education, including 'a form of study for people at work' and the form of education in which eye contact between teacher and student is lacking. His chapter subjects to scrutiny managerial and analytical formulations about this form of education which have characterized the decade.

Moore, from the American Centre for Study of Distance Education, investigates the concepts of distance, of interaction and what happens in education when there is no class. Also from North America came one of the most important books on the theory of distance education of the decade, *Le savoir à domicile*. Published only in French, the book has had less attention than it merited. The extract translated here gives the views of the two editors, Henri from the Télé-université in French Canada and Kaye of the Open University in England, on what is essential to this form of education.

Ljoså, first President of the European Distance Education Network with a background in Scandinavian thinking, sees distance education as a service

industry. Barker and his colleagues from the United States anticipate the
influence of an electronic future on theoretical positions.

REFERENCES

Devlin, T. (1993) 'Distance Training' in D. Keegan (ed) *Theoretical Principles of Distance Education*, London: Routledge, 254–68.

Dieuzeide, H. (1985) 'Les enjeux politiques', in F. Henri and A. Kaye (eds) *Le savoir à domicile*, Québec: Presses de l'Université du Québec and Télé-université.

Peters, O. (1967) *Das Fernstudium an Universitäten und Hochschulen: Didaktische Struktur und Vergleichende Interpretation. Ein Beitrag zur Theorie der Fernlehre*, Weinheim: Beltz.

Sewart, D., Keegan, D. and Holmberg, B. (eds) (1983) *Distance Education: International Perspectives*, London: Croom Helm.

Sparkes, J. (1983) 'The problem of creating a discipline of distance education', *Distance Education* 4 (2), 197–205.

Van den Brande, L. (1993) *Flexible and Distance Learning*, Chichester: Wiley.

1 Understanding distance education

Otto Peters

INTRODUCTION

Due to the unusual origin of distance education, the peculiarity of its methods, and its rapid unprecedented growth during the last twenty years, the question of its basic character and true nature has been dealt with several times. It may also well be that practitioners and scholars like to ponder on this phenomenon. The result is quite a number of theoretical explanations (Moore 1973, Wedemeyer 1977, Sewart 1978, Bååth 1980, Holmberg and Schümer 1980).

I do not want to deal with these explanations of the nature of distance education, nor do I wish to present a new theory of it, although it would certainly be appropriate and necessary to redefine its possible functions in the post-modern society. This, however, must remain a desideratum for the time being. Rather, I should like to conduct an experiment.

'COMMON-SENSE KNOWLEDGE' AND 'LAY THEORIES'

In the 1980s, we have learnt or have been reminded again that the behaviours of people are, as a rule, not governed by elaborate theories but just by assumptions and notions which grow out of experience. They form our view of the world and influence our actions. As such, they are especially important for the analysis of our behaviour. These assumptions and notions are part of our 'common-sense knowledge'. As they implicitly contain special views, ways of thinking and even conceptual elements, social psychologists call them 'subjective' or 'lay' theories (Furnham 1988). Lay theories can become influential when they are adopted by other people and assume the functions of stereotypes or clichés. They can be analysed but, of course, not to the same degree as objective or scientific theories. They are implicit rather than explicit. They are incoherent and inconsistent, and can, consequently, contradict themselves. But in spite of this, some researchers (Gröben *et al.* 1988) see analogies and parallels between lay and scientific theories. They are important for us as we generally are not influenced by the facts in our world of everyday life but basically by our assumptions of and subjective theories about these facts.

With regard to the theme of this chapter, I should like to analyse subjective theories about distance education. In order to do this, I shall examine a number of designations of distance education which have been used widely. I assume that someone who 'invents' a name for distance education must have a certain concept and understanding of its nature. This holds true also for many people who accept and use this name.

Furthermore, I should like to refer to some stereotypes which have been derived from theories of distance education. As a rule, these theories are often reduced to a few words or phrases or catchwords in everyday practice. They start a career of their own – independently from their original theories. Here I am not interested in the original objective theories, but rather in the lay theories which have been developed by people who are using those stereotypes. My hypothesis is that there might be a lot of sound thinking in those lay theories in spite of their not being explicit and consistent. I hope that if we summarize various outcomes of these lay theories we learn something more about what really matters when dealing with distance education. We might recognize a way of understanding which is really shared by the people concerned with this particular form of education.

DESIGNATIONS

We are aware of quite a number of different designations of 'distance education' in various languages. There are also different designations for the same phenomenon in one language, especially in American English. Dealing with them we have to accept the premise that different designations mean different ways of looking at distance education and of attaching importance to different elements of this form of education. Let us try to describe them.

Fernunterricht (Instruction at a distance)

The German word *Fernunterricht* characterizes the phenomenon by pointing at a striking difference from face-to-face education: the apartness of teacher and learner. It stresses the physical distance between them which does not allow direct interaction.

A number of associations are still attached to this word, most of them originating in the nineteenth century or the first half of the twentieth century. These associations include the use and misuse of the term in connection with profit-led organizations, and the opportunity it offers to ambitious and gifted but underprivileged people who are denied the possibility of obtaining an education through the usual channels. Strangely enough, if these people engage themselves in instruction at a distance they are quite often still looked at with a mixture of admiration and condescension.

Fernstudium (Learning at a distance in higher education)

The distinctive term *fern* (trs. 'distance') proved to be so successful that it was also applied in higher education when it became possible to study at a university without attending classes. Further, it was also translated into English and is now internationally recognized.

The notions evoked by this term are partly similar to those of *Fernunterricht*. Here we think of individuals, discontent with their socio-economic status who try to change it in the face of many difficulties. Many people are impressed by these individuals who try to elevate themselves in the social strata or just between the more and less educated. However, again they are looked at with mixed feelings – with admiration, envy, suspicion and disdain. Not all people, especially workers, find it really appropriate to take advantage of this new form of education.

As most institutions of distance study are state institutions, this term is not tainted by associations with profit-making organizations.

Correspondence study

Those who decided to use this term were undoubtedly impressed by a new communication medium in the middle of the last century: the letter (or postcard) in connection with the railway system, which guaranteed quick and reliable delivery. Here the concept of the teacher and the learner who send letters, instead of talking to each other, was in the foreground. The term was so successful that it was adopted in the Romance languages and also in Chinese, in which *han shou* means 'teaching by letters'. It dominated the conception of the new form of tuition for nearly a century.

The most important association attached to this designation is the teacher who instructs by writing and the student who learns by reading. Thus, it popularized a new teaching and learning behaviour.

Open learning

This term when being used to designate distance education emphasizes the 'openness' of the teaching-learning process as compared to the 'closeness' of learning in traditional schools. It stresses that access to this kind of learning is easier ('open access') and that the students are allowed to operate with a degree of autonomy and self-direction. This does not refer only to decisions with regard to the place, time, duration and circumstances of their learning but in some cases also with regard to the curriculum, as the students are free to select from pre-planned curricula or to develop curricula of their own.

Home study

This term suggests that the teaching and learning does not take place in the class or lecture room but at home. It generates pleasant feelings connected to one's home: privacy, familiarity, cosiness – as opposed to the often unpleasant experiences at schools or colleges: publicity, the necessity to deal with many (unknown or not well-known) persons, the uncomfortableness of rooms, impersonality.

Angeleitetes Selbststudium (Guided self-study)

Here, 'self-study' is qualified by 'guided'. Clearly, this term is to minimize the difference between distance education and teaching and learning at a university by referring to a highly valued element of advanced higher education. As it is the tacit goal of higher education to produce scholars who work independently and mainly by themselves, self-study has a tradition and is in no way questionable. Much of post-graduate work is done in this way with only occasional guidance by a professor. Seen in this way it is not so alien, so frighteningly different from academic tradition.

Zaochny

This is the Russian word for 'distance' in distance education. It is remarkable as it means – etymologically speaking – 'without eye contact'. This implies that the decisive criterion according to which distance education can be distinguished from conventional teaching and learning is the lack of eye contact. Distance education does not take place 'eyeball to eyeball' as Wedemeyer (1971: 135) once called it. As the eye is the organ of man's innermost feelings, this aspect of apartness is surely significant. We become aware that a whole emotional dimension of the interaction of the teacher and learner is lacking in distance education. The new form of teaching and learning is defined and characterized by pointing to a severe deficiency, as in a court when the judgement is announced without the accused being present.

Study without leaving production

This designation is, indeed, telling. Obviously it was invented by bureaucrats of a state-planning institution. For them, the most important feature of distance study is the possibility that students can study without discontinuing their work. It shows how much work in production is valued and how much the products of the working force are needed. It is easy to see that this designation was coined in a socialist country: the [former] USSR. From there it was taken over by other socialist countries. There is no other designation for distance study which points to its economic advantage so bluntly. On the other hand one should not overlook the fact that it has strong ideological overtones which are important with regard to the general goal of education. This form of study appeared as an ideal solution to the problem of how practice and theory – the world of work and of theoretical investigation – can be combined and united. Small wonder that 'study without leaving production' was considered to be the main and regular form of higher education in the USSR for some years.

CATCHPHRASES

Guided didactic conversation

Obviously, this phrase suggests that there is a communication between the teacher and the learner going on in distance education and that it is the most important structural element of it. The choice of the word 'conversation' reminds us that dialogue, as the basic traditional form of all teaching, applies also to distance education. The phrase suggests strongly that distance education is not simple self-study as it is organized according to the traditional pattern of teaching and learning. This phrase emphasizes the similarities between traditional face-to-face teaching and distance education rather than the differences. Implicitly, it means that without 'guided didactic conversation', distance education ceases to be distance education.

Two-way communication in distance education

Two-way communication became the catchphrase in distance education in the 1980s, as Keegan (1983: 83) once remarked. The people who used it again and again wanted to stress this particular attribute of distance education in order to demonstrate that again distance education is not just self-study, that the separation of student and teacher does not mean that communication between them is cut off altogether, that there are many tricks of the trade to establish and maintain two-way communication. Clearly, this phrase has been coined and is understood as an opposite to the 'one-way communication' of television. Perhaps this is the reason for its tremendous impact.

The first motive of those who invented this phrase and possibly also of those who use it frequently is the desire to defend distance education. They want to criticize the opinion that in distance education the student is left alone with his or her learning material, which, as we all know, is quite often the case. They want to drive home the idea that distance education is much more similar to face-to-face education than, for instance, televised instruction.

The second motive behind the propagation of this phrase is the desire to show and mark the way in which much of the current distance education practice should and could be improved considerably.

'Continuity of concern' in distance education

This is another phrase often used. It stresses a feature of distance education which is considered to be of vital importance and which by no means should be neglected. Those who advocate this phrase are opposed to the idea that learning packages could be really self-instructive and that the students should just work for themselves. Therefore, they consider face-to-face tutorials as constituent elements of distance education – being the bridge between the teaching material and the individual learner or a group of learners. Accordingly, they are strongly in favour of study centres. Again we can say: if this element is missing, distance education is no longer distance education. And again we can note that those who are in favour of this phrase are strongly convinced that it is necessary and possible to improve distance education.

Independent study

Here, the liberation of the student from the fetters of school or college routine is emphasized. According to this notion of distance education, it is the student who determines the when, where and how of his or her learning. This phrase suggests that the student assumes more responsibility for his or her own learning than is possible in face-to-face situations. Studying in this way, the student is no longer forced to follow the lead of a teacher and is no longer subjected to the conformity pressure of the learning or peer group.

The success of this term can only be explained by referring to strong educational and political reform movement. In this respect, it has an ideological bias.

Industrialized form of instruction

This characterization of distance study is being referred to quite often. Implicitly, it underlines the fact that distance study must be carefully pre-planned, prepared and organized, and that there is a division of labour, a growing use of technical equipment to work with, and the necessity of formalized evaluations. People become aware that these and other features of distance study are structurally the same as those that can be found in an industrialized production process. Explicitly, these ideas are expressed by using the image of a teacher in the classroom working like a craftsman, as opposed to a teacher being a part of a complicated teaching-learning system organized like an industrialized process. The catchphrase 'industrialized form of instruction' helps to recognize structural elements which are typical for distance study.

LAY THEORIES AS THEORIES OF LEGITIMATION

If we add up the designations referred to we get a composite picture of the content of the term 'distance education'. This picture must be necessarily illuminative. For whereas the catchphrases quoted tried to explain distance education by referring to one – considered to be the most characteristic or important – element, this composite picture will refer to seven of these elements. According to them, distance education is a special form of education in which:

- teachers and students work apart from each other – 'at a distance';
- teachers and students do not communicate 'eyeball to eyeball' with each other;
- letters (and other printed material) are exchanged with the help of the mailing system;
- the learning usually takes place in the homes of the students;
- the teaching-learning process assumes the form of self-study, however guided by the teacher;
- the teaching-learning process allows a degree of openness with regard to access, goals and methods;
- the student does not cease to work for a living as it is a study alongside work.

Evaluating this list of descriptive aspects we can see easily that distance education is not a common, but still an extraordinary way of teaching and learning. One of its characteristic features is that because of the apartness of teacher and learner certain emotional dimensions and overtones of instructional interaction are cut off. Hence it is depersonalized to a certain degree. Clearly, this is a deficiency.

On the other hand, the second characteristic feature is clearly an advantage: the student can study alongside work. This opens up the world of learning also to adults and the underprivileged who otherwise are denied the opportunity to learn and to get or continue their education.

Finally, it should be noted that there still is some ambiguity attached to the term. It generates feelings of appreciation and depreciation at the same time. It is depreciated because it is considered to be merely a substitute for 'real' and that means face-to-face teaching, a surrogate, an emergency measure in situations in which no traditional way of learning is possible.

Let us also summarize the catchphrases. Each of them was coined to characterize distance education by emphazising its most important aspect. The first four of them have something in common: the intention of improving distance education. They do not depict it as it is, but rather as it should be. They are prescriptive. Accordingly, distance education is to be developed after the pattern of a 'guided didactic conversation', must necessarily be based on 'two-way communication', must be 'continuously concerned' about the learner's progress, and emancipate the learner from traditional restrictions of time, place and persons by developing a truly 'independent study' which is open enough to allow for a 'degree of autonomy and self-direction'.

The fifth catchphrase ('industrialized form of instruction') is basically descriptive. It characterizes distance education as a form of study which, because of its typical features, is the product of a particular period in the development of our culture: industrialization. It is useful for discerning and understanding particular features in which it does differ from face-to-face education.

Finally, I should like to mention another aspect of this summary. Normally, we are not aware of our 'common-sense' knowledge and of our subjective theories. It is only in critical situations that they are considered and reflected upon consciously. The number of different designations for 'distance education', the long debate about changing the designation 'correspondence education' into 'distance education' and the various attempts and efforts to improve distance education by defining it in reformatory terms show clearly that distance education has always been in a critical situation. For a long time, it was not recognized and not appreciated at all in other areas of education. Hence, some of the subjective theories referred to in this chapter usually have a strong apologetical trend. They mirror the efforts to gain status. Therefore, most of them can be called theories of legitimation.

Has the experiment been worthwhile? I should like to respond to this question by mentioning the following three points.

1 One can be impressed by the many aspects of distance education inherent in the lay theories referred to. Certainly, they can be useful in qualifying and differentiating the lay theories of our own – which are very likely to be also derived from one aspect only.

2 We can see that the composite picture of distance education is not very progressive in outlook – e.g. modern technological communications

media including television and computer are missing. Maybe common-sense knowledge is necessarily rather conservative by nature.

3 Nevertheless, the comprehensive overview of common-sense knowledge about distance education shows that it seems to be advisable to take note of it. Before developing objective theories about distance education, one should have examined the respective lay theories.

REFERENCES

Bååth, J. A. (1980) 'Postal two way communication in correspondence education', *Epistolodidaktika* 1–2: 11–41.

Furnham, A. (1988) *Lay Theories: Everyday Understanding of Problems in the Social Sciences*, Oxford: Pergamon.

Gröben, N., Wahl, D., Schlee, J. and Scheele, B. (1988) *Das Forschungsprogramm Subjektive Theorien: eine Einführung in die Psychologie des reflexiven Subjekts*, Tübingen: Francke.

Holmberg, B. and Schümer, R. (1980) *Methoden des gelenkten didaktischen Gesprächs*, Hagen: FernUniversität, ZIFF.

Keegan, D. (1983) *Six Distance Education Theorists*, Hagen: FernUniversität, ZIFF.

Moore, M. G. (1973) 'Toward a theory of independent learning and teaching', *Journal of Higher Education*, 44: 661–79.

Sewart, D. (1978) *Continuity of Concern for Students in a System of Learning at a Distance*, Hagen: FernUniversität, ZIFF (ZIFF Papiere, 22).

Wedemeyer, C. (1971) 'With whom will you dance? The new educational technology', in O. Mackenzie and E. L. Christensen (eds) *The Changing World of Correspondence Study*, University Park: The Pennsylvania State University Press, 133–40.

Wedemeyer, C. (1977) 'Independent study', in A. S. Knowles (ed.) *The International Encyclopedia of Higher Education*, Boston: CIHED, 548–57.

2 Three types of interaction

Michael G. Moore

Many of the greatest problems of communicating about concepts, and, therefore, practice in distance education, arise from our use of crude hypothetical constructs-terms like 'distance', 'independence', and 'interaction', which are used in very imprecise and general ways, each having acquired a multiplicity of meanings. Most seriously, the same terms are commonly used at both generic and more specific levels. For example, the generic concept 'independence' is frequently confused with its species, independence of learners from instructors in space and time and independence of learners to control their means of study. These are further confused with the many subspecies of each type of independence. The same could be said of the concept and term 'distance' itself, which is commonly used in the most general sense to describe education characterized by separation between learner and instructor, but by too few users in the more technical and specific meanings as discussed, for example, by Moore (1984), Saba (1988), Keegan (1988), or Shale (1988). 'Interaction' is another important term that carries so many meanings as to be almost useless unless specific submeanings can be defined and generally agreed upon.

Progress in this direction was made in a panel discussion convened by the Divisions of Independent Study and Educational Telecommunications of the National University Continuing Education Association at its annual meeting in Salt Lake City on 16 April 1989. Chaired by Shirley Davis of Purdue University, the panel was titled: 'Interaction: that perplexing component of distance education'. The panel, Arnold Seigal, Ellen Wagner, Nofflet Williams and myself, debated such questions as: What level of interaction is essential for effective learning? What is good interaction? How can we achieve it? What does real-time interaction contribute? Is it worth the cost?

For my contribution I suggested that, as a minimum, distance educators need to agree on the distinctions between three types of interaction, which I labelled learner-content interaction, learner-instructor interaction, and learner-learner interaction. To distinguish among these three types will have benefits conceptually, but will also do much to overcome the misunderstandings between educators who use different media. (For example, see the debate between Pittman (1987) and Duning (1987)).

LEARNER-CONTENT INTERACTION

The first type of interaction is interaction between the learner and the content or subject of study. This is a defining characteristic of education. Without it there cannot be education, since it is the process of intellectually interacting with content that results in changes in the learner's understanding, the learner's perspective, or the cognitive structures of the learner's mind. It is this type of interaction that I believe is at least partly involved in what Holmberg (1986) calls the 'internal didactic conversation' when learners 'talk to themselves' about the information and ideas they encounter in a text, television programme, lecture, or elsewhere.

The oldest form of distance teaching that aimed to facilitate interaction with content was the didactic text. In medieval times, nearly all texts were aimed at instructing, not merely informing, and certainly not at entertaining. In the nineteenth century, the use of print for teaching was advanced by the invention of home study guides that accompanied a text, providing explanations of it and directions for its study. In more recent times, learners have interacted with content broadcast on radio and television programmes, and with electronic recordings on audiotape, videotape, and computer software. Interactive videodisc is the most advanced form of didactic interaction invented so far.

Some learning programmes are solely content-interactive in nature. They are one-way communications with a subject expert (sometimes assisted by an instructional designer), intended to help distant learners in their study of the subject. No other professional teaching expertise is provided, and learning is largely self-directed. According to the findings of adult education research, the majority of the adult population who undertake further education do so through self-directed study (Tough 1971, Penland 1977, and Hiemstra 1982).

LEARNER-INSTRUCTOR INTERACTION

The second type of interaction – regarded as essential by many educators, and as highly desirable by many learners – is interaction between the learner and the expert who prepared the subject material, or some other expert acting as instructor. In this interaction, distance instructors attempt to achieve aims held in common with all other educators. First, having planned or been given a curriculum, a programme of content to be taught, they seek to stimulate or at least maintain the student's interest in what is to be taught, to motivate the student to learn, to enhance and maintain the learner's interest, including self-direction and self-motivation.

Then instructors make presentations – or cause them to be made. These may be presentations of information, demonstrations of skill, or modelling of certain attitudes and values. Next, instructors try to organize students' application of what is being learned, either the practice of skills that have been demonstrated, or manipulation of information and ideas that have been presented. Instructors organize evaluation to ascertain if learners are making progress, and to help decide whether to change strategies. Finally, instructors provide counsel, support, and encouragement to each learner, though the extent and nature of this support varies according to the educational level of the learners, the teacher's personality and philosophy, and other factors.

The frequency and intensity of the teacher's influence on learners when there is learner-teacher interaction is much greater than when there is only learner-content interaction. In preparing instruction for learner-content interaction, the educator can design written and recorded material that aims to motivate, make presentations, facilitate application, evaluate, and even provide a degree of student affective support. However, the lack of feedback from individual learner to educator makes these teaching procedures highly generalized, not individual, leaving ultimate responsibility for maintaining motivation, for interacting with the presentation, for analysing the success of application and for diagnosing the difficulty on the learners themselves, requiring a high degree of learner autonomy.

Where interaction between learner and teacher is possible through correspondence or teleconference, the learner comes under the influence of a professional instructor and is able to draw on the experience of the professional to interact with the content in the manner that is most effective for that particular individual learner. The long recognized advantage of correspondence instruction is its individual nature. When the correspondence instructor sits with a set of student papers, there is no class; instead, the instructor enters into a dialogue with each individual, perhaps attending to the motivational aspect with one student and to the explanation of a misunderstanding with another. While the students and their instructor are attending to a common piece of presentation (usually in a set text, but quite likely on audio- or videotape), each student's response to the presentation is different and so the response to each student is different. To some a misunderstanding is explained, to others elaborations are given, to others simplifications; for one analogies are drawn, for another supplementary readings suggested.

The instructor is especially valuable in responding to the learners' application of knowledge. Whatever self-directed learners can do alone for self-motivation and interaction with content presented, they are vulnerable at the point of application. They do not know enough about the subject to be sure that they are applying it correctly, applying it as intensively or extensively as possible or desirable, nor are they aware of all the potential areas of application. It is for reality testing and feedback that interaction with an instructor is likely to be most valuable.

LEARNER-LEARNER INTERACTION

It is the third form of interaction, a new dimension of distance education, that will be a challenge to our thinking and practice in the 1990s. This is inter-learner interaction, between one learner and other learners, alone or in group settings, with or without the real-time presence of an instructor.

Through the history of education, the class or educational group has more often than not been organized for reasons that have nothing to do with learners' needs. At present, many classes are organized because the class is the only organizational form known to most teachers and because in the short term – though not usually the long term – it is the cheapest way of delivering the teaching acts of stimulation, presentation, application, evaluation and student support.

However, learner-learner interaction among members of a class or other group is sometimes an extremely valuable resource for learning, and is sometimes even essential. Phillips, Santoro, and Kuehn (1988) describe the importance of interaction among members of an undergraduate class who had to learn skills of group interaction. With the rationale that skilled committee and other group work is essential for functioning in modern society, especially in business, Phillips *et al.* taught principles of, and trained students in, effective group functioning. This is an example of content that makes group interaction especially valuable. One could study the presentation of principles of group leadership and group membership alone, or in interaction with an instructor. However, at the point of application and evaluation, the availability of a group of fellow learners becomes invaluable for learner and instructor alike. Interestingly, the researchers found they could not effectively facilitate interaction among members of a large undergraduate class in face-to-face classrooms, and turned to distance education techniques, using recorded video and computer interaction to achieve higher performance in group behaviours than they had been able to obtain in live groups. Thus, these educators gave their students the advantage of individual interaction with the instructor by electronic correspondence, and the benefits of peer group interaction by asynchronous e-mail and by synchronous computer 'chatting'.

Apart from teaching interaction itself, when else is inter-learner group interaction between students highly desirable? The answer to this question depends largely on the circumstances of the learners and their age, experience, and level of learner autonomy. For younger learners, the teaching task of stimulation and motivation will be assisted by peer-group interaction, though this is not particularly important for most adult and advanced learners, who tend to be self-motivated.

It is most useful for some types of presentations, such as up-to-the-minute reports from experts, and for purposes of application and evaluation. In my audio and interactive video classes, weekly presentations are shared by two or more students and last typically for an hour. This is followed by peer discussion and analysis in small groups and then feedback and further discussion. This process is successful because of the level of self-management that adult graduate students possess, and it not only acknowledges and encourages the development of their expertise but also tests it, and teaches important principles regarding the nature of knowledge and the role of the scholar as a maker of knowledge.

APPLICATIONS

A significant characteristic of distance education, and a major contribution to the field of education, has been an awareness of the benefits of division of labour in teaching. With the rapid expansion of telecommunications in American education, the principle of specialization of teaching activity and use of communication medium must be applied to distinguish more deliberately among the three types of interaction described above. Educators need to organize programmes to ensure maximum effectiveness of each type of interaction, and ensure they provide the type of interaction that is most suitable for the various teaching tasks of different subject areas, and for learners at different stages of development.

The main weakness of many distance education programmes is their commitment to only one type of medium; the combination of one-way satellite video and two-way audio is increasingly dominant. When there is only one medium it is probable that only one kind of interaction is permitted or done well. While correspondence gives superior learner-content interaction and good, though slow, learner-instructor interaction, it gives no learner-learner interaction. The teleconference group is excellent for learner-learner interaction, and for some types of instructor-learner interaction, but is frequently misused for instructor presentations that could be done better by print or recorded media. In the time saved by avoiding such presentations, a teleconference could stimulate and facilitate learner-learner interaction that has been difficult or impossible to achieve in distance education until now.

In short, it is vitally important that distance educators in all media do more to plan for all three kinds of interaction, and use the expertise of educators and communication specialists in both traditional media – printed, broadcast, or recorded – and newer teleconference media.

REFERENCES

Duning, B. (1987) 'Independent study in higher education: a captive of legendary resilience', *American Journal of Distance Education* 1, 1: 37–46.

Hiemstra, R. (ed.) (1982) *Self-directed Adult Learning: Some Implications for Practice,* Syracuse: Adult Education Program, School of Education.

Holmberg, B. (1986) *Growth and Structure of Distance Education,* London: Croom Helm.

Keegan, D. (1988) 'Problems in defining the field of distance education', *American Journal of Distance Education* 2, 2: 4–11.

Moore, M. G. (1984), 'Independent study', in R. D. Boyd and J. W. Apps (eds) *Redefining the Discipline of Adult Education,* San Francisco: Jossey Bass, 16–31.

Penland, P. R. (1977) *Individual Self-planned Learning in America,* Pittsburgh: Graduate School of Library and Information Sciences, University of Pittsburgh.

Pittman, V. V. (1987) 'The persistence of print: correspondence study and the new media', *American Journal of Distance Education* 1, 1: 31–6.

Phillips, G. M., Santoro, G. M. and Kuehn, S. A. (1988) 'The use of computer-mediated communication in training students in group problem solving and decision-making techniques', *American Journal of Distance Education* 2, 1: 38–51.

Saba, F. (1988) 'Integrated telecommunications systems and instructional transaction', *American Journal of Distance Education* 2, 3: 17–24.

Shale, D. (1988) 'Toward a reconceptualization of distance education', *American Journal of Distance Education* 2, 3: 25–35.

Tough, A. (1971) *The Adults Learning Projects: a Fresh Approach to Theory and Practice in Adult Learning,* Toronto: Ontario Institute for Studies in Education.

3 Problems of distance education

France Henri and Anthony Kaye

The numerous problems of distance education could be said to include both internal and external problems. Internal problems are related to the demands of distance education in relation to the characteristics of the culture of the teaching environment. External problems are concerned with the nature and actual vocation of distance education.

The culture of teaching environments, and especially that of the university environment, revolves around the principle of freedom of practice. Academics freely draw up and structure their teaching. They have the recognized competence that allows them to choose the content of the teaching that is bestowed on students. Their work is not commissioned and they are not agents. The university tradition also encourages academics to teach courses relating to their personal research interests. This ensures quality in university education. The academic, therefore, undoubtedly holds responsibility for the teaching process. This is an indisputable fact.

The demands of distance education exert numerous constraints on this freedom of practice traditionally recognized in the teaching profession. In order to be profitable, distance education has to both address the public at large and recruit a large number of students. In this perspective, the nature and content of education programmes and courses is crucial. In realizing their business objectives, managers of distance education institutions can be tempted, and in certain cases succumb, to impose upon academics the content of their teaching. This content is dictated by either circumstantial or selective tastes discovered by market research rather than as a function of the requirements of the discipline to be taught or the training to be given. Distance learning courses with low enrolment levels are generally not in favour with managers of distance education institutions. The pressures of distance education systems, in search of economic profitability, tend to reduce the academic freedom greatly defended by teachers in traditional education. Is it acceptable in distance education for market research and marketing demands to be considered as facts governing academic life?

The necessity of attaining a critical mass for the distribution of distance education products is not the only concern of distance education. The pedagogical process must also endure another constraint unknown in traditional education. The final product of distance education is rarely the fruit of one person's work. Most models of course creation rely on the collaboration of several specialists (Mason and Goodenough 1981: 110). The person responsible for creating a course is thus placed in a situation where he must submit his work to be commented upon, criticized, restructured and transformed by the expertise of other specialists. One sees in this phenomenon disguised means of controlling and censuring the pedagogical process. Many problems arising within course teams stem from the injured feelings of members whose work and ideas are submitted to the demands of their colleagues and collaborators, with whom they may not be in full agreement. Power struggles occur which may lead to serious confrontations. Distance education can thus become the fruit of compromise, of happy or unhappy adjustments and of arbitrary decisions that are never desirable in a context of cooperation and collegiality.

Another aspect of the internal problems in distance education relates to where the responsibility lies. In the cases where course creation is shared amongst several people, responsibilities are ideally taken collectively. But as confrontations arise, as struggles of power become firmly established and an attempt is made to control the teaching from all directions, disillusionment almost inevitably takes over. The process is bureaucratized and shared responsibility is no longer part of the spirit. Team members become demotivated, which leads to collective irresponsibility. The collaborators are no longer partners in creating collective work and they dissociate themselves from the final product, which is more than likely to be different from the initially expected product.

The external problems in distance education call into question the nature and actual vocation of distance education. Teaching at a distance to a large number of people through the mass media has no possible comparison with traditional education. The latter is a private act, nearly intimate, and takes place within the walls of a classroom, a laboratory or even a lecture theatre. To teach at a distance is to take a public stand and to expose oneself to criticism. On the other hand, traditional education is more concealed and since it does not use means of mass communication it is not exposed to public opinion. It is known that the teaching aids of traditional education, such as the distribution of class notes to students, do not give an accurate picture of the professor's strategies or of his competence as a teacher and of what really goes on in the classroom. Teaching aids generally present organized and structured knowledge which, at the actual time of teaching, are enriched by the professor's critical comments, relationships, résumés and explanations.

In the traditional environment, the teaching process takes on its *true meaning* during viva voce interventions in the classroom or elsewhere. Knowledge is placed in context and both the learner and teacher give it meaning. The teacher allows himself to contextualize knowledge, and as he adopts a tone of 'professional confidence' (Vandenberg 1982), he communicates intimate thoughts to the students. Hence the teaching process tends to render knowledge more significant and closer to 'real life'.

In distance education, mediated teaching takes a formal shape. The 'subjective' speech and comments of the professor in front of his students are clearly eliminated. Content is 'objectively' presented. Under the pretext of knowledge validity, 'subjective' speech is avoided for fear of being accused of an ideological bias or of being tendentious. Students are deprived of 'the model of the subjective use of an objective conceptual structure' (Vandenberg 1982). There is therefore the risk that distance education only leads to learning of facts, which in turn does not help students to, at a personal level, develop as students. The latter would enable students to develop a critical mind, to deal 'subjectively' with the knowledge that they receive and to establish their own connections within a frame of reference that their education should help them to develop.

External problems of distance education are therefore linked not only to the pedagogical products that it creates, but also to the effects that these products have on society and on the relationship of knowledge that distance education proposes. External problems are also linked to the hidden contradictions between the mandate that distance education wishes to adopt and that which it actually practises. Distance education is concerned with accessibility, in other words, with the 'opening' of education programmes to a larger number of people. For this, several institutions have given themselves liberal entry policies that abolish the academic prerequisites generally required in traditional systems. Moreover, the flexibility characteristic of distance education enables students to choose their pace of learning, determine their course of study and progress to the mastery of specialized and high level knowledge. Thus the innovation of distance education does not consist in presenting students with new content but rather in organizing the delivery of education outside the constraints imposed by traditional systems. To achieve this, the preparation of courses is subjected to rational and systematic planning, as well as to an industrialized or partially industrialized production system. The contribution of educational technology has been significant in this. Consequently, new ground has been broken as regards the form of teaching rather than as regards the content, and in such a way that distance education programmes resemble those of traditional education, and often perpetuate an élitist nature.

Moreover, the mass distribution of distance education programmes risks the *de facto* establishment of a certain standardization of knowledge. Distance learning materials are even used in traditional education. Certain institutions use them as manuals or reference books for lectures. There is thus a risk of standardising certain areas of knowledge and certain learning processes. The autonomy that distance education claims to promote is therefore seriously compromised. To avoid such a situation happening, distance education should offer students possibilities of reacting and of being critical and creative towards their course content. The difficulty distance education comes up against is that of reproducing the dialogue that enables students to be critical and personal in their learning. Students should be able to enter into exchanges in order to understand, criticize, adapt and finally use the knowledge that has been given to them and which they have made their own.

Adult learners, in distance education, seem deprived of such exchanges. Could learners themselves restore worthwhile educational relationships? How can the complex communication network of distance education succeed in supporting students whilst respecting the unique nature of their development?

LEARNING AT A DISTANCE

Deschooling, as taken to broadly mean the bringing of adults into the educational process, implies a real cultural revolution in education. It breaks down the barriers between education, work and leisure and demands a return to the different adult roles through educational activities. It calls for a redefinition of the roles and responsibilities of student support staff, especially tutors, in adult education. The specific characteristics of the adult world should not be ignored by continuing to map the school's education system on to the educational practices of adults. 'Deschooling' requires the deployment of new modes of participation which postulates that adults have the knowledge and abilities essential for contribution. Above all, deschooling is based on the belief that the 'responsible autonomy' of adults must be promoted and that a significant place must be reserved for them in the educational process (Gouvernement du Québec 1982: 21).

Amongst other methods, distance education can be a way of deschooling adult educational activities since it places students in direct contact with a field of knowledge. Having access to this knowledge, students can take responsibility for the organization of their own learning programmes by using, as required, other available resources. This method of taking responsibility for the organization of one's education radically changes the nature of the relationship that the student has with the teacher in traditional education. It is generally considered that the educational relationship should be dynamic and interpersonal and that it is an important part of the pedagogical process. Its richness is due to the fact that it revolves around several factors: communication of knowledge, personal development, emotional and social relationships, awareness, the arousal of curiosity, and so on. It contributes to the development of 'knowing how to do' and 'knowing how to share' and is not restricted to the simple transmission of knowledge. What of the educational relationship in distance learning? Without the physical presence of a tutor, is it even feasible to talk of a relationship? To what extent is distance education able to ensure a relationship as rich as that found in the best examples of traditional education?

The following analysis of the way in which the educational relationship is formed and structured answers these questions. This relationship is not without dynamism and richness and, far from seeking its exclusiveness, it uses a network of resources developed in a 'deschooled' environment. In traditional education, barriers confine the educational relationship to a limited number of people and to a particular place and time (school and university establishments with fixed hours do not exist in distance education). The educational relationship exists both between the learner and his environment (including learning activities, the didactic materials and student support systems) and between the learner and the distance education institution. Surrounding the student there exists a complex network of relationships which, in the best examples, provides educational relationships and high quality exchanges.

THE EDUCATIONAL RELATIONSHIP

The absence of direct intervention from the teacher and the dispensation of education through mediated materials deeply modifies the nature of the educational relationship in distance education. Teacher intervention is situated above the student's learning processes. Once a course has been created and the institution has delivered it, the students are unable to communicate directly with the course developer. They are unable to question the choices, values and options that the course developer has made in his mediated teaching. Neither can they ask him to explain certain obscure or difficult passages. And finally, students are unable to discuss the personal synthesis of their newly acquired knowledge.

The complexity of the relationship

Despite the apparent lack of communication, the educational relationship exists in distance education and it is certainly more complex than in traditional education. Figure 3.1 represents the various components of this

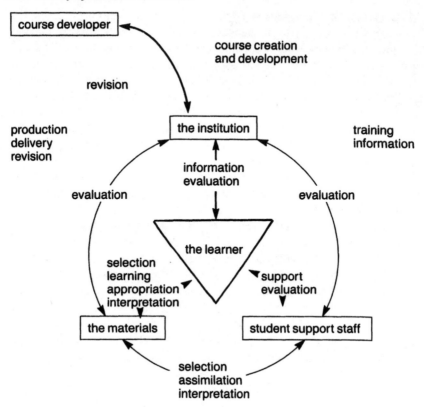

Figure 3.1   The components of the educational relationship in distance education

relationship, that is to say, the relationships that the students have with the following.

- *The distance education institution*: administrative communications, admission requirements, evaluation procedures, assessment, etc. It is in these relationships that the principles and philosophy of the education conveyed by an institution take shape.
- *The didactic materials*: this component of the relationship is perceived differently by each learner according to student motivation, student learning strategies, the presence or absence of evaluation procedures and the pedagogical choices influencing the creation of teaching materials (should students learn course contents off by heart to be reproduced in an exam or should they use the materials as a resource amongst others to realize a personal learning project?).
- *Student support staff*: all distance learning systems attach vital importance

to human student support systems. These intermediaries have numerous relationships with students and carry out the following functions: counselling, tutoring, evaluating, correcting, and helping learning processes. These relationships are generally very different to those of the classic teacher-pupil relationship.

• *The learner*: in the centre is the student who, outside the institutional context, develops in a personal environment (family, social, professional, economic, geographic). In this natural setting comes the learning environment which is nurtured by the former. In traditional education, the educational process generally takes place in a specially developed environment which is different to the student's home environment, such as the classroom, lecture theatre, laboratory and library. Distance education institutions do not offer this classic environment though students are occasionally invited to training courses and seminars in study centres. Thus the educational process essentially takes place in a decompartmentalized (and deschooled) environment. For most students, this environment is the home. Family, social and professional exchanges represent (or do not represent) the main occasions to discuss study related subjects.

To this can be added the contacts that students on the same study programme have with each other. Group seminars (with or without a tutor or moderator) can be fairly frequent and important in certain distance learning programmes. These exchanges, whether they be compulsory or optional, formal or informal, at a distance (teleconferencing, mail, telematic networks) or face-to-face, are perceived differently by students. Some students have a marked interest in them, whereas others find that they do not correspond to their expectations, motivations and learning strategies. To compensate for the infrequent contacts students have with each other, many institutions have played a large part in the setting up of student associations. Many of these publish their own student bulletins or journals (for example, the bulletin *Le trait d'union* published by the Télé-université of Québec and *Sesame* published by the British Open University).

REFERENCES

Gouvernement du Québec (1982) *Apprendre: une Action Volontaire et Responsable*, Québec: Presses du Gouvernement.
Mason, J. and Goodenough, S. (1981) 'Course creation', in A. Kaye and G. Rumble (eds) *Distance Teaching for Higher and Adult Education*, London: Croom Helm.
Vandenberg, D. (1982) *Charlatans, Knowledge, Curriculum and Phenomenological Research*, Brisbane: University of Queensland.

4 Distance education in the society of the future: from partial understanding to conceptual frameworks

Erling Ljoså

What exactly is it we are trying to understand when we talk about understanding distance education?

Somewhere out there is a student. The student has a wife, or a husband, perhaps a child. They like to come together with friends now and then, and with relatives at other occasions. The student also has an employer and some colleagues, and many other relations with other people. Being a student means that this person also has a relationship with an educational institution, in this case at a distance. Somebody has prepared study materials. The student sends assignments to his or her teacher, and may have other contacts as well with staff from the institution. In some cases it is possible to follow local classes or to get advice from somebody by telephone or by personal visit to a study centre. Distance education is a process going on with relations between a number of persons, who are more or less involved in the process or have some impact on it.

Usually, there is more than one student in the course. All the relations I have mentioned repeat themselves, although with considerable variation, each time we enrol a new student. Consequently, distance education is an aggregation of such processes. And this aggregation goes further to include all the processes in other courses within the institution. In NKS (Norsk korrespondanseskole) we have about 70,000 distance education processes going on at the same time. Although Norway is a small country, there are several other distance education institutions, with other students, other courses, other technologies, other administrative systems and procedures. We must continue the aggregation of processes to include other countries, other cultures, other educational systems and traditions. There is an almost overwhelming complexity and variation involved when we are trying to understand distance education.

LEVELS OF UNDERSTANDING

I believe it is useful to distinguish between three levels of understanding:

- the intuitive, 'common-sense' understanding we have as participants in or observers of distance education activities;
- reflective analysis based on experience, communication and comparison;
- systematic research and theory building.

An individual's intuitive understanding of what is going on in distance education is of course dependent on the individual's own role in the process. But it also depends on his or her previous experience of similar situations. An event needs interpretation, and individuals derive meaning for events from their everyday understanding of the world, the persons and situations involved.

The next level implies the development of concepts and expression of relations between concepts. The intuitive interpretation of events is confirmed, refined, corrected and expanded through the accumulation of experience and through communication with other people. The concepts and the way you use the concepts express your personal 'picture' of what distance education is all about.

On the third level, researchers work even more systematically and according to accepted methods and rules, to derive meaning for their data from concepts, models and theories. But these research activities are also dependent on the understanding achieved at the two other levels to establish concepts and theories which they can confront with the data available.

These three levels of understanding are interrelated and depend on each other. Our concepts are developed from our experience and intuitive understanding of events and situations. The theories and models which we develop give new insight and help us understand the everyday situations better. Therefore, concepts and theories influence what is going on in the everyday world, at the same time as they are picturing and explaining it. The struggle about words and definitions is not only a theoretical battlefield.

This is easy to see when you consider the discussions provoked by Peters' description of distance education as an industrialized form of education (Peters 1973). It is also an important aspect when Garrison describes the 'three generations' of distance education, referring to systems based on communication by mail, by telecommunication and by computer communication (Garrison 1989). In many cases, concepts and descriptions serve a purpose. They promote and advocate something – or they are used for such a purpose. They may even have a moral aspect, and try to tell us how things ought to be and how distance education should develop. It is an illusion to believe that understanding is neutral. Understanding usually has a purpose.

PARTIAL UNDERSTANDING AND COMPLEMENTARITY

Since our understanding of distance education is rooted in experience and interpretations of this experience, it is always a partial understanding. St Paul, by some historians presented as the first distance educator, realized that knowledge and understanding is partial, and never absolute. The student's experience is different from the teacher's experience, and both the administrator's and the researcher's experience reflect their particular perspectives, which are again different from the perspectives of the student or the teacher.

This situation is, in my opinion, of epistemological significance. The Danish physicist, Niels Bohr, has put a label on it, known as the principle of complementarity. In quantum physics, different explanations of phenomena, explanations which are derived from different observational situations, seem to be mutually exclusive, but are nevertheless necessary to cater for all the experimental observations. The famous example is the complementary explanations of quantum phenomena in terms of classical models – on the one hand waves, on the other hand particles.

The principle of complementarity, which meant a fundamental shift of paradigm in physical science, was influenced by Bohr's study of the American psychologist William James. In his book *The Principles of Psychology*, James described the paradox of self-observation – of analyzing one's own stream of thought. Bohr often referred to this as the paradox of being at the same time an observer and a participant of the scene of life. These complementary roles could also be described as on the one hand analysis and the search for causal explanations, on the other hand immediacy and feeling of finality and purpose.

Bohr's idea of complementarity has been made use of by sociologists and anthropologists reflecting on the methodological aspects of participative observation in the study of cultures and social relations. In a ZIFF paper, Rothe has discussed complementarity as a link between quantitative and qualitative research in distance education, or between an 'inside' and 'outside' viewpoint on individuals and situations – where the 'inside' view represents experiential knowledge of the everyday world, and the 'outside' view represents accepted generalized understanding of human actions (Rothe 1985). These two complementary approaches should, according to Rothe, be combined to form a holistic, representative picture of educational phenomena.

THE PROBLEM AND POTENTIAL OF GENERALIZATION

A similar problem reveals itself when we consider that research, be it based on qualitative or quantitative methods, aims at generalization. It looks for common aspects and structures – shared by individual events and situations. The Danish philosopher Søren Kierkegaard coined the expression 'Subjectivity is the truth', which became a basic principle in existentialist thinking. Although I will not argue against objectivity (or inter-subjectivity) in research, we should consider that generalization is in a way complementary to the search for individual truth and meaning. One could therefore ask to what extent research is possible in social science, or better: What do we lose and what do we win when we look for generalization? Is the authenticity of the individual event maintained when we concentrate on what it has in common with other events?

The knowledge acquired through research can never be complete knowledge. It is partial in perspective, it is subjective in conceptualization, and it is incomplete as a result of generalization. However, the loss of completeness is compensated by the number of cases where the knowledge can be applied, and that is the reason why systematic research is such a powerful tool in our endeavour to understand reality.

The search for understanding is firmly based in the nature of human existence, and the value of research may be derived from this general search for understanding. However, I believe that the case for research is even stronger when its power of generalization is used to optimalize existing systems of distance education at any level of aggregation.

ASPECTS OF MY UNDERSTANDING OF DISTANCE EDUCATION

I started by asking what we mean by distance education, referring to the complexity of the activities and relations involved. According to my understanding, the core of distance education is an interactive, educational process between two people, student and teacher, separated by physical distance.

The student is an individual, and has an individual everyday context. To the student, the process represents a unique relationship with a particular distance education system and all the persons involved. The student's focus is on the object of study – or its representation in form of course material – and on his/ her individual process of study. The teacher is, of course, also an individual. But to the teacher, the relationship with the student is far from unique. The student is one among a number, and the teacher may tend to apprehend the student more as a case than as an individual.

Together with other teachers, he/she will perform a role within the particularly designed distance education system, with a limited freedom of action. The teacher's focus will be more on the product and outcome of the student's efforts than on the student as a person – but also on the feedback that is adequate from the teacher to the student in order to support the student's learning process.

My own perspective is not from any side of the student-teacher relationship, but from the system context of the teacher. My focus is on the frameworks laid by my institution's organization and system design on the processes which are going on between students, teachers and a number of other people and elements in the system. I am interested in the optimal operation of the system, and in its development in order to serve future students.

DISTANCE EDUCATION AS VALUE-ORIENTED SERVICE SYSTEMS

Personally, I have made Peters' description of distance education as an industrialized type of education part of my own understanding. At the same time, however, I have advocated that we go a step further and look at distance education as a service industry. According to service management theory, the direct delivery of service takes place when the individual customer meets with a service carrier, one of the front-line staff, in what is called 'the moment of truth'. The decisive impression of service and quality comes from such moments – for instance, when a student phones the institution, or receives the corrected assignment from the teacher, or attends a tutorial seminar.

The fundamental problem of the service industries is to combine the two words: *service*, which means taking care of an individual with her/his individual goals and needs; and *industry*, which means standardization, division of labour, and mass production.

Service management theories offer some tools for analysing services, systems and organizations – for instance, in terms of market segment, service package, delivery system, image, and culture. An additional useful method is value chain analysis, as presented by Woudstra and Powell (1989) with examples from Athabasca University. The important aspect of both these approaches is that they put the emphasis not on the inherent efficiency of the system as a goal in itself, but on the values and services offered to the students.

FRAMEWORKS FOR THE FUTURE

Garrison has recently published a stimulating book called *Understanding Distance Education: Frameworks for the Future*. Space does not permit me to present or discuss his main ideas. I agree with many of them, but believe that he underestimates the role of systems and organizations, and I am not quite happy with his discussion of various technologies. Garrison's main issue is very important. When we are thinking of and planning the future of distance education, we are often limited by our own frameworks and ways of understanding. It is similar to the situation when the inventors of the automobile tried to imagine the car as a sort of carriage with something in front of it which was not a horse. Distance education is also very often compared to what it is similar to, but still is not like.

The issue includes the question whether 'distance education' as a term will be obsolete as distance education merges into the so-called 'mainstream' of educational systems that is supposed to open up and incorporate the use of modern communication technologies. I believe in this merger if it means that distance education should be seen as part of education, and will be used increasingly by conventional educational institutions in combination and coexistence with other methods. But I also believe that distance education will continue to be both a distinct and meaningful term and a particular field of study and practice.

On the other hand, it may be useful to study educational processes at various levels of aggregation. Distance education is only one possible delineation of a set of study objects. I believe it is useful to develop theories of distance education. But it may be of equal relevance to study particular types of distance education, as well as more general phenomena like adult education. It remains to be seen how useful the criterion of distance actually is from a theoretical viewpoint in delineating a separate field of study.

I do not look at the development of distance education as a succession of 'generations' of technologies and forms. I think of it more as a set of different system structures, made possible through the availability and successive refinement of different technologies which at least partly overcome the problem of physical distance between learners and between learners and teachers. It is important that we continue our efforts to understand these structures, their roles in our developing societies, and their opportunities and limitations for providing effective, high quality education now and in the future.

REFERENCES

Bohr, N. (1957) *Atomfysik og Menneskelig Erkendelse*, Köbenhavn: Schultz.
Garrison, D. R. (1989) *Understanding Distance Education: Frameworks for the Future*, London: Routledge.
Gjessing, G. (1968) *Complementarity, Value and Socio-cultural Field*, Oslo: Universitetsforlaget.
Holmberg, B. (1990) *On the Rationale, Typology and Methodology of Research and Scholarship: a Practitioner's Understanding of Epistemology*, Hagen: FernUniversität.
Holy Bible, St Paul: The First Letter to the Corinthians.

James, W. (1890) *The Principles of Psychology*, London: Macmillan, 2 vols.

Jammer, M. (1966) *The Conceptual Development of Quantum Mechanics*, New York: McGraw Hill.

Kierkegaard, S. (1846) *Afsluttende Uvidenskabelig Efterskrift*, Köbenhavn: Los C. A. Reitzel, Universitets-Boghandler.

Ljoså, E. (1986) 'Service management in distance education', *Epistolodidaktika* 1986/1: 37–50.

Nörretranders, T. (1985) *Det Udelelige: Niels Bohrs Aktualitet i Fysik, Mystik og Politik*, Köbenhavn: Gyldendal.

Peters, O. (1973) *Die didaktische Struktur des Fernunterrichts: Untersuchungen zu einer industrialisierten Form des Lehrens und Lernens*, Weinheim: Beltz.

Petersen, A. (1968) *Quantum Physics and the Philosophical Tradition*, New York: Belfer Graduate School of Science, Yeshiva University.

Rothe, J. P. (1985) *Linking Quantitative Distance Education Research through Complementarity*, Hagen: FernUniversität. (ZIFF Papiere 56).

Woudstra, A. and Powell, R. (1989) 'Value chain analysis: a framework for management of distance education', *American Journal of Distance Education* 3, 3: 7–21.

5 Broadening the definition of distance education in light of the new telecommunications technologies

Bruce O. Barker, Anthony G. Frisbie and Kenneth R. Patrick

The 1980s have witnessed an explosion of alternative instructional delivery systems for American public education (*School Tech News* 1986). Distance learning projects utilizing telecommunications technologies such as cable television, fibre optics, microwave, slow scan television, satellites and microcomputer networking have opened up opportunities for school districts to coordinate schedules and to share resources, thereby providing an expansion of curricular offerings and educational opportunities for students (Barker 1987a and Kitchen and Russell 1987). Fuelled by state-sponsored curriculum reform intended to upgrade high school graduation requirements, the concept of 'distance education' has caught the attention of both national and state education officials (Anderson 1986). Many higher education administrators are also showing keen interest in distance education as they face the challenges of declining enrolments, an ageing student population, and reduced levels of state funding. While interest in distance education continues to grow, efforts to define the concept remain inconsistent, and in many cases dated and incomplete. This is particularly true of some current writers in the field who continue to link distance education chiefly to correspondence study whereby the student:

- is physically separated from the teacher,
- is separated in time from the teacher, and
- learns independent of contact with the teacher or with other students (Beaudoin 1986, Keegan 1986 and Moore 1987).

Distance education has its historical foundation in correspondence study and the aforementioned aspects of a definition still have value, and are correct when applied to traditional correspondence study. Nevertheless, the introduction of telecommunications technology to distance education necessitates a restructuring of the definition. The term 'distance education' is being used more frequently by educators and legislative policy makers around the country. In most cases, reference is intended to mean the simultaneous telecommunicated delivery of instruction from a host site or classroom to distant sites, coupled with live audio and/or video interaction between teacher and student(s) – not to correspondence study (Falsone 1986, Barker 1987a, Benson and Hirschen 1987, Garrison and Shale 1987 and Paulsen 1987). A broadening of the definition of 'distance education' is needed in order to clarify the inherent strengths that new technologies bring to the field, to recruit new audiences to the benefits of distance learning, and to guide further study and research in this aspect of outreach education. In this chapter, we present a categorization of distance education methodologies in the form of a taxonomy intended to compare correspondence study-based distance education approaches with telecommunications-based approaches. The basis of our comparison is on teacher–student and student–student interaction in the distance learning process. At the conclusion of this chapter, we also suggest elements for a definition of 'distance education' more in harmony with current practice and understanding.

A TAXONOMY OF DISTANCE EDUCATION

By definition, a taxonomy is a scientific and orderly method of classification that arranges objects, processes, or ideas into related groups based on shared commonalities. Normal organization of a taxonomic grouping is hierarchical, going from general to specific. When applying a taxonomic process to education, two subdivisions immediately present themselves: (1) traditional classroom or residence instruction, and (2) distance learning. Both residential instruction and distance learning are intended to present valid, useful information in a manner that is sufficiently dynamic and interactive to promote learning on the part of the student. In addition, both should provide a feedback mechanism that permits a dialogue of some sort between student and teacher beyond the normal interactivity of assignments, testing, and grading. It is the method of delivery and level of interactivity that marks the major differences between these two approaches to education.

Residential instruction occurs at a set time and in a predetermined location where both teacher and students meet together. This traditional and well-accepted approach permits relatively easy interaction and dialogue between an individual student or groups of students and the teacher, and makes assessment of student performance fairly immediate. Distance learning, on the other hand, is generally accepted as teaching in which the instructor and the student(s) are separated in terms of physical location and are frequently separated relative to time. The instructor and student(s) can be in different rooms, different buildings, different cities, different states, or even different countries. The desired end result in distance education has been to provide an educational opportunity equal to that provided in traditional classroom teaching. A major factor in the growing interest in distance education is the ability to conduct live, real-time instruction between teacher and student(s) made possible by technology. This ability to simulate, as closely as possible, a traditional classroom teaching–learning experience permitting live teacher–student exchanges and student–student exchanges – irrespective of geographical distance – is changing the scope and definition of distance education. The use of new technologies permits live interaction and allows for immediate feedback and interaction between teacher and student(s). Differing technological approaches permit assorted levels of interactivity that in essence 'bridge' the geographical distance between instructor and student. It is this added component of live interaction that breaks the field of distance education into two major categories – correspondence-based distance education and telecommunications-based distance education (see Table 5.1). The list of approaches starts with the most interactive levels and proceeds to those that are the least interactive.

Table 5.1   Distance education approaches from low to high levels of teacher–student interaction

---

Category 1   Correspondence-based distance education

- Correspondence study based on print materials supported by audiotapes and/or videotapes (higher interaction)
- Correspondence study based on print materials supported by broadcast signals (radio or television) but with no 'real-time' communication
- Correspondence study based on print materials only (lower interaction)

Category 2   Telecommunications-based distance education

- Two-way voice link, two-way video (full-motion) link (higher interaction)
- Two-way voice link, two-way video (freeze frame) link
- Two-way voice link, one-way video (full-motion) link
- Two-way voice link, one-way video (freeze frame) link
- Two-way voice link only (lower interaction)

Traditional distance learning has tended to be correspondence-based and to be individually oriented. The level of interactivity practised with this type of delivery has generally been very slow and low level. Days or even weeks might pass between a student's submitted assignment or question(s) and the instructor's written response. Administrators of correspondence study programmes might argue that correspondence study students are highly interactive with their instructor because they must respond directly, in writing, to each question in their course study guide. Under ideal conditions this is true, yet extensive exchanges via written communication requires a much larger time investment (and delay) for instructor and student than do live, verbal interactions. In addition, it is not unusual for many correspondence study instructors to write very little or, in some cases, no comments on students' submitted work. The inclusion of radio and television broadcasts into a correspondence-study approach has definitely improved the coverage of content and likely increased educational accessibility. Nevertheless, the issue of teacher–student interaction has not been affected overall. While the merging of audiotapes and videotapes to the format of many correspondence courses has improved, the opportunity for more detailed verbal exchange between instructor and student, the delay in 'turnaround time' has not been appreciably altered. Furthermore, in each of the three levels of correspondence-based distance education listed in Table 5.1, individual student contact with other students who are taking the same course is essentially non-existent, or at best limited. Generally, individual correspondence study students are not networked in any way with other students taking the same course.

Telecommunications-based distance education approaches are an extension beyond the limits of correspondence study. The teaching–learning experience for both instructor and student(s) occurs simultaneously – it is contiguous in time. When an audio and/or video communications link is employed, the opportunity for live teacher–student exchanges in real time is possible, thereby permitting immediate response to student inquiries and comments. Much like a traditional classroom setting, students can seek on-the-spot clarification from the teacher. Opportunities for teacher–student interaction also promote greater spontaneity for all participants in the teaching–learning process. Within these more interactive approaches there is a further breakdown of the degree or level of interactivity possible, depending on the type of telecommunications technology and system configuration used. Lower level interactive systems employ two separate voice links, usually in the form of audio teleconferencing. To obtain higher levels of interactivity, two-way voice links are combined with video links. Present configurations use either a one-way video or a two-way video format. The video link may be real-life freeze frame images transmitted via slow scan television, computer-generated, freeze-frame graphics relayed via microcomputer, or a full-motion television image over microwave, ITFS, cable, fibre optics, or satellite delivery. The ideal, and typically the most expensive configuration, is two-way voice with two-way full-motion video.

Another important aspect of telecommunication distance education delivery is the potential for student-to-student interaction. Use of an audio and/or video bridge to link several distant sites simultaneously with each other and with the host instructional site allows students an opportunity to interact not only with their teacher, but also with other students at different sites. Along with teacher–student interaction, the opportunity for student-to-student interpersonal communication and social interaction – albeit electronically – is a significant advantage of ongoing telecommunicated distance education approaches in contrast to correspondence-based approaches (Paulsen 1987). Telecommunicated distance education projects are not focused on an individualized instructional model as is the case with correspondence-based distance education. Instead, the focus is on small groups or clusters of students at different locations networked together for real-time audio interaction with the instructor and with each other (in some cases video is also included). The prospect of student-to-student exchanges not only increases the likelihood of socialization between students but also fosters the potential for peer tutoring and small group study.

THE GROWING INTEREST IN TELECOMMUNICATED DISTANCE EDUCATION

Interest in telecommunicated distance education is growing so rapidly that it is impossible to accurately document the many projects presently under way or being considered in the United States. Only three-and-a-half years ago, interactive satellite broadcasts of high school credit courses began in Texas, California, Utah, Arkansas, and Oklahoma (Holt 1985, Falsone 1986 and Barker 1987b). Several networks now broadcast live, full motion video over satellite transponder to subscribing high schools in over twenty-five states (Barker 1987a). Audio talk-back by students is transmitted over regular telephone lines linked to the classroom studio. In addition, state-wide networks for interactive satellite instruction have been established in Kentucky, Missouri, and North Carolina (Gardner 1987, Smith 1987, and Clauss 1988). State education administrators across the country are showing keen interest in this telecommunicated approach to distance education.

Numerous two-way, full-motion interactive television projects are operating between cooperating high schools in Minnesota, Wisconsin, Iowa, Illinois, New York, and other states (Barker and Muse 1985, Robinson, Collins, and West 1985, Lanier 1986, and Wall 1986). In most two-way interactive TV systems, each participating school has a fully equipped classroom that allows a teacher in one location and students at one or more distant schools to both see and hear each other during instruction. Transmission is typically over cable, fibre optics, or microwave. The usual model is a cooperative arrangement between two to five school districts to form a telecommunications cooperative. The network co-ops human, financial, and equipment resources in order to provide fully interactive television programming over several channels between member schools. Not only are students able to interact with their TV teacher, but they are also able to see, hear, and communicate freely with their TV classmates at different schools.

Slow-scan TV systems, sometimes referred to as freeze-frame video, are widespread in many states (Davison 1985 and Sleight and Tueller 1985). Depending on the extent of technology used, either one-way or two-way still-frame TV imagery can be transmitted from one site to multiple receiving sites over regular telephone lines. Audio interaction between teacher and students and student-to-student(s) is over a second set of dedicated phone lines. A related technology, also using telephone lines as the communication medium, is being used to transmit computer-generated graphics via modem from a host site to distant site locations. Audio interaction is over speaker telephones at each of the distant sites. Known as micro-computer audiographic teleteaching, the concept has been successfully field-tested for five years in Pennsylvania with over 1,600 students participating. Use of microcomputer audiographic teleteaching has expanded to New York, Alaska, Utah, Nevada, and Texas (Wydra 1987). As with other telecommunications approaches, it is anticipated that this technique to deliver distance education will continue to experience rapid growth.

The cost of establishing and maintaining interactive telecommunication networks for instructional purposes is high and varies significantly between types of technology used and the size of the network desired. Microcomputer audiographic teleteaching and slow-scan video are among the less expensive systems, while interactive satellite and two-way interactive television are much more costly. In most cases, the monetary cost for schools to use telecommunicated distance education alternatives is much higher than that for correspondence-based distance education delivery. As with the entire telecommunications industry, however, costs have been and are continuing to drop. Although pricing is definitely important, the potential for interactive teaching/learning and the fact that geographically dispersed student bodies can be served simultaneously are appealing factors that have sparked state and national interest in telecommunicated distance education. As individual networks grow, costs will continue to drop as expenses are distributed among more users. The research base, though scant at present, suggests that students who study via telecommunicated distance education approaches perform as well as their counterparts in traditional classroom settings (Morehouse, Hoaglund, and Schmidt 1987, Whittington 1987 and Wydra 1987). Without question, telecommunicated teaching is an effective means to reach out to geographically isolated settings and new, vast audiences who otherwise would not be afforded educational equity.

CONCLUSION

In this chapter, we have attempted to differentiate between correspondence-based distance education and telecommunications-based distance education. Distinction between these two general approaches to outreach delivery has been developed around the level of interactivity afforded between teacher and student and that provided for student-to-student exchange. We readily acknowledge that distance education is a concept that is difficult to define, and we recognize that other professionals in the field may not fully agree with our stated views or may want to modify or add to them. We feel that additional dialogue is needed on this topic in order to

- help promote distance education alternatives as feasible methodologies for teaching and learning, and
- help guide the use of technology in a manner that will best benefit the learning of students.

State-sponsored education reforms, reduced state fiscal revenues, impending teacher shortages, and advances in telecommunications technology have spawned great interest in distance education as an alternative delivery methodology in the United States. The opportunity for live, teacher–student interaction through technology has caught the attention of many state and national education and policy decision makers. The increased interest and growth in distance education is usually in reference to telecommunicated instruction. Present use and practice necessitates a distinction between correspondence-based distance education and telecommunications-based distance education. The latter is best defined as the live, simultaneous transmission of a master teacher's lessons from a host classroom or studio to multiple receiving site classrooms in distant locations. Two-way live communication in real time, whether audio or video, between the teacher and students, permits the instruction to be interactive. This definition implies that instruction is oriented more toward small groups or clusters of students at different sites than to an individual student. Under ideal conditions, students at any one site are not only provided with two-way audio and visual contact with their instructor, but also are able to communicate directly with students at other sites during the instructional process.

To conclude, we affirm that correspondence-based approaches to distance education have been and will continue to be a viable means of educational delivery to reach out to students who otherwise might not be afforded an opportunity to achieve their educational goals. Yet, despite present and past research to support the efficacy of correspondence study as a bona fide methodology, it is well known that this approach is generally held with low regard (Almeda 1985 and Feasley 1985). The use of new and emerging technologies in distance education that foster live, teacher–student and student-to-student interactivity will enable distance education to assume its rightful and respected role in the educational process.

REFERENCES

Almeda, M. B. (1985) 'Upgrading the image', *Continuum* 49, 3: 198–202.
Anderson, B. (1986) 'Educational problems facing the region', address delivered at the Shaping Education Through Coalitions Conference sponsored by the Southwest Educational Development Laboratory, November 1986, Austin, Texas.
Barker, B. O. (1987a) *Interactive Distance Learning Technologies for Rural and Small Schools: a Resource Guide*, Las Cruces: New Mexico State University, ERIC Clearing house for Rural Education and Small Schools (ERIC Mini-Review).
Barker, B. O. (1987b) 'Interactive learning by satellite', *The Clearing House* 61, 1: 13–16.
Barker, B.O. and Muse, I. D. (1985) 'Innovative programs in America's rural schools', *The Rural Educator* 7, 1: 1–3.
Beaudoin, M. F. (1986) 'Distance learning does work', *Education Digest* 51, 5: 56–7.
Benson, G. M. and Hirschen, W. (1987) 'Distance learning: new windows for education', *T. H. E. Journal* 15, 1: 63–7.
Clauss, W. (1988) Personal communication, 19 January.
Davison, D. M. (1985) 'Using new technology to provide inservice education for rural teachers', *The Small School Forum* 6, 3: 21–2.
'Distance learning seen sweeping country' (1986) *School Tech News* 3, 7: 1, 5.
Falsone, A. M. (1986) *Distance Learning: a Practical Solution for Small or Low Budget Schools to Meet the Needs of Every Student*, Haxiun, Colorado: Highlighter, Inc..
Feasley, C. E. (1985) 'Research for improving the image of distance education', *Continuum* 49, 3: 203–8.
Gardner, H. (1987) Personal communication, 10 April.
Garrison, D. R. and Shale, D. (1987) 'Mapping the boundaries of distance education: problems in defining the field', *American Journal of Distance Education* 1, 1: 7–13.
Holt, S. (1985) 'Arts and sciences network for public school programming', *Counterpoint* 5, 1: 1, 18.
Keegan, D. (1986) *The Foundations of Distance Education*, London: Croom Helm.
Kitchen, K., and Russell, J. T. (1987) 'Educational telecommunications: an overview of Minnesota's state funded projects', *T. H. E. Journal* 14, 8; 55–6.
Lanier, R. (1986) 'Interactive telesystem breaks new ground', *E-ITV* 18, 6: 35–7.
Moore, M. G. (1987) 'University distance education of adults', *Tech Trends* 32, 4: 13–18.
Morehouse, D. L., Hoaglund, M. L. and Schmidt, R. H. (1987) 'Interactive television: findings, issues and recommendations', paper presented at the Vision for Rural and

Small Schools Conference sponsored by the Illinois State Board of Education, 17 September 1987, Springfield, Illinois.

Paulsen, M. F. (1987/88) 'In search of a virtual school', *T. H. E. Journal* 15, 5: 74–6.
Robinson, R. S., Collins, K. M. and West, P. C. (1985) 'No funds? No teachers? Share advanced courses with other schools via interactive cable television', *Tech Trends* 30, 2: 17–19.
Sleight, W. and Tueller, R. L. (1985) 'A new telecommunication system: teaming the electronic writing board with slow-scan TV', paper presented at the Applying New Technologies in Higher Education Conference, 4–5 March 1985, Orlando, Florida.
Smith, P. (1987) Personal communication, 10 April.
Wall, M. (1986) 'Technological options for rural schools', *Educational Leadership* 43, 6: 50–2.
Whittington, N. (1987) 'Is instructional television educationally effective? A research review', *American Journal of Distance Education* 1, 1: 47–57.
Wydra, D. (1987) 'The Pennsylvania audiographic teleteaching project', address delivered at the 8th Annual Conference for Administrators of Community Schools, 1 December 1987, Lubbock, Texas.

Part II
Organization and structures

Introduction

In 1982, the name of the International Council for Correspondence Education was changed to the International Council for Distance Education. The event is often described as a watershed, signifying the emergence of the multimedia approach to distance education to challenge the former supremacy of the traditional correspondence education approach. But its significance is greater than this. It also reflected the tremendous growth of distance education during the previous decade which was beginning to be reflected in the expanding membership of the organization. Particularly notable amongst new participants in the international conference scene were the autonomous national distance teaching universities, of which a dozen were set up during the 1970s. This type of institution provided the dominant model during the 1970s. More such institutions were established in the 1980s and a few others are planned or talked of even now, but other, potentially more flexible, models are more characteristic of the late 1980s and the 1990s. The distance teaching universities were the influential, high profile institutions, which gave to distance education the credibility it had not previously possessed.

The 1982 ICDE Conference is also significant because it reflects a new level of international interest by institutions in one another's activities. Prior to the 1970s, the total volume of distance education activity was much smaller than today's and communications in the first half of the century were also much less developed. One of the outstanding features of distance education at the present day is the multiplicity of international organizations of distance teaching institutions. There is communication between institutions at national, regional and international level, both at official level and between individuals, as well as unilaterally between institutions. Much more notice is taken of trends in distance education; institutions are created or expanded with an increased awareness of what is taking place in other parts of the world, there is substantial inter-institutional contact, and scholars and postgraduate students are widely concerned with comparative studies and with the analysis of international developments.

The proliferation of distance education in the 1980s and 1990s following the establishment of the distance teaching universities has been characterized by diversity and change. The potential of distance education for educational and training purposes, and in some instances for generating profit, is now recognized not only by educationists but also by international agencies, governments, and the private sector. Projects and programmes, both large and small, centrally organized and decentralized, have been set up in many countries in many subject areas to address a variety of problems. The potency of distance education is now generally recognized; it is potentially a powerful weapon against the problems which beset developing countries, particularly in Africa and Eastern Europe, if the resources can be found to release it and if realistic plans can be produced and implemented.

Daniel's chapter (Chapter 6), which first appeared in *Higher Education in Europe*, a journal published by the UNESCO European Centre for Higher Education in Bucharest, Romania, attempts to re-focus attention on the problems of the 1990s and the potential of distance education in the twenty-first century. Daniel is concerned particularly with what distance education could achieve for the nations of Eastern and Central Europe. He looks one step beyond the aspirations of organizations such as the Commonwealth of Learning, whose mission is to improve study opportunities for people in developing countries by facilitating the exchange and transfer of courses and materials. He proposes an international force along the lines of a United Nations peace-keeping force, which would have the responsibility for developing distance education provision to meet specific requirements and towards the ultimate goal of the creation of 'a common European home'.

In his book *Foundations of Distance Education*, of which an extract appears in this section (Chapter 7), Keegan presents a series of models of distance teaching institutions, based on a typology of existing institutions and organizations world-wide. No model is admitted to the classification unless a substantial number of institutions can be identified as being within it. It is indicative of the pace of change and of the influence of political events on education that in the short time since the book was published, the very existence of one of the models has been placed in jeopardy as a consequence of the recent dramatic events in Eastern and Central Europe. The 'consultation model', which has been central to the education systems established in Eastern bloc countries, is set to disappear in the changed social and political ethos of the reformed nations. Developments in Australia have also dramatically affected higher distance education provision and the 'Australian model'. In providing a typology of distance teaching institutions, Keegan has mapped an area whose boundaries are inevitably as susceptible to change as the boundaries of nation states.

The chapter by Taylor *et al.* (Chapter 8), originally published in *Distance*

Education, presents the findings of an international research project involving institutions from Australia, Canada, Pakistan and the South Pacific. The research topic is student persistence in distance education. The project report is particularly interesting not only for the research findings *per se*, but because it illustrates and points up the very considerable differences between institutions. The point is made very strongly that institutional contexts must be regarded as extremely important in any comparisons which are attempted between institutions.

The final chapter in this section is by Rumble, sometime Planning Officer of the UK Open University, who has for many years been concerned with issues relating to the costs of distance education. The area has proved a contentious one over the years, particularly because of the diversity of institutions involved in distance teaching and because of the multitude of different ways of estimating costs. This chapter, originally published in the Unesco journal *Prospects*, presents an internationally based account of how costs are estimated in various areas of distance teaching institutions. It provides evidence supporting the contention that distance education can be cheaper than conventional education.

6 A duty for distance education in the 1990s

John S. Daniel

INTRODUCTION

Börje Holmberg introduced a very fecund notion into the practice of distance education when he suggested that the aim of correspondence education was the establishment of a 'guided didactic' conversation with the learner. From this simple idea has grown an extensive literature on two-way communication in distance education. Those involved with the monitoring and the counselling of students, who are most directly responsible for maintaining instructional conversations at a distance and guiding their didactics, have created an especially active international network. Otto Peters formulated a more controversial concept when he described distance education as an 'industrial form of education', a term viewed as an oxymoron by those unsympathetic to mass education outside the classroom.

Despite widespread scepticism and occasional outright hostility from the educational establishment, these ideas of Holmberg and Peters have given rise to a burgeoning new form of teaching. Individuals desirous of enhancing their own opportunities and governments seeking greater returns on public investment in education have embraced the methods of distance education with enthusiasm. These methods make possible the rapid and inexpensive provision of instruction of consistent quality to large and scattered populations.

So far, however, distance education systems have usually been organized within national borders – like their conventional classroom counterparts. Moreover, the instructional material for distance teaching is also mostly home-grown. A trickle of materials transfer is occurring between countries, but the adoption of courses from other nations is still a rarity. Not-invented-here protectionism can still be rationalized and camouflaged by appealing to the importance of cultural appropriateness in education – even though the élites who make this appeal do not invoke it for their own families.

The thesis of this chapter is that the geopolitics of the 1990s challenge distance education to abandon parochialism. It has a duty to play a leading didactic role in the development of the new European world that could emerge now that the Berlin Wall has been breached and Germany reunited.

IF NATION SPEAKS PEACE UNTO NATION ...

Only a short time ago, '2000' was being date-stamped on blueprints for the future. 'Vision 2000', 'Toward 2000', 'Distance Learning in the Year 2000' – these were the typical titles of attempts at strategic planning. After a ritual acknowledgement of the pace of change, the 1990s designs for the future blithely ignored the 1990s in order to aim for the beckoning glamour of the twenty-first century. The target was overly distant. Such plans now resemble a boomerang that has spun back to land at the feet of the thrower. Suddenly, it is clear that the 1990s may be the most interesting decade of this century – and possibly the most hopeful.

This chapter is not the place in which to review in any detail the dramatic changes occurring in our world as it enters the 1990s. That task is for newspapers, for they admit the uncertainty of their forecasts. However, for the international distance education community, some trends seem clear and important.

First, the war of ideologies is over. This does not mean the end of history or of economic and political thought. But it does mean that the confrontation between capitalism ('read pluralistic market economies') and communism (read 'centrally-planned command economies') has ended. The tension beween the superpowers has diminished. Second, the new atmosphere of constructive dialogue between the superpowers – vividly evident in the United Nations – is hastening the trend to a multipolar world of economic blocs. Third, mankind has not lost its propensity to translate differences of class, ethnicity, and religion into violent conflict. Such conflicts seem more numerous than ever. The new concern is that these disputes now occur within countries rather than between them.

These trends create an unprecedented educational challenge because they demand monumental paradigmatic shifts in societies around the world. Before they can help their people make these intellectual shifts, educators themselves must first adopt new frameworks of thought. Such situations have occurred before, on a modest scale, when national school curricula have changed. In such cases, distance education has proved to be the best method for equipping teachers not simply to cope with changes, but to embrace them with enthusiasm. In Canada, for example, distance education was used in the 1970s to convert teachers to the new mathematics; in the United Kingdom, it is now helping teachers make the transition to the new national curriculum; and in the developing world, distance teaching methods are a mainstay of teacher training systems. The urgency and the scale of this new challenge create an historic opportunity for distance education.

Holmberg invented the term 'guided didactic conversation' for the two-way communication between correspondence school and individual learner. The times call for didactic conversations on a massive scale. Modern technology has transformed the simple techniques of correspondence tuition into the powerful teaching medium of contemporary distance education. This medium now provides the best means for guiding the didactic conversations between peoples so as to make them the best guarantors of prosperity and of peace.

WHAT SHOULD THE CONVERSATION BE ABOUT?

The fundamental need most clearly apparent in eastern Europe is for educational opportunities that can help equip and empower people to effect quiet revolutions in their local or national political economies. Programmes and courses that were unimaginable during the ideological war come to mind. In the communist world, the teaching of market economics or of business management used to be subversive. In the pluralist countries, instruction in political science included large doses of national self-justification, if not of self-glorification. Although these biases have not yet been completely eliminated, we can now imagine courses in economics and in management that could help the already well-educated people of eastern Europe steer their countries out of the economic doldrums without succumbing to the temptations of Peronism. It is even possible to imagine courses in political science based on a genuine search for appropriate democratic structures other than on the assumption that if eastern Europe simply adopted the political institutions of the United Kingdom, the United States, or Germany, all would be well.

In the evolving economic bloc that is western Europe, the need is for courses that will give intellectual substance to the claims that a new European spirit exists. This does not mean the creation of an ersatz culture cobbled together from the lowest common denominator of diverse national experiences, but an attempt to give people of all ages a more lively appreciation of the different intellectual traditions that exist within Europe.

In North America, the social need is to narrow the growing gaps between the life experiences of rich and poor, white and non-white, urban and suburban. Distance education can do some of this directly, with special courses for disadvantaged groups, but it has greater potential to help indirectly, by improving the schools. The wealthier class is fleeing the urban public schools for private education. Greater use of distance education courses in the public schools would help to enhance choice, improve consistency, and facilitate the professional upgrading of teachers.

In southeast Asia, distance education is already contributing strongly to the quiet revolution that has made it the most economically dynamic region of the world. Distance education seems to find particularly fertile soil in rapidly industrializing societies, which should not surprise us since it is, in Peters' words, an industrial form of education.

It should also not surprise us that in Africa and in Latin America distance education is only developing in fits and starts. Most of the countries on these continents lack the industrial and organizational traditions on which distance education finds its most comfortable foundations. Nor has the piecemeal approach of international aid agencies provided optimal support. Experts such as Holmberg have observed the tendency to launch one new project on top of another instead of supporting fewer projects consistently.

However, certain recent developments bode well for the future. The last decade has seen increasing cooperation between the countries of Latin America. The triennial world conference of the International Council for Distance Education will be held in Latin America for the first time in 1990. Many expect this event to symbolize the coming of age of distance education in this region.

For the developing countries of the Commonwealth, particularly those of Africa, a newly created cooperative mechanism holds promise. This is the Commonwealth of Learning, a network of countries and institutions established in 1988 to help poorer countries build up an indigenous capacity for distance education. Among its activities are the facilitation of staff training as well as the transfer and the joint development of course materials. The Commonwealth of Learning could be a useful model for cooperation in distance education in Europe in the 1990s.

WHY NOT AN INSTRUCTIONAL PEACE-MAKING FORCE?

Whenever one society helps another respond to its educational needs, grumbles about imperialism or hegemony may be heard. A way to avoid such criticism is to internationalize the assistance. Is the world's distance education community capable of mounting an effort, in the intellectual arena, to promote economic effectiveness and peaceful politics in eastern Europe? Throughout history, mankind has taken internationalism for granted in activities of high priority. Indeed, the rise of nationalism in a particular area of endeavour is a warning that its priority may be slipping. In medieval times, when Christendom and civilization were synonymous in the West, the appointment of an Italian to an English bishopric caused no surprise. In modern times, when rocketry and power became synonymous in the Cold

War, the recruitment of the best German scientists by the USA was applauded. As economic prosperity became a higher priority, business became multinational. Now that environmental repair is urgent, scientists are crisscrossing the world to study global trends.

Distance education is at a stage of development aud priority at which internationalism is taken for granted. For example, Börje Holmberg was appointed to lead research on distance education in Germany after a distinguished career as a practitioner in Sweden. Many distance education professionals have changed jobs across the Atlantic in both directions. More recently, there has been similar mobility within Africa and Asia. Another measure of internationalism is that the membership of the International Council for Distance Education has diversified dramatically since the 1960s. Today, its ratio of countries represented to total membership is exceptionally high for a voluntary international association. Finally, the industrial dynamic of distance education has meant that its growth has been concentrated in only a few institutions in each country. These conditions are very propitious for the launching of an international effort to assist eastern European countries and institutions that seek help with the paradigmatic shift which these revolutionary times require.

What are the principles on which the distance education community should base such an initiative? Three guiding ideas seem important.

First, there is a useful analogy with the peace-keeping forces of the United Nations. The UN does not recruit troops directly. It puts its blue berets on contingents supplied voluntarily by member states. In a similar way, any international coordinating mechanism for distance education should use courses and personnel supplied by existing institutions rather than develop its own capacity.

Second, the principle of subsidiarity should apply. Operations should be carried out as close to the learner as possible. Specifically, this would mean delivering courses and programmes through concerned institutions in the eastern European countries. Only in this way will an indigenous capacity to continue the process be established.

Third, since our particular purpose is to fill a vacuum created by the long absence of instruction in free market economics, pluralist political theory, and private business management, the operation itself must reflect the values of free enterprise and pluralism. A balance must be achieved between the need to establish viable mechanisms for making courses available and the imperative not to create institutional or ideological monopolies.

TO ASSIST CHANGE IN EASTERN EUROPE

The challenge for distance education in eastern Europe is most closely analagous to the in-service training of teachers in industrial countries. Eastern European countries already have educated workforces, trained teachers at all levels, and extensive networks of institutions, including some distance teaching establishments. The goal is simply to show people new ways of thinking about economic, political and managerial issues and to re-equip them with some of the professional skills that the transition to market economies will require. The operation is one of retraining, not of initial training.

The first essential element for the operation is money. This does not appear to pose a problem. Western nations have already built up a substantial fund to help the economies of eastern Europe. Indeed, a current worry is that since these economies have previously misallocated their financial resources, it may be difficult for them to spend international funds without worsening the existing structural problems. There is, therefore, a direct analogy with two decades of experience of international aid projects in the Third World. This experience has led international donor agencies to place increasing emphasis on the importance of human resource development as a *sine qua non* for other forms of progress. For this reason, Western governments are likely to favour spending money on an effective educational means for the preparation of the people of eastern Europe for work in economies based on free-market assumptions.

The second necessary element is a mechanism for coordinating the acquisition or creation of appropriate distance education packages and the liaison required with the institutions in each country that will provide student support. This role could be undertaken directly by an international governmental organization, such as the European Community, or indirectly by contracting to an international non-governmental organization or voluntary association. The European Association of Distance Teaching Universities (EADTU) is an obvious candidate in the second category, since much of the teaching required will be at the post-secondary level. The long-established correspondence schools in the Scandinavian countries might be appropriate bodies to coordinate non-university work.

The potential diversity of such an operation, in terms of subjects, countries, and languages, is such that the most promising approach would be to start quickly on a modest scale and then to build on success. This is not the place to propose a planning schedule for the operation we have sketched out here. However, the importance of particular aspects of the preparations required is worth emphasizing. We can assume that a wide variety of courses will be made available by institutions around the world once the project is launched, even if most of them will have to be translated. For this reason, work should begin at the other end of the process, namely the identification of institutions in eastern Europe with the capacity and desire to participate. These would not all need to be existing distance teaching operations, for some conventional institutions might wish to take this opportunity to begin offering programmes in a dual mode.

If, as is likely, the potential institutional participants in the East are also numerous, choices will have to be made. The quality of support they are likely to provide to students should be the main criterion for adjudicating among competing bids.

Another important constituency for the project will be the businesses that elect to expand in eastern Europe in order to obtain their share of the available markets and to contribute to the transformation of the economies. These firms, which will likely have eager workforces with urgent training needs, could be powerful allies for the public institutions involved.

A further reason for beginning with the demand-side of the instructional equation is to face immediately the questions of credit transfer and equivalency that will have to be resolved. In this respect, the work on credit coordination already accomplished by the European Community will be a useful starting-point.

A guiding principle in the implementation of the project should be the creation of a process that is sustainable, once launched, without ongoing special funds. Doing so should not be difficult since institutions in eastern Europe could soon acquire the skills to adapt and to revise by themselves the distance education courses that they are enabled to offer through this mechanism. The project must ensure that the conditions under which Western institutions provide courses do not impede this process. At a later stage, the participating institutions in eastern Europe will be able to develop their own courses on the subjects that are the focus of this proposal and build up fully-functioning distance education programmes.

CONCLUSION

Thanks to the intellectual underpinnings provided by scholar–practitioners such as Holmberg and Peters, distance education has already created two waves of success in the second half of this century. In the 1960s and 1970s, modern media technologies were blended with older correspondence techniques to create open universities in industrial countries.

In the 1970s and 1980s, the developing and industrializing countries of Asia took the open university concept and applied it on a huge scale, with student numbers in the hundreds of thousands and public expenditures low enough to break the vicious spiral of rising educational costs that has bedevilled conventional universities in the developing world.

In the 1990s, distance education will have the historic opportunity to facilitate the last great movement of the twentieth century, the creation of a common European home. In helping the countries of eastern Europe to catch up on lost time, the institutions and countries of the West will find that their own appreciation of the rich traditions of the other nations of Europe is enhanced.

7   A typology of distance teaching systems

Desmond Keegan

There are distance teaching universities only in South Africa and the USSR.

Otto Peters 1965

BACKGROUND

It used to be accepted that distance teaching started in 1840. Holmberg (1960: 3) gives that as the date when Isaac Pitman offered tuition by post in shorthand to students in England. In 1856, Charles Toussaint and Gustave Langenscheidt commenced language teaching by correspondence in Germany. Delling (1979: 13), however, has argued convincingly that institutions which exhibit all the characteristics suggested above (Keegan 1986) are little more than a century old.

Today, a listing of distance institutions would embrace most countries of the world and all levels of education. A stringent listing of systemic characteristics has been proposed whereby only those institutions exhibiting certain academic and administrative peculiarities, which are reflected in decisions about physical plant, are considered to be distance education institutions for the purpose of this study. Even then the field remaining is vast (Harry 1984) and there is great variety of provision. Global statements about distance education as a whole are rarely valid and most general statements must be hedged with qualifications. The need to provide the reader with groupings or classifications about which at least some general statements may be made with confidence is pressing.

CONDITIONS FOR A VIABLE TYPOLOGY

The classification in this study is based on the following premises for the construction of a usable typology.

- It should be helpful to the readers, enabling them to focus on a range of institutions within the field of 'distance teaching institutions' about which statements can be made that identify what this grouping of institutions has in common, and what it is that distinguishes it from the other groupings.
- To be helpful it should not be artificial – each grouping should contain dozens, preferably hundreds, of institutions.
- It should not be artificial with regard to students – each grouping should enrol thousands, preferably millions, of students.
- It should not be artificial with regard to time – each grouping should have been identifiable for at least a decade, preferably longer.
- It should try to encompass all distance teaching institutions, public and private, at all levels from primary schooling to postgraduate levels – and not just concentrate on distance education at university level.
- It should only include those distance teaching institutions or departments of existing institutions which exhibit both the major characteristic sub- systems of distance institutions (course development and student support services) – for without this limitation the variants are legion. Institutions or departments which are considered not to exhibit both these operational subsystems are excluded (though some of them have made excellent contributions to distance education).

Fundamental to the classification proposed here is the acceptance (with Neil, Keegan and Rumble) that the basic distinction is between *autonomous distance teaching institutions* and *distance subsections of conventional institutions* (see Figure 7.1). As an explanation of 'autonomous', Neil's (1981: 140) listing of autonomy in (a) finance, (b) examination and accreditation, (c) curriculum and materials, and (d) delivery and student support systems, is accepted as accurate.

It is a question of autonomy at the institutional level because autonomous distance institutions like the Open University of the UK, the Centre National d'Enseignement à Distance in France, and the New South Wales College of External Studies in Australia are components of state or national education systems. Neil explains: 'Although the OUUK is enmeshed in, and utterly dependent upon, the United Kingdom infrastructure, its relationships with other organizations are basically contractual and commercial in nature' (1981: 139).

Once these two basic groupings have been established, further division within the two groupings is by didactic structure, that is the linking structures that the groupings of institutions provide between learning materials and learning. It is when institutions are classified in this way that it starts to become possible to make general statements about the groupings which have some validity. Distance education is too rich and diversified a field of

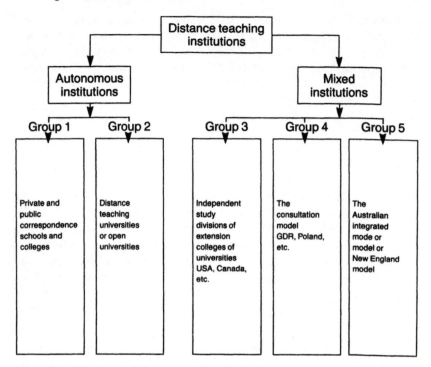

Figure 7.1   Typology of distance teaching institutions

education for more general statements of the type 'all distance institutions do this' to be possible without so many nuances and qualifications as to be virtually unintelligible.

AUTONOMOUS DISTANCE TEACHING INSTITUTIONS

The autonomous distance teaching institutions have been divided into two groups for the purpose of this study. Group 1 is called 'Public and private correspondence schools and colleges' and Group 2 'Distance teaching universities'. The division between the two groups is based on complexity of didactic structure and level of provision.

In very general terms the link between learning materials and learning provided by Group 1 institutions tends to be less complex than by those of Group 2, especially in the use of 'big media' (Schramm 1977) and face-to-face meetings. Group 1 institutions, whether public or private, sometimes state that students enrol with them precisely because they wish to avoid face-to-face contact. Group 2 institutions sometimes have the intention of supporting the distance learner by as rich a provision of support services as possible.

In terms of level of provision, Group 1 institutions normally provide courses for children and adults at lower than university level. Group 2 institutions are called distance teaching universities. The division is not watertight, however, as many Group 1 institutions offer some university level courses, while most distance teaching universities offer courses below university level.

Autonomous distance teaching institutions which provide a full range of courses from basic adult education to university programmes are of particular importance. Rather than create a new category for these multi-level providers they will be regarded here as having a mixture of characteristics from the two groupings identified.

Public and private correspondence schools and colleges (Group 1)

Correspondence schools and colleges are autonomous distance teaching institutions. They control or have authority over staffing, finance, accreditation, development of materials, and student services, even when they are part of a state-wide or nation-wide system.

This model is used widely throughout the world both by government-sponsored and by proprietary institutions. Schools and colleges of this type have existed for over 100 years and today there are examples in nearly every country of the Western world. Examples are found particularly amongst government-sponsored schools at primary and secondary level, and both publicly sponsored and privately supported colleges at technical, vocational, and further education levels. Some well-known examples are the National Extension College, Cambridge; Leidse Onderweijsinstellingen, Leiden; and the New South Wales College of External Studies, Sydney. In Australia, Canada, and New Zealand this has been the chosen model for government correspondence schools for nearly seventy years, with the Alberta Correspondence School, founded in 1923, reaching 60,330 annual enrolments by 1986 (Turnbull 1987: 108). Karow (1979) listed 144 Group 1 institutions (all proprietary) in the Federal Republic of Germany and there must be at least as many in France.

Group 1 is an institutional structure which emphasizes the correspondence element in distance education. It might be represented diagrammatically as in Figure 7.2. The didactic structure is frequently patterned thus: the correspondence schools and colleges develop or purchase learning materials and send them by post to the student. The student studies the materials and posts assignments back to the institution, which marks and comments on them and

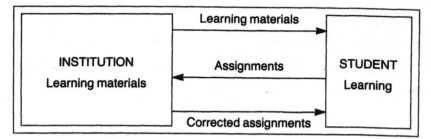

Figure 7.2   A correspondence school or college model (Group 1)

posts them back to the student. The student studies the comments, completes the next assignment and the process is repeated.

Print tends to be the didactic medium with some use of audio-cassettes. From this description and the diagrammatic representation in Figure 7.2 it can be indicated that the environment for student learning provided by this model can be fragile. The student's main contact with the representatives of the institution is by post so that isolation can become a problem.

As many correspondence schools and colleges have a philosophy that suggests that students enrol with them because 'they want to be left alone', it can be maintained that student support services and face-to-face sessions can infringe learner autonomy or the independence of the adult learner. Gone are peer group support and the presence of the teacher. The drop-out rate can be enormous.

There are, nevertheless, institutions which have turned these disadvantages into factors to benefit student learning. There is evidence to claim (Bååth and Wångdahl 1976, Bååth 1979, Holmberg 1981 and Rekkedal 1981) that the dedication of the correspondence tutor can forge with the distant student by letter and by telephone such a creative link that a correspondence course can become a form of privileged one-to-one study. A type of one-on-one bonding has often been created that is difficult to achieve in lecture or tutorial.

Distance teaching universities (Group 2)

In 1965, Otto Peters wrote 'The Republic of South Africa and the USSR are the only countries with distance teaching universities'. The scene was quite different twenty years later.

Distance education started the decade of the 1970s as the Cinderella of the education spectrum: it was practically unknown as a segment of national education provision and at times criticized for the malpractice of some of its representatives. It emerged in the 1980s with the possibility of a radical change of image. The foundation of the open universities was a major element in this fairy tale-like transformation, together with the growing privatization of urban society which characterized the decade and the benefits of industrialization in a period of growing financial stringency.

At the head of the list of distance teaching universities stands the Open University of the United Kingdom (OUUK) at Milton Keynes which received its Royal Charter in 1969 and taught its first students in 1971. Each commentator will have a personal list of the constituents of the OUUK's immediate success, but amongst them were brilliant political and educational leadership, an unswerving concentration on the needs of students studying at a distance and a national backlog of intelligent adults for whom the provisions of face-to-face universities were not fully relevant. These factors and others quickly brought this non-traditional university structure the status of a permanent provider of university education in the UK with an annual enrolment of 100,000.

The OUUK was followed by a series of foundations in both developed and developing countries of similar institutions called 'Fernuniversitäten', 'open universities' or 'universidades de educación a distancia'. Not only does the foundation of these universities mark a watershed in distance education, it provides the most advanced stage yet in the evolution of the concept of a university.

These universities do not have students in residence, neither do they have full-time day-time students, nor even part-time night-time students. They place their students at home. One looks in vain for students as one walks around the campus at Milton Keynes. Many of the other universities are off-putting, factory-like buildings and there is little or nothing for students to do at them. Gone too is the concept of the university library with places for undergraduate and postgraduate research, gone are the lecture rooms, tutorial rooms, seminar rooms, laboratories for student research, and facilities for the student community.

These are universities of a nation or a state, not of a city like Oxford or Bologna. Frequently they are universities on tens or hundreds of sites spread throughout the nation.

These universities present the most radical challenge yet to the idea of a university enunciated by John H. Newman and developed in the Western world. They represent the final democratization of the concept of a university by opening up the possibility of university studies to many who were formerly barred from enrolling by the timetabling of lectures and the necessity of set periods of research at the universities' facilities. Full-time workers, the disabled, imprisoned, and hospitalized, together with those tied to the home, can now enrol at a university if it teaches at a distance.

In didactic structure, Group 2 institutions attempt to provide a more comprehensive linking between learning materials and student learning. This might be represented as in Figure 7.3.

Distance teaching universities differ from Group 1 institutions in the following three ways.

1 *The level of provision.* Correspondence schools and colleges in Group 1 concentrate on education for school-children and further education for adults. The distance teaching universities focus on the provision of university degrees at a distance, though most of the group offer further education courses as well.

2 *The use of media.* A study by Keegan and Rumble (1982: 213) shows a movement towards a more extensive use of educational media by the distance teaching universities. In general, Group 2 institutions make a more comprehensive use of non-print educational media than Group 1 institutions.

3 *The didactic link.* Group 2 institutions profess to provide a more coherent link between learning materials and learning so that a satisfactory university-level educational experience is provided.

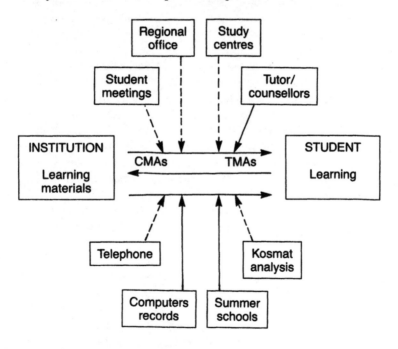

Key: ---- optional ——— obligatory

Figure 7.3   A distance teaching university model (Group 2)

DISTANCE EDUCATION DEPARTMENTS OF CONVENTIONAL INSTITUTIONS

For the purpose of this study, three types of a distance education department or section within the structures of a conventional institution have been distinguished. These are:

- independent study divisions of a conventional college or university (Group 3);
- distance education departments of institutions in the socialist republics of Central and Eastern Europe – the consultation model (Group 4); and
- the Australian integrated mode – New England model (Group 5).

It is felt that these three groupings can be satisfactorily distinguished one from the other both administratively and didactically, though it is clear that they share many common characteristics.

Institutions within each of these three groupings have been in existence for many decades. They have enrolled many tens of thousands of students studying at a distance. Each grouping contains dozens of institutions which teach, normally, at higher education level.

Independent study divisions of a conventional college or university (Group 3)

Examples of independent study divisions are numerous and have been in existence for almost a century. Noteworthy among them are the Independent Study Divisions of Extension Colleges of American and Canadian universities. In the early 1980s, sixty-four American universities had independent study departments and there were twenty similar structures in Canada. In France, the Centres de télé-enseignement universitaire (CTUs) at nearly twenty universities fall within this category. In Sweden, distance education is organized in this way from a number of Swedish universities. Many universities in India and Latin America have correspondence or distance departments within this category.

Recent studies have been published of a number of these institutional arrangements, notably by Markowitz (1983) on the independent study departments of United States universities, by Willén (1983) on distance education in Swedish universities, by Escotet (1983) on the Latin American provision, and by Singh (1980) and Carr (1983) on India.

One of the administrative structures of these universities is the Continuing Education or Extension College. The Department of Independent Study or Correspondence Study is usually one of the divisions of the Extension

College. Departments of Independent Study offer courses in ten major delivery modes within the field of distance education:

Correspondence lessons
Credit by examination
Contract alternative
Directed individual study
Special programmes for groups
Television courses
Video-cassette courses
Radio courses
Audio-cassette courses
University without walls.

Course development is usually by university faculty paid overload to produce the courses, though a smaller number of faculty (called adjunct faculty) come from other universities, and occasionally from other sectors of the academic community. Tuition is also provided by the university faculty and the students study for degrees or certificates awarded by the university. However, there are limitations on the use of independent study credits for degree programmes in certain departments or schools of the university, and in many cases, one is not permitted to complete a full degree by independent study.

The consultation model (Group 4) to 1990

Peters' (1971) classification of two basic structures for distance education, print-based with correspondence feedback in the West and print-based with consultations in the East, was a valid analysis of distance education in the 1960s and still has its uses today. In this study, however, the autonomous distance teaching universities of the USSR are placed in Group 2 (the distance teaching universities) and a special category (Group 4) is created for the consultation model when it is a subset of a mixed institution which teaches both on-campus and at a distance.

The consultation model has been documented for the German Democratic Republic by Schwartz (1978), Möhle (1978), and Dietze (1979), for the USSR by Gorochov (1979) and Ilyin (1983), for Bulgaria by Christow and Mutojischiew (1979), for Hungary by Fekete and Nahlik (1979), and for Yugoslavia by Krajnc (1988).

The didactic model of Group 4 is quite different from Western systems and 'correspondence' usually plays little role in it. In some systems students, on enrolment, are allocated both to the institution from which they will get their degree (which may be far away) and to a consultation centre at an institution near to their home and work. In other systems the enrolment and the consultation centre are at the same university.

Study commences with a residential seminar on-campus. After this, students study at home from the learning materials provided. This home study is interspersed at regular intervals (often once a fortnight) by consultations which are frequently compulsory. A consultation consists of a day's work on campus in which the student receives face-to-face guidance in each of the subjects being studied.

The consultation model highlights characteristics of distance education that are not found, or are not found so clearly, in Groups 1, 2, 3, and 5. Amongst these are the following.

- Distance education is seen as a democratization of educational provision by opening up to all adults, irrespective of their place of work, access to university qualifications at all levels.
- Distance education provides for the nation a means of training the work-force without withdrawing students from contributing to the Gross National Product throughout the length of their studies.
- Distance education is linked to the students' work and there is constant interaction between work and study.
- Of the major types of distance education provision it is the one which is closest to face-to-face provision.

Ilyin (1983) gives a presentation of the consultation model in the USSR. Apart from the fourteen distance teaching universities (classified as Group 2 institutions in this study), he refers to no fewer than '800 distance subsidiaries and branches of full-time universities and institutes'.

In the German Democratic Republic, the ratio of face-to-face consultations to individual study at home is 20 per cent as the 1:1 rhythm of equal attendance on-campus and private study expected of conventional students is replaced by a 5:1 rhythm in Fernstudium.

Besides the learning materials there are three other major components of the didactic structure: private study, the students' workplace, and regular seminars (consultations). The students' workplace plays an important role in the study programme. Students are usually sponsored by their firm. They receive by law 48 days' paid study leave per year. Their thesis is usually on some aspect of the company's product or management. They are, in effect, practically guaranteed a promotion position upon graduation.

Schwartz (1978) and Möhle (1978) present the didactic structure schematically as in Figure 7.4. It is claimed that this interaction of work and study provides a unique blending of theoretical and practical learning that is not paralleled in ordinary education.

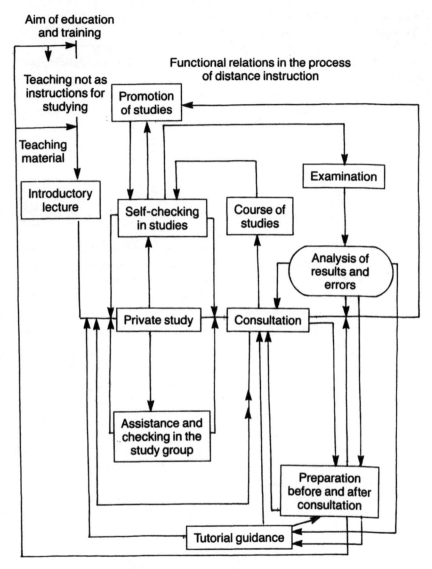

Figure 7.4   A consultation system model (Group 4)
Source: Adapted and translated from Schwarz (1978), Möhle (1978)

The Australian integrated mode – New England model (Group 5)

A distinct form of distance education department within a conventional college or university has evolved in Australia. It is known as the 'New

England model' (New England is an area in New South Wales, 300 km NW of Sydney) or the 'Australian integrated mode'. It has been extensively presented: Sheath (1965, 1973), Dahllöf (1978), Smith (1979, 1984), Laverty (1980), Guiton (1981), Ortmeier (1981), White (1982) and Shott (1983a, b). It is found, with variations, in Australian colleges of advanced education and universities that teach at a distance. Systems in Zambia, Fiji, Papua New Guinea, and Jamaica have been modelled on it.

There had been a long history of distance education in Australia prior to the founding of the University of New England at Armidale in 1955, but all from Group 1 or Group 3 structures. Individual Australian universities or colleges do not have sufficient distance students to warrant the foundation of an autonomous institution.

In 1955, the University of New England commenced teaching both on campus and externally. A unique staffing structure and an attempt to preserve as much on-campus provision for students as possible was evolved for the distance teaching system. The university's lecturers were given a dual mandate and allocated groups of both internal and external students in equal numbers. Lecture notes and even audio-cassette tapes recorded live in on-campus lectures were sent to students and a requirement of compulsory periods of time on-campus was built into the distance study programme. This model is presented schematically in Figure 7.5.

The system maintains that the academic staff of the university or college are to be responsible for the total teaching/learning process of writing courses, teaching them through a combination of independent study materials and face-to-face tuition and assessing the students by way of assignments and formal examinations.

The external studies department is therefore an administrative one which organizes for students a series of interactive activities, including at least a brief period of traditional university or college life as a full-time student in residence.

Thus external and internal teaching are integrated. The same academic staff teach and assess both sets of students. Students are enrolled in the same courses, take the same examinations, and qualify for the same degrees and diplomas.

Because academic staff have internal teaching commitments to conventional students, besides the responsibility of developing learning materials for external studies and then tutoring them, an External Studies Department is set up to relieve them of administrative details. This department frequently has no teaching function but looks after the production and distribution of course material, student records, statistics, and student support services.

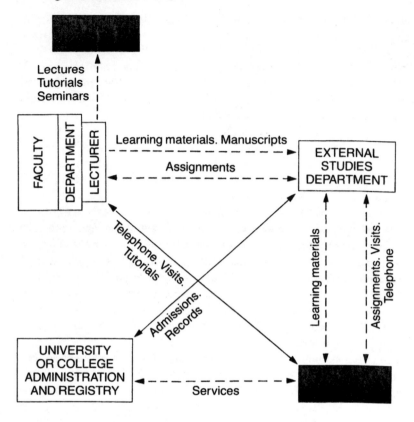

Figure 7.5   Australian integrated mode model (Group 5)

OTHER STRUCTURES

Distance education institutions, as defined in this book, are institutions which teach students. They parallel ordinary schools, colleges, and universities in that they enrol students, teach, assess, and evaluate them and provide a total learning experience for them in every way. They also have a second function, which is not paralleled by ordinary schools, colleges, and universities. They prepare for (some scholars would use the verb 'teach' here too) future students. They prepare printed, audio, video, and/or computer-based learning materials for students who will enrol in the future – next year or in two to ten years in the future.

The demands of a viable typology that would comprise groupings of institutions large enough for practical use have eliminated from consideration a number of institutions that are often associated with the evolution of distance education. These include (a) some accrediting institutions; (b) some materials production centres; and (c) certain audio-video and television programmes.

REFERENCES

Bååth, J. (1979) *Postal Two-Way Communication in Correspondence Education*, Malmö: LiberHermods.

Bååth, J. and Wångdahl, A. (1976) *The Tutor as an Agent of Motivation in Correspondence Education*, Lund: University of Lund. (Pedagogical reports 8)

Carr, R. (1983) 'Distance education in Indian universities: a change of direction?', *Distance Education* 4, 2: 101–19.

Christow, J. and Mutojischiew, L. (1979) 'Die Entwicklung des Fernstudiums in der Volksrepublik Bulgarien', in G. Dietze (ed.) *IVe Internationales Wissenschaftliches Seminar zum Hochschulfernstudium*, Dresden: Zentralstelle für das Hochschulfernstudium des Ministeriums für Hoch-und Fachschulwesens, 22–30.

Dahllöf, U. (1978) *Reforming Higher Education and External Studies in Sweden and Australia*, Stockholm: Almqvist & Wiksell.

Delling, R. (1979) *Lehrbrief als Fernlehrgelegenheit*, Hagen: FernUniversität.

Dietze, G. (ed.) (1979) *IVe Internationales Wissenschaftliches Seminar zum Hochschulfernstudium*, Dresden: Zentralstelle für das Hochschulfernstudium des Ministeriums für Hoch-und Fachschulwesens.

Escotet, M. (1983) 'Adverse factors in the development of an open university in Latin America', in D. Sewart, D. Keegan and B. Holmberg (eds) *Distance Education: International Perspectives*, London: Croom Helm.

Fekete, J. and Nahlik, J. (1979) 'Ungarn', in G. Dietze (ed.) *IVe Internationales Wissenschaftliches Seminar zum Hochschulfernstudium*, Dresden: Zentralstelle für das Hochschulfernstudium des Ministeriums für Hoch-und Fachschulwesens.

Gorochov, W. A. (1979) 'Hauptwege zur Vorrollkommung des Fernstudiums in der USSR', in G. Dietze (ed.) *IVe Internationales Wissenschaftliches Seminar zum Hochschulfernstudium*, Dresden: Zentralstelle für das Hochschulfernstudium des Ministeriums für Hoch-und Fachschulwesens.

Guiton, P. (1981) 'Australian distance teaching systems', paper to Conference of Universiti Sains Malaysia, Penang, Malaysia.

Harry, K. (1984) 'The International Centre for Distance Learning's new computerized database', *International Council for Distance Education Bulletin* 6: 6–7.

Holmberg, B. (1960) *On the Methods of Teaching by Correspondence*, Lund: Gleerup.

Holmberg, B. (1981) *Status and Trends of Distance Education*, London: Kogan Page.

Ilyin, V. V. (1983) 'The USSR Financial and Economic Institute for Education', *Distance Education* 4, 2: 142–8.

76   *Organization and structures*

Karow, W. (1979) *Privater Fernunterricht in der Bundesrepublik Deutschland und in Ausland*, Berlin: DIBB.
Keegan, D. (1986) *Foundations of Distance Education*, London: Croom Helm.
Keegan, D. and Rumble, G. (1982) 'Distance teaching at university level', in G. Rumble and K. Harry (eds) *The Distance Teaching Universities*, London: Croom Helm.
Krajnc, A. (1988) *Social Isolation and Learning Effectiveness in Distance Education*, Hagen: FernUniversität. (ZIFF Papiere 71)
Laverty, J. (1980) 'Kevin C. Smith's "External studies at New England" ', *Distance Education* 1, 2: 207–14.
Markowitz, H. (1983) 'Independent study by correspondence in American universities', *Distance Education* 4, 2: 149–70.
Möhle, H. (1978) *Das in das einheitliche sozialistische Bildungswesen der DDR integrierte Hochschulfernstudium*, Leipzig: Karl-Marx Universität.
Neil, M. (1981) *The Education of Adults at a Distance*, London: Kogan Page.
Ortmeier, A. (1981) *Das Fernstudium an den Universitäten und Fachhochschulen Australiens*, Tübingen: Deutsches Institut für Fernstudienforschung.
Peters, O. (1965) *Der Fernunterricht*, Weinheim: Beltz.
Peters, O. (1971) *Texte zum Hochschulfernstudium*, Weinheim: Beltz.
Rekkedal, T. (1981) *Introducing the Personal Tutor Counsellor in a System of Distance Education*, Stabekk: NKI Norway.
Schramm, W. (1977) *Big Media, Little Media*, London: Sage.
Schwartz, R. (1978) 'Die Konsultation in Studienprozess des Fernstudiums', in H. Möhle (ed.) *Hoch-und Fachschulfernstudium in der DDR und in entwicklungsländern Afrikas*, Leipzig: Karl-Marx Universität.
Sheath, H. (1965) *External Studies at New England: the First Ten Years*, Armidale, NSW: University of New England.
Sheath, H. (1973) *Report on External Studies*, Armidale, NSW: University of New England.
Shott, M. (1983a) 'External studies in Australia at the cross-roads?', *Australian and South Pacific External Studies Association Newsletter* 9, 2: 2–9.
Shott, M. (1983b) 'Final report to the ASPESA Executive', *Australian and South Pacific External Studies Association Newsletter* 9, 3: 15–17.
Singh, B. (1980) *Correspondence Education at Indian Universities*, Patiala: Punjabi University.
Smith, K. C. (1979) *External Studies at New England: a Silver Jubilee Review 1955–1979*, Armidale, NSW: University of New England.
Smith, K. C. (1984) *Diversity Down Under in Distance Education*, Toowoomba, Queensland: Darling Downs Institute of Advanced Education.
Turnbull, A. (1987) 'Distance education: the trendsetter', *Media in Education and Development* 20, 3: 108–12.
White, M. (1982) 'A history of external studies in Australia', *Distance Education* 4, 2: 101–21.
Willén, B. (1983) 'Distance education in Swedish universities', *Distance Education* 4. 2: 211–22.

8 Student persistence in distance education: a cross-cultural multi-institutional perspective

*James C. Taylor, Les J. Barker, Vernon J. White,
Garry Gillard, David Kaufman, Ahmed Noor Khan
and Ross Mezger*

Following the Twelfth World Conference of ICDE (Vancouver, 1982), the author was invited to coordinate a project aimed at operationalizing a research methodology that was discussed during the conference. The essence of the proposed methodology was to conduct essentially the same empirical study in a variety of distance education settings. It was thought that such an approach could engender an objective synthesis of research results that might lead to a significant contribution being made to the empirical basis for distance education.

It was agreed that the study should focus on something of practical importance to distance educators. It was further agreed that the study could not be of too specialized a theoretical nature because of the need to involve a number of institutions across a wide range of cultural settings. It was finally agreed that the study should take a lead from Rekkedal's (1973) study on turnaround time.

Major contributions to this first ICDE International Research Project were made by L. J. Barker and V. J. White (Darling Downs Institute of Advanced Education, Australia), G. Gillard (University of the South Pacific, Fiji), D. Kaufman (Open Learning Institute, Canada), A. N. Khan (Allama Iqbal Open University, Pakistan), R. Mezger (Tasmanian State Institute of Technology, Australia) and the ICDE Research Committee regional coordinators.

INTRODUCTION

The recommendation to use Rekkedal's (1973) study as the starting-point placed the project in the broader context of the problem of student drop out (Woodley and Parlett 1983), which has generated a great deal of discussion and argument among distance educators. Typical of the interest in the low completion rates of many distance education students are relatively recent studies by Kember (1981), Scales (1984), Roberts (1984), Thompson (1984) and the re-publication (in 1984) of the aforementioned Rekkedal study. A review of this latter study revealed the major conclusion that it was quite likely that drop-out rates can be lowered by reducing turnaround time (1984: 250). In Rekkedal's study, turnaround time was defined as the time from the moment the student mails in the homework assignment for a study unit until it is received by the student with the tutor's corrections and comments (1984: 232).

During the course of Rekkedal's study, turnaround time was manipulated experimentally so that one group of students, classified as the Quick Group, had a median turnaround time of 5.6 days, while the other group (the Delayed Group) experienced a turnaround which had as its median 8.3 days. The overall range of turnaround times in the experiment was between 2 days and 10 days or more. Obviously the nature of the assignments involved is a critical factor in determining turnaround time. Rekkedal's study was undertaken within the context of a basic course in mathematics, where one would assume that marking time may not be excessive. Further, the course was aimed at students with 'very poor training' or those students who 'feel that they are so unsure of their knowledge that they wish to repeat basic materials' (1984: 238). The extent to which such findings can be readily generalized to other distance education contexts (for example, those for undergraduate students in an accredited degree course) is somewhat problematic. Indeed, this concern for the lack of generalizability of much of the research in distance education was one of the reasons for undertaking the current project. It seems likely that relatively weak students in an area like basic mathematics would perhaps be more dependent on a rapid turnaround time than more mature students studying a range of other disciplines who had experienced a successful high school education. Indeed, it might be somewhat surprising were Rekkedal's results to be generally applicable to distance education, given the apparently limited range of turnaround times evident in his study.

Without denigrating the value of Rekkedal's study, part of the problem of generalizing such research to other settings is the fact that the study is generally devoid of any theoretical underpinning. Several potentially useful models of student attrition have been developed since the time that Rekkedal's study was undertaken. Recent reviews of the literature (Tinto 1975 and Terenzini and Pascarella 1980) have agreed on several generalizations emanating from research on student attrition. First, it is clear that no single factor explains attrition in higher education. Second, it is clear that the research on attrition would be better conducted using a theoretical model rather than a descriptive approach. Several theoretical models including those of Spady and Tinto (1975) have been developed and have subsequently generated empirical work. The present study was based on Tinto's model which conceptualizes attrition as a product of the student's characteristics, abilities and goal commitments interacting with the institutional environment. This interaction is usually described in terms of the academic and social integration of students into the academic environment and social substructure of the institution. In short, integration produces student commitment to the institution and a strengthened commitment to attaining his or her educational goals, whereas a lack of integration leads to withdrawal from the institution.

These theoretical notions of academic and social integration have obviously been inspired by concerns for traditional on-campus students rather than for those enrolled in distance education. In reviewing the limits of theory and practice in student attrition, Tinto (1982) defined academic and social interaction primarily in terms of contacts (both formal and informal) between faculty and students. He subsequently recommended that institutions should encourage those contacts whenever and wherever possible (Tinto 1982: 697). This emphasis on optimizing social and academic interactions between students and faculty appears to be worthy of investigation in the distance education arena.

Whereas the social and academic integration of on-campus students seems likely to be enhanced by regular attendance at lectures, tutorials and regular contacts with academic staff and other students, the integration of off-campus students can be seen to be dependent on the model of distance education used by a particular institution. Such models vary from those that are perhaps purely self-instructional, entailing minimal interpersonal interaction with students, to those institutions which attempt to maximize interpersonal interactions by either employing local tutors (who meet regularly with students) or by running weekend schools on a regular basis with attendance for students being compulsory. Other institutions make extensive use of telephone tutorials, residential schools and the like. The extent of social and academic integration with an institution then seems likely to be largely dependent upon the model of distance education employed. In most distance education systems, such interactions are often optional, whereas it is compulsory for students to interact with faculty via work submitted for assessment. Thus, the number of assignments and the timing of assignments throughout a period of study could well be common significant aspects of integration when viewed from a distance education perspective.

In the present study, the notion of integration of students was investigated in light of the number and timing of required contacts between the faculty and students. These required contacts were investigated in terms of the number of assignments submitted, the turnaround time on these assignments, and the 'feedback interval' between assignments, which was defined as the elapsed time (in days) between the receipt of feedback on consecutive assignments. Such required contacts were therefore examined in terms of the pace of interaction (turnaround time) and the density of feedback (feedback interval). Additionally, attempts were made to monitor the number of contacts between the student and the institution during the course of study. From Tinto's (1975, 1982) perspective, it could be argued that students who were exposed to regular, rapid contacts during their distance education experience might well be expected to exhibit persistence in their studies, compared to those whose contacts with the institution were perhaps somewhat sporadic and rather slow.

This point of view must be regarded as somewhat truncated, since no allowance is made for the quality of interaction in determining the social and academic integration of students. It is acknowledged that the quality of interpersonal contact (and its interaction with various student characteristics, Thompson 1984) will have a significant impact on social and academic integration. At the same time, however, any research project must be sensitive to logistical and practical constraints. The valid and reliable measurement of quality interaction in the context of a cross-cultural multi-institutional study is at the present time nigh impossible. Similarly, the complete explanation of social and academic integration would inevitably demand a focus on learner characteristics such as level of previous education, age, sex, motivation, time available for study and so on.

Many distance education institutions, however, are not in a position to screen prospective students thoroughly and tend to operationalize admission policies based largely on a minimal acceptable level of previous education, rather than on other potentially important personal characteristics such as living and employment conditions, which are inevitably outside the control of the institution. Add to this the tendency of many distance education institutions to endorse some form of open access policy for mature age students, who may not have the required standard of previous education, and it becomes evident that a focus primarily on institutionally controllable variables is a defensible pragmatic approach to research. In short, given the complexity of conducting a cross-cultural multi-institutional study, it seems reasonable to adopt an orientation towards research in which learners are regarded as relatively fixed inputs into the system, and improvement in the persistence of students is seen to be a function largely of institutionally manipulable variables.

The present project therefore concentrated on those aspects of social and academic integration which are, primarily, under relatively ready institutional control, namely: turnaround time and feedback interval. Further, data on these variables is often collected by distance education systems in the day-to-day monitoring of the efficiency of their operations thus facilitating data collection for the project. An effort was also made to collect other readily available data on basic student characteristics. namely age and sex. An attempt to collect data on additional contacts was also made, since such data is important from Tinto's (1975, 1982) theoretical perspective; though it was anticipated that not all participating institutions would be able to supply such information.

PROJECT MANAGEMENT

The manageability of the project was enhanced by focusing on the issue of student persistence at the level of a unit of study, as Rekkedal (1973) had done. The scope of the empirical study was further delimited by the elimination of non-starters from the sample. The elimination of this group of students from the project meant that students included in the project were those who had sufficient motivation to forward at least one assignment during their course of study and excluded those who enrolled but did not appear to participate further in their studies. Given the well-documented phenomenon of the first year drop out, an effort was made to focus on first year students in their initial contact with the distance education system, where the drop out phenomenon is accentuated. To further delimit contextual variables, data was collected at the level of undergraduate studies, leading to a formally accredited award at the Bachelor degree level. As mentioned previously, however, such parameters are probably less significant than the model of distance education used by participating institutions in teaching the unit of study selected for perusal. A brief description of the major contextual variables, including reference to the model of distance education of each of the participating institutions, follows.

Allama Iqbal Open University (AIOU)

The jurisdiction of AIOU extends to the whole of Pakistan: in effect, its campus is a national one. It provides facilities for the educational uplift of the masses, including those who are unable to attend conventional institutions, by bringing it to their door-steps. Its programmes offer a wide choice of courses at a variety of levels for the general public as well as for professional people.

The AIOU aims to provide them with an opportunity for further education through organizing the following learning activities: systematic study of correspondence texts by students at their homes; regular hearing and viewing facilities of radio and television lessons at study centres; contact with tutors at study centres; and written assignments, final written examinations and practical work with special home experiment kits, etc.

Students in the AIOU sample were those studying the unit Pakistan Studies, an elective in the Bachelor of Arts degree. While data was supplied on 1,411 students, data on only 664 students was coded and subsequently analysed due to a resource constraint. Such a sample was regarded as sufficiently representative of AIOU's operations to warrant its valid inclusion in the project. Of the 664 students for whom data on age was available, the majority were in the range of 20–35 years, 530 being male and 134 female.

Darling Downs Institute of Advanced Education (DDIAE)

Since its foundation in 1967, the Institute has developed as a comprehensive multilevel, regional college of advanced education offering courses in engineering, education, applied science, arts and business studies. Courses are offered which lead to awards of associate diploma, diploma, Bachelor's degree and graduate diploma. While it emphasizes its commitment to the community of the Darling Downs, the Institute enrols its students from all areas of Queensland and beyond. Through its extensive distance education courses, the Institute has offered opportunities for higher education to many persons whose personal or vocational circumstances do not permit them to enrol as on-campus students. Since 1982, the proportion of the Institute's total student body (approximately 6,000) studying at a distance has been just over 50 per cent.

The Institute operates a dual-mode teaching system with academic staff members being responsible for teaching the same unit of study to both off-campus and on-campus students. In the distance education mode, the teaching staff make extensive use of telephone tutorials, which link the main campus with several of the Institute's fifteen study centres located throughout Queensland. These study centres are supported by twenty regional liaison officers, who play an important role in facilitating communication between students and the Institute. Unlike some institutions, which appoint tutorial staff to fulfil an academic role in these regional centres, the regional liaison officers act as administrative support officers, assisting with the organization of telephone tutorials, conducting evaluative telephone surveys, enhancing communication and maintaining a booking sheet for the Institute's computer managed learning (CML) system.

The CML system is based on the use of microcomputers in the Institute's study centres (Barker, White and Taylor 1985). The unit of study selected for scrutiny in the present project was a foundation unit, Introduction to Law, in the Bachelor of Business degree. This unit is one of over forty units which makes use of the CML system. During the semester, students are required to complete seven CML tests on contract law. In using the microcomputer, students receive immediate diagnostic feedback on their performance on the tests, with turnaround time being effectively reduced to a few seconds. Those students who cannot gain easy access to the microcomputers are required to submit computer-marked answer sheets, which are processed on campus, with students ultimately receiving diagnostic feedback in the form of a letter printed by the computer. Institutional response time for such letters is usually no more than two days.

Students enrolled in this unit may therefore experience somewhat different instructional treatments, which may be accentuated by their choice to attend an optional five-day residential school held at the main campus during the mid-semester break for on-campus students. Apart from these variations in treatment, students receive a self-instructional package specially prepared by a unit team consisting of a subject matter specialist, an instructional designer and an education officer. The package for the law unit in question consists of a study book, a book of readings, a computer-managed learning booklet, and an audiotape containing an introduction to the unit as well as answers to the self-assessment questions which are embedded in the study book.

The students enrolled in the unit were primarily resident in Queensland. Most of the 241 students who embarked on the unit were male (165), with 76 females completing the total. The mean age of these students was 29.3 years, though it is worth noting that 39 students were aged 21 years or under, while 24 students were aged 40 years or over. The youngest student was 17 years and the oldest 51 years.

The Open Learning Institute of British Columbia (OLI)

Since its establishment in 1978, OLI has become a well-developed organization providing programmes in adult basic education, in career–technical–vocational areas, in continuing education and leading to undergraduate degrees in arts and sciences. OLI's distance education system caters for the needs of British Columbia's population of approximately two-and-a-half million spread over an area of almost 370,000 square miles. In a province of this size, OLI had to face the difficulty of the limited extent to which face-to-face contact between tutors and students would be viable. Tutors were therefore provided with an Institute telephone which facilitated contact with students, who were able to make contact without charge. Additionally, the Institute established an advising service, whereby advice is provided to students in various parts of the province on a variety of matters, including programme planning, registration, financial aid and problems (not specifically academic) related to their interaction with the Institute.

From a teaching–learning perspective, the instructional packages forwarded to students are as self-contained as possible, and endorse principles of self-instruction. Nevertheless, an important point of contact between students and tutors is written comments on submitted assignments. Additionally, in cooperation with Simon Fraser University, OLI devised a scheme for providing a reasonably extensive library service to distance students. The students in the sample (drawn from a range of undergraduate courses) therefore had access to a useful range of support systems. Due to the extensive decentralized nature of these services, however, it was not logistically feasible to monitor the number of additional contacts students had with officers of the Institute. Similarly, no data was available on the age or sex of students included in the sample.

Tasmanian State Institute of Technology (TSIT)

Formerly established in 1968 as the Tasmanian College of Advanced Education, TSIT is a multidisciplinary college located in Launceston, with study centres at Burnie, Hobart and Devonport. The external studies programme covers an extensive range of associate diploma, Bachelor's degree and graduate diploma courses, including those in education, applied science, business studies, computing and arts. While it concentrates its efforts on Tasmanian residents, under special circumstances exceptions are made for students living in other Australian states.

The Institute operates a dual-mode teaching system with academic staff teaching the unit to both on-campus and external students. The three study centres are permanently staffed by full-time academic staff, who conduct regular tutorials of two hours' duration every four weeks throughout the year. These tutorials are, however, optional. Some students depend solely on the self-instructional study guides and audio-cassette tapes that constitute the core of the instructional package which is mailed to them. Written feedback on submitted assignments is a significant aspect of the distance education experience of the student.

Students in the TSIT sample were those studying the unit Introduction to Accounting, a foundation unit of the Bachelor of Business degree. Of the 131 students, 82 were male and 49 female. The mean age of these students was 28 years; of these, 24 were aged 21 years or younger, while 11 were aged 40 years or more. The youngest student was 18 years and the oldest 50 years. Complete data on turnaround time, feedback interval and additional contacts was available for the TSIT sample.

University of the South Pacific (USP)

Since its establishment in 1968 (Interim Council 1967), USP has developed a sophisticated support system for its extension students scattered over more than one million square kilometres of the South Pacific ocean. USP has well-established extension centres in the following nine countries: Cook Islands, Fiji Islands, Kiribati, Niue, Solomon Islands, Tonga, Tuvalu, Vanuatu and Western Samoa. The staff at each centre normally consists of a centre director, a lecturer, a secretary and a satellite operator. In Nauru, however, the Director of Education assists in administering extension study courses. The region served by USP has an estimated 60 cultures with about 300 languages. English, the language of instruction, is normally the second or even the third language for most of the students.

By using various means of communication, including printed study materials and audiotapes sent through the mail, and a radio satellite network for two-way communication between centres, USP has been able to bridge the gap between distance students and the institution. Regular written communication between the institution and many students is nevertheless logistically restricted by the great distances involved. Thus the submission of regular assignments cannot constitute a major aspect of many courses, which must be primarily based on self-instructional principles. The range of courses offered is extensive, including introductory and foundation programmes, vocationally oriented programmes and degree programmes. The subjects in the USP sample were drawn from the Bachelor of Education programme, specifically from the unit Human Development. Due to obvious logistical problems, it was not possible to gather data on additional contacts between students and the institution. Nor was it possible to collect data on the age and sex of the students. Further, the limited number of assignment submissions meant that the treatment of the feedback interval data was somewhat restricted.

COLLECTION AND TREATMENT OF DATA

As well as these important inter-institutional variations, attention must be drawn to the point that students do not experience equivalent distance education treatment even when enrolled in the same unit of study at a particular institution. Certainly, staff of most institutions would no doubt endorse a philosophy based on all students receiving equitable treatment. Nevertheless, due to the vagaries of mail systems, geographical locations and the demands made on academic staff marking large numbers of assignments, it is inevitable that students receive different treatments, especially in regard to turnaround time and feedback interval.

Furthermore, students will not make the same use of the system. For instance, some students will prefer to work independently without making additional demands for support on the institution, and will submit assignments and attend examinations without making further requests for assistance by letter or telephone. In this sense, their distance education experience could be quite different from that of students who seek regular additional contacts with institutional personnel.

The extent to which students experience different distance education treatment in terms of turnaround time, feedback interval and additional contacts may or may not have a significant influence on the persistence of students. It seems reasonable to argue that there may be a number of highly motivated students with high need-achievement, who are likely to persevere with their studies irrespective of their treatment by the institution. Such students will probably complete the basic task requirements of a unit of study. On the other hand, it seems that turnaround time and feedback interval could well be significant aspects of the distance education experience for those students who may not be so motivated or confident in their ability to succeed, as in the case of Rekkedal's (1973) study.

In summary, efforts were made to examine the relationships between persistence at the unit level and factors associated with social and academic integration (turnaround time, feedback interval, and the number of additional contacts between student and institution beyond those demanded by the submission of assignments). The influence of the age and sex of students was also examined. Analysis of data from each separate institution was under-taken in an effort to investigate potential common trends emanating from each institution relative to a particular model of distance education and in a specific context. Should any common trend emerge across contexts, then it would seem likely that such a trend could be acknowledged as an empiri-cally-derived generalizable principle upon which distance education could be based.

Following communication with the institutional project leaders during the latter months of 1983, data was collected primarily during the first semester of 1984. The two data collection formats for the project were designed to focus on required contacts related to written assignments and additional contacts respectively. One form focused on the dates of assignment receipt and despatch (institutional response time) and the typical mail service response time for students in various geographical locations, enabling com-putation of turnaround time, which was defined as the elapsed time (in days) from mailing an assignment to receiving the corrected assignment. This focus on the pattern of assignment receipt and despatch also allowed for computa-tion of the feedback interval, which was defined as the elapsed time (in days) between the receipt of feedback on consecutive written assignments. The other form focused on additional contacts which simply described the num-ber of contacts between the student and the institution (whether student-initiated or institution-initiated) which occurred in addition to those demanded by assessment requirements in a given period. Apart from these three aforementioned independent variables, the dependent variable under scrutiny was persistence, measured simply in terms of whether a student completed all the required assignments for the selected unit of study.

All participating institutions provided data on turnaround time and feedback interval respectively. As anticipated, two of the participating institutions (Open Learning Institute and University of the South Pacific) were unable to collect data on additional contacts due to their styles of operation. The standard data collection formats were returned to the project coordinator, who completed the data analysis phase of the project using the computing resources of the Darling Downs Institute of Advanced Education. Using the SPSS software package (Nie *et al.* 1975), descriptive statistics were computed for each of the four major variables. Relationships between these variables were investigated in terms of cross-tabulated data and an appropriate test of statistical significance (chi-square) (see Table 8.1).

DISCUSSION

The results relevant to the examination of the relationship between turnaround time and persistence demonstrate no consistent trend even though the DDIAE data is consistent with Rekkedal's (1973) conclusion that low turnaround time is likely to increase persistence. Of the 82 students who failed to complete requirements, 55 of these experienced high turnaround time, whereas of the 110 students who succeeded in completing requirements, only 29 experienced a high turnaround, while 81 students had low turnaround time. This pattern of results could be reasonably interpreted as pointing to the potential efficacy of turnaround time in influencing persistence. In the other four institutional contexts, however, there is no such indication of a significant statistical relationship, although the data for TSIT was tending to be compatible with that of DDIAE, with 44 of the 70 students who failed to complete requirements experiencing high turnaround time, which could well have had a deleterious effect on student persistence. In the three other institutional contexts, however, no such patterns emerged; rather, the results could be reasonably interpreted as being indicative of no salient relationship between turnaround time and persistence.

A similar pattern of inter-institutional contextual variations was evident in the consideration of the relationship between persistence and feedback interval. The DDIAE data is consonant with Tinto's (1975) model, which would tend to support the notion that regular feedback is likely to enhance persistence. Of the 85 students who failed to complete requirements, 59 experienced relatively delayed feedback (high feedback intervals), whereas of the 68 students who fulfilled requirements, only 7 experienced delayed feedback, while 61 experienced relatively rapid feedback. A similar pattern of results was evident in the TSIT data, with 45 of the 60 successful students experiencing relatively rapid feedback. The pattern of results for the remaining two institutions for which sufficient data was available, AIOU and OLI

Table 8.1 Major descriptive statistics from the five participating institutions

Institution	Unit of study	No. of students	No. of assignments submitted	Average turnaround time	Average feedback interval	Average additional contacts	Completion rate (%)
AIOU	Pakistan studies	674	4	8 days	26 days	5.6	90.7
DDIAE	Introduction to law	241	10	14 days	14 days	8.8	53.5
OLI	Various courses	202	5	13 days	25 days	n.a.	32.2
TSIT	Introduction to accounting	131	5	25 days	24 days	11.8	45.8
USP	Human development	144	2	24 days	30 days	n.a.	43.8

respectively, was not generally supportive of any significant relationship between persistence and feedback interval. Thus, results from the latter two institutions were not compatible with Tinto's (1975) rationale.

The data available on the relationship between persistence and number of additional contacts needs to be interpreted with some caution, since students who do not complete requirements may drop out sufficiently early in the semester to limit contacts with the institution compared to those students who remain active throughout the total period of the course. The fact that results for all institutions appear to be consistent with Tinto's (1975) rationale (that increased contacts would be likely to enhance integration and subsequent persistence) should therefore be treated with some caution. The aforementioned body of students who might be expected to persist largely irrespective of additional contacts with the institution (other than those demanded) could also complicate the interpretation of these results. In the case of AIOU and DDIAE, the relatively small number of high contact students, who eventually failed to persist, however, is generally supportive of Tinto's perspective. Further analysis of data revealed no clear pattern with regard to whether these contacts were student-initiated or institution-initiated. The actual number of contacts was apparently more important than the source of initiation.

CONCLUSION

The most obvious conclusion that can be drawn from the project is that one should be extremely cautious in generalizing the results of research studies across institutional contexts. There was enough variation in outcomes to suggest that the specific institutional context in which a study is undertaken has a major influence on relationships between the variables under investigation. While some results were consistent with the conclusions drawn from Rekkedal's (1973) early experimental study on turnaround time, and while some results were consonant with inferences drawn from the extrapolation of Tinto's (1975) model to the distance education arena, there was certainly no consistent empirical evidence that could suggest a generalizable principle upon which distance education systems could be based.

The importance of the immediate institutional context in action research projects is not surprising, however, since each institution inevitably responds to a variety of local influences and comes up with a practical operational system, dependent on its own unique circumstances. More often than not, certain over-riding practical, economic, social or political factors tend to determine to a significant extent the basic features of the model of distance education used by a particular institution. The use of pre-active meta-analysis to generate cross-institutional comparisons, however, has the advantage of highlighting such contextual influences, and while no consistent pattern of results emerged, some practical issues apparently worthy of consideration emerged from the project.

With regard to the relationship between turnaround time and persistence, the support for Rekkedal's (1973) findings in the DDIAE context suggested that some students may have been disadvantaged by relatively tardy return of assignments. A component of this difference in turnaround time among students is the geographical location of students, with mail service response times varying between 2 and 6 days in the case of DDIAE students. This range is no doubt greater in the case of institutions like USP, where students are spread over a vast geographical area. Despite this inequitable distance education experience of students, there does not appear to be any effort to sort assignments by geographical region so that turnaround time might be optimized for students disadvantaged by living long distances from the institution. Some form of colour coding of assignment covers could minimize the need for additional resources to support this initiative, were it to be pursued in the interests of providing equitable distance education experiences for all students.

An alternative approach would be for institutions to provide markers in regional centres so that turnaround time could be minimized for all students. If a component of this marking could be handled by micro-computers in regional study centres (as in the case of DDIAE), such minimization of turnaround time could be facilitated with potentially positive results for all students. The use of microcomputers in this way is obviously somewhat dependent on the type of subject matter and the instructional objectives of the unit of study. Further, the use of such technology also has major resource implications, and is ultimately dependent on the feasibility of the support systems available in particular contexts.

The DDIAE experience of using microcomputer-based, computer-managed learning initiatives to increase contacts with students and to provide students with performance-related feedback was no doubt important in generating the support for Tinto's (1975) model, which highlighted the likely significance of generating regular interaction to enhance the integration of students with the institution. The TSIT data was supportive of this trend also, and in this context such interaction was entirely interpersonal. The DDIAE experience, however, suggests that integration of students could well be supported by machine-mediated (computer-based) interaction as well as by interpersonal contacts. It should be noted that rational use of a computer-managed learning system can provide for relatively personal, diagnostic-prescriptive feedback, which can amplify productive student–institution contacts without being too dependent on the availability of teaching staff. Once again, the feasibility of such initiatives has major resource implications, which will be relative to particular contextual constraints. The apparent importance of the interval between contacts related to assignment submission and return appears to be worthy of further investigation. As mentioned previously, however, such research should try to incorporate measures of the quality, as well as the quantity, of feedback.

Such a consideration is also relevant to the examination of the relationship between persistence of students and additional contacts over and above those demanded to meet the requirements associated with completing a unit of study. While some caution is required in drawing conclusions from the results of this aspect of the project, one obvious practical consideration is whether institutions should monitor the number of additional contacts with students, and subsequently make an effort to contact those students who are not seeking additional advice in case they are in danger of dropping out. Overall, though, this approach may not make the best use of available resources, since it was evident from the data that a significant proportion of students managed to meet requirements without seeking much additional contact with the institution. Such an outcome highlights the need for an approach to research based on consideration of aptitude–treatment–interaction.

While the present project, largely for logistical reasons, concentrated on variables that were manipulable by the institution, and tended to regard students as relatively fixed inputs, there is potentially more value in endeavouring to classify students in some way and to subsequently evaluate their reaction to a particular distance education treatment. This type of research, commonly referred to as aptitude–treatment–interaction (Cronbach and Snow 1977), is based on the persuasive rationale that instructional treatments are differentially effective due to variations in learner aptitude. It seems likely, however, that such an approach would be more likely to be productive at the level of a single institution rather than in a cross-cultural multi-institutional setting, since aptitude–treatment–interaction findings tend to be problematic in that they are difficult to measure and relatively unstable (Sherman 1985).

In retrospect, it seems reasonable to argue that a variety of approaches to research in distance education is desirable. There is clearly some value in conducting cross-cultural multi-instructional studies, if only to highlight the caution required in generalizing the results of research studies across institutional contexts. Such studies, however, tend to be somewhat determined by the practical constraints imposed by conducting research across widely different systems and settings – especially when such research is conducted at a distance. It appears that more control over empirical investigations could obviously be engendered by allocating limited resources to the conduct of research at the level of a single institution. Such research seems likely to provide information that is primarily useful to the institution concerned, rather than to be readily generalizable across settings. Nevertheless, both types of research appear to be capable of crystallising practical issues which confront decision makers working in distance education settings. Both types of research, however, must be conducted within the complex context of ongoing distance education systems, usually operating under significant resource constraints. From this perspective, it seems unlikely that decisions about distance education will have the benefit of a clearly established empirical rationale for some years to come. Decision makers will have to continue to allocate resources on the basis of less than complete information. There is no doubt, however, that benefits can accrue from contacts among distance education institutions facing similar problems under different contextual constraints. Indeed, although the logistics of conducting a cross-cultural, multi-institutional research project at a distance tended to somewhat limit the potential value of the outcomes, there can be no doubting the value of increased inter-institutional contact and associated insights into the complexity of the distance education arena that emanated from the project. Such outcomes are entirely consistent with the objectives of the International Council for Distance Education.

REFERENCES

Barker, L. J., White, V. J. and Taylor, J. C. (1985) 'Computer managed learning in tertiary education: an organisational development perspective', *Australian Journal of Adult Education* 25, 1: 20–9.

Cronbach, L. and Snow, R. (1977) *Aptitudes and Instructional Methods: a Handbook for Research on Interactions,* New York: Irvington.

Getzlal, S. B., Sedlacek, G. M., Kearney, K. A. and Blackwell, J. M. (1984) 'Two types of voluntary undergraduate attrition: application of Tinto's model', *Research in Higher Education* 20, 3: 257–68.

Kember, D. (1981) 'Some factors affecting attrition and performance in a distance education course at the University of Papua New Guinea', *Distance Education* 2, 2: 164–88.

Nie, N. H. *et al.* (1975) *Statistical Package for the Social Sciences,* 2nd edn, New York: McGraw Hill.

Pascarella, E. T. and Terenzini, P. T. (1980) 'Predicting freshman persistence and voluntary dropout decisions from a theoretical model', *Journal of Higher Education* 51: 60–75.

Rekkedal, T. (1973), (1984) *The Written Assignments in Correspondence Education: Effects of Reducing Turn-around Time: an Experimental Study,* Oslo: NKI-skolen Undervisningssentrum. English translation, *Distance Education* 4, 2: 231–52.

Roberts, D. (1984) 'Ways and means of reducing early student drop-out rates', *Distance Education* 5, 1: 50–71.

Scales, K. (1984) 'A study of the relationship between telephone contact and persistence', *Distance Education* 5, 2: 268–76.

Sherman, T. M. (1985) 'Learning improvement programs: a review of controllable influences', *Journal of Higher Education* 56: 85–100.

Terenzini. P. T. and Pascarella, E. T. (1980) 'Toward the validation of Tinto's model of college student attrition: a review of recent research', *Research in Higher Education* 12: 271–82.

Thompson, G. (1984) 'The cognitive style of field-dependence as an explanatory construct in distance education drop-out', *Distance Education 5*, 2: 286–93.

Tinto, V. (1975) 'Drop-out from higher education: a theoretical synthesis of recent research', *Review of Educational Research* 45: 89–125.

Tinto, V. (1982) 'Limits of theory and practice in student attrition', *Journal of Higher Education* 53, 6: 688–700.

Woodley, A. and Parlett, M. (1983) 'Student drop-out', *Teaching at a Distance* 24: 22–3.

9 The economics of mass distance education

Greville Rumble

There is a belief that distance education is cheaper than traditional forms of education. What is usually meant by this is that the cost per student and/or per graduate is less than in traditional forms of education. Since students can progress at different rates (either full-time or part-time), the cost per student is often expressed in some kind of standard measure such as the cost per student-hour or cost per full-time student equivalent.

It is not always easy to compare the costs of distance and traditional systems. They may have different objectives; they may teach different subjects, or the same subjects in very different ways; the previous educational qualifications of the students entering the systems may be different, and this may affect their success in producing graduates; and the quality of the teaching may be different. Any one of these variables may affect costs and the way we view them. Generally, however, cost comparisons are confined to institutions teaching at the same level (primary, secondary or tertiary) and the assumption is made that the quality of the education offered is similar.

Of course, distance-education systems are not set up just because they are believed to be cheaper. However, cost is an important factor, and those responsible for their establishmeht rightly point out that they can be cheaper. The organizing committee of the Venezuelan Universidad Nacional Abierta stated its belief that the institution would 'contribute in significantly reducing the annual cost per student and the social cost per graduate' (COUNA 1979). The Andhra Pradesh Committee on the Establishment of an Open University (1982) cited evidence drawn from early cost studies of the British Open University to the effect that the average recurrent and capital cost per student in the latter was less than that found in conventional British universities, and implied that the foundation of a distance-teaching university in Andhra Pradesh would be cheaper than any alternative course of action open to the state government.

Unfortunately the hopes of politicians and planners are not always realized. There are examples of distance-teaching schemes where the cost per student or cost per graduate, and sometimes both, has been higher than costs in traditional systems doing comparable tasks, just as there are plenty of examples of distance teaching systems which have been cheaper (Perraton 1982).

The cost structures of distance and traditional education are so different that those setting up distance systems experience considerable difficulty in describing the operation and economics of their institution to officials in government and funding agencies (Snowden and Daniel 1980).

To understand why this is so, and why distance systems may be both cheaper and more expensive than traditional ones, it is necessary to have some knowledge of the way educational costs behave.

THE BASIC COST FUNCTION

The total costs of an enterprise are made up of both fixed and variable costs. Fixed costs do not vary continuously in relation to changes in volume of activities, although they may change if activities are ended or if there are very significant changes in volumes. (What is a significant change in volume needs to be defined within the context of the enterprise.) Variable costs tend to increase or decrease directly (linearly) with fluctuations in the volume of activity.

The basic cost function for any educational system is

$$T = S\Omega + C\delta + P\pi + F$$

where T is the total cost, S is the number of students, C is the number of courses which are being developed, P is the number of courses being presented to students, F is the fixed cost of the system (administrative costs and other overheads), Ω is the direct cost per student, δ is the direct cost of developing a course, and π is the direct course-related cost of presenting a course. The total direct cost of teaching students is $S\Omega$, the total direct cost of courses in development is $C\delta$, and the total direct cost of courses in presentation is $P\pi$. The variables for which volumes of activity are identified here as being of significance are S, C and P. There may be others which are of importance in particular distance education systems: for example, the number of local study centres at which teaching takes place. However, the model used in this chapter ignores the influence of other variables. All the costs on the right-hand side of the equation are dependent on management choice.

In distance-education systems, student-related costs include the costs of materials supplied to students, the costs of distributing materials where these are sent to each student, the costs of paying tutors to mark students' assignments and examination scripts, and the costs of any face-to-face tuition.

Obviously, the cost per student goes up if one gives students more rather than less material, while the cost per student of tuition, for example, will vary depending on the amount of tuition given and the student–tutor ratio.

The direct costs of developing a course will include labour costs (payments to authors, editors, designers, broadcast producers) as well as the development and production costs of producing 'master copies' or prototypes of course materials (for example, payments to consultants, payments for rights, cost of editing broadcasts and preparing master tapes, etc.). The way a cost behaves can be changed by management decision. The cost of producing copies of the materials which are given to the students is a direct student cost, while the cost of producing a stock of materials which one lends to students while they are registered on a particular course is a direct course cost. For example, if one gives students the video-cassettes associated with a course, the cost of this copy is a direct cost which is incurred for each student; if one has a stock of video-cassettes from which one loans a copy to each student, then the cost of the stock of copies is a direct cost of the course.

The direct course-related costs of presenting a course include such items of expenditure as the cost of transmitting broadcasts associated with the course, re-writing examination questions, monitoring the course, and generally updating and clarifying the materials.

Overhead costs are more or less self-evident, covering the costs of management functions (personnel, finance, management services, administration, institutional planning and evaluation, etc.). The more sophisticated the management and control system, the greater these costs are likely to be. Overhead costs may also include an allowance for the replacement of capital (studio and transmission equipment, computers, etc.), all of which will in due course wear out and need to be replaced. There are a number of ways of treating capital costs, but for practical purposes what is really important is the cost to the enterprise of replacing the capital item when it is worn out with a new item which will fulfil a similar function.

The use of media and the problems of managing distance-taught students means that the overhead costs of the institution (F), the costs of developing a course (δ), and the course related costs of presenting courses (π), are in general higher in distance teaching institutions than in traditional institutions with comparable student numbers. However, the relatively limited amount of support given to students means that the direct cost per student (Ω) is lower. This is because much of the managerial and academic effort of the institution is being put into the development and maintenance of educational materials and administrative systems for the control of distance students. This then represents a form of capital investment which replaces direct student–teacher contact, and which can be used to teach many times the numbers of students who can be catered for in such traditional forms of education as the (face-to-face) lecture, seminar and tutorial. In essence, capital replaces labour, offering to educationists what Wagner (1982) described as 'a mass production alternative to the traditional craft approach'.

The extent to which fixed (capital) costs can predominate in distance education was shown in a comparative study of the costs of courses at conventional British universities and at the distance-teaching Open University: whereas the ratio of variable to fixed course costs at conventional British universities was about 1:8, at the Open University it was about 1:2,000 (Laidlaw and Layard 1974).

THE COSTS OF DEVELOPING, PRODUCING AND DISTRIBUTING COURSE MATERIALS

A particular feature of distance-education systems is the level of investment required in the system before a single student can be enrolled. The investment in capital items (buildings, equipment, etc.) can be considerable, particularly if studio-based technologies and satellite or terrestrial broadcasting are used, and these facilities have to be built, as opposed to being hired as required. Use of computer-based technologies for teaching and administration also adds significantly to cost. Provision needs to be made for the warehousing and handling of course materials, so warehouses may have to be built and will certainly need to be equipped to meet the institution's needs. Additional costs will be incurred if it is decided to set up an in-house print shop rather than use existing commercial printers.

A range of course materials sufficient to meet the academic objectives of the institution and provide potential students with an element of choice has to be designed and produced. The most significant cost here is likely to be the cost of the academic and related staff required to develop the materials. Sparkes (1984) has suggested that whereas it takes from 1 to 10 hours of staff time to develop one hour of small group teaching, and from 2 to 10 hours to prepare a one-hour lecture, it will take from 3 to 10 hours to prepare one hour of tutored video instruction (TVI), 50 to 100 hours to prepare a teaching text which will occupy a student for one hour, 100 hours or more to develop a 'broadcast quality' 60–minute television programme, 200 hours or more to prepare one hour's worth of computer-aided learning, and 300 hours or more to prepare one hour's worth of material on interactive videodisc.

These figures need to be treated with some care. Broadly speaking, there are four approaches to the creation of distance learning materials. The first of these is to look around for some existing material which can be used either as it stands or in adapted form to meet the needs of distance-taught students. It is quite common, for example, for an institution to recommend certain textbooks to its students, which they are then required to buy in order to take the course. Obviously, this vastly reduces the costs of the institution, which then only has to prepare a few notes of guidance and some assessment questions in order to begin teaching. This approach involves hardly any creative effort on the part of the teaching institution, and is a very cheap way of proceeding. It is used by some commercial correspondence colleges preparing students for professional and other examinations. It rarely produces good self-instructional teaching materials, but it does allow a wide range of courses to be developed at very little cost. It is also used in a modified form in some high-level Open University courses, where the amount of self-instructional materials produced to support student learning is limited.

The second approach is to 'tack' the distance teaching system on to a conventional teaching system by video-recording lectures given to conventional students and preparing lecture notes to accompany the videos. The lecture notes can be reproduced (in modified form) as lecture hand-outs, examples written up on blackboards, flipcharts or overhead projector acetates, photographic slides, etc. Once lecture theatres have been equipped with video cameras and recording equipment, the additional per capita costs of preparing videos and lecture notes for use by off-campus students can be very little, as Wagner (1975) showed in respect of the off-campus graduate engineering programme at Colorado State University, and Leslie (1979) demonstrated in respect of the University of Waterloo Correspondence Programme. A vast library of video material can be built up rapidly for relatively little total cost. While the quality of these videos may not be very high, they are adequate for their purpose. Broadcast by satellite, they can enable students spread over very wide geographical areas to 'listen in' to lectures providing up-to-date information on technological advances. Students may also be able to participate in the lectures through telephone links (tutored video instruction, or TVI). Such approaches are now being used by a number of universities including the National Technological University in the United States.

Both the third and fourth approaches are based on the development of special self-instructional materials (print, audio-visual, broadcast, etc.) designed to teach distance students. There is little doubt that the quality of specially designed and produced distance teaching materials can be very high indeed.

The third approach is to plan the curriculum and to specify course content in broad outline, and then appoint academic consultants to develop the written materials and scripts for broadcasts and audio-visual materials. This kind of approach was adopted by the Universidad Estatal a Distancia in Costa Rica. It has the great advantage that payment is by results. The academics are not permanent members of full-time staff, so there is no long-term commitment to train them, provide them with time to undertake research, deal with staff problems arizing from low productivity or obsolescence of knowledge relative to institutional needs, etc. Curriculum planners specify the aims, objectives and broad content of new programmes of study, and academic editors and educational technologists turn the consultants' drafts into finished products. If the authors fail to deliver the goods, they do not get paid. Advance notification of a course may be given, but sometimes (as at the Open Learning Institute in British Columbia), a course is only announced after all the materials have been handed over for production. The process has more in common with a publishing house than a university. Commercial correspondence colleges which create their own materials use consultants because this is obviously a relatively cheap and flexible way of employing academic course writers and broadcast and audio-visual producers. The cost of employing an author on contract can nevertheless vary, depending on 'supply'. In some countries or in some subject areas suitable authors can be hard to find and they may command high fees.

The fourth approach is to employ a core of full-time academic staff to create the course materials. Such staff may be appointed on permanent or temporary contracts. Where the appointments are permanent, the staff need to keep themselves abreast with their subjects areas, hence they need time off for study and possibly research. After a time, permanent staff may acquire many of the skills of instructional designers and educational technologists. Unlike temporary staff, they are not always looking towards the next job, but bad appointments may become a long-term liability, particularly in systems where there is tenure.

The total salary bill also depends on how the academic staff are deployed. Institutions such as the Open University, Athabasca University in Canada, and Deakin University in Australia, which have adopted a course team approach (in which groups of academic and technical staff work together on a project team to develop a course) need higher levels of staffing than those that require the staff merely to stick to their own specialist task. On the other hand, while the course team approach is expensive in staff time and hence pushes costs up, it does enable staff to work in a very creative environment. Of these four approaches, the first is the cheapest and the last the most expensive.

A further factor to be taken into account in considering the cost of the course development, production and presentation system is the choice of media. Here again, management choice can greatly influence the cost of the system.

We have already noted Sparkes's contention that the time required to develop material designed to serve one hour of student learning varies significantly depending on the choice of media. The costs of developing the material are, however, not the only costs. Printed material needs to be designed, edited, typeset, printed and distributed; video and audio material has to be disseminated through appropriate channels and received on appropriate equipment; computer-based systems require extensive equipment and access to networks, as well as a great deal of investment in software.

To take the case of print, all material will require editing and design work. The cost of editing an author's manuscript into a form suitable for a self-instructional learning package is likely to be greater if contract authors are used. The cost of design can vary significantly, depending on the extent to which illustrations and artwork are incorporated into the text. The way the text is set affects costs. Offset lithography from typed originals is generally cheaper than letterpress printing from hot-metal type. Use of word processors instead of typewriters makes the preparation of camera-ready copy even easier, and can affect authoring costs. Timmers (1986) reckoned that the use of word processors at the Vancouver-based Open Learning Institute cut the time taken to develop and prepare for production a page of text from 120 hours to 50. On the other hand, where texts have to be handwritten, costs can escalate. The Allama Iqbal Open University pays its calligraphers on the same scale as university lecturers. Some institutions, such as the Sri Lankan Open University, prepare their texts in more than one language, thus incurring the costs of translation. The costs of printing can also vary. Paper costs differ from country to country; different grades of paper may be used; and the costs of printing change depending on the method used. The costs of the offset litho process are affected by whether paper or metal plates are used. The former are cheaper but are good for only about 500 copies. The use of colour adds greatly to the costs of printing. Variations in distribution costs can be so significant that it is difficult to make generalizations, but obviously it depends on whether the materials are mailed direct to individual students' homes, as happens at the British Open University, or are dispatched to local centres for collection by students, as happens at the Universidad Estatal a Distancia in Costa Rica. Finally, printing costs are susceptible to economies of scale. The length of the print run makes a great deal of difference to the unit cost per title. On the other hand, where more than one year's stock is printed, the costs of storage will also need to be taken into account.

The production costs of video vary enormously too. The cost per hour of video-taped lectures is much less than broadcast-quality television. The latter is expensive for a number of reasons. The cost of equipment to produce broadcast-quality television is greater than that required to produce video. Broadcasting unions in some countries have pushed the rates of pay to very high levels, and in many cases this has been coupled with agreements on staffing levels which have also exacerbated costs. What constitutes broadcast-quality television is also subject to different standards. In the United States the Public Broadcasting Service broadcasts three-quarter-inch

Lo-band Umatic tape generated material, which is cheaper to produce than the three-quarter-inch High-band tape material used by the television companies in the United Kingdom. It is perfectly feasible to produce 'broadcastable' educational material at low cost. The National Technological University, for example, broadcasts low-cost videotape lectures by satellite which is perfectly adequate for its purpose.

The distribution costs of video can also vary significantly, depending on whether video-cassettes or terrestrial or satellite-based systems are used (the latter encompassing both direct broadcasting by satellite (DBS) and satellite to cable head ends), and the extent to which the distance-education institution is responsible for meeting the capital costs of the distribution system or has access to transmission time at economic or marginal costs. In general, television is an expensive medium and cannot be justified in circumstances where the basic infrastructure to support it (maintenance services and trained manpower) are lacking or a significant proportion of homes are not equipped with television sets (Eicher *et al.* 1982). The costs of home-based video systems, in which individual students are expected to equip themselves with video players and either record off-air or play cassettes which have been provided by the teaching institution on loan or for purchase can also be significant. The Open University found that it was cheaper to give each student a 60–minute video-cassette than transmit over the air provided that there were fewer than 133 students on the course. Between 134 and 233 students it was cheaper to loan a cassette to each student, paying the costs of postage each way. Over this level, it was cheaper to transmit once using the national television channels of the BBC. These cross-over points were obtained using cost-volume charts and, of course, apply only to the situation and costs in the Open University at the time the study was undertaken (1984). However, selling the cassettes to students merely puts increased costs on them.

Video-cassette recorders can, of course, be installed in local centres with students accessing cassettes from a library of tapes held at the centre. The overall costs of such a system will be lower but there are drawbacks, not least the needs for the institution to maintain the equipment, ensure its safe-keeping, and provide sufficient players and quiet rooms so that students do not have to wait too long to view the cassette of their choice, and for students to travel to the centre at times when it is open.

Radio and audio-cassettes have the advantage that they are relatively cheap, and audio-cassettes can be used in imaginative ways with printed material to provide an audio-visual element. Eicher *et al.* (1982) were nevertheless sceptical about the cost-efficiency of radio in systems with under 2,000 students, while the Open University found that for courses with under 1,000 students, it was cheaper to provide audio-cassettes to each student rather than transmit radio programmes over the air.

The comments on the use of cassettes versus over-the-air transmission relate to costs and not to the educational effectiveness of the two modes of distribution. There is little doubt that distribution by cassette or systems where students record off-air onto cassette are educationally more effective since students can replay, as well as stop and start, the cassettes at will.

The costs of computer-based systems have been insufficiently studied to date, but the experience of the Open University, which has some 75,000 students taking degree-level courses, has been that the cost of providing each student with a personal computer is such that the institution itself cannot hope to fund the project. Even if the University restricted itself to providing computers to students taking courses where a significant level of computing is deemed to be academically essential, it would quickly have to provide for the needs of at least 13,000 students. A machine which meets the needs of the University (basically MS DOS operating system, 512K memory and VT 100 communications capability) costs in the region of $900–1,000 at 1987 prices, so the University cannot afford to equip students with personal computers. In view of this the University has recently instituted a policy under which it hopes that students will either buy the machines outright at a negotiated rate of discount, with or without a bank loan, or hire them from the University at a rate which still makes student purchase an attractive option for those students who can foresee the need to have a machine for several years.

THE PROBLEM OF STUDENT VARIABLE COSTS

Another factor which affects the costs of distance education systems is the extent to which students are provided with access to support systems. The cheapest form of distance education is found in those systems which register students for an examination, provide them with details of the syllabus and a list of books which will help them, and leave them to prepare themselves. This approach is that used by the University of London external degree system. With the exception of those taking the economics degree, students who wish to receive tuition have to enrol with a commercial correspondence college which provides them with lecture notes, set assignments, and arranges for these to be marked and commented on by a tutor. When students are ready, they present themselves for the examination. The cost of tuition is paid by the student. On the other hand, many of the new wave of distance-teaching universities founded in the 1970s and 1980s in the wake of the British Open University have developed a sophisticated system based on the provision not only of educational course materials but also of student support services including counselling, correspondence tuition and face-to-face tuition (Rumble and Harry 1982). The cost of tuition and counselling is either a direct (variable) student cost or a semi-variable cost related to the number of students taken on by tutors and counsellors. Clearly, the provision of such services represents a reversion to the labour-intensive methods found in traditional education. The higher the direct variable or semi-variable cost per student, the nearer the teaching cost of distance education will approach that of traditional forms of education. Thus, for example, one of the Open University's early geography courses had a direct variable cost per student that was much higher than the variable cost of social science courses in traditional British universities, thus preventing the Open University from reaping any of the economies of scale said to be present in distance education, at least on this course (Laidlaw and Layard 1974).

Obviously, as the amount of face-to-face tuition provided increases, so a basic characteristic of distance teaching, the physical separation between the teacher and the learner, is lost. Ultimately, the situation occurs in which conventional classroom-based teaching, whether provided by regular teachers or by semi-trained *animateurs*, is being supported by centrally produced materials. There are or have been numerous systems of this kind, particularly at primary and secondary level (for example the Radio Mathematics Project in Nicaragua, the Mauritius College of the Air, the El Salvador Educational Television project, Telescundaria in Mexico, etc.). Schemes of this kind may have a lower cost per student because the additional cost per student of developing, producing and distributing the centrally produced materials is more than offset by reductions in cost arising from the use of semi-trained *animateurs*. However, they are not distance education systems.

THE COSTS OF THE CURRICULUM

A further factor which influences the costs of distance education is the number of courses which the institution offers. Each course represents an investment in course materials. The more courses on offer, the greater the total investment and the greater the cost of maintaining them, or eventually replacing them with new versions or with entirely different courses.

The number of courses is determined to some extent by the number of subject areas to be covered, the extent to which students pursue a single subject in depth (for example a specialized single-subject degree course) or a combination of subjects, and the extent to which a range of optional courses is provided.

The most efficient distance-education system will be one with a relatively small range of courses and large numbers of students. The distance-teaching programme of the Universidad Pedagogica Nacional in Mexico is a good example. Dedicated to the in-service training of primary-and secondary-school teachers, the range of courses offered by the University is relatively limited and the numbers of students (60,000 in 1980) substantial, thus ensuring that each course has a large number of students.

As more courses are added to the curriculum, so the numbers of students per course will decline, provided the total number of students remains constant or does not increase pro rata to the increase in course options. For example, the British Open University was established in 1971. From the start it was assumed that it would grow quickly in size. In its first year it took in 25,000 students, registered on four courses. But by its second year, with course numbers increasing rapidly and student numbers still climbing, Laidlaw and Layard (1974) were already able to foresee that the case for developing higher-level courses with relatively small numbers of students would have to be justified 'on the grounds that they are an integral part of a system providing wider access to complete degree courses rather than that they are a cheap way of doing this'. By 1976 Wagner (1977) could point out that the economies of scale reaped by the Open University had been achieved in its first years of operation, since when it has been following the conventional university pattern of little increase in productivity. Wagner argues that the major reason why this was so was that the University had been using the economies of scale produced by rising student numbers to increase the overall number of courses offered to students.

However, there were limits to the extent that the Open University could justify increases in its course offerings at the expense of economies of scale. Early in its development, the University prepared an academic plan which aimed at presenting an undergraduate academic profile equivalent to 111 credits (each credit equivalent to about 420 to 450 hours of student work). It quickly became apparent that it could not develop and support this load within existing or likely resource levels, and accordingly a more modest plan for the presentation of 87 credits was approved. This plan, with minor modifications, still forms the basis for the Open University's undergraduate academic plan. It is accepted that the University's first degree is a general degree, and that students will not be able to specialize in a particular subject area. Moreover, it is recognized that further expansion of the profile of courses will have to be accomplished through the development of inexpensive courses or be accompanied by an increase in student numbers.

One way of minimizing the costs of a profile is to extend the life of a course so that the costs of development can be written off over more years. Again the experience of the Open University is instructive. Originally it planned to replace its courses every four years. It rapidly became obvious that it could not both sustain this aim and increase the number of courses on offer to students. Courses now routinely have to last for from eight to ten years, with all the implications this has for credibility as course content becomes dated. It is only fair to say that the University is very conscious of this problem.

Commercial correspondence colleges have solved these problems by only presenting courses with comparatively low development and production costs, concentrating on courses that will not rapidly become outdated, and resolutely not developing courses which will attract relatively few students over their life. The new videotape lecture systems such as that developed by the National Technological University in the United States have solved the problem of presenting state-of-the-art material which dates rapidly by video-taping lectures given in conventional universities, but the videos fall far short of the standards of self-instructional teaching material adopted by the best distance education systems.

ABSOLUTE COSTS, AVERAGE COSTS, EFFICIENCY AND EFFECTIVENESS

The many examples given above show not only how difficult it is to cost distance education in the abstract, but also how the costs of particular systems can be affected by management decisions. For this reason, relatively few costs have been cited in this chapter.

The absolute cost of a system can be very high. On the other hand, the cost per student can be brought down below that found in traditional systems operating at the same educational level. Whether this happens may well depend upon the number of students attracted into the system. The chances of the Venezuelan Universidad Nacional Abierta reducing its average costs to a level where it could achieve its planners' aim that it should bring down the annual cost per student and reduce the social cost per graduate was threatened by the disastrously high drop-out rates it experienced in its early years (only 22.6 per cent of the 1978 intake passed the introductory course), and the fact that the number of students attracted into the University actually fell between 1978 and 1981 while course offerings increased (Siqueira and Lynch 1986). With an annual enrolment of about 4,400, the costs per course enrolment at Athabasca University were comparable with those found in conventional Albertan universities, while in 1972 the average cost per student at the more capital-intensive British Open University was found to equal that in conventional British universities when the university had 21,700 students (Laidlaw and Layard 1974). (At the time of this study, it already had over 31,000 students.)

Most economic studies measure the relative cost-efficiency of distance and traditional educational systems. Efficiency is concerned with the cost of achieving outputs: an organization is efficient relative to another enterprise if its output costs less per unit than that of the other institution. It becomes more efficient to the extent that it maintains outputs with a less than proportionate increase in inputs. The fact that a distance-education institution has a low cost per student, credit hour or graduate does not necessarily mean that the institution is as efficient as it could be. It may well be able to reduce its unit costs by increasing its internal efficiency through changes in practice and cost reductions, as Mace (1978) commented in respect of the British Open University.

Generally, in making a comparison, it is assumed that the quality of the output of systems operating at the same educational level is comparable. This is not always the case. There is, however, some concrete evidence that the level of comprehension of students completing traditionally taught economics courses at Heriot Watt University in the United Kingdom and those completing distance taught economics courses at the Open University was similar (Lumsden and Scott 1982). More generally, however, 'planners will be disappointed at the amount of evidence available' (Eicher *et al.* 1982), since what there is suggests that motivated students can learn from any medium provided it is competently used and adapted to their needs (Eicher *et al.* 1982; Wells 1976).

This chapter has shown why, given the differences in the structure of costs between distance and traditional education systems, the former can be cheaper per student, credit hour or graduate than the latter. Distance education can also be as good as traditional forms of education in terms of the quality of what is learnt. Whether distance education is actually cheaper depends on a number of factors, including choice of media, the number of subject areas covered and courses offered, the extent to which the direct variable student cost is kept below the level found in traditional forms of education, and, of course, the number of students. It has also shown that the issue of who pays (student, employer, or government) is an important one which has a bearing on both what is taught and access, and it has been suggested that, as new technologies develop, so the technologization of distance education will put increasing costs on to students, with further implications for access. Third World countries, it is suggested, may be unable to exploit the new 'high tech' forms of distance education now being developed in the advanced industrialized countries.

REFERENCES

Committee on the Establishment of an Open University (1982) *Towards an Open Learning System,* Hyderabad: Osmania University Department of Publication and Press.

COUNA (Organizing Commission of the National Open University) (1979) *The National Open University of Venezuela,* Caracas: Universidad Nacional.

Eicher, J-C., Hawkridge, D., McAnany, E., Mariet, F. and Orivel, F. (1982) *The Economics of New Educational Media.* 3: *Cost and Effectiveness Overview and Synthesis,* Paris: Unesco.

Laidlaw, B. and Layard, R. (1974) 'Traditional versus Open University teaching methods: a cost comparison', *Higher Education* 3: 439–68.

Leslie, J. D. (1979) 'The University of Waterloo model for distance education', *Canadian Journal of University Continuing Education* 6: 33–41.

Lumsden, R. and Scott, A. (1982) 'An output comparison of Open University and conventional university students' *Higher Education* 11: 573–91.

Mace, J. (1978) 'Mythology in the making: is the Open University really cost-effective?' *Higher Education* 7: 295–309.

Perraton, H. (1982) *The Cost of Distance Education,* Cambridge: International Extension College.

Rumble, G. and Harry, K. (eds) (1982) *The Distance Teaching Universities,* London: Croom Helm.

Siqueira de Freitas, R. and Lynch, P. (1986) 'Factors affecting student success at the National Open University, Venezuela', *Distance Education* 7: 191–200.

Snowden, B. L. and Daniel, J. S. (1980) 'The economics and management of small post-secondary distance education systems', *Distance Education* 1, 1: 68–91.

Sparkes, J. (1984) 'Pedagogic difference between media'. in A. W. Bates (ed.)*The Role of Technology in Distance Education,* London: Croom Helm.

Timmers, S. (1986) 'Microcomputers in course development', *Programmed Learning and Educational Technology* 23, 1: 15–23.

Wagner, L. (1975) 'Television video-tape systems for off-campus education: a cost analysis of SURGE', *Instructional Science* 4: 315–32.

Wagner, L. (1977) 'The economics of the Open University revisited', *Higher Education* 6: 359–81.

Wagner, L. (1982) *The Economics of Educational Media,* London: Macmillan.

Wells, S. (1976) 'Evaluation criteria and the effectiveness of instructional technology in higher education', *Higher Education* 5, 253–75.

Part III
Administration of distance education

Introduction

Institutions which teach at a distance inevitably face many of the same administrative problems as conventional institutions which teach only face-to-face. Conventional institutions must have in place, for example, arrangements to deal with the registration of students, teaching, and the provision of support. Distance teaching institutions must also deal with arrangements for registration and teaching, and the great majority also provide student support services. There are, however, many differences between the nature of the tasks as they are actually performed. This distinction applies not only between conventional and distance teaching institutions but also between individual distance teaching institutions, since the latter exist in so many diverse forms and sizes and operate in so many different ways.

Differences exist, however, not only in detailed arrangements for coping with the intake and progress of students, but on the philosophical level. Paul's chapter (Chapter 10) looks at the concepts of 'open learning' and 'distance education' and then examines the extent to which the principles which underlie them are carried into practice in institutions in their decision making and priority setting. Although his immediate focus is 'open universities', autonomous, degree-granting institutions, his arguments transcend the educational level. Paul is a North American who brings extensive international experience as well as an international sense of humour to bear on his topic.

One of the major differences between conventional and distance teaching institutions is in the area of the teaching of courses. This applies regardless of whether the distance teaching institution is autonomous or whether it is a type of dual mode institution. Whereas in conventional institutions, administrative arrangements centre around the scheduling of lectures and seminars, distance teaching institutions develop, produce and deliver their own courses, often employing a variety of media, including radio, television, audio- or video- cassettes, computer software, or home experiment kits, to support specially prepared printed materials. The literature contains many examples of how-to-do-it guides to the writing of distance teaching materials and to a variety of other aspects of distance education. Marland and Store's chapter (Chapter 12) represents a contrast to this type of guide. It is a meticulous, research-based piece of work which examines in considerable detail the possible functions in printed distance teaching materials of a series of instructional devices and strategies.

The development of courses may be considered from at least two perspectives: in relation to the logistical arrangements necessary for the development and delivery of courses, and in relation to the pedagogical factors to be borne in mind in the creation of materials. In terms of logistics, the best-known means of creating distance-taught courses is probably the course team method introduced by the UK Open University. This involves a cooperative process resulting in materials which are the product of a team rather than of a series of individuals. This model has been followed to a greater or lesser degree by a number of distance teaching institutions; in practice its feasibility is greatly affected by the academic traditions which pertain in the country into which it is introduced. An alternative model, which in view of the world-wide economic downturn might have been adopted in a number of countries including the UK had they commenced operations a few years later, involves the use of external consultants to create materials which are then developed by instructional designers into distance teaching materials.

The delivery of courses presents major administrative challenges which conventional institutions do not face. Once course materials have been produced they must be stored and then delivered to students, either through the mail, via study centres, or where appropriate through the medium of broadcasting organizations. Students must also have a means of submitting assignments and having them marked and returned.

In terms of pedagogy, a major current concern is how students learn and how best materials can be written and structured most effectively to meet their requirements. The principal teaching medium in virtually all distance teaching institutions, with the exception of many in the United States, is print. Many institutions prepare their own printed instructional materials, the best of which include a variety of devices designed to incorporate the highest possible level of interactivity and to help students assess their progress. Additionally, many institutions produce integrated multi-media materials which are intended to enrich the student's learning experience. Vertecchi's chapter (Chapter 11), which appears here for the first time in English, presents an Italian perspective on the introduction of a mastery learning strategy into the development of distance teaching materials.

Student support services take a wide variety of forms, but frequently offer students the opportunity to visit study centres for tutorial and counselling support, to meet fellow students, and to use facilities unavailable to them at home. Library services, including a postal loan service of books and videos, are offered in some countries. Advice and support is frequently offered, not only during the period of study but also prior to enrolment. Guidance to potential students is particularly important in institutions with open admission policies where students may be admitted with no educational qualifications. Vivian's chapter (Chapter 13), presented here in edited form, reports the introduction into an Australian distance teaching system of a new medium, electronic mail, in an attempt to speed up transactional processes between primary and secondary level students and their teachers and to provide an improved learning environment. The chapter is unusual in that it records students' experience as well as presenting the teachers' perspective.

10 Open universities – the test of all models

Ross H. Paul

THE PHILOSOPHY OF OPEN LEARNING

Open learning is an elusive term, meaning many different things to different people. In the most general sense, it is a relative term, referring to degrees of openness compared to some existing practice. Hence, an open-admissions policy is one which places few or no restrictions on entry, in contrast to those applying strict selection criteria.

In practice, no educational institution is completely open, for an institution on the absolute open end on all dimensions of a closed–open continuum would not be an institution at all. Instead, one would have achieved the complete 'deschooling' advocated by Illich (1971).

Nevertheless, the history of education and, most recently, of higher education, has seen a strong trend towards a philosophy of 'more open' learning. Fletcher's description (1968) of the evolution of the modern university provides a useful overview of why this has come about.

He traces the evolution of Oxford and Cambridge, with their emphasis on the collegiate system, to earlier monasteries where 'groups of scholars committed to a love of scholarship in the setting of a community life' were assembled (1968: 14). The twelfth-century Italian Cathedral Schools introduced the notion of self-government and professional education, the seventeenth century brought research, and the nineteenth saw the development of teacher-training and technical universities and colleges (1968: 15–17).

In the important work, *A Cultural History of Western Education*, Butts traces the social and intellectual roots of our modern educational system. The value of education for the liberation, enlightenment and equality of all people can be traced from Plato and Aristotle, through the social humanitarianism of Rousseau and the Encyclopaedists in France, to Jefferson, Mann and Dewey in the USA.

It is the twentieth century, however, which has seen strong movement towards the expansion and democratization of higher education. Many of the factors in this trend, according to Fletcher (1968: 19–44) have had more to do with pragmatism and economic development than social altruism and idealism.

It has been only since about 1900 that economists have been interested in the relationship between economic investment and economic progress, finding that 'return from investment in education is much higher than was generally supposed' (Fletcher 1968: 24). This lesson was learned in the first half of the century through the rapid expansion of secondary education, and there are few, if any, governments which do not accept a fundamental relationship between investment in education and economic return. Other economic forces which have had an impact on the expansion of higher education have been the rise of the professions and new technology which combine to make demands for new, highly trained specialists and better researchers.

Major powers have also seen higher education as a crucial factor in nation building, both in terms of seeking international competitive advantage and enhancing military power, which has emphasized science and technology, and of developing foreign-service and diplomatic corps, which has encouraged such disciplines as history, economics, languages, political science and sociology. The apparent relationship between investment in higher education and economic and political success has encouraged developing countries to follow suit.

The opening up of higher education has not been exclusively for such utilitarian purposes, however. Nineteenth-century egalitarianism was the first to break down the exclusiveness of admission to higher education (Fletcher 1968: 38) and the twentieth century has seen unmistakable trends towards the democratization of education, so that universal primary and secondary education is a reality in most countries, and the proportion of the population attending higher-educational institutions is growing steadily almost everywhere.

Open learning is merely one of the most recent manifestations of a gradual trend towards the democratization of education. The use of the term 'open' admits that education and learning have traditionally been 'closed' by various barriers – entrance requirements, time constraints, financial demands, geographical distances, and, much more subtly, social and cultural barriers, as well as those of gender.

An open-learning institution is one dedicated to helping individuals overcome these barriers to their further education. Our primary interest here is in open universities, institutions which provide open admission to adult students and, through flexible policies and a variety of delivery mechanisms, notably distance education, provide access to and success in university education to those previously denied such opportunity.

The institutions known as 'open universities' vary considerably in form and structure, and some are more open than others. Their common characteristics are the following.

- A commitment to the belief that most adult students, regardless of age, gender, economic status, geographic location, employment status, and previous educational experience, given the opportunity and support, can succeed in studies at the university level.
- A concomitant commitment to providing structures, processes and services which assist such students in overcoming these various barriers to university access and support.
- At the risk of circular reasoning, we can say that open universities are most obviously those institutions which choose to define themselves in that way. It does not necessarily follow that they are more open on any specific dimension than any other institution, but this definition simply indicates that a commitment to the dimensions of open learning suggested immediately above is fundamental and central to their *raison d'être*.

There are enough loopholes and ambiguities in this discussion already to suggest that terms like 'open learning', 'distance education' and 'open-learning institution' may be more elusive than first meets the eye.

DIMENSIONS OF OPENNESS

The literature and current debate suggest considerable confusion among a number of similar terms, including open learning, distance education and flexible learning. A major variable in a model of 'openness' is the extent to which the learner controls the educational process – its content, how it is learned (organization of materials, various media and teaching methods), where it is learned (home, regional centre, on campus), when it is learned (start dates, self- or institutionally paced) and whether and how it is assessed.

For purposes of this Chapter, open learning is depicted as an ideal-type, a construct which incorporates a number of fundamental values. From this perspective, almost no formalized provision of education will reach the ideal on all the continua suggested, for the extreme would not be an institution at all but some form of what Ivan Illich envisioned in his *Deschooling Society* (1971). The point is not so much whether or not a particular educational system can be classified as 'open' but whether it is more open than a previous alternative on the following dimensions.

by the prevailing behaviourist or educational-technology
ourse development (Inglis 1985 and Thompson 1989).

ngest barriers to openness is the emphasis placed on quality
on by universities and colleges. Morrison (1989:9) notes that
pposed concern with quality which underpins the accreditation
re to do with exclusion, selection and tracking. It follows that
nstitution would not offer credit courses. However, given that
ing context for post-secondary education is within the credit
s of openness can be measured in terms of:

tion of courses accredited by other institutions for transfer

f students to 'challenge' for course credit through special
ns designed for that purpose;
or 'experiential learning', the granting of credit on the basis of
ient of the individual's life experiences.

the gap between promise and reality

tral to the concept of open learning, the above concepts should
sion making and priority setting within open learning institu-
ver, the process of implementation is one that frequently
commitment, and no institution comes near to matching the
all dimensions.
rge, then, institutions claiming to be open are simply more open
ore conventional counterparts on specified and sometimes quite
nsions of openness. Lewis has done a useful job of illustrating
1990), and Rumble has forced the question of the relative
of one or more dimensions, notably access (1989: 33).
ish preoccupation with the debate about open learning and
ucation, which has received a lot of attention in recent editions of
ing and in several new textbooks (Thorpe and Grugeon 1987,
, has strong political connotations in that country, but it has also
used more attention on our use of these terms in other applica-
efulness has been primarily to challenge justifiable pride in what
ing institutions have achieved to date and to force those of us
n them to identify significant gaps between theory and practice,
o suggest ways in which they could be much more open.

Accessibility

Open learning is characterized by a commitment to helping students, especially adults, overcome such traditional barriers to a post-secondary
education as the following.

Prior academic credentials

Open learning means a commitment to open admissions, a belief that most
adult students lacking formal qualifications can succeed in university-level
studies if given the (or another) opportunity. They are admitted on a 'first
come, first served' basis, limited only by the availability of the appropriate
programme or of course places (usually governed by availability of course
materials or staff rather than physical space).

Time

Many adult students, because of work and/or family responsibilities, cannot
manage the full-time (usually also 'day' time) commitment that most degree
programmes require. Open learning includes a commitment to helping the
student to find ways to study in his or her own time.

Physical location

In open learning, the institution comes to the student rather than vice versa,
and thus provides access to those located in communities not otherwise
served by formal educational institutions. This is usually provided through
printed study materials prepared especially for home study with the support
of a great variety of media and services, including tutoring by correspondence, telephone or teleconferencing, and using such information
technologies as computer-assisted learning, interactive videodisc and satellite television.

Financial constraints

By allowing students to study in their own time and place, and on a full- or
part-time basis, open learning assists them to overcome financial barriers to
formal education by allowing them to study while holding a full-time job or
raising a family. It may also provide the requisite study materials more
cheaply than would normally be the case.

Personal characteristics

An area that has not received as much attention in this sort of analysis is the collection of barriers to learning erected by the students themselves. The argument here is that a true commitment to open learning takes these into account. Too often, adult students tend to blame themselves rather than the institution for their failures, and this presents a formidable challenge to the latter in helping students overcome their insecurities and deficiencies, a challenge that must be met if the open door is to be more than a revolving one.

Social responsibility

Such institutions usually have a deliberate orientation towards the traditionally disadvantaged – those from lower socio-economic strata or aboriginal groups, prison inmates and others traditionally denied places at a university. As with so many other attempts to provide for a more open society, however, this element of openness is often less prevalent than is admitted, and research almost inevitably demonstrates that the proportion of students from disadvantaged strata is significantly below that held out for such institutions at the time of their inception (Woolfe 1974 and Woodley 1986).

Flexibility

Institutionalized flexibility is an integral part of an open learning system, but it is a more fundamental issue than simply increasing accessibility. It stems from a strong commitment to the learner as the starting-point for all learning.

In the traditional institution, the main task of the administrator is to ensure that the right learner is in the right classroom at the right time with the right professor. What happens then is left up to the latter (and only sometimes to the student). In a truly open learning institution, these factors are governed much more directly by the student, who has far more control over the learning environment than is usually the case. In practice, however, this may also be a bit of an illusion. Writing in the context of Britain's Open University, Harris cautions against this common assumption:

> Despite the promise of a radical departure from existing practice, in the name of liberating the learner, there is a risk of merely modernising existing practice and subjecting the learner to more rational and individualised controls.

(Harris 1988: 14)

Among the characteristics of inst
following.

Frequent admission periods

Instead of two or three semesters a
ence of the organization of classe
individually and more frequently,

Self-pacing

Students may frequently be able
predetermined time period), submitt
own schedules and writing examir
(rather than when the institution sch

Optional support services

The institution attempts to provide a b
including tutoring, counselling and ad
whether or not he or she takes advant

Learner control over content and st

In the optimum case, the student is ab
to learn on an individual basis. The stud
in which various topics are approached
Typically, so-called open-learning insti
tive in these areas than they have b
flexibility in modes of course delivery,
curricula, evaluation and accreditation f

Choice of delivery systems

In the optimum open-learning institution
to choose delivery systems and learning
her individual requirements. Not everyon
person learns in different ways under diff
subject matter. A challenge for all educat
delivery systems to individual learning
problem for distance-learning institutions,

well addressed
approaches to

Accreditation

One of the stro
and accreditati
much of the su
system has mo
the most open
the overwhelm
system, degre

- the recogn
  credit;
- the right
  examinatio
- provision
  an assessm

Conclusion:

As values ce
drive all dec
tions. Howe
threatens thi
ideal type or
By and la
than their m
limited dime
this (1986,
importance
The Bri
distance edu
Open Lear
Paine 1988
usefully fo
tions. Its us
open learn
employed
and hence

DEFINITIONS

For purposes of this chapter, 'open learning' is an ideal-type construct against which various institutions can be measured (see the dimensions set out above). It is not an absolute concept which distinguishes some institutions from others, although, as Rumble has observed, many have successfully promoted themselves as such in order to capitalize on government funding and support for such institutions (1989: 37).

'Distance education' is one means towards the end of open learning. It describes non-contiguous learning whereby the learning process takes place 'away' from the institution, although, again, it is not an absolute term. Escotet's statement, cited in Rumble (1989: 34), provides a good summary of this position:

> *Open education* is particularly characterized by the removal of restrictions, exclusions and privileges; by the accreditation of students' previous experience; by the flexibility of the management of the time variable; and by substantial changes in the traditional relationships between professors and students. On the other hand, *distance education* is a modality which permits the delivery of a group of didactic media without the necessity of regular class participation, where the individual is responsible for his own learning.

These definitions notwithstanding, terms such as 'open-learning institution', 'open university' and 'distance-teaching institution' are used quite freely throughout this chapter. In these cases, the reference is to educational institutions which formally identify themselves in this way (for example, Athabasca University, the Open University, the Indira Gandhi National Open University) and does not necessarily imply that they are more open than some other institutions on any particular dimension.

'Open management' is an approach to the management of such organizations which is modelled on the value systems on which they are based.

INSTITUTIONAL BARRIERS TO OPENNESS

While open-learning institutions have been established to help students overcome such barriers to a further education as geographical distance, financial and time constraints, and restrictive admission policies, there are other less obvious barriers, some of which emanate from the institutions themselves.

It is one thing to adopt a policy of openness and quite another to carry it out successfully. It is ironic that some of the following are derived directly from attempts to institutionalize open learning.

Traditional staff

Given their relative newness, it is not surprising that open-learning institutions are staffed mainly from the ranks of traditional universities and colleges. While there are strong elements of self-selection, it is also frequently the case that academics apply for and accept positions in such institutions more because of job availability than dedication to the principles of open learning. Especially given the power of faculty in any university, such staff may dominate university governance, resulting in much more conservative institutions than was originally intended.

Traditional students

Harris writes persuasively about the 'hidden curriculum' which arises from resource limitations, from the unintended consequences of various assessment schemes and, most strongly, from the 'unstated but powerful and often highly conventional expectations of pupils or colleagues in practice' (1988: 14). This suggests that our institutions have to educate their students not only in the formal curriculum but about open learning as well.

Invisible students

In many open learning situations, the student is seldom or never 'on campus'. While some academics sardonically refer to this as one of the great benefits of such institutions, in practice, it is a major problem. Staff who are not in daily contact with students can quickly lose their primary student orientation, so that registry clerks may be slower in responding to problems, faculty take longer to mark assignments, and tutors do not have the same commitment to an individual they would have in face-to-face situations. Senior administrators may be even further removed from the day-to-day problems faced by their students than they are at a campus-based institution. This invisibility may be particularly important in adult education where institutional staff need to be reminded from time to time that their students usually lead very busy lives, with several other identities (spouse, parent, career) often taking precedence over that of student (unlike the pattern for most full-time students aged between 18 and 22). Adult students may lack the skills to organize their competing priorities and may require assistance from the institution in ways which they may find difficult to articulate.

Never-ending academic year

In cases where students can enrol at the beginning of any month (as at

Athabasca University), there is no formal beginning or end to the academic year. After a while, this can be very demoralizing for staff, for whom the work never ceases. In the traditional semester system, even if it has been a 'bad' year, at least it comes to an end; the lecturer can sigh, say 'Thank goodness, it's over', and enjoy a break before getting a fresh start in the new year.

Fiscal factors

Given that open-learning systems are often justified in terms of their cost efficiency and effectiveness, there may be a tendency to cut back on resources required for student support, so that a critical component of the commitment to open learning, support for the individual student, is compromised. For example, liberal extension and suspension policies which allow students to buy extra time for the completion of their courses may penalize other students waiting for a course place and may reduce success rates by tacitly encouraging procrastination. This is a sensible argument for reducing or eliminating them, but it may be at a cost to the openness and flexibility that is supposedly driving all decision making.

While there is an implicit assumption that 'open' is usually better than 'closed', it does not necessarily follow that a specific educational provision is always better the more open it is. It has already been noted that a completely open programme would not require an institution at all, and virtually every so-called open institution has elements that are quite closed.

For example, a specific training programme for the employees of a given company is obviously closed in its admissions, and yet may be very open in every other way. Other projects might have open admissions but quite rigid requirements as to when the students attend classes or take centralized examinations.

As Lewis (1990) and others have demonstrated, one can establish an ideal type against which existing institutions can be measured to determine their degrees of openness. While it may be an interesting intellectual exercise to compare various institutions in terms of their degree of openness, debates over which institutions are more open than others are trivial at best.

In each case, the ultimate test should be that the rationale for a given provision or requirement is seen as being in the best interests of the particular student group for whom it is intended. There will, of course, always be great debate about this – many institutional arrangements supposedly for the students' 'own good' have a lot more to do with convenience to their staff or to fiscal concerns. It is all too easy to dismiss these, but there will always be practical and resource-based limitations on openness and flexibility.

Furthermore, some restrictions and limitations can be justified as being in the students' own interests. For example, it is usually reasonable to require students to take a prerequisite course before admitting them to a course which they otherwise have almost no hope of passing. Subject matter which requires social interaction may not be conducive to home study or may require educational media which are not necessarily accessible to everyone.

The ideal-type presented above for open learning, combined with the notion of 'value-driven leadership', offers a useful model for the management of open learning. The values are derived from the ideal type, and it is up to each institution to be very clear on where it stands on each (for example, open admissions, degree of flexibility in learning systems, control of content). Once defined, these values can then be set out as criteria for planning and decision making in the organization.

It is argued here that if our institutions are to be as open as we say they are (and it does not take very much insight to recognize that they are not), management too must be open and driven by the same values which are represented in the organization's mission statements and strategic plans.

REFERENCES

Butts, R. F. (1955) *A Cultural History of Western Education: its Social and Intellectual Foundations,* New York: McGraw-Hill.
Escotet, M. (1980) 'Adverse factors in the development of an open university in Latin America', *Programmed Learning and Educational Technology* 17, 4: 144.
Fletcher, B. (1968) *Universities in the Modern World,* London: Pergamon Press.
Harris, D. (1988) 'The micro-politics of openness', *Open Learning* 3, 2: 14.
Illich, I. D. (1971) *Deschooling Society,* London: Calder & Boyars.
Inglis, P. (1985) 'Promoting positive learning attitudes through personalizing external studies: a study of the learning experiences of 50 Weipa (far North Queensland) students', paper presented at the Thirteenth World Conference of the International Council for Distance Education, Melbourne, August 1985, no. 1039.
Lewis, R. (1986) 'What is open learning?', *Open Learning* 1, 2: 5–10.
Lewis, R. (1990) 'Open learning and the misuse of language: a response to Greville Rumble', *Open Learning* 5, 1: 3–8.
MacIntosh, N. and Morrison, V. (1974), 'Student demand, progress and withdrawal: The Open University's first four years', *Higher Education Review* 7: 37–66.
Morrison, T. R. (1989) 'Beyond legitimacy: facing the future in distance education', *International Journal of Lifelong Education* 8, 1: 9.
Paine, N. (ed.) (1988) *Open Learning in Transition: an Agenda for Action,* Cambridge: National Extension College.
Rumble, G. (1989) '"Open learning", "distance learning", and the misuse of language" ', *Open Learning* 4, 2: 32–40.
Thompson, G. (1989) 'Provision of student support services in distance education: do we know what they need?' in R. Sweet (ed.) *Post-secondary Distance Education in Canada,* Athabasca: Athabasca University and Canadian Society for Studies in Education. 43–50.

Accessibility

Open learning is characterized by a commitment to helping students, especially adults, overcome such traditional barriers to a post-secondary education as the following.

Prior academic credentials

Open learning means a commitment to open admissions, a belief that most adult students lacking formal qualifications can succeed in university-level studies if given the (or another) opportunity. They are admitted on a 'first come, first served' basis, limited only by the availability of the appropriate programme or of course places (usually governed by availability of course materials or staff rather than physical space).

Time

Many adult students, because of work and/or family responsibilities, cannot manage the full-time (usually also 'day' time) commitment that most degree programmes require. Open learning includes a commitment to helping the student to find ways to study in his or her own time.

Physical location

In open learning, the institution comes to the student rather than vice versa, and thus provides access to those located in communities not otherwise served by formal educational institutions. This is usually provided through printed study materials prepared especially for home study with the support of a great variety of media and services, including tutoring by correspondence, telephone or teleconferencing, and using such information technologies as computer-assisted learning, interactive videodisc and satellite television.

Financial constraints

By allowing students to study in their own time and place, and on a full- or part-time basis, open learning assists them to overcome financial barriers to formal education by allowing them to study while holding a full-time job or raising a family. It may also provide the requisite study materials more cheaply than would normally be the case.

Personal characteristics

An area that has not received as much attention in this sort of analysis is the collection of barriers to learning erected by the students themselves. The argument here is that a true commitment to open learning takes these into account. Too often, adult students tend to blame themselves rather than the institution for their failures, and this presents a formidable challenge to the latter in helping students overcome their insecurities and deficiencies, a challenge that must be met if the open door is to be more than a revolving one.

Social responsibility

Such institutions usually have a deliberate orientation towards the traditionally disadvantaged – those from lower socio-economic strata or aboriginal groups, prison inmates and others traditionally denied places at a university. As with so many other attempts to provide for a more open society, however, this element of openness is often less prevalent than is admitted, and research almost inevitably demonstrates that the proportion of students from disadvantaged strata is significantly below that held out for such institutions at the time of their inception (Woolfe 1974 and Woodley 1986).

Flexibility

Institutionalized flexibility is an integral part of an open learning system, but it is a more fundamental issue than simply increasing accessibility. It stems from a strong commitment to the learner as the starting-point for all learning.

In the traditional institution, the main task of the administrator is to ensure that the right learner is in the right classroom at the right time with the right professor. What happens then is left up to the latter (and only sometimes to the student). In a truly open learning institution, these factors are governed much more directly by the student, who has far more control over the learning environment than is usually the case. In practice, however, this may also be a bit of an illusion. Writing in the context of Britain's Open University, Harris cautions against this common assumption:

> Despite the promise of a radical departure from existing practice, in the name of liberating the learner, there is a risk of merely modernising existing practice and subjecting the learner to more rational and individualised controls.
>
> (Harris 1988: 14)

Among the characteristics of institutions which are more open, then, are the following.

Frequent admission periods

Instead of two or three semesters a year scheduled primarily for the convenience of the organization of classes, students may be able to start courses individually and more frequently, say, at the beginning of any month.

Self-pacing

Students may frequently be able to work at their own rates (within a predetermined time period), submitting essays and papers according to their own schedules and writing examinations when they feel ready for them (rather than when the institution schedules them).

Optional support services

The institution attempts to provide a broad range of student-support services, including tutoring, counselling and advising, but it is left up to the individual whether or not he or she takes advantage of these.

Learner control over content and structure

In the optimum case, the student is able to negotiate what he or she wishes to learn on an individual basis. The student is also able to determine the order in which various topics are approached, and how he or she is to be assessed. Typically, so-called open-learning institutions have been far more conservative in these areas than they have been in providing accessibility and flexibility in modes of course delivery, as they have depended on control of curricula, evaluation and accreditation for their academic credibility.

Choice of delivery systems

In the optimum open-learning institution, the student has maximum ability to choose delivery systems and learning processes most appropriate to his or her individual requirements. Not everyone learns the same way, and the same person learns in different ways under different circumstances or for different subject matter. A challenge for all educational institutions, the matching of delivery systems to individual learning needs and styles is a particular problem for distance-learning institutions, especially as it is not particularly well addressed by the prevailing behaviourist or educational-technology approaches to course development (Inglis 1985 and Thompson 1989).

Accreditation

One of the strongest barriers to openness is the emphasis placed on quality and accreditation by universities and colleges. Morrison (1989:9) notes that much of the supposed concern with quality which underpins the accreditation system has more to do with exclusion, selection and tracking. It follows that the most open institution would not offer credit courses. However, given that the overwhelming context for post-secondary education is within the credit system, degrees of openness can be measured in terms of:

- the recognition of courses accredited by other institutions for transfer credit;
- the right of students to 'challenge' for course credit through special examinations designed for that purpose;
- provision for 'experiential learning', the granting of credit on the basis of an assessment of the individual's life experiences.

Conclusion: the gap between promise and reality

As values central to the concept of open learning, the above concepts should drive all decision making and priority setting within open learning institutions. However, the process of implementation is one that frequently threatens this commitment, and no institution comes near to matching the ideal type on all dimensions.

By and large, then, institutions claiming to be open are simply more open than their more conventional counterparts on specified and sometimes quite limited dimensions of openness. Lewis has done a useful job of illustrating this (1986, 1990), and Rumble has forced the question of the relative importance of one or more dimensions, notably access (1989: 33).

The British preoccupation with the debate about open learning and distance education, which has received a lot of attention in recent editions of *Open Learning* and in several new textbooks (Thorpe and Grugeon 1987, Paine 1988), has strong political connotations in that country, but it has also usefully focused more attention on our use of these terms in other applications. Its usefulness has been primarily to challenge justifiable pride in what open learning institutions have achieved to date and to force those of us employed in them to identify significant gaps between theory and practice, and hence to suggest ways in which they could be much more open.

DEFINITIONS

For purposes of this chapter, 'open learning' is an ideal-type construct against which various institutions can be measured (see the dimensions set out above). It is not an absolute concept which distinguishes some institutions from others, although, as Rumble has observed, many have successfully promoted themselves as such in order to capitalize on government funding and support for such institutions (1989: 37).

'Distance education' is one means towards the end of open learning. It describes non-contiguous learning whereby the learning process takes place 'away' from the institution, although, again, it is not an absolute term. Escotet's statement, cited in Rumble (1989: 34), provides a good summary of this position:

> *Open education* is particularly characterized by the removal of restrictions, exclusions and privileges; by the accreditation of students' previous experience; by the flexibility of the management of the time variable; and by substantial changes in the traditional relationships between professors and students. On the other hand, *distance education* is a modality which permits the delivery of a group of didactic media without the necessity of regular class participation, where the individual is responsible for his own learning.

These definitions notwithstanding, terms such as 'open-learning institution', 'open university' and 'distance-teaching institution' are used quite freely throughout this chapter. In these cases, the reference is to educational institutions which formally identify themselves in this way (for example, Athabasca University, the Open University, the Indira Gandhi National Open University) and does not necessarily imply that they are more open than some other institutions on any particular dimension.

'Open management' is an approach to the management of such organizations which is modelled on the value systems on which they are based.

INSTITUTIONAL BARRIERS TO OPENNESS

While open-learning institutions have been established to help students overcome such barriers to a further education as geographical distance, financial and time constraints, and restrictive admission policies, there are other less obvious barriers, some of which emanate from the institutions themselves.

It is one thing to adopt a policy of openness and quite another to carry it out successfully. It is ironic that some of the following are derived directly from attempts to institutionalize open learning.

Traditional staff

Given their relative newness, it is not surprising that open-learning institutions are staffed mainly from the ranks of traditional universities and colleges. While there are strong elements of self-selection, it is also frequently the case that academics apply for and accept positions in such institutions more because of job availability than dedication to the principles of open learning. Especially given the power of faculty in any university, such staff may dominate university governance, resulting in much more conservative institutions than was originally intended.

Traditional students

Harris writes persuasively about the 'hidden curriculum' which arises from resource limitations, from the unintended consequences of various assessment schemes and, most strongly, from the 'unstated but powerful and often highly conventional expectations of pupils or colleagues in practice' (1988: 14). This suggests that our institutions have to educate their students not only in the formal curriculum but about open learning as well.

Invisible students

In many open learning situations, the student is seldom or never 'on campus'. While some academics sardonically refer to this as one of the great benefits of such institutions, in practice, it is a major problem. Staff who are not in daily contact with students can quickly lose their primary student orientation, so that registry clerks may be slower in responding to problems, faculty take longer to mark assignments, and tutors do not have the same commitment to an individual they would have in face-to-face situations. Senior administrators may be even further removed from the day-to-day problems faced by their students than they are at a campus-based institution. This invisibility may be particularly important in adult education where institutional staff need to be reminded from time to time that their students usually lead very busy lives, with several other identities (spouse, parent, career) often taking precedence over that of student (unlike the pattern for most full-time students aged between 18 and 22). Adult students may lack the skills to organize their competing priorities and may require assistance from the institution in ways which they may find difficult to articulate.

Never-ending academic year

In cases where students can enrol at the beginning of any month (as at

Athabasca University), there is no formal beginning or end to the academic year. After a while, this can be very demoralizing for staff, for whom the work never ceases. In the traditional semester system, even if it has been a 'bad' year, at least it comes to an end; the lecturer can sigh, say 'Thank goodness, it's over', and enjoy a break before getting a fresh start in the new year.

Fiscal factors

Given that open-learning systems are often justified in terms of their cost efficiency and effectiveness, there may be a tendency to cut back on resources required for student support, so that a critical component of the commitment to open learning, support for the individual student, is compromised. For example, liberal extension and suspension policies which allow students to buy extra time for the completion of their courses may penalize other students waiting for a course place and may reduce success rates by tacitly encouraging procrastination. This is a sensible argument for reducing or eliminating them, but it may be at a cost to the openness and flexibility that is supposedly driving all decision making.

While there is an implicit assumption that 'open' is usually better than 'closed', it does not necessarily follow that a specific educational provision is always better the more open it is. It has already been noted that a completely open programme would not require an institution at all, and virtually every so-called open institution has elements that are quite closed.

For example, a specific training programme for the employees of a given company is obviously closed in its admissions, and yet may be very open in every other way. Other projects might have open admissions but quite rigid requirements as to when the students attend classes or take centralized examinations.

As Lewis (1990) and others have demonstrated, one can establish an ideal type against which existing institutions can be measured to determine their degrees of openness. While it may be an interesting intellectual exercise to compare various institutions in terms of their degree of openness, debates over which institutions are more open than others are trivial at best.

In each case, the ultimate test should be that the rationale for a given provision or requirement is seen as being in the best interests of the particular student group for whom it is intended. There will, of course, always be great debate about this – many institutional arrangements supposedly for the students' 'own good' have a lot more to do with convenience to their staff or to fiscal concerns. It is all too easy to dismiss these, but there will always be practical and resource-based limitations on openness and flexibility.

124   *Administration of distance education*

Furthermore, some restrictions and limitations can be justified as being in the students' own interests. For example, it is usually reasonable to require students to take a prerequisite course before admitting them to a course which they otherwise have almost no hope of passing. Subject matter which requires social interaction may not be conducive to home study or may require educational media which are not necessarily accessible to everyone.

The ideal-type presented above for open learning, combined with the notion of 'value-driven leadership', offers a useful model for the management of open learning. The values are derived from the ideal type, and it is up to each institution to be very clear on where it stands on each (for example, open admissions, degree of flexibility in learning systems, control of content). Once defined, these values can then be set out as criteria for planning and decision making in the organization.

It is argued here that if our institutions are to be as open as we say they are (and it does not take very much insight to recognize that they are not), management too must be open and driven by the same values which are represented in the organization's mission statements and strategic plans.

REFERENCES

45 We
Butts, R. F. (1955) *A Cultural History of Western Education: its Social and Intellectual Foundations,* New York: McGraw-Hill.
Escotet, M. (1980) 'Adverse factors in the development of an open university in Latin America', *Programmed Learning and Educational Technology* 17, 4: 144.
Fletcher, B. (1968) *Universities in the Modern World,* London: Pergamon Press.
Harris, D. (1988) 'The micro-politics of openness', *Open Learning* 3, 2: 14.
Illich, I. D. (1971) *Deschooling Society,* London: Calder & Boyars.
Inglis, P. (1985) 'Promoting positive learning attitudes through personalizing external studies: a study of the learning experiences of 50 Weipa (far North Queensland) students', paper presented at the Thirteenth World Conference of the International Council for Distance Education, Melbourne, August 1985, no. 1039.
Lewis, R. (1986) 'What is open learning?', *Open Learning* 1, 2: 5–10.
Lewis, R. (1990) 'Open learning and the misuse of language: a response to Greville Rumble', *Open Learning* 5, 1: 3–8.
MacIntosh, N. and Morrison, V. (1974), 'Student demand, progress and withdrawal: The Open University's first four years', *Higher Education Review* 7: 37–66.
Morrison, T. R. (1989) 'Beyond legitimacy: facing the future in distance education', *International Journal of Lifelong Education* 8, 1: 9.
Paine, N. (ed.) (1988) *Open Learning in Transition: an Agenda for Action,* Cambridge: National Extension College.
Rumble, G. (1989) '"Open learning", "distance learning", and the misuse of language" ', *Open Learning* 4, 2: 32–40.
Thompson, G. (1989) 'Provision of student support services in distance education: do we know what they need?' in R. Sweet (ed.) *Post-secondary Distance Education in Canada,* Athabasca: Athabasca University and Canadian Society for Studies in Education. 43–50.

Thorpe, M. and Grugeon, D. (1987) *Open Learning for Adults,* London: Longman.
Woodley, A. (1986) 'Distance students in the United Kingdom', *Open Learning*, 1, 2: 11–13.
Woolfe, R. (1974) 'Social equality as an Open University objective', *Teaching at a Distance* 1: 41–4.

11 A two-level strategy for mastery learning in distance education

Benedetto Vertecchi

Distance education provides a particularly favourable context for the verification of didactic models and for the elaboration and trial of new hypotheses. First of all, it is clear that very little of classical educational methodology can be applied in an instructional situation such as distance education, where the spatio-temporal contiguity between teachers and students does not exist.

A large part of classical educational methodology puts the focus of its activity more on the interpretation of the relationship involved in an educational situation than on the criteria for the organization of learning. But even when the aim of the methodological proposal is to promote the development of the learning activity, the teacher's part has always been prominent in determining the spatio-temporal conditions of the process and in defining the quantity and the frequency of interaction with the students and between students. Put simply, we could say that classical methodology appeared 'liberal' when the teachers were urged to qualify the space of the educational activity and 'authoritarian' when attention was drawn to the organization of time.

If one considers the organizational models which have played a determining role in the development of European education, it is easy to identify a strong attention to educational time, while little attention is paid to location. Thus, if one reads Ignatius of Loyola's *Ratio atque institutio studiorum*, the work in which he lays down the principles and organizational structure of Jesuit colleges, one finds a detailed description of the temporal sequence of educational activities and only a few references to the physical space.

The same approach characterizes the regulations of the Gymnasium at Sturm, the regulations of a Napoleonic lycée or the organization of a British public school. In general terms, when time is the central category in the planning of educational decisions, it implies an institutionalized idea of education in which the main aim is to obtain uniform behaviour, with little concern for the individual needs of the student.

Very often, criticism of educational models focused on time (especially because of the excess of authoritativeness that they manifest) has been formulated by stressing the concept of space: it can be a theoretically-defined space as in Rousseau's *Emile*, but also a physical space designed for precise educational conditions as in Neill's experiences at Summerhill and in many educational projects promoted by anti-authoritarian groups in the twentieth century.

Classical educational methodology drew up its didactic proposals adapting the spatio-temporal dimensions in which such an activity had to find its concrete realization to certain educational interpretative hypotheses. This approach has entailed educational solutions with a common tendency to prize uniformity of behaviour. In other words, classical methodology proceeded mainly along deductive lines, either when the purpose was to explain educational behaviours in accordance with moral principle or general theories, or when the purpose was to try to apply results attained in various fields of experimental research to educational practices.

The crisis of classical methodology became more and more noticeable as the educational task became more complicated with the general enforcement of compulsory schooling in contemporary society. It became evident that the attractive hypothesis of finding a valid strategy to satisfy the educational needs of a population of students potentially equal to the whole demographic cohort of the same age, was immediately blocked by the difficulties created by the concrete conditions of the educational intervention. When the population of students potentially coincided with the whole demographic class then the variability of the characteristics of such a population is extremely high, both in cognitive and affective dimensions. Thus it was most improbable that a concrete solution, even when carefully planned and articulated, could satisfy the needs of such a diverse student body.

Educational research's response to the crisis of classical methodology consisted of an attempt to find didactic strategies that would allow the educational offering to be adapted to the individual characteristics of students. This opened the way to a major redefinition of the teaching–learning processes: it was no longer a question of defining the educational offering with the implicit idea that it should match the needs of a large part of the students, with the hope that the remaining group could adapt to it. On the contrary, the educational proposal had to be flexible enough to adapt to the characteristics of all the students or, at least, to almost all of them. Thus educational research has been involved in its Copernican revolution: the focus which previously was on the educational structure was now placed on the student. In the past, the student was asked to adapt to the educational offering: now the latter has to correspond to the educational needs of the individual.

The road which leads to educational individualization is long and difficult.

One of the major difficulties is the framework of the spatio-temporal relationship in which the educational process takes place. In fact, when the process is based on uniformity, its realization is simplified because the spatio-temporal references are unified. The individualization of the educational process, on the contrary, is based on the fact that the learning process of different individuals requires a different amount of time and does not necessarily take place at the same place. Educational activities planned for a group of students (lectures, exercises, laboratory experiments) proceed at regular times and in fixed locations (lecture theatres, classrooms, specially equipped locations). The whole scheme becomes much more complicated if the activities are individualized.

In this latter situation temporal unity must be abandoned as each student follows his/her own learning rhythm and each student receives different educational stimuli which are organized in theoretically, and sometimes physically, different places. Thus the teachers' task becomes much more complicated because of the fact that both the teaching strategy and its realization lose their unity: the individualization of the educational process not only requires a planning framework which defines the objectives of the activity but also a different strategy for each student to reach the stated objectives, in theory, at least, equal to the number of students. Besides, these strategies can only be conjectured at the planning stage because they are determined by the students' characteristics which are almost unknown at the beginning of the process and can be discovered only little by little during its development. For each student, the educational process is defined during the development of the process by the decisions the teachers are able to make.

Consciousness of the difficulties connected with educational individualization entails a practical consequence: a gap between acknowledgement of the necessity of individualization and its concrete realization. In school practice, at least, individualization has concerned only some restricted aspects of teaching and the predominant pattern is still represented by unindividualized models. B. S. Bloom's '*mastery learning*' is an excellent example of educational strategy based on individualization. Starting from the finding that in an unindividualized educational situation the distribution of results corresponds to the characteristics of the students at the start of the learning activity, mastery learning provides a core of educational activities through which students should acquire determined skills and an array of diversified learning opportunities. In this approach it is possible to plan a common activity and, at the same time, to consider the personal needs of each student. In such a strategy, emphasis is place on two educational functions: assessment and compensation (or catching up). These two functions are linked so that information obtained from assessment activates the compensation/catching up and determines its content. It is an educational application of feedback theory: the student is individualized in his/her learning process and is encouraged to undertake tasks from which it is possible to understand whether he/she reached the required level of performance related to a specific segment of the learning activity.

When the student is not able to answer an intermediate test satisfactorily (such tests are called *formative* because they occur during a learning activity and influence its subsequent character), the structure provides for an intervention which allows the student to overcome his/her difficulties (see Figure 11.1). The effectiveness of the individualization depends mainly on how analytic the evaluation is and the timeliness of the activation of the compensatory intervention. It is important that the student does not develop a gap which could become stable and difficult to remove later.

For this reason, great emphasis is placed on an analysis of the cognitive predispositions of the student: that is, the abilities and skills he/she possesses when embarking on a learning activity. The difficulties identified in testing for the necessary prerequisites must receive immediate compensation to allow each student to undertake the educational activity with a good chance of successful completion.

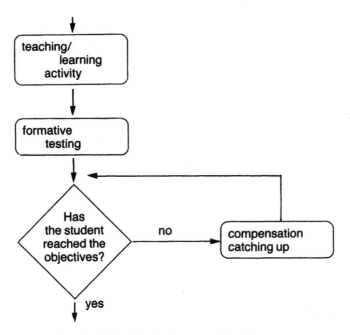

Figure 11.1 Individualization in mastery learning

Mastery learning strategies represent a positive compromise between a group-based educational process and the need to consider personal characteristics. The vertical axis of the diagram presented as Figure 11.1 shows the development of collective activities; the horizontal axis represents the individualized activities.

If the learning activity developed along the vertical axis alone, as in approaches consonant with models based on classical methodology, the tendency of the distribution of the final results (at least when the group is large enough) would be casual. A large majority of students would reach an intermediate level: smaller groups would have medium high and medium low results and at the two extremes would be found the two smallest groups with excellent or very bad results. (See Figure 11.2 in which the percentage values shown refer to the frequencies contained in the intervals of a standard deviation that would be obtained by rounding off the figures if the distribution were normal.) The hypothesis which is fundamental to mastery learning

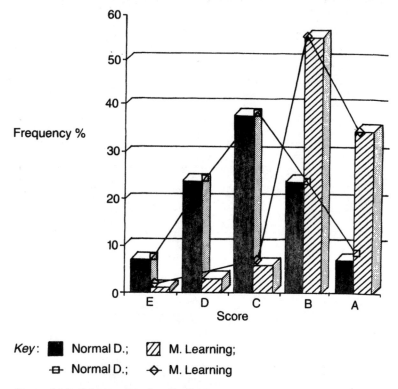

Figure 11.2 Mastery learning distribution

strategies is that a decisive improvement in the final results can be achieved by individualized intervention: about 90 per cent of the students should master objectives that could be mastered by only a third of the group without individualization.

Classical methodology focused essentially on behaviours which had to characterize the teaching process: mastery learning, on the contrary, has in particular developed functions which define the formal structures of an educational process. In other terms, in mastery learning the teachers' behaviour can and does vary because the coherence of the procedure and its capacity to reach stated objectives is entrusted to the clarity of the formal structure. Its superiority to classical methodology is clear when one considers that individualization breaks up temporal unity – and spatial unity too, when it is necessary to differentiate the activities.

Mastery learning strategies can easily be applied to the field of distance education. In fact, distance education is characterized by the absence of the very spatio-temporal references which characterize face-to-face education. Moreover, on the one hand, distance education models based on mastery learning strategies can more easily than others overcome the difficulties caused by the absence of spatio-temporal dimensions. On the other hand, they allow for the simulation of a school situation. Mastery learning, in a face-to-face situation, is based on the possibility of building a frequent interaction between students and teachers. In distance education the situation does not change except for one aspect: a collective teacher, represented by the educational structure, projects, designs and implements the educational process and replaces the different teachers identified by face-to-face students as physical individuals.

From this point of view, distance education can be regarded as a simulation of classroom activity: its quality depends to a large extent on the frequency and the quality of the interaction it can provide to students. The achievement of the results hypothesized for mastery learning (the distribution of such results is shown in Figure 11.3) provides both quantitative and qualitative verification that the interactions necessary for providing each student with the individualized educational offering that he/she actually needs, has in fact taken place.

It is worth stressing that in face-to-face education the explicit interactions, (that is, those which are intentionally produced during an educational process), are integrated with a large number of implicit interactions. These two forms of interaction make the students' adaptation to the learning task easier and, at least in part, adapt the learning process to their personal characteristics. In face-to-face learning, a flow of communication, non-vocal to a large extent, is set up between teacher and student and this allows the teacher to adapt the educational message to the students by modifying the contents,

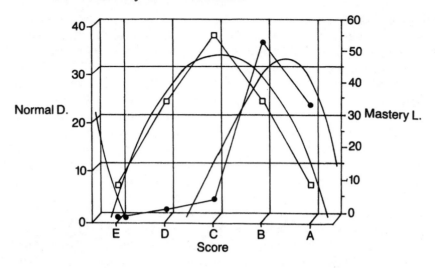

Key: -□- Normal D.
        -•- Mastery L.

Figure 11.3 Normal distribution and mastery learning

the expositions and the pacing of the activities. The teachers become aware if the level is suitable for the students, sense the approach of difficulties, perceive the development of attitudes unfavourable to the learning task. As a result teachers modify their approach, consciously or unconsciously: they go back over subjects that some of the students followed with difficulty; they slacken the study rate or speed it up; they re-present with a different approach parts of the course they consider particularly important. It is clear that this cannot actually be considered to be individualization because the teachers' attitude towards the group remains undifferentiated. From this constant adaptation, however, the learning task is constantly fine-tuned.

In distance education implicit interactions which would simplify the learning process cannot be relied on. One must, therefore, multiply the explicit interactions to make the learning task really suitable to the students' needs. In many cases the level of individualization which is achieved by offering compensatory activities to those in difficulties is inadequate, whether it is an initial compensation at the beginning of the educational process to compensate for lack of the prerequisites or compensation/ catching up after failure in formative tests. To achieve the best results, it is necessary that individualization no longer be restricted to compensation but extended to the whole learning process.

Research on students taking postgraduate courses in the Department of Educational Sciences at the University of Rome 1, 'La Sapienza', shows that the method proposed by Bloom is inadequate when the distribution of the prerequisites related to the study of a certain course unit shows excessive dispersion. Unit 5 of the course, *Methods of School Evaluation*, is a case in point. This is a course on statistics for data collection, measurement and data analysis. It is a central unit in the structure of the course. In the first four units, students study the context and theoretical analysis of problems of educational evaluation. In the fifth unit, they are trained in the acquisition of the conceptual and statistical skills necessary for the operational activities in educational evaluation of units 6 to 10. It is precisely in unit 5 that a notable dispersion in the characteristics of the students enrolled in the course is found: their backgrounds are very heterogeneous. The study of unit 5 is not difficult for students who are competent mathematicians, but it is irksome for others. The difficulties are connected not only with their university background but also with the secondary school programme followed. It is evident that a graduate in such subjects as mathematics, physics, biology, economics finds it easier to cope with statistics than a graduate in humanities or pedagogy. But the root of the problem often lies in difficulties which derive from the secondary school programme. The mathematical knowledge of students who followed a matriculation science programme has an incomparably more solid mathematical formation than a student who went to an *istituto magistrale* (vocational school for primary teachers).

These considerations suggested the development of a specific educational strategy of offering each student an individualized course corresponding to his/her characteristics. In practice, the provision of personalized learning paths for each student required an intervention on the vertical axis of the procedure illustrated in Figure 11.1. The goal was to provide for each student a study text specially designed for his/her needs. It was considered that the best educational strategy for achieving this was to double mastery learning (see Figure 11.4). The role of evaluation and catch-up/compensation procedures of classical mastery learning strategies remain unaltered, but the way in which the learning process is organized is completely modified.

There are logistical problems in the personalization of learning materials. In reality it is inconceivable to write a different version of the study text for each student: if more than 300 students enrolled and the study unit consisted of about 100 pages, it would be necessary to write 30,000 pages! Thus the implementation of double mastery learning strategies required a technological solution: a procedure that automatically produced personalized texts. In broad outline, these are the steps needed:

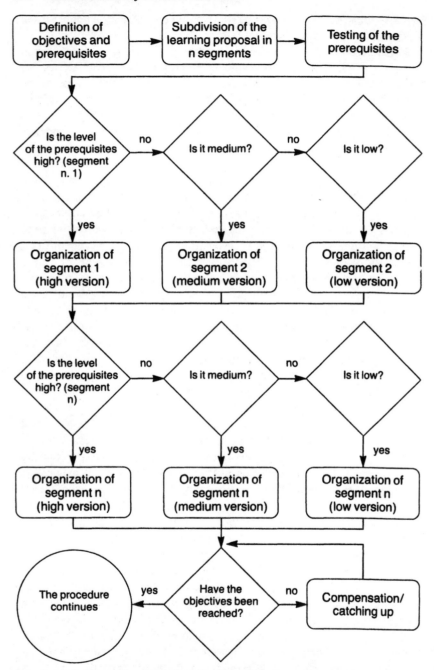

Figure 11.4 Flow chart of double mastery learning

- First, the learning objectives have to be defined with great accuracy.
- For each objective it is necessary to find the corresponding cognitive prerequisites.
- A test for the prerequisites is given to all students.
- The learning path of the unit is then subdivided into segments, with each segment corresponding to a specific objective and to a few cognitive prerequisites.
- Each segment is written in three different versions, at high, medium and low levels respectively.
- The results of the prerequisites test show which version (high, medium, low) of each segment is most suitable for each student.

The operations described in the last step are completely computerized. The textual variants and the data from the students' responses to the prerequisites test are stored in the computer. The computer then proceeds to the production of the text. In the case in point – unit 5 of *Methods of School Evaluation*, the text was divided into fifteen segments. As each segment is written in three different versions, the computer could theoretically produce 14,348,907 different personalized texts (La Torre 1991).

Double mastery learning is at present being evaluated at the Department of Educational Sciences at the University of Rome. The project design comprises:

- Students enrolled in unit 5 are split into two groups and at random assigned to the experimental group (E) or the control group (C). In both groups there are 150 students.
- Both groups do the prerequisites test. All the students know we are implementing an educational experiment but they do not know their role in it.
- The data from the prerequisites test are processed. We anticipate that the distribution of group E will be identical to that of group C.
- Two sets of learning materials are produced. The experimental group is provided with personalized texts (in theory we could have 150 different texts. The first data needed, in fact, differentiated texts for more than 90 per cent of the students). The control group all received the medium level of each segment as their version of the text.
- The students study the course materials as usual, fulfil the assignments and send in their intermediate tests. From the student's point of view, there is no difference between the study of unit 5 and the study of all the other units. The students know that an experiment is in progress because they were told about it and because of the rigour of the prerequisites test. In the study material, there is nothing to indicate whether they are in the experimental or the control group. We were very careful in constituting

the groups and in dealing with the students to avoid parasitical variables in the experimental data caused by differences in the attitude of the students of both groups to the course objectives.

* The results of students in the experimental group will be compared with the results of the other group. The hypothesis is clearly that the results of the E group will be significantly better than the C group. If the experiment is successful, it will entail interesting consequences both in the theoretical definition of the concept of individualization of the educational process, and in the planning and design of distance education courses.

REFERENCE

La Torre, M. (1991) 'Unità didattiche "su misura": modelli strutturali', *Istruzione a Distanza*, 3, 2: 11–18.

12 Some instructional strategies for improved learning from distance teaching materials

Percy W. Marland and Ronald E. Store

In distance teaching we are usually concerned with indirect methods of interacting with learners, using for the most part the written word. Quality of learning in distance education ought therefore to be closely related to the quality of textual materials provided to students. In this chapter we examine some ways of facilitating learning at a distance. We begin by noting the current dearth of models for teaching through text and make a plea for diversity and experimentation in this area. Some traditional instructional strategies (including advance organizers, overviews, pretests, objectives and inserted questions) from the dominant approach to distance teaching are examined along with devices in typography and graphics. Guidelines for their use are developed, based on research, everyday rationality, and from an embryonic conceptualization of distance learning

INTRODUCTION

All teachers without exception have to grapple with several perennial issues including motivation of students, specifications of goals, the provision of worthwhile learning activities, giving effective feedback, and inducing an appropriate disposition towards learning in students. In responding to these issues, classroom teachers can call on an abundant literature which addresses the issues either separately or collectively within the framework of carefully articulated and reasonably comprehensive approaches to teaching. Classroom teachers can similarly select from a wide range of in-service programmes to enhance their existing skills or develop new ones.

No such luxury awaits the distance teacher. Distance education has not captured the attention of those involved in educational research, and its literature has a short history and remains slight, with little theoretical discussion and little documentation of instructional practices; in fact, it is only during the last decade that distance teaching has become the focus of much discourse at all.

An examination of the literature of distance education and of many samples of distance teaching materials currently being used will show a preference for one particular approach to teaching through text. This approach incorporates use of devices which have been derived from, or can be readily aligned with, a traditional approach to teaching in which, typically, specific goals are defined for students; content and resources are presented by the teacher; interactive processes and patterns are largely initiated, guided, and controlled by the teacher; obligatory assessment activities are set by the teacher; and feedback is provided by the teacher. These devices are considered by Macdonald-Ross (1979) to be the 'cultural descendants' of tightly structured programmed learning materials. Clearly they signal an approach to distance teaching which is heavily teacher-directed and which casts the teacher in the roles of manipulator, controller, and director. Such an approach posits a close analogy between teaching and manufacturing. Some have criticized it because of the value it places on efficiency, cost-effectiveness, product orientation, and marketability of the product at the expense of diversity, individuality, and a humanistic approach. Surprisingly, the pervasiveness of this approach in distance teaching has not provoked much comment to date, but it does invite investigation since this one-model dominance conflicts with a generally accepted proposition at the classroom level that there is not just one 'right' way to teach.

The reasons for the dominance of this approach are probably varied and complex. It does *seem* to give the teacher more control of what the student does, how he learns, and in what order he does it. The sense of control over learning that it imparts might be a palliative for those distance teachers troubled by their physical remoteness from learners and their inability to influence learners directly. However, this sense of control may be misleading. The evidence on this issue, as we shall show in this chapter, is not yet all in and, even where there has been a fair degree of research, conclusions can only be tentatively drawn. Certainly we would not want to suggest that it is the best approach to distance teaching. We would rather argue for more eclecticism and more experimentation than seems presently to exist amongst many distance-teaching enterprises. Diversity in instructional approach is warranted in view of the clearly established need to vary instructional strategies to suit differences in instructional goals, the demands of specific knowledge domains, and the needs of learners such as those arising from differences in cognitive style and cultural backgrounds. In particular, we would advocate the extension of developmental work begun by Bååth (1979) in delineating different instructional approaches in the distance teaching field, and which parallels the efforts of Joyce and Weil (1972, 1980) on teaching in conventional classrooms.

We also believe that there is a need to structure materials in a way which will provide the student with greater access to the content. In discussing this concept we have drawn considerably on the work of Waller and Macdonald-Ross of the Open University (UK). 'Access structure' refers to the 'co-ordinated use of typographically signalled structural cues that help students to read texts using selective sampling strategies' (Waller 1979: 175). These cues help the reader to find his or her way about in the text. We believe that for too long we have ignored the fact that students at a distance read instructional texts *selectively*.

Another theme which has informed our thinking is that of the 'veto power' over learning which students at a distance can exercise. They are able to make decisions about how they will deal with an instructional package, instructional decisions which are usually denied the internal student. Good design of instructional text will recognize this veto power.

The main task we have set ourselves in this chapter, however, is to examine a number of the devices which have been used in instructional text for tertiary level distance learners. In particular, we focus on the devices which orient the learner and introduce the textual material (advance organizers, overviews, pretests and objectives), on the insertion of questions, and presentation techniques which have instructional consequences, including graphics and typographical cues. These seem to us to be major areas of concern. Anyone designing instructional text will usually make decisions about how to introduce materials and orient learners, how to provide appropriate questions to assist learners, and how to present the text in such a way that it will facilitate learning. Where appropriate, we have drawn on research and research reviews. On other occasions, we have resorted to intuition, our own experience, and everyday rationality. Where possible we have tried to derive guidelines for those involved in the day to day preparation of distance teaching materials. Two caveats are in order here. First, the guidelines which we propose are in many respects general ones. Their application in specific contexts should be made only after consideration has been given to the goals achieved, features of the particular context (including the nature of the subject matter) in which they are to be used, and characteristics of learner groups. Second, these guidelines do not apply to the preparation of the subject matter discourse but to instructional devices which are embedded in the text and which are intended as aids to facilitate students' use of the text.

ORIENTING THE LEARNER

The writer of distance teaching materials has available a range of devices for introducing students to learning tasks. These devices usually appear in the introductory sections of textual material and include easily distinguishable forms such as advance organizers, overviews, pretests, and objectives.

Writers generally tend not to put all their eggs in one basket but rather use a combination of these devices. In our view, there are good reasons for encouraging this practice. Our investigation of introductory material in some examples of distance teaching texts showed that it was even more multi-faceted than we expected.

In addition to the four components listed above, we found: statements containing a rationale for the objectives; pictorial and graphic material attempting to present an overview of the contents of the text; brief bio-graphies of writers; statements on the writers' value positions and biases; advice to students on how to process the text; exhortations about the import-ance of adopting a sceptical frame of mind when reading and studying; and even a motto which sounded a similar warning – *Caveat emptor*: Let the buyer beware. We believe that each of these forms of introductory material has its own intrinsic merits from a pedagogical standpoint and, while we could not find one jot of research evidence in respect of any of them, in contrast to those listed in the previous paragraph, we consider that they would satisfy the discerning eye of the educational connoisseur.

The diversity within and across those examples reviewed is quite high and their richness and potential for assisting learners seem impressive to us. We see no reason for not using a range of orienting devices. At the same time, diversity for its own sake is purposeless, especially where one device simply duplicates the effects and functions of another.

Advance organizers

Form and functions

It has been argued that, just as in the construction and fitting out of a new building, the first stage involves the erection of a shell or framework based on a master plan, so, in assisting learners to acquire the content of disciplines, there is a need either to provide them with a framework of ideas (an ideational framework) or to make explicit an already existing framework to which new ideas in the material to be learnt can be anchored. Such an approach is based on the premise that 'the most important factor influencing the meaningful learning of any new idea is the state of the individual's existing cognitive structure at the time of learning' (Ausubel and Robinson 1969: 143). The notion of presenting learners with an ideational structure prior to actual presentation of the material to be learnt was first developed by Ausubel in the context of his theory of meaningful verbal learning. Since then, many other writers have endorsed this proposition and it has also been the focus of considerable research. The term coined by Ausubel for this preparatory framework was 'advance organizer'.

The term advance organizer is used, then, to describe deliberately structured sets of ideas presented to learners prior to the material to be learnt. The intention is to provide them with a conceptual framework for facilitating learning and retention of the new material by making available an organization of old or familiar ideas to which the new ideas can be related and anchored. The framework provided by the advance organizer has therefore to encompass all the ideas in the new material (that is, the material to be presented subsequently), and so has to be more general and more abstract than the new material. In essence, then, advance organizers as distinct from summaries have to be higher levels of generality, abstraction, and inclusiveness than the material to be presented subsequently to students for their learning. The basic proposition is that if an advance organizer contains ideas which are familiar to and understood by students, and which are relatable to the ideas in the material to be presented, then learning and retention of the new material will be enhanced. To be maximally effective, advance organizers 'must be formulated in terms of language and concepts already familiar, and use appropriate illustrations and analogies if developmentally necessary' (Ausubel and Robinson 1969: 316).

Two kinds of advance organizers have been proposed by Ausubel (Ausubel and Robinson 1969).

- Expository organizers (for example, a definition of a concept or a generalization), which are recommended for use when the material to be presented to learners is completely unfamiliar to them. An expository advance organizer contains knowledge already established in learners' cognitive structures that is relatable to the new information they are to learn and that can make the new material more plausible and comprehensible.
- Comparative advance organizers (for example, an analogy), which are to be used when the new material is not completely novel as would occur, for example, when students, having previously examined one theory of learning, encounter another theory of learning. In this case, a comparative advance organizer would make explicit similarities and differences between the two theories of learning.

Research on advance organizers

In addition to reports in the early 1960s by Ausubel and his co-workers of their research into the facilitative effects of advance organizers, several major reviews of recent vintage have been undertaken (Barnes and Clawson 1975, Faw and Waller 1976, Hartley and Davies 1976, Lawton and Wanska 1977, Mayer 1979, and Luiten, Ames, and Ackerson 1980). Of these, the most comprehensive review in terms of number of studies was the meta-analysis by Luiten *et al.* of 135 advance organizer studies undertaken in the period 1960–79. The general conclusion reached in this meta-analysis was that, taking the research studies as a whole, 'advance organizers have a facilitative effect on learning and retention' (Luiten, Ames and Ackerson 1980: 213). The majority of the reviewers cited above had earlier reached a similar conclusion though one or two retained a healthy scepticism and wanted to reserve judgement until more research had been completed. Barnes and Clawson dissented from general opinion, asserting that 'advance organizers, as presently constructed, generally do not facilitate learning'. However, serious flaws in their analysis have been exposed by Lawton and Wanska (1977).

Though the general conclusion cited above is of significance *per se*, it also provides an important backdrop for what follows, because the issue that is of particular interest in this chapter is reviewers' conclusions relating to the effects of advance organizers in textual materials on tertiary level students. Some tentative conclusions have been ventured, but their authors have been quick to point out the very limited empirical basis in which they have been grounded. Briefly, the conclusions are as follows.

- University students comprise one section of a group of students that appear to derive more benefit from advance organizers than others (Hartley and Davies 1976).
- Advance organizers appear to facilitate both learning at the higher cognitive levels and retention (Hartley and Davies 1976, Hudgins 1977 and Luiten *et al.* 1980).
- Advance organizer formats other than continuous prose (for example, simulations, models, graphs, maps, and networks) should be considered (Hartley and Davies 1976).
- Advance organizer treatment groups derive a permanent rather than a short-term advantage in terms of retention of material (Luiten *et al.* 1980).
- Advance organizers have the strongest positive effect on transfer of knowledge rather than retention (Mayer 1979).
- Subject areas in which advance organizers appear to be most facilitative are mathematics and science (Mayer 1979).

Discussion

Our position is that these conclusions have relevance for writers of distance teaching materials in spite of the ecological differences between distance-learning contexts and those in which most advance organizer studies have been done. In fact these studies involved neither distance teaching materials nor distance learners. So we are playing a hunch; but given the fact that many studies involved the students in just reading the advance organizer and then the text, we believe that the likelihood is slight that the facilitative effects of advance organizers would be noticeably or significantly depressed by features of distance learning contexts such as isolation, learner independence, and lack of immediate feedback. Apparently, however, mode of presentation of the advance organizer does make a difference. Luiten *et al.* have claimed that studies in which the advance organizer has been presented orally 'show a much greater effect size than studies using only a written presentation mode for the advance organizer, especially at the college level' (1980: 27). Nevertheless we are still prepared to recommend use of advance organizers to writers of distance teaching materials.

In spite of the qualified research support for advance organizers, it appears that they have been used on only a very limited scale to date. Our examination of a small sample of readily available distance teaching material from the UK and Australia provides partial confirmation of this. Joyce and Weil (1980) also reported finding only one curriculum project, the Anthropology Curriculum Project developed at the University of Georgia, in which design of learning materials had been based on an advanced organizer strategy.

Two reasons probably account for this low level of usage.

- Advance organizers have not been operationally defined. Hartley and Davies (1976) point out there is no clear-cut technology for the formulation of advance organizers as there is for behavioural objectives.
- Advance organizers are difficult to formulate.

Neither of these problems appears insoluble, however, and, because of the degree of research vindication for advance organizers, serious efforts to alleviate these problems seem warranted. Such an effort is discussed later where guidelines for writers of textual materials in distance education programmes have been proposed. Some, but not all of these guidelines, have an empirical basis, at least in part, but others are grounded in practical experience and considered opinion.

Guidelines

When to use advance organizers

We recommend that advance organizers be used when materials to be learned can be differentiated, step by step, into units and sub-units which become progressively more specific, more concrete, and less inclusive; that is, when material to be learned can be organized hierarchically along three dimensions simultaneously: general to specific; abstract to concrete; more inclusive to less inclusive. For example, a study of different ways of teaching can begin with a definition of a model of teaching (advance organizer), an abstract, general and highly inclusive statement, and proceed through a consideration of different families of models and sub-families to a detailed study of specific examples of models of teaching, one at a time.

A second example, in which the hierarchical structure of material to be taught is represented diagrammatically, appears in Figure 12.1 (Eggen *et al.* 1979: 303). In this case, the advance organizer would be another definition, this time of the term 'minerals'.

Advance organizers should be used when it is important for students to have a conceptual framework for subsequent use in clarifying the task ahead. For example, Ausubel and Robinson (1969), in preparing students familiar with the tenets of Christianity to study Buddhism, provided a comparative organizer setting out the similarities and differences between the two religions. When learning material possesses a structure which can readily be integrated with students' existing knowledge, an advance organizer seems appropriate. The use of an advance organizer also seems appropriate when learning material is entirely unfamiliar and students are either: without relevant past experiences and ideas for relating to and integrating with new material; or unaware that they have specifically relevant ideas in cognitive structure.

How to use advance organizers

Use visual aids (for example, concept maps, diagrams, graphs) in conjunction with advance organizers in verbal form. See, for example, Figure 12.1. An advance organizer could also be presented orally using an audio-cassette or take the form of a simulation, demonstration, film, or chart. Precede the advance organizer with a statement of objectives for the unit, overview, etc. Following presentation of the advance organizer, define criterial attributes of concepts, illustrate with examples, point out similarities and differences, encourage students to link new material with their own experiences, and relate new information to the advance organizer.

How to formulate advance organizers

Become familiar with the subject area. Conceptualize subject area, topic, or field of study as a series of hierarchically organized concepts or propositions. Represent this structure diagrammatically. See, for example, Figure 12.1.

Prepare the advance organizer, which can take the following forms.

• Definition of a concept, for example, 'landforms (concept) are land

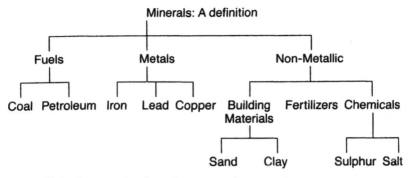

Figure 12.1   An example of an advance organizer

surfaces that have characteristic shapes and composition' (Eggen *et al.* 1979: 260).
- Generalization, for example, 'culture may be viewed as sets of solutions to problems. Diffcrent cultures solve problems in different ways ' (Joyce and Weil 1972: 174).
- Analogy, for example, a prose passage explaining functions of a computer in terms of filing cabinets and sorting baskets together with a concrete model (Mayer 1979).

Overviews

Form and functions

Overviews are highly condensed content outlines which emphasize salient points and may contain a glossary of key terms. They are different from advance organizers in that the substance of the overview is at the same level of abstraction, generality, and inclusiveness as the subsequent material. Overviews can also take various forms, for example, verbal, pictorial or graphic, though the same presumed effects of overviews might also be achieved by employing typographic devices such as a system of headings and subheadings to segment texts.

The principal purpose of an overview is to familiarize students with the scope and broad structural features of the material to be presented – its central themes, generalizations, divisions, and classificatory systems, for example. It achieves its purpose by rendering down the material to be presented into a simple, coarse-grained form – what might be called a content map in which are displayed only the most prominent features of the content.

It seems likely that this map of the content might be appreciated by readers because it would allow students access to topics relevant to their needs and interests. Overviews, then, may be valuable to students as a form of access structure (Macdonald-Ross 1979), a device which is not so much for assisting comprehension as for assisting the reader to find his or her way about within the text. Overviews also probably provide ready-made organizing centres for rehearsal and mental storage of the elaborated material in text, and so may assist recall and hence the higher cognitive functions for which information recall is a prerequisite.

Research

Apparently, little formal enquiry into the general effects of overviews on learning from text has been undertaken. What research has been done on overviews has occurred mainly in relation to films and has produced the seemingly inevitable division of opinion as to their worthwhileness, though Hartley and Davies (1976) reported that positive effects of overviews were found in a majority of these studies. Very little research seems to have been done on the effects of overviews on distance learning.

Guidelines

Our advice on use of overviews in instructional text will probably conform with common practice but will make explicit some of the principles tacitly followed in the preparation of overviews. We suggest the following.

- Overviews should be used where material to be learnt can be segmented or organized into units that help define the nature of the material (where material can be structured hierarchically, an advance organizer could be more appropriate).
- The structure made explicit in the overview should be used in the presentation of subsequent material.
- Overviews should be brief, highly condensed outlines of teaching subject matter, and contain explanations of key terms.
- Pictorial and graphic devices that can illustrate overview content, or represent it more economically, should accompany or supplement verbal overviews.
- Stage-by-stage overviews should be used in preference to, or in addition to. mass overviews.

Pretests

Functions

Pretesting, that is, administering a pre-instructional test to learners, is an instructional technique which has support in educational discourse if not in practice. Advocates of pretests claim that they can be used to determine what students, at the start of instruction, already know about material to be taught or whether or not students have the prerequisite knowledge and skills for acquiring what is to be taught. Pretesting, therefore, would allow for a more economical use of teaching effort. It seems, too, that pretesting may have additional dividends such as orienting learners to the content to be presented and alerting them to performance standards expected of students, gaps in their knowledge, and essential learning tasks. This last-mentioned function is very likely an important one for distance learners who might have to be selective in their reading and study of instructional text because of limited time.

But all of these benefits are alleged ones. Hartley and Davies (1976) cited only six investigations into the effects of pretesting on post-instructional performance. In the majority of these studies effects were not discernible, prompting the suggestion that, like overviews, the real value of pretests resides, not in their capacity to facilitate actual comprehension of learning materials, but in their potential to function as access devices.

Guidelines

If pretests are to be used by text writers (and we see no reason why they should not), it would be advisable for writers to keep clearly in mind the probable range of functions served by pretests and to use them principally as devices for providing students with access to the text, and as cues about performance standards and salient material. Intending users of pretests can take heart from the fact that, in the context of educational measurement, the state of the art is relatively advanced. A technology for test development exists and is well respected, and the problems and pitfalls of administration and evaluation are well known.

As with so many other guidelines appearing in this chapter, the ones we offer below on pretests should be viewed more as hypotheses to be tested rather than hard and fast rules.

- In the first place, we suggest using pretests in conjunction with other instructional devices such as objectives and overviews, always being clear about the content and processes which you wish to test.
- It seems appropriate to view pretests as one of a variety of devices for

providing *access* to instructional material, and to use each where the appropriate situation presents itself.

- Situations which are most amenable to the use of pretests in distance teaching are those where prerequisite knowledge and skills or material to be taught can be tested by means of objective test items (multiple choice, true–false, and short-answer questions), and performance can then be readily assessed by students from marking keys; for example, mathematical skill prerequisites for a course in research statistics.
- Use several shorter pretests, locating them before the relevant text units, rather than one large pretest.
- Students should be made aware of how to use pretests to assist their learning.

Objectives

To those familiar with instructional planning and teacher education the next two statements will come as no surprise: first, the empirical and prescriptive literature on instructional planning is replete with advice and research reports about objectives but, in comparison, other facets of planning are poorly served. Second, prospective teachers are generally required to spend numerous hours in pre-service courses learning about the virtues of objectives and how to formulate them.

Both these conditions are symptomatic of a general obsession in educational planning with objectives. It emanates from a strong commitment to a model of planning which stresses the importance of rationality and ends–means logic and which asserts the primacy of objectives in planning for effective teaching and learning. Proponents of this model argue for a high level of precision in formulating objectives, with some advocating the use of behavioural objectives which represent the ultimate in precision.

Their conviction about the need for clear, unambiguous objectives stems from two beliefs. The first is that precise objectives provide teachers with clear guidelines for selecting instructional means and evaluative criteria; the second is that providing students with these objectives will increase their motivation and learning.

The second proposition has been debated vigorously and has been tested in experimental research but the issue has not been satisfactorily resolved. Instead, the research has revealed the complexity of relationships between use of objectives and learning and has raised many other issues requiring resolution. According to Macdonald-Ross (1979), this whole area is in a state of confusion which no simple summary can sort out. While such a warning cannot be overlooked, the practice of writing objectives into instructional text continues, so text writers will continue to look for answers to perennial dilemmas relating to level of specificity, location in text, number and distribution throughout the text, when to use them and, even, whether to use them at all. There is a need, therefore, to review evidence and opinion about the effects, functions, and value to students of objectives, and then to generate some guidelines on their use.

Research

Research and theories about instructional objectives from within two different research traditions will be reviewed. Those two traditions are as follows.

1 An experimental research tradition, owing much to behavioural psychology. Studies conducted within this tradition, of which there are many, have been undertaken in contrived learning-from-text situations, involving mainly tertiary and upper secondary students.
2 A descriptive research tradition with allegiances to ethno-methodology and a cognitive view of learning.

Very little research relating to this second tradition has been reported but its goals are to assess student responses to objectives in natural study settings and to trace the actual processes engaged in by students when using objectives. As might be expected, these reviews lead to two sets of conclusions which are not easily reconciled.

It was stated earlier that experimental research into the facilitative effects of objectives on overall learning (that is, intentional and incidental learning) is equivocal. This is the general opinion of most reviewers (see, for example, Faw and Waller 1976, Hartley and Davies 1976 and Macdonald-Ross 1979). If a simple vote-counting procedure were used, there probably would be a slight advantage for research showing positive effects from objectives (see, for example, Melton 1978), but the result is certainly not clear-cut. If effects of objectives on intentional learning only were considered, the weight of evidence in favour of objectives increases but it is still not convincing.

This failure of research to provide clear confirmation of a popularly-held belief about the value of objectives has prompted attempts to pinpoint reasons for the unexpected result. Some blame has been attributed to flaws in research design and statistical techniques but many other plausible reasons have been advanced to account for the ambivalence in research results. Inferences about conditions when objectives could be effective aids to learning have also been generated. These conjectural statements have been summarized in Table 12.1 and may assist readers of the chapter to make decisions in respect of their own use of objectives.

From Table 12.1 it is clear that a variety of complex conditions govern whether or not objectives enhance relevant and incidental learning. So far,

150 *Administration of distance education*

Table 12.1 Effects of objectives on learning – some inferences from reviews of research

Independent Variable	+ Pos	0 Nil	– Neg	Comment
Characteristics of objectives	✓			
Specific objectives				Enhances intentional learning but effect is not clear cut; enhances learning of material not considered important by learner
			✓	Decreases incidental learning (varying the topic or subject matter will not change the nature of the effect)
General objectives		✓		
Large number of specific objectives			✓	
Specific objectives distributed with each section of text	✓			
Specific objectives located at one point in text			✓	
Specific objectives requiring high level of cognition (that is, difficult objectives)	✓			
Specific objectives requiring low level of cognition (that is, easy objectives)		✓		
Specific objectives and text				
Specific objectives in text with low degree of structure	✓			Where text is highly structured specific objectives have no additive effect
Specific objectives and student characteristics				
Specific objectives with students whose past experiences with objectives have been:				
•rewarding	✓			
•unrewarding		✓		
Specific objectives with students trained in the use of objectives versus those not so trained		✓		
Specific objectives with students interested in objectives versus students with little or no interest	✓			Results favour students interested in objectives
Students who use objectives to search text for relevant material versus those not using objectives	✓			Results favour students using objectives to search text for relevant material

Sources: Duchastel, P. (1979); Duchastel, P. and Merrill, P. (1973); Faw, H. and Waller, T. (1976); Gage, N. and Berliner, D. (1975); Hartley, J. and Davies, I. (1976); Kaplan, R. (1976); Macdonald-Ross, M. (1979) and Melton, R. (1978).

few insights have been obtained into the precise combinations of conditions that must prevail for desirable effects to occur. One inference about a main effect which is set down with less hesitation and trepidation than are most in this area of educational research is that specific objectives enhance relevant learning but decrease incidental learning (Faw and Waller 1976 and Duchastel 1979). On this 'finding' has been built a selective attention hypothesis which proposes that objectives direct attention to objective-relevant material and away from material which is not related to objectives. It is also frequently claimed that objectives, assuming students accept them as helpful and know how to use them, provide students with clear goals which assist them to organize more efficiently their learning activities and reduce time spent on misdirected effort. It is also claimed that they offer a basis for student self-evaluation in the course. These attributions have not been confirmed by self-report data or other means, but enjoy a measure of credibility at the moment due to circumstantial evidence from research studies and the intellectual appeal of the logic underpinning them.

When we turn to descriptive research and the inferences generated from it, we see objectives from quite a different perspective. Though there is very little research to report, what there is indicates that, as with inserted questions, students do not use objectives as intended by those who have written them. The evidence from survey studies conducted at the Open University (UK) (Macdonald-Ross 1979) suggests that students do not use objectives as attention-directors or as goal statements for problem solving, but as means for assisting them to find their way about in the instructional text. This, and a view of the student as an active and selective reader, has led to a radically different conception of in-text instructional devices. Objectives, like inserted questions and overviews, are seen as 'access devices', providing students with different points-of-entry to the instructional material and allowing them to chart their own ways through it. Seen in this light, objectives would no longer serve as direct aids to learning and would not be fulfilling the role ascribed to them in the rational, ends–means model of planning.

It might be thought, then, that they need not be placed early in the text. However, if they are to serve effectively as part of the access structure they would still need to be in a prominent place and students would have to be alerted to their presence. Macdonald-Ross (1979) and, before him, Kaplan and Simmons (1974) proposed that '(objectives) be placed at the end of the teaching material as a check list . . . with page numbers for back reference' (Macdonald-Ross, 1979: 251). In that case they would appear to be duplicating a function of inserted questions or self-assessment checks. It then raises the question of whether they should be used in place of, or in addition to, either of the other two devices.

Guidelines

The foregoing analysis makes it abundantly clear that generating guidelines on the use of objectives for writers of instructional text has many problems and pitfalls. There are no definitive answers from research, just a few clues or straws to clutch at, but even these lose much of their significance because of the disparities between research and study settings. The guidelines supplied here are therefore rules of thumb to be used cautiously.

- It would appear that objectives probably do serve some useful functions for students provided they are clear and precise and so are worth considering as an instructional aid in distance teaching texts. This should not be taken to mean that they can or should be used all the time. Their use in conjunction with other instructional devices still must be justified in the light of specific conditions and requirements applying in each case.
- It appears also that their use is more warranted when learning tasks are complex and difficult (that is, require high level cognitive skills) and/or when important learning tasks are not clearly distinguishable. At the same time, there is no evidence that there are specific groups of learners for which, or specific subjects in which, objectives work best.
- Actual use of objectives by students is also likely to be, in some respects, different from and more diverse than intended use. It is important for writers to recognize that such diversity of usage exists. One consequence of this diversity is that location of objectives in text in terms of a simple choice between start of teaching materials and end of teaching materials becomes a non-issue, because location in text does not determine whether or how students use objectives. Students will use objectives to suit their own purposes irrespective of their location. There is, however, another aspect of in-text location of objectives, arising from consideration about frequency of insertion or density of objectives. Dispersing objectives throughout text in small sets in company with the relevant material seems to be a sensible practice to follow. Placing a large number may cause students to feel overwhelmed and frustrated and discourage them from using objectives.
- Another guideline which we believe has some merit concerns advising students on the purposes for which objectives have been inserted in text and how they might be used by students. It is assumed that writers who use objectives in text do so with some clear preconceptions about how those objectives should be used. There are also good grounds for stating that students use them in those and other ways. Our position is that making explicit the intended and likely functions served by objectives could help students improve their study skills, thereby enabling them to derive greater benefit from objectives and the instructional material. Remaining

silent about such functions would not achieve anything, but it may account in part for lack of use by students of objectives and may impede refinements that could be made to objectives as an instructional device.

Finally, a comment about objectives and incidental learning. Writers, if they plan to use objectives, would be well advised to consider the implications of the selective attention hypothesis mentioned earlier, which proposes that objectives cause students to be selective in their text processing and focus only on objective-relevant material. Writers could take two basic positions:

1 promote student attainment of prespecified objectives only, and accept the possibility of depressed incidental learning; or
2 adopt the view that prespecified objectives represent a common core of student learning which is to be extended where possible.

Adoption of the second position would require the use of instructional strategies to consciously promote extension of learning horizons beyond those represented by the prespecified objectives.

Our position is that a policy of ignoring, discouraging or discrediting incidental learning is indefensible. Learning experiences will inevitably lead to unanticipated outcomes – sound or unsound, relevant or irrelevant, acceptable or unacceptable. Instructional science has not reached the point (perhaps it should not strive for it either) where it can control learning so that only targeted objectives are attained and unanticipated outcomes suppressed, even the unwelcome ones. Writers of distance teaching materials should acknowledge this and contemplate how they might monitor incidental learning, negate or counteract undesirable incidental outcomes and help students derive benefit from the positive incidental outcomes. Conventional strategies could be used such as specially designated self-assessment items which test extended or allied objectives, that is, learning beyond the range of prescribed objectives. Writers might also encourage incidental learning by giving greater emphasis to expressive objectives, that is, unanticipated learnings which are 'expressed' from the educational encounters with the instructional materials. For example, writers could indicate areas in which expressive objectives could be attained, seek evidence of learning attainment through self-reports or contractual assignments, and provide feedback.

CONCLUSIONS

In preparing this chapter we have tried as far as possible to bring together the evidence of research and the wisdom of practice in developing useful guidelines for those involved in the difficult task of writing instructional text. Some readers may be offended by the advice which we proffer, and label it a 'recipe approach'. We make no apology for our approach as it is the sort of advice which we wish had been conveniently summarized for us when we were neophytes in the preparation of external studies materials. Further, although research on the design of instructional text is still in its infancy and not always very helpful, we believe that there is a body of knowledge which can be distilled into a useful form.

We would not want to suggest, however, that these guidelines which we have presented should be assumed always to be applicable. Nothing can replace the construction–trial–rewrite–trial cycle. And we are pragmatists. We know that often constraints such as deadlines and costs will influence how a writer of instructional text will be able to use the various devices which we have described. We are also aware that there are many devices and unanswered questions which we have not been able to deal with in this chapter.

We would also want to suggest that, as with any written communication, no matter what devices are used, it is possible to do it well or poorly. If we have suggested an embryonic technology, we also believe that there is still much art which should go into the design of the instructional text.

REFERENCES

Anderson, R. C. and Biddle, W. B. (1975) 'On asking people questions about what they are reading', in G. H. Bower (ed.) *Psychology of Learning and Motivation 9, New York: Academic Press.*

Anderson, R. C., Reynolds, R. E., Schallert, D. L. and Goetz, E. T. (1977) 'Frameworks for comprehending discourse', *American Educational Research Journal* 14, 4: 367–81.

Ausubel, D. P. and Robinson, F. G. (1969) *School Learning: an Introduction to Educational Psychology*, New York: Holt, Rinehart and Winston.

Bååth, J. A. (1979) *Correspondence Education in the Light of a Number of Contemporary Teaching Models*, Malmö: LiberHermods.

Barnes, B. R. and Clawson, E. U. (1975) 'Do advance organizers facilitate learning? Recommendations for further research based on an analysis of thirty-two studies', *Review of Educational Research* 45, 4: 637–59.

Burnhill P., Hartley, J. and Young, M. (1976) 'Tables in text', *Applied Ergonomics* 7, 1: 13–18.

Crooks, B., Rowntree, D. and Waller, R. (1979) 'Writing your lesson', in D. Rowntree and B. Connors (eds) *How to Develop Self-Instructional Teaching: a Self-Instructional Guide to the Writing of Self-Instructional Materials*, Milton Keynes: The Centre for International Co-operation and Services, The Open University.

Duchastel, P. (1979) 'Learning objectives and the organization of prose', *Journal of Educational Psychology* 71, 1: 100–6.

Duchastel, P. (1981) 'Illustrations in text: a retentional role', *Programmed Learning and Educational Technology* 18, 1: 11–15.

Duchastel, P. and Merrill, P. (1973) 'The effects of behavioural objectives on learning: a review of empirical studies', *Review of Educational Research* 43: 53–69.

Duchastel P. and Whitehead, D. (1980) 'Exploring student reactions to inserted questions in text', *Programmed Learning and Educational Technology* 17, 1: 41–7.

Eggen, P. O., Kauchak, D. P. and Harder, R. J. (1979) *Strategies for Teachers: Information Processing Models in the Classroom*, Englewood Cliffs, N. J. : Prentice Hall.

Faw, H. W. and Waller, T. G. (1976) 'Mathemagenic behaviours and efficiency in learning from prose materials: review, critique and recommendations', *Review of Educational Research* 46, 4: 691–720.

Frase, L. T. and Schwartz, B. J. (1979) 'Typographical cues that facilitate comprehension', *Journal of Educational Psychology* 71, 2: 197–206.

Gage, N. L. and Berliner, D. C. (1975) *Educational Psychology*, Chicago: Rand McNally.

Glynn, S. M. and Di Vesta, F. J. (1979) 'Control of prose processing via instructional and typographical cues', *Journal of Educational Psychology* 71, 5: 595–603.

Haber, R. N. and Fried, A. (1975) *An Introduction to Psychology*, New York: Holt, Rinehart and Winston.

Hartley, J. (1978) *Designing Instructional Text*, London: Kogan Page.

Hartley, J. and Burnhill, P. (1977a) 'Fifty guidelines for improving instructional text', *Programmed Learning and Educational Technology* 14, 1: 65–73.

Hartley, J. and Burnhill, P. (1977b) 'Understanding instructional text: typography, layout and design', in M. J. A. Howe (ed.) *Adult Learning: Psychological Research and Applications*, London: Wiley.

Hartley, J. and Davies, I. K. (1976) 'Pre-instructional strategies: the role of pretests, behavioural objectives, overviews and advance organizers', *Review of Educational Research* 46, 2: 239–65.

Henry J. (1981) Personal communication.

Hudgins, B. B. (1977) *Learning and Teaching: a Primer for Teachers*, Itasca, Ill. : Peacock.

Joyce, B. R. and Weil, M. (1972) *Models of Teaching*, Englewood Cliffs, N. J. : Prentice Hall.

Joyce, B. R. and Weil, M. (1980) *Models of Teaching*, 2nd edn. Englewood Cliffs, N. J. : Prentice Hall.

Kaplan, R. (1976) 'Effects of grouping and response characteristics of instructional objectives when learning from prose', *Journal of Educational Psychology* 68, 4: 424–30.

Lawton, J. T. and Wanska, S. K. (1977) 'Advance organizers as a teaching strategy: a reply to Barnes and Clawson', *Review of Educational Research* 47, 1: 233–44.

Luiten, J., Ames, W. and Ackerson, G. (1980) 'A meta-analysis of the effects of advance organizers on learning and retention', *American Educational Research Journal* 17, 2: 211–18.

Lockwood, F. (1978) *A Rationale for the Use of Formative Assessment Components (ITQs, SAQs, activities, FTMAs) with Actual Examples of Each*, Milton Keynes: Institute of Educational Technology, The Open University, mimeograph.

Macdonald-Ross, M. (1977a) 'Graphics in text', in Shulman, L. S. (ed.) *Review of Research in Education 5*. Itasca, Ill. : Peacock.

Macdonald-Ross, M. (1977b) 'How numbers are shown: a review of research on the presentation of quantitative data in texts', *Audio Visual Communication Review*, 23: 359–409.

Macdonald-Ross, M. (1979) 'Language in texts', in L. S. Shulman (ed.) *Review of Research in Education, 6.* Itasca, Ill. : Peacock.

Macdonald-Ross, M. and Waller, R. H. W. (1975) 'Criticisms, alternatives and tests: a framework for improving typography', *Programmed Learning and Educational Technology* 12, 2: 75–83.

Mayer, R. E. (1979) 'Can advance organizers influence meaningful learning?' *Review of Educational Research* 49: 371–83.

Melton, R. F. (1978) 'Resolution of conflicting claims concerning the effect of behavioural objectives in student learning', *Review of Educational Research* 48: 291–302.

Reigeluth, C. N., Merrill, M. D. and Bunderson, C. V. (1978) 'The structure of subject matter, content and its instructional design implications', *Instructional Science* 7, 2: 107–26.

Rickards, J. P. and Denner, P. R. (1978) 'Inserted questions as aids to reading text', *Instructional Science* 7, 3: 313–46.

Rothkopf, E. Z. (1965) 'Some theoretical and experimental approaches to problems in written instruction', in J. D. Krumboltz (ed.) *Learning and the Educational Process,* Chicago: Rand McNally.

Rothkopf, E. Z. (1970) 'The concept of mathemagenic behaviours', *Review of Educational Research* 40, 3: 325–36.

Rothkopf, E. Z. and Bloom, R. D. (1970) 'Effects of interpersonal interaction on the instructional value of adjunct questions in learning from written material', *Journal of Educational Psychology* 61, 6: 417–22.

Rowntree, D. and Connors, B. (eds) (1979) *How to Develop Self-instructional Teaching: a Self-instructional guide to the Writing of Self-instructional Materials,* Milton Keynes: The Centre for International Co-operation and Services, The Open University.

Szlichcinski, K. P. (1979) 'Diagrams and illustrations as aids to problem solving', *Instructional Science* 8, 3: 253–74.

Waller, R. (1977a) *Numbering Systems in Text.* Milton Keynes: Institute of Educational Technology, The Open University, mimeograph (Notes on transforming, 4).

Waller, R. (1977b) *Three Functions of Text Presentation,* Milton Keynes: Institute of Educational Technology, The Open University, mimeograph (Notes on transforming, 2).

Waller, R. (1979) 'Typographical access structures for educational texts', in P. A. Kolers, M. E. Wrolstad and H. Bouma, (eds) *Processing of Visible Language,* New York: Plenum Press, 1.

Waller, R. (1981) Personal communication.

Wright, P. (1977) 'Presenting technical information: a survey of research findings', *Instructional Science* 6, 2: 93–134.

13 Electronic mail in a children's distance course: trial and evaluation

Vicki Vivian

This chapter describes and evaluates a project involving children from nine isolated families connected with an Australian correspondence school. Staff and students used videotex, facsimile, 1200/75 baud modems, IBM personal computers with colour monitors, and the telephone. Though subject to unforeseen problems, the project was rated a great success.

HOW DID THE PROJECT COME ABOUT?

It has long been felt that a major difficulty in correspondence teaching is the time lag between the teacher sending the pupil's work, the work being done in the pupil's home, the teacher responding to that piece of work and the pupil receiving the corrected work back again. Turnaround time can be anything from two to six weeks depending on several factors, the most obvious of which are the pupil's location and the nature of the mail service. Communications technologies incorporating electronic mail facilities seemed to offer a potential solution to slow turnaround time.

With the appointment to the correspondence school of an educational technology development officer in late 1983 came the opportunity to begin to explore the new communications technologies in relation to the school's needs. In 1984, an electronic mail trial was conducted for a small group of 7-year-old isolated children. From the experiences of this trial, a set of recommendations was formulated which became the basis of the 1985 trial. The Australian Commonwealth Advisory Committee on the Educational Use of Communications Technology was approached and a grant of $13, 100 was given to the school, matched by the New South Wales Department of Education in salaries of teachers and clerical assistants and supply of support materials.

The 1984 trial had used videotex, facsimile, 1200/75 baud modems and videotex terminals as the method of delivery. The 1985 trial additionally used IBM personal computers as terminals. This change in terminals was brought about as the result of the 1984 trial participants seeing the need for more interaction between teacher and pupil/supervisor.

Several members of staff were committed to the idea that material should be written for the trial which would test the technology's suitability in delivering up-to-date learning activities. A team of three teachers wrote a block of nine weeks' lessons in Language and Mathematics with this in mind.

The following aims were formulated for the 1985 electronic mail trial:

* to reduce the turnaround time of pupils' work, thus providing faster feedback; identify which learning techniques can be successfully applied using these communications technologies; evaluate the potential of these communications technologies as an aid to the implementation of current child-centred curriculum guidelines; evaluate videotex and facsimile as an electronic mail system in primary distance education in New South Wales; compare the costs of delivery and return of learning materials by surface mail and electronic mail;
* to explore the different organizational structures that electronic mail will demand at the school level; provide easier communication between teacher, pupil and supervisor to help overcome isolation and distance.

WHAT WERE THE DAY TO DAY WORKINGS OF THE PROJECT?

Part A: Preparation for the trial

During Term 1, nine families were asked to participate in the trial. They were chosen by the school based on two criteria: (i) the child to be included in the trial group was approximately ten years old and within a certain range on the school's existing Mathematics and Language courses, and (ii) the family was willing to participate and had previously demonstrated a good return of work.

The six teachers to be involved in the trial were automatically selected by virtue of already teaching the children who were targeted and whose families had agreed to proceed. No families rejected the offer to participate. All children were geographically isolated home pupils (see Figure 13.1).

Telecom was requested to visit each homestead to check the phone line's capacity to transmit data, as well as to install a plug to take the facsimile machine. Two 008 lines (cost of a local call) were installed; one at the school and one at the database, ICL Computers at North Sydney.

Newly-written courses in Mathematics and Language were put into the videotex database at ICL. These courses were subsequently edited at the school by one of the trial teachers. Editing proved a time-consuming process

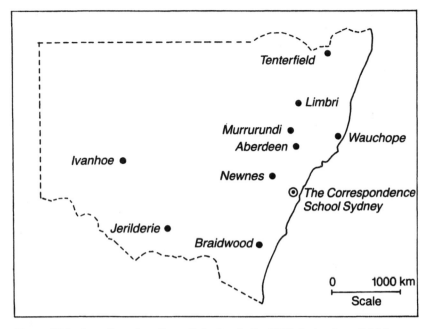

Figure 13.1   Location of pupils participating in the 1985 electronic mail trial

which it would not be constructive to repeat. The courses were to last for 44 days (nine school weeks) and took 700 frames of videotex to present.

The group of trial teachers, course writers and administrators prepared a videotape giving an introduction to the trial for parents and children. The tape was sent to each family at the end of Term 1. Each family had previously been supplied with a television monitor and VCR by the federally-funded Isolated Children's Loan Video Scheme.

One of the course writers prepared a second videotape explaining how to set up and operate the equipment. This, along with other lesson support materials e.g. videotapes, audiotapes and books, was sent to families in early Term 2.

The hardware (facsimile machine, modem, personal computer with separate keyboard and colour monitor) was sent to homesteads by courier in week 5 of Term 2. This was four weeks later than anticipated, but the fitting of videotex cards to the personal computers at the IBM workshop and the visiting of each homestead by Telecom took time. The trial eventually started in week 6 of Term 2.

The nature of some families' isolation is illustrated by a phone call to the school from an anxious Telecom technician, who said: 'Could you please tell me quickly how long the cord needs to be for the fax machine. The clouds are gathering here and if it rains I mightn't get out for a week.' Meanwhile, at the school, teachers met to discuss the new trial courses and to learn how to operate the facsimile and computer.

Part B: The trial under way

Once the equipment had arrived at homesteads and had been assembled, it was time to phone the database (a 008 toll-free call) to get the week's lessons. These were saved on disk while on line in order to be played back when the pupil did his/her lessons. Parents were asked to phone the database at 'off-peak' times where possible, in order to save phone costs. At certain stages in the lessons the request 'fax to your teacher' would appear. It was then time to send that piece of work to the school (again by a 008 call). Again, this was often done at night. The teacher would respond to the work and fax back a reply, if appropriate, making amendments to the lessons where necessary. This faxing process necessitated voice contact by phone, and much building of rapport as well as some teaching were achieved in this impromptu way.

In the lead-up to the trial, parents and children had been asked to keep a daily journal as a record of all their experiences, both positive and negative. They reveal in day-to-day language that planned procedures rarely happened and indeed varied greatly from family to family and from day to day.

TECHNOLOGY

The following subsections describe the day-to-day functioning of the equipment:

Phone lines

Of the nine families, only one did not manage either to send or receive any data. In this case, the quality of the phone line could not sustain data transmission. The teacher reported:

> I wondered just how much educational benefit was happening! In the case of my child, his self-esteem dropped, he became anxious and his general work declined. Hence I began to wonder what we were teaching him . . . how to accept technical breakdowns?

Another family in the Ivanhoe region and on a manual telephone exchange found consistent difficulty in contacting Sydney.

For the remaining seven families, the efficiency of the phone contact varied from excellent to having an occasional interruption. Indeed some developed a very friendly relationship with the local Telecom technician. Five of the nine families called in Telecom for at least one follow-up visit.

Facsimile machines

There was a great range of success rate in the use of the facsimile machines. Three of the nine families had perfect facsimile operation and as well as sending to the school were able, on several occasions, to fax work to each other. In this way the children were able to comment on each other's work for the first time. Four families needed to send their machines in for repair.

Computers

Approximately two weeks into the trial, the school contacted the Faculty of Education at Sydney University for assistance with evaluation procedures. This new liaison brought about the involvement in the trial of a tutor from the university as a part-time consultant. Up to this point, the IBM personal computers were being used only as videotex terminals. Although the colour monitor provided an excellent display of videotex and the keyboard allowed us to edit screens of videotex, the actual computer was not being used to its capacity. Plans were made to amend the trial so that the capabilities of the computer could be used. Four families were supplied with word processing programs and later on with communications packages (PC-Talk) so that file transfer (screen-to-screen communications between computers) could occur.

At least two computers required adjustment to cards, which had to be done by families. In one instance, the school's computer consultant described the repair of the inside of a computer to a mother 500 km to the north in blow-by-blow terms: 'See the second screw from the right'. This 'repair' took two hours by phone.

Diskettes

Diskettes formatted for DOS 2.1 Videotex had been sent to families. It became apparent that, unless these were double-sided double-density, they were liable to become corrupt. This happened in several cases.

Power supply

Five out of nine families did not have state grid power and so relied on generators to power the equipment for the trial. A recent survey of all isolated home pupils in New South Wales. found that only 42 per cent were on state grid power. Thus the trial sample of nine was quite representative. Two families who were using large generators found the demands of the equipment too expensive or inconvenient and were sent small generators by the school from the resources of the Loan Video Program. One parent reported that the extra use of the generator which was also connected to a cold store was causing the contents of the cold store to freeze, while another stated: 'The children watch their videos while I do the ironing. We can't afford to have the generator on all morning just for the computer'.

Videotex

The presentation of work in colour was a motivating factor to the children. Also, the IBM colour monitor used this year gave slightly better quality and had a bigger screen. However, videotex was unable to represent a suitable oblique line or curve and this was a distinct disadvantage in mathematics.

The process of calling up the database and storing screens of work on diskette was time-consuming, especially for families experiencing phone-line interruptions. It was estimated that each screen took 11 seconds to access (by an experienced operator). If we assume the median length of a day's work to be twenty pages or screens, then for a week this means $(11 \times 20 \times 5)$ seconds' telephone time, approximately 18 minutes, per week. At Subscriber Trunk Dialling rates, this is expensive.

Parents also found that not having a paper copy of the day's or week's work made it that much more difficult to skim through the lessons in advance in order to make adequate preparation. This had to be done by calling up each screen. Hard copies would have been possible if each family had been provided with a printer, but only three families had printers supplied.

It can be seen from the foregoing analysis of the functioning of equipment that each of the families was at a different stage of being 'operational' throughout the trial, ranging from not-at-all to running perfectly.

COURSES

The following subsections describe the day-to-day encounters with the courses and electronic mail facilities by pupils, parents and teachers.

Faxing

There was a highly motivating factor for the children in receiving their work back in a matter of hours.

Two major issues surfaced for teachers and course writers in relation to faxing. First, not everything needed to be 'faxed back'. Just as a general comment will often suffice for feedback in the regular classroom, so, specific immediate communication is not always necessary in the correspondence setting. Also, communicating at STD rates made teachers weigh the decision further. Second, our facsimile only registered in black and white, so when writing a comment on say, a child's story, basic legibility became a problem on the 'returned fax'. Teachers soon abandoned this and either typed out children's work on which they would then write comments or wrote separate notes altogether. The lack of colour e.g. children's drawing, use of coloured pens, was seen as a minus also.

Being tied to the phone/school room

Several parents mentioned that schoolwork with the electronic equipment limited their mobility. Other parents mentioned the difficulty of leaving the phone, eg. for necessary visits to town or neighbours, when they were scheduled for a return fax from the teacher. Teachers also found the phone ringing to be an interruption. Although some scheduling was organized, it was not always possible to stick to this. Some teachers complained of what they called 'electronic nagging'.

Process writing and word processing

Most parents and teachers reported a significant positive development in their children's writing during the trial. Children who did not have a word-processing package (four of the nine families had been supplied with PFS-WRITE) showed improvement, as well as those who were using the computer as a tool for story-writing. The newly-written language course was literature-based and thematic and also incorporated the elements of conference process writing. These seemed to form a sound basis for heightened interest and performance in writing, while the addition of a word-processing facility developed these even further. One of the practical advantages of the word processor is that re-writing of drafts is obviously faster than handwriting the whole piece.

Many questions were raised at the school about the relationship between conference process writing and electronic mail. When encouraging children to write in this way while using surface mail, the whole notion of conferencing work with the teacher becomes so long-winded as to be almost a non-event. Having access to more speedy turnaround time, so that the teacher's response to the child's first draft is relatively immediate, changes the whole face of conference process writing by correspondence.

Much was also achieved in this area by means of the *ad hoc* voice contact by phone, which was necessary for the sending of a fax or a computer file.

The question really still remains as to how 'conference writing' can be done without voice, even given the faster turnaround of the written page.

Mathematics changes

The mathematics written for the trial emphasized two of a number of current curriculum changes in that subject area. The first was the use of concrete materials for as long as the child might need them to develop his/her understanding. The second was a focus on relevant and everyday problem-solving rather than computation for its own sake. Factors such as the increasing availability and use of electronic calculators have been major influences here.

One child in particular found the trial mathematics course work to be 'too easy', at least in the early stages. An overview of addition, subtraction, multiplication and division operations was provided for the children, emphasizing understanding by using numeration blocks. While this did not stimulate those who had already developed understanding in these areas, it was nevertheless most beneficial to others.

The lack of stimulation for the particular child above may also be explained by the 'core' nature of the course. Due to pressure of time in writing, no extension or remediation elements were incorporated. This means that one of the potential benefits of a faster turnaround time, namely, the capacity to modify the course according to the child's needs, was not explored. As puzzles, games and brain-teasers began to appear in the daily activities, all children found a stimulating challenge.

Mathematics presented with a greater emphasis on simplifying concepts via concrete materials and employing a relevant problem-solving approach was to one girl nothing short of enlightening: 'For my daughter, it was as if all the pieces fell into place for the first time' (Father/Supervisor).

Although there were some dissatisfactions with the trial courses, the overall response was one of enthusiasm for the changes. As with all innovation, we are in something of a dilemma when trying to pinpoint the reasons for this apparent success. Was it the thrill of the technology or the inherent soundness of the course or the heightened involvement of supervisors and teachers? We have no clear-cut answers to these questions, of course. Further training accompanied by informed and energetic discussion is necessary to bring us closer to an acceptable consensus.

WHAT DID WE LEARN FROM THE PROJECT?

The following list is an attempt to synthesize, both in terms of our original aims and in terms of the unintended outcomes, the learning that was produced by the project.

Turnaround time

The turnaround time of lessons was dramatically reduced from 2–4 weeks to a matter of days, hours or occasionally even minutes. Of course, this all depended heavily on the efficient, reliable functioning of the technology. Where this was no problem, the sense of 'connectedness' between teacher and pupil was greatly enhanced.

One of the main aims of speeding up the turnaround time is to provide the teacher's feedback to the pupil within a time scale that is constructive to learning. This feedback could, under regular classroom conditions, involve the changing of the learning activities in some way. Were the lessons too easy, too difficult, inappropriate in content, etc.?

This central function of good teaching, the ability to adjust lessons to the child's needs, was not addressed fully in the trial due to lack of time for course preparation. However, it was more flexible than the regular posted course to some degree in that a family could call up the database when 'out of work' and not await the postman.

Easier personal communications

Four children on the trial were successful in sending their work to each other by facsimile or computer file transfer (via PC-TALK). This interaction with other pupils is obviously a boon to isolated correspondence students, giving them the opportunity to share ideas and support one another in their studies. A drawback here is that the phone costs had to be paid by individual families. On a larger scale, with mostly more than one child in the family, this would be prohibitive.

Another aspect of personal communications centred around the telephone. Phone contact is currently not a feature of correspondence teaching in New South Wales except for emergencies. The setting up of fax machines ready for transmission and, for some families, the sending of screen-to-screen computer files, had all to be organized by a prior phone call.

Learning activities not appropriate to electronic mail

In recent years, the use of audiotapes, both studio-produced and spontaneous teacher-made personal tapes, has been a growing positive feature of correspondence teaching. Indeed, the trial language course, though in videotex mode, used audiotapes as support material, and required the children to tape-record activities in return. At the outset, it would be a retrograde step to omit voice contact from correspondence teaching/learning.

We would indeed need to think laterally in order to find our way round the electronic mail presentation of our music course, for example. Art is, it seems, another area unsuitable to this mode of transmission. During the trial, a class teacher prepared a very successful integrated art course which could have been transmitted by videotex had time permitted. What was prepared by the children in response were paintings, collages and creations that had to be returned to the school by regular mail.

Electronic mail is not, it seems, an across-the-board substitute for regular mail. The nature of the subject area and the planned learning outcomes will determine its suitability.

Gender

Of our random sample of nine children, six were girls and three were boys, although this does not reflect our overall enrolment. There appeared to be no difference between girls and boys in handling the technology. As computers are introduced to schools there seems to be a difference in girls' willingness to approach computers and it is speculated that much of this is due to peer pressure relating to traditional role stereotypes. An hypothesis is that isolated children do not suffer this peer pressure to such an extent and, provided the family environment is supportive, have more freedom to move outside the sex role stereotypes.

Journals

Parents and children were invited to write a daily journal both as a way of experiencing daily writing for the children and keeping track of blow-by-blow responses to the project for all of the family. Most families used this process and much was gained by having detailed observations and feelings recorded in this way.

Trial organization

The administration of anything at a distance is, by its nature, more difficult than something in front of you. In the correspondence situation, such an apparently simple school administrative task as counting the number of children in a class who were not 'attending' on a given day entails much more than simply 'hands up the people in 4Z who were away on Tuesday.' But we know this; and mostly we are prepared for the extra planning it entails.

The electronic mail trial got off to a bumpy start. At the next to last moment the Educational Technology Development Officer was transferred to other duties, which left a less-informed cohort to take over. Although more was learned about more by more people in the long run, the 'pioneer group' certainly felt stress of a notably high level in the early days at the school.

Most unfortunately, the rushed and uncertain start caused quite some discomfort at the homesteads too, for parents and children. However, people were tolerant and helpful on every side. 'Lead-time' is an essential in an innovation as complex and dynamic as this. It seems that being pioneers is enough to deal with, without having to be pioneers whose wagons have only three wheels and whose stores have been unavoidably delayed. At times the 'trial' became a 'tribulation' to all.

Two points emerging from this experience are as follows.

1 Any innovation means that we must all be learners. It is a sobering experience for adults (teachers and parents) to be placed in that position alongside the children for whom they are 'responsible'. However, what happened by virtue of this enforced, common starting-point, was that each person in the 'innovation community', children included, became both teacher and learner. This function of challenging established roles could be one of the new technology's most exciting contributions. Not only will the teacher's new role become one of facilitator, but, necessarily, one of co-learner.

2 It is often healthy to have a 'belief in the ignorance of experts'. In this project there were no 'outside experts' who knew more than the participants about the whole set of issues which were being explored. This meant that regular discussion and collaboration were necessary; by communications technology to the families and face-to-face at the school. Although this was both time and money consuming, it is suspected that this level of interaction created a heightened commitment to the investigations. Also an airing of concerns and building of constructive working relationships occurred, which could be further developed.

Staff development

One teacher commented that a positive outcome of the project was 'the changed attitudes of most staff members who, before the trial began, were techno-phobic, or at least techno-nervous'. It is certainly true that, notwithstanding the pressure of innovation, many teachers have developed knowledge and skills relating to communication technologies that they did not have before. The comparative lack of techno-phobia is also apparent.

Although several of the staff kept journals, and many meetings took place, it would still be true to say that a 'final conclusion' about the issues of the project would be hard to find amongst staff.

As one teacher said, 'It's as though we have just peered through a chink in the wall at computers'. Some of the aspects still to be explored include:

- process conference writing by electronic mail;
- electronic mail and voice communication: how do they co-exist?
- course-writing using computers and word-processing;
- what does faster turnaround time mean to daily organization, i.e. use of phones, scheduling, etc?
- what does faster turnaround time mean to course organization?
- must we have 'electronic nagging'?
- how can teachers develop their own technology skills faster?
- the computer as a tool or a way of life?

Costs

It has been widely accepted that, at least in the foreseeable future, surface post will remain necessary for art, audiotapes, library books, etc. The potential of electronic mail is in learning activities which require faster feedback, can be mostly print-based and are, to some degree, sequential.

At the time of the project, the maximum cost of a return posting per week was A$6.80, while the minimum was A$2.75. Such a posting would typically contain leaflets, audiotapes and books. Electronic mail costs using a videotex database, facsimile or computer file transfer, as in this project, are at STD rates. A skilled operator took a minimum of 18 minutes per week to phone the database for lessons, which took up to an hour or more in some cases. Other phone costs were in sending facsimile (four minutes per page) or file transfers to the school and receiving them back again. For an estimated 48 minutes per week, the STD costs would be between a minimum of A$10.56 and a maximum of A$23.04.

Some points to consider are as follows.

- The lack of 'lead-time' of the project meant that operators' skills were learned 'on-the-job'. Skilled users would need less time on line.
- The facsimile machines were not 'state of the art'. An up-to-date machine can transmit an A4 page in 15 seconds, regardless of distance.
- The number of pages to be faxed back becomes more of an issue when potential increase in cost and 'electronic nagging' are considered. Does the teacher really need to see that particular page in a 'hurry'? Should the family be 'interrupted' with a phone communication at this moment?
- Computer file transfer takes a matter of seconds per page. This facility

was introduced for a few families in the second half of the trial. Again, skills took time to learn.

Many questions still remain to be answered about electronic mail in distance education. The most important element seems to be having our educational priorities clear.

CONCLUSION

What correspondence teachers and their clients lack is face-to-face interaction. At present their interactions are by means of post, audiotape, some videotape, the occasional phone call and the very occasional visit.

When a child and teacher are together in a regular classroom, the child's work can be *looked at* by the teacher and the child simultaneously, *discussed, modified*, i.e. the teacher can re-teach, extend or take another approach or content sample. Electronic mail permits us to 'look at' the child's work much closer to the moment of its completion. The teacher then has to decide what kind of response is appropriate (the 'discussion' stage). A general comment, some praise and encouragement, for instance, has been easily possible by facsimile or file transfer. But, unlike work returned by surface post, a voice reply (audiotape) was not generally possible.

At this point, it is appropriate to ask the 'innovation community' whether the faster turnaround which electronic mail provided for the written work in this trial is worth the loss of voice contact which is linked to the written word, i.e. the *status quo*. This has to happen once the word and voice are out of sync.

The third process which occurs with teacher and child in the regular classroom is that the child's work can be modified as a result of teacher–child interaction. This modifying already happens in the correspondence situation, but there is an unacceptable time lag. An obvious advantage of electronic mail is that this process can happen within hours, if necessary. What is necessary, however, are courses stored in a database, which are not linear and core only, but where extensive choice of level of difficulty, content and style is available. This would involve a complete restructuring of the correspondence school's course planning, and would still not solve the voice contact problem.

So far, the process of electronic mail has been discussed only from a teaching/learning viewpoint in this section. It is as well to recall the 'people and technology' nexus which necessitates answering the phone when it rings, no matter what else you are doing; sitting at screens for long periods and learning keyboard and 'fixit' skills; and dependence on the reliability of phone lines and technology.

At least some of the good feeling about this electronic mail trial was generated by the specially-written courses. Most children seemed to enjoy the fresh approach. In addition, there has been positive spin-off at the school for teachers and course planners.

The use of computers in the trial for purposes other than as videotex terminals has brought the correspondence school into line with other schools which are trying to understand how computers fit into today's education in terms of both philosophy and action. The further issue of how computers fit into distance education would mean linking them with electronic mail, should that be adopted. It is important, I think, to keep those two issues (electronic mail and computers in schools) separate for a time at least, until a better understanding of computers in education is reached than that which seems currently to exist across the wider community.

A lively, informed and constructively critical dialogue needs to be encouraged, based on current educational thinking with its increasing emphasis on processes for learning rather than fact-collection, on life skills rather than merely academic exercises, on humanitarian rather than purely competitive, materialistic themes.

There seems a strong possibility that the computer for children could be a liberating tool rather than just another consumer item. The idea of access to vast banks of information at the speed of light and the choice that this would offer is exciting. But, as with all choice, we need to have a rationale to underpin it or else risk being swamped with randomness and 'kneejerk' responses. Since we are at the beginning of Toffler's 'Third Wave' (i.e. the Technological Revolution) let us rely on our potential for openness, reflection and careful consideration on behalf of our children.

Part IV
Media in distance education

Introduction

In distance education, a communications medium enables the learning group to be dispersed in time and/or space so that the educational interaction can take place at a distance. In recent decades, wonderful new electronics communications technologies have been added to the original mechanical media which are still, no doubt, being used with success in many parts of the world.

The literature on the use of media in distance education is rich and varied and reflects the variety of institutional choices for cost-effective and educationally-effective media in distance education down the decades and across the nations. During the last decade, Media in Distance Education was one of the most vibrant, and one of the most active, sub-fields of this research area.

From many aspects, the decade of the 1970s could be characterized as the decade of television with a major focus on that medium by policies introduced at the Open University of the United Kingdom. Allied to this was the promotion of educational/instructional television in schools by international agencies like UNESCO and the World Bank.

In a similar way, the telephone could be labelled the medium of the 1980s. That decade saw the introduction of a variety of new developments with far-reaching educational consequences: the fax machine, the widespread use of modems, improvements in loudspeaking receivers and transmitters, leading to the blossoming of audioconferencing, videoconferencing and computer conferencing.

The telecommunications industry has undergone changes so swift and so complex in recent years that the reader who is not a specialist will welcome a guide to the developments that have occurred. This will provide a backdrop to the readings that have been selected as a guideline to the use of media in distance education in the early to mid-1990s.

The changes of the last decade can be attributed to three factors: an urge to deregulate, the speeding up of chips and the introduction of broadband technology.

A decade ago, governments regarded telecommunications as a lucrative, monopoly industry linked to secret defence installations. There was total regulation. Policies, however, associated with Margaret Thatcher in the United Kingdom led to open tenders and a seeking for better services and better value for money. Policies associated with Ronald Reagan in the United States led to the breaking of monopolies, especially for new cellular licences. Telecommunications became consumer driven.

Computing technology was introduced into telecommunication in the 1960s with the first public analog software switchboards dating from the mid-1970s. These were digitalized almost immediately and followed by the development of Integrated Services Digitalized Networking (ISDN) in the 1980s. In the 1990s, seamless digitalized connections between fixed and air networks are being aimed at. In all these developments, the ever-increasing speed of chips was crucial.

A current focus of the telecommunications industry is the development of broadband technology. This is of great importance for distance education because one needs extensive bandwidth for pictures. Fibre optic cabling can provide the bandwidth required for the transmission of still and moving images so that broadband ISDN will provide the technology for the transmission of voice, data, video and other digitalized services.

These developments in the 1990s are of vital interest to educators and the coming together of television and telephone technologies offers the possibility of teaching face-to-face at a distance in virtual classrooms via compressed video or full bandwidth links together with a wondrous range of new interactive and non-interactive educational possibilities.

The chapter from Bates (Chapter 14), originally from the UK Open University and now at the Open Learning Agency in Canada, provides the reader with a comprehensive and unemotional overview of the use of media in distance education from the mid-1980s to the mid-1990s.

The remaining four chapters discuss the marvels of teleconferencing technology in its four distance education structures: one-way audio; two-way audio; one-way video and two-way audio; two-way video and two-way audio.

The role of one-way and two-way audio is analysed by Robinson in the context of the Open University of the United Kingdom (Chapter 15). The author previews the use of these media in post-1992 European distance education, introducing a complex series of issues that occur when distance teaching transcends national boundaries and appears uninvited in the printed, audio, video or data networks of another state.

Extensive work has been done on two-way audio systems by Garrison of the University of Calgary, Canada. They have been used by him as the basis for the considerable contribution to distance education analysis made by this author in the last decade (see Chapter 16).

One-way video, two-way audio systems are analysed by Duning from the United States. Her chapter (Chapter 17), which is slightly shortened from the original here, leads the way to reflection on the complex interplay of corporate and educational providers in the use of electronic communications media in distance education in the 1990s.

The road to an already-present future is provided in the final selection on two-way audio and two-way video teaching systems (Chapter 18). Virtual or electronic classrooms are linked in this structure by compressed video codec technology along fibre optic telephone lines enabling a class of students to be divided between two cities or two countries. The lecturer can see and hear not only the students present at the class but all the other students at the other sites hundreds or thousands of kilometres away. In the same way, all the students at all the locations can see and hear not only the lecturer but all other students in the system. All the interaction of face-to-face education has been re-created electronically: any student can question or interrupt the teacher or another student just like a normal classroom. It is now possible electronically to teach face-to-face at a distance.

14 Technology for distance education: a ten-year prospective

Anthony Bates

We are living through an exciting time regarding technological developments of relevance to distance education. There is, to say the least, a lot happening – artificial intelligence, compact discs, electronic publishing, home computers, satellites and videodiscs, to name but a few examples. What is the potential of these and other technological developments for distance education? Perhaps even more importantly, what steps should European distance teaching institutions take to ensure that the 'right' media are chosen and are properly harnessed and used to increase the effectiveness of distance education in Europe?

GAZING INTO THE CRYSTAL BALL: PAST EXPERIENCE

Any attempt to look into the future is, by definition, speculative; it is also influenced by personal views and experience, which, in my case, is weighted towards audio-visual media. This chapter should, then, be seen as a basis for discussion, and not as a definitive statement of the future ten years from now.

We can learn a lot about the future by looking back into the past. In 1977, a colleague and I produced a report: *Alternative Media Technologies for the Open University* (Bates and Kern 1977). This looked at new technologies in the pipe-line, and at already existing technologies that were not being used – including audio-cassettes, floppy audio-discs, audio-records, super 8 mm film, video-cassettes, telephone teaching, viewdata, the electronic blackboard, digital cassette vision (Cyclops), and home computer terminals linked by telephone to mainframe computers.

It is salutary to note that, despite the potential of these new technologies, the only major change – and certainly the most cost-effective – in the UK Open University's technology over the last decade has been the introduction of audio-cassettes, which have virtually replaced radio.

There are important lessons to be learned from this. Audio-cassettes are low cost; all students already have facilities at home; they are easy for academics to produce, and cheap and simple to distribute; students find them convenient to use; and, when designed properly, they encourage student activity. (UKOU audio-cassettes are rarely lectures.) These factors are likely to apply just as forcibly to any new technologies that become integrated into distance education over the next ten years.

A more consoling point is that it has taken a decade before some of the technologies being discussed in 1977 have become a practical reality for distance education. For instance, video-cassette recorders and home computers are only now at a point where they are feasible for extensive use in distance learning. There are several reasons for this incubation period. Home-based technologies have to be very low cost and easy to use. It can take ten years from the introduction of a technology into the market place before it becomes available in most homes. Furthermore, it usually takes several years from the time that a distance teaching institution positively assesses the potential of a technology to the time it is actually introduced, even on a small scale, into its teaching.

The reason that this is consoling is because it means that the future is with us now: the technologies that are going to be in widespread use in the late 1990s already exist, at least in prototype form. Any major new developments that arise over the next ten years, and are not yet known about, are unlikely to be at a stage where they will be practically useful for distance education by 1997.

A FRAMEWORK FOR ASSESSING TECHNOLOGY

First, several distinctions need to be made between the following.

- Technologies for *teaching* and technologies for *operational* purposes. For instance, technologies for teaching are much more influenced by the likely home (or student work) environment, and, therefore, have to be relatively low cost. Technologies for operational purposes (e.g. student registration and publishing), however, are more likely to be introduced to improve institutional efficiency; although cost remains an important factor, a high cost of investment for operational purposes may well be justified in terms of increased efficiency.
- Technologies used *within* a distance teaching system and technologies used for communicating *between* different systems. The latter is particularly important with respect to European cooperation.
- Different levels, types of courses and students. Some courses (e.g. Foundation level and/or science courses) are likely to need a different mix of media from other courses (e.g. third level and/or arts courses). Similarly, some students, such as professional engineers requiring updating, will

require different technologies from others, such as housewives wishing to return to work.

It is also important to identify the most useful *criteria* for deciding on the potential of new technologies. Cost is obviously one important criterion, and learning effectiveness another. But there are other equally important factors, such as availability to students, user friendliness and the organizational environment.

There will also be major variations from country to country in the speed at which various technologies are likely to be available – not so much for operational purposes, but for teaching purposes. For instance, the number (and type) of micro-computers in homes in France or Germany is likely to be different from that in Spain or Portugal over the next ten years. In this respect, technology is more likely to increase inequalities between countries than reduce them, as far as the provision of distance education is concerned.

Another factor which needs to be considered, and to which little attention is usually paid, is the organizational environment necessary for successful innovation. There are basically two ways in which a new technology may be used within a system. The first is for it to be *added* to an existing system. This usually means that it does not play a central role and adds cost to the system. The second is for it to *replace* an existing technology. This normally means not only changing technologies but also methods of working. Changes in technologies will need to be accompanied by *structural* changes within the organization, as well as changes in individual work practices, to ensure that resources and decision-making powers match the requirements of the new technology. This is usually the main barrier to innovation, since those with decision-making powers are often those who control the resources associated with the 'old' technologies that are under threat.

Lastly, and most importantly, there remain the educational and operational rationales for using technology. What learning or teaching or administrative benefits will they bring? What benefits would be lost by replacing 'older' technologies, such as print? For these questions to be answered, it is necessary to make decisions about what kind of teaching and learning we want. Similar decisions also need to be made about what kind of work environment we want for staff involved in distance teaching. Choice of technology, therefore, is not just a technical decision, but requires value judgements as well.

While it is impossible for me to cover all these questions in this chapter, they do provide a framework for making judgements about the appropriate choice of technology; and my personal responses to some of these issues have influenced my interpretation of significant future developments.

THE TECHNOLOGIES

Text

Electronic publishing will be a major development in distance teaching. Over the next decade, I would expect at least 70 per cent of the various steps in publishing to be carried out electronically in most European distance teaching institutions. It will, in fact, be technically possible for electronic publishing to cover all the stages, from author's first draft right through to access by students. However, 100 per cent electronic publishing is still likely to be rare. There will probably be some re-keying, particularly for first drafts; but many institutions will still prefer to paste-up graphics, where colour or high-quality graphics are required, and most institutions will still print hard copy for distribution by mail to students for reasons given later. However, electronic publishing can both reduce the costs and increase the speed of production of core texts, which can be updated more easily, permitting 'demand printing' each year; and it also allows supplementary materials to be renewed annually at far less cost.

The move to electronic publishing will have major implications for work roles, requiring cooperation from the workforce. It will need a considerable training programme, not only for publishing staff such as editors, but also for academic or subject-expert staff.

One consequence of electronic publishing is that it will give institutions more flexibility for contracting in subject expertise from outside the institution. It will enable an author at any location in Europe to prepare materials for a distance teaching institution. This will require a reappraisal of the benefits and disadvantages of full-time, permanent academic staff. Indeed, electronic publishing (combined with electronic mail and conferencing) opens up the possibility of small, independent, commercial institutions providing distance learning courses – possibly run by academic staff made redundant by a change to contract hiring! While the power of accreditation will be an important factor in maintaining the popularity of distance teaching universities, the competition from small, independent commercial companies designed specifically to exploit the potential of electronic publishing and communications – and, therefore, able to offer low-cost and flexible learning packages – should not be underestimated.

Therefore, I expect that core texts, while prepared electronically, will still be printed, but that supplementary materials which change each year (e.g. assignment questions and cut-off dates) will be delivered to students electronically. Nevertheless, the pressure to move to 100 per cent electronic delivery, once the high initial costs of electronic publishing and home computing have been met, is likely to be strong. The relative advantages and disadvantages of print over electronic text, in terms of learning effectiveness, do need to be researched more thoroughly to provide stronger empirical grounds for decision-making.

Lastly, electronic publishing should facilitate considerably joint production, sharing or adaptation of materials between different institutions – at least where the same language is used – since draft texts can be electronically distributed and edited across different centres.

Audio-visual media

While nearly all European distance teaching institutions currently depend on large quantities of textual material for at least undergraduate teaching at a distance, there is a good deal of variety among them in the use of audio-visual media. For instance, the UK Open University makes substantial use of television and audio, unlike the FernUniversität in West Germany.

The value of audio-visual media, in relation to their cost, is still a controversial issue in distance education. There is no doubt, in my view, that well-designed audio-cassettes, combined with printed material, are an extremely cost-effective medium; and that television has valuable and unique roles to play in distance education, but requires high levels of expenditure on production to exploit its unique characteristics. For me, the argument is not about whether or not to use audio-visual media, but in which forms to use them. (See Bates (1988) for a full discussion of the value of television in distance education.)

Terrestrial broadcast television and radio

Broadcast television, and to a lesser extent radio, could still have a useful role to play in distance education, even in the late 1990s. Broadcasting will still be an extremely valuable form of publicity for distance teaching institutions; and it will continue to be one of the few methods of distribution guaranteed to be available to all students anywhere in a single country. However, both these roles are dependent on getting access to national broadcast channels at convenient and popular times. Also, it will remain the cheapest way to deliver audio-visual material to large numbers of students (i.e. over 500 students per course for television and 1,000 students per course for radio); and it will still be valuable for introducing students to a subject, for providing an overview and for raising awareness. These latter roles are less dependent on good quality transmission times, since off-air recording facilities will be available to most students in many European countries in ten years' time.

The key question, however, is whether it will be possible *politically* to get access to any form of terrestrial broadcast television for educational purposes in the late 1990s. The advent of satellite and cable trends toward deregulation and competition, and the relatively small numbers of students following any particular course at any one time, are all likely to discourage terrestrial broadcasting organizations from giving a regular quality commitment to transmission of distance teaching programmes.

Terrestrial broadcasting is also limited to national communications, although some cross-border traffic is beginning (e.g. UK programmes are now also relayed on cable in Belgium and Norway; Belgium can receive broadcasts from Holland, West Germany, France and Luxembourg, as well as the UK). These are not European-wide communications, though, but are limited to neighbouring countries.

Lastly, production for terrestrial broadcasting is likely to remain extremely expensive, because of the professional production standards required by broadcasting organizations. Other forms of distribution, such as cable and video-cassette, do allow for more flexible and experimental low-cost production, such as tutored video instruction or the use of low-cost portable equipment for collecting and editing material. At the same time, there is a high risk that poor quality production, in professional terms, may also lead to poor quality material in educational terms.

Nevertheless, this is an open issue. The dramatic reduction in the cost of production equipment for television, and the increasing availability of alternative means of distribution to terrestrial broadcasting, do mean that video production is now a more realistic possibility for many distance teaching institutions, at least in terms of cost.

Video-cassettes

Broadcasting is an ephemeral medium. This has caused a number of problems for learners within the UKOU system. For example, the loss of quality transmission time caused serious difficulties in the early 1980s. In 1977, viewing on transmission averaged 65 per cent (i.e. on average, a student would watch about two-thirds of the programmes on a course; or two-thirds of the students on a course would watch each programme, on average); but by 1984, this had dropped to 48 per cent. The situation, however, was saved by the arrival in an increasing number of homes of the video-cassette recorder (VCR). The overall viewing rate is now around 60 per cent (combining both viewing on transmission and on cassette).

Table 14.1 gives figures for video-cassette ownership in Europe in 1986 and 1987. In a survey carried out at the end of 1986 (Kirkwood 1987), 60 per cent of UKOU students on new courses had a VCR in their own homes, and 77 per cent reported that they either had access at home or 'convenient access elsewhere'. The rate of growth of UKOU students' ownership of VCRs over the last five years has, if anything, increased; thus, I expect that over 80 per cent will have their own VCRs by 1990. It may be worth pointing out that this will far exceed students' ownership of home computers, and there is no problem of standardization on VCRs. (VHS seems to rule supreme.) Furthermore, studies by the BBC Audience Research Department have found that ownership of VCRs in Britain is not income-related (except for the unemployed), while ownership of home computers is. If the trend in Britain is followed elsewhere in Europe, it seems reasonable to assume that nearly all students will have access to video-recording equipment at home (or at least convenient access elsewhere) by the end of 1997, in most countries represented by the European Association of Distance Teaching Universities.

Table 14.1   European home video-recorder access, 1986 and 1987

Country	1986(%)	1987(%)
Belgium	18	22
Denmark	28	24
France	23	30
German Federal Republic	36	44
Ireland	39	44
Italy	8	14
Netherlands	37	44
Norway	31	37
Portugal	38	39
Spain	21	28
United Kingdom	51	61
EEC (average)	31	38

Source: Screen Digest, 1987

The value of the video-cassette lies not just in its ability to allow students to view programmes at more convenient times; it also enables learning from television to be much more effective. Indeed, the video-cassette is to the broadcast what the book is to the lecture. Table 14.2 compares the control characteristics of broadcasts and cassettes.

If a major value of television to students is its ability to link concrete examples to abstract ideas, and to enable learners to interpret and analyse material, it would seem essential that learners can access the television material at the appropriate point in their studies, that they can stop and reflect on what they have just seen before moving on to the next part of the

Table 14.2 Broadcast vs. recorded television

Broadcast	Cassette
Fixed time to view	Available when needed
Ephemeral/once only	Repetition/search/mastery
Difficult to reflect	Analysis/relating/reflection
One speed	Individually paced
Integration more difficult	Integration easier

programme, and that they can watch the same scene as many times as necessary to interpret it.

One lesson learned from audio-cassettes is that changing the technology of distribution also has implications for the design of the teaching materials. At the UKOU, we are experimenting with certain design features to encourage students to make better use of the control characteristics of vidco-cassettcs. (Scc Tablc 14.3.)

The increased availability of video-cassettes will have three major implications. First, there should be a marked improvement in the learning effectiveness of television, if the control characteristics are properly exploited; second, video-cassettes offer alternative distribution possibilities for distance teaching institutions without access to broadcasting; and third, lower production costs for video compared with national broadcasting will make television a more practical possibility for some distance teaching institutions. Once again, though, quality control will be important.

Table 14.3 Implications for programme design of video-cassettes

– Use of segments
– Clear stopping points
– Use of activities
– Indexing
– Close integration with other media (e.g. text, discussion)
– Concentration on audio-visual aspects

Satellite

The 1980s have been dominated by the expansion of video-cassette ownership in Europe. The 1990s will be dominated by the expansion of satellite broadcasting. To what extent will satellite (or cable) provide alternatives to terrestrial broadcasting?

There are basically two kinds of satellites – low-powered and high-powered, the latter usually being called direct broadcast satellites or DBS. Essentially, though, DBS transmissions can be received directly in homes using small and cheap dish aerials, while low-powered satellites require a larger and more expensive dish, with television signals usually being redistributed by cable or terrestrial transmitters to people's homes. Satellites, however, can also transmit voice and data signals, using a fraction of the capacity of a television channel and hence at far less cost – a point of particular significance for distance education.

Ariane, the launch rocket of the European Space Agency (ESA), has the demanding schedule of one satellite launch a month over a period of several years, starting in September 1987. A substantial proportion will be European satellites, both low-powered and DBS. With a one in fifteen chance of a launch failure, a lot could go wrong. Nevertheless, there will almost certainly be a rapid expansion in satellite capacity in Europe – from the current twenty-one television channel capacity to somewhere around 100 channels within the next five years (CIT Research 1987).

Transmission costs for full bandwidth television range from free up-link and transmission facilities for educational users (on Olympus) to £1,800 (US$2,880) an hour on Eutelsat (including transponder charges) for peak evening transmission. While not insignificant, transmission costs will, however, usually be minor compared to the costs of production, administration and ground support services. Neither reception nor transmission costs are likely to be a significant barrier to the use of satellites for distance education in Europe, compared with finding suitable programming, and paying for it.

Cable

Probably no other medium will vary as much in its availability among different European countries as cable television. Some countries (such as Holland and Belgium) already have extensive provision; in others, such as the UK, France and West Germany, cable penetration is low, and is unlikely to reach 50 per cent within ten years, even under the most optimistic estimates.

There has been a lot of high pressure sales activity about the interactive possibilities of cable television for education. However, the interaction possible on co-axial cable systems is extremely limited; fibre-optic cabling will permit greater interaction, but there will be very few homes with a direct, two-way fibre optic cable link. Distribution is likely to be via fibre optic cable for the trunking, but the links into individual houses are likely to remain co-axial, for cost reasons. 'Star' fibre-optic capability, whereby any single point on the system can link to any other point at full television bandwidth, will almost certainly be limited to intra-and inter-institutional communications, and even these are likely to be few and far between by 1997.

Cable television is essentially a local distribution facility. It has potential for campus-based higher education institutions to extend their teaching off-campus, in the areas covered by a cable network, or for local support (tutorials, discussion groups, etc.) for national distance teaching institutions. Cable may also be used as a means of distributing video programmes nationally, where terrestrial broadcasting facilities are not available.

Videodiscs

Videodiscs have great potential for education and, especially, training. They can either be used in a stand-alone form – in the same way as a video-cassette, but with much more precise and convenient control – or combined with a micro-computer. The latter can be used for video-enhanced, pre-programmed computer based learning and/or as a huge audio-visual database, with the computer enabling access according to any pre-specified criterion.

Computer technology

Until recently, it has been necessary to use local centres to deliver computer-based distance teaching, either on terminals linked to a central mainframe computer or on stand-alone micro-computers located at the local centre. Considerable problems have been encountered in this method of delivery, such as queueing, inconvenience, or students being physically unable to reach the local centres at the time when the service is available. This has been a major restriction on the extensive use of computers for distance education.

However, in February 1988, the UKOU will offer three courses requiring students to have a home computer, one of which will have 1,500 students; and in 1989, it will offer the foundation course in technology to approximately 4,000 students which will also require each student to have a home computer. This has been made possible primarily by the reduction in costs of 'business standard' (i.e. MS-DOS) computing equipment to a level which allows students to purchase or rent machines, and by some additional funding from government sources to subsidize the courses.

It is important to distinguish the different potential uses of home computers in distance education. I consider these briefly below in what is, in my view, their order of importance: teaching about computers; computers as study tools; educational communications; administration; pre-programmed computer-based learning.

Teaching about computers

There is a great demand for courses which improve people's knowledge, understanding and skills in using computer technology. Whether it involves learning about programming, computer hardware or computer systems, access to computer equipment is essential for this kind of course.

Computers as study tools

Another important role for computers is as a general tool for helping the study process. Word processing, spread sheets and access to databases can help students with note-taking, essay writing and bibliographies. It is unlikely that students would be required to have access for this sole purpose, but they will increasingly acquire computers voluntarily for this reason.

Educational communications

Because written or graphic information entered through a computer keyboard, or even a television camera, can be digitalized, computers can also transfer words and still pictures between different sites. In fact, data transmission works out much more cheaply per word than voice transmission. This is because, being digitalized, it can be recoded and packed tightly, then sent very quickly to the other end, where it is decoded and unpacked into 'normal' text and pictures – thus occupying less capacity on the telephone system than speech.

Electronic communication has several advantages. First, it is relatively easy for both students and tutors to use. Second, there are no 'up-front' production costs, as with pre-programmed computer-based learning. The teaching and learning occurs through natural communication between teachers and learners. Third, electronic communication allows for other forms of communication besides didactic teaching – such as discussions and socializing with other students, albeit at a distance. Fourth, it allows for a more open-ended and social form of learning than pre-programmed computer-based learning, thus being more appropriate for subject areas where interpretation and controversy are important.

At the moment, the UKOU is using electronic communication as an additional service for students; it is possible, though, to envisage certain advanced-level courses where the course design would be radically different, with far greater emphasis on student–tutor communication, both by telephone and electronically, and with far less emphasis on specially prepared texts. This will have major implications for course design and will radically change the role of the academic and the cost structure of a course.

Administration

Once students and tutors have electronic communication, this can be used for administrative purposes as well. Student registration, fee payment via credit card, assignment grades and delivery of updated course or university information are all possible electronically. The potential for reducing administrative costs are substantial; however, there are also major implications in respect of redesigning admission and registration procedures, staff re-training and changes in organizational structures. It is for these reasons that I suspect that the role of electronic communication for administrative purposes is likely to take some time to occur, and is likely to follow academic developments.

Pre-programmed computer-based learning

Pre-programmed computer-based learning refers to any form of teaching where the learner is directed by, and interacts with, pre-programmed teaching material contained in the computer software. This is called variously CAL (computer-assisted learning), CBT (computer-based training), CAI (computer-assisted instruction), etc. I shall use the term CBL (computer-based learning). The distinction between CBL and electronic communication is that, in the latter case, the interaction is *through* a computer terminal but *with* other sources – such as another learner, tutor or administrator – and not with the computer program itself.

THE DOMINANT TECHNOLOGIES

What technologies then are likely to dominate distance education over the next ten years, and what are the implications for distance education?

Home-based learning

For this group, availability of equipment in the home is, in my view, the most important criterion. If distance teaching is to be home-based, and as open as possible to all kinds of students, account must be taken of the limited technology available in the homes for every potential student.

As indicated in Table 14.4, home-based learning will still be limited in some European countries to very few technologies for all potential students – namely, print and audio-cassettes. For other European countries, the telephone, terrestrial broadcasting (but not for European-wide education), video-cassettes and home computing (for selected courses) will also be possible for all potential students. Compact disc players are also expected to

Table 14.4   Home access to technology (Western Europe)

Type of technology	Now (%)	1997 (%)
Print (via mail)	→100	100
Terrestrial broadcasts (radio and TV)	→100	?
Audio-cassettes	90–99	99
Telephone	50–90	70–99
Cable TV	10–80	20–80
Video-cassettes	30–60	50–99
Viewdata	1–40	5–90
Home computer	1–40	10–70
Compact disc	5–35	50–90
Satellite TV	0–5	5–63
Videodisc player	0–1	5–35

reach high penetration in some EEC countries by 1997, but whether this will still be sound and data only, or video as well, is uncertain.

However, there will be difficulties in home-based access for several other technologies. Neither satellite television reception nor home computing is expected to be in more than 70 per cent of homes in any European country by 1997. This could mean that for some home-based target groups (particularly the unemployed and the less educated), these technologies will still be inappropriate for home learning, unless special provision can be made. It also seems unlikely that videodiscs will be a serious proposition for home-based learning in the near future. Lastly, there are very large national variations, particularly regarding cable television and viewdata (i.e. telephone-based teletext services).

It can be seen that increased dependence on technology for teaching can not only widen the difference between provision in different European countries but also reduce the openness of an individual institution. On the other hand, technology does make possible (and indeed requires) a wider variety of course design. I foresee three main kinds of course, with a variety of intermediate positions:

1   the current, primarily text-based course, but with greater use of electronic publishing;
2   'lecture-based' courses, using cable-, satellite- or video-cassette-based technology, supplemented by set reading (textbooks, etc.);
3   electronic courses, using the telephone and electronic communication, with limited textual support, based primarily on interaction between tutors and students on a regular and on-going basis.

It is likely that these different kinds of courses will be directed at different kinds of students.

Centre- or work-based learning

To some extent, this decision will depend on what technology is already available for other purposes. For instance, if every employee to be trained already has access to his/her own computer terminal and screen for work purposes, then this can be used also for training purposes. Certainly, education and training located at the work-bench or in local centres will be less restricted. For instance, at a reception or work-station cost of between UK £400 and £1000, satellite television and computer-based learning become realistic propositions for individuals at their workplace or in local centres. Even videodiscs become viable where they can be shared by several users, or in businesses where they are likely to have another function as well (such as marketing holidays in travel agents).

Communications within and between systems

There are far fewer restrictions on the use of technology here. Virtually anything should be possible by 1997. Technology can be used for training of tutors and regional staff, for joint production of courses, and for developing joint policies, all at a distance. For instance, using a combination of telephone teleconferencing and electronic mail, 'meetings' could be held without any staff having to travel from their desks.

However, for this to happen, a number of steps need to be taken. Policy-makers and academics in each institution need workplace micro-equipment and electronic communication facilities; there need to be common standards agreed for electronic mail; and governments and the EEC need to be lobbied regarding satellite regulation. These are primarily technical issues, but they depend on policy regarding cooperation among institutions being put into place first.

CONCLUSIONS

Technology for home-based learning will still be relatively restricted in a number of countries, even ten years from now. For some countries, there will be a wider range of technologies for distance teaching and greater potential for cross-national delivery of courses. This could lead to a much wider variety of course design and delivery, with major implications for organizational structures and work roles. There is a danger, however, that too great a commitment to new technologies could limit the openness of distance teaching institutions. Communication within and between institutions will be considerably eased by technology, although steps need to be taken now to standardize technology and procedures between different institutions.

Technology will change the nature of the distance learning experience. Technological developments need to be preceded and accompanied by research and evaluation, to monitor carefully not only the learning but also the cost and organizational implications. It is important that research priorities are carefully defined. At the moment, governments are giving priority to basic research in the area of artificial intelligence and for the development of interactive video. However, distance teaching institutions should be investing in more immediate and practical issues, such as monitoring student access to equipment, studying the design implications of video-cassettes, evaluating new types of course design based on new technology, and studying the cost and organizational implications of introducing new technology.

The main point to emerge, though, is that technological decisions need to be preceded by policy and educational decisions, although at the same time it needs to be recognized that the availability of new technology does allow for major changes in the way we teach at a distance. The choice to be made, however, is not 'what technology', but 'what kind of teaching we want to provide'.

REFERENCES

Bates, A. W. (1987) *Satellites for Commonwealth Education: Some Policy Issues. Main report,* London: Commonwealth Secretariat.

Bates, A. W. (1988) 'Television, learning and distance education', *International Council for Distance Education Bulletin* 16: 29–38.

Bates, A. W. and Kern, L. (1977) *Alternative Media Technologies for the Open University,* Milton Keynes: Institute of Educational Technology, The Open University.

CIT Research (1987) *New Satellite Communications in Western Europe,* London: CIT.

Kirkwood, A. (1987) *Access to Video Equipment for Study Purposes – Undergraduate Students in 1986,* Milton Keynes: Institute of Educational Technology, The Open University.

Mason, R. (1988) 'Computer conferencing and the university community', *Open Learning* 3, 2: 37–40.

Organization for Economic Co-operation and Development. Centre for Educational Research and Innovation (1983) *Project on Education and the New Information Technologies,* Paris: OECD.

Tydeman, J. (1987) *Cable and Satellite Television Reception in West Europe,* Luxembourg: Société Européene des Satellites.

Weizenbaum, J. (1985) *Computer Power and Human Reason,* London: Penguin.

'World video markets review' (1987) *Screen Digest* November: 249–56.

15 Telephone teaching and audio-conferencing at the British Open University

Bernadette Robinson

THE CONTEXT OF TELEPHONE TEACHING IN THE BRITISH OPEN UNIVERSITY

Telephone teaching at the Open University takes two forms: one-to-one telephone tutoring; and small-group audioconferencing. Neither is used to deliver course content. Its use is designed to help students to learn from their printed and other materials, to resolve their difficulties, and to provide them with access to a tutor or counsellor. Audioconferencing at the Open University is essentially a small-scale, small-group activity (with up to eight or nine participants), which replicates via telecommunications the kind of small-group activity that goes on at face-to-face tutorials. This use contrasts with large-scale, delivery-based systems such as that of the University of Wisconsin Extension, USA (see Parker and Olgren 1984 for further details of the Wisconsin system).

Telephone tutoring and audioconferencing form part of the regionally organized tutorial support services provided for students and are financed from individual regional budgets. There are thirteen Open University regions, each responsible for its tutorial provision. It is staff in the regions, which vary considerably in size, public transport availability and costs, student populations on different courses and their dispersal, who decide the best way to use the money for tutorial provision. This results in wide variability across regions in the use of different media for tutoring. Tutoring most often takes the form of face-to-face meetings, but is also done via telephone, audio-cassette, correspondence, and more recently, by computer-conferencing on a small number of courses.

Tutorials in the Open University are optional for students. They generally take the form of small group meetings at study centres at evenings and weekends. Study centre meetings are fairly infrequent for post-foundation courses; some students are unable to attend them anyway because of problems of distance and accessibility, or because they are disabled or home-bound. Telephone tutorials, whether one-to-one or audioconference, enable students to interact with their tutor and with other students in real time. For some students they provide the only means of immediate or direct contact. Expenditure on telephone tutorials, whether conference or individual, represents only a small part of the university's tutorial budget, but its function is significant for a proportion of students. It is their main means of interacting with tutors, other than through correspondence tutoring on written assignments; for example in Scotland, some 2,000 students are tutored only by telephone apart from their written exchanges in the form of correspondence tuition.

TEACHING ROLES FOR TELEPHONE TEACHING AT THE OPEN UNIVERSITY

One-to-one telephone tutoring

This is very common in the Open University. It provides a means of developing a relationship between tutor and student, a humanizing 'real voice–real person' element in the system. All students are given tutors' home or, less often, work telephone numbers and are encouraged to contact them when they need help or if they have a query. Tutors are encouraged to telephone students occasionally, especially if the latter do not attend tutorials or if their written work indicates particular problems. More formal tutorial arrangements are also made as part of the tutor's allocated tutorial hours and paid for by the university, for remote or disadvantaged students or for students on project work courses where the need is for individual tuition.

Audioconferencing

British Telecom's Conference Call Service is used for audio conferences (with the exception of the Welsh Region which can arrange calls through its own conferencing bridge). Regional bookings are made with British Telecom for each meeting which can link three to eight separate locations into a common but temporary telecommunications network, allowing two-way speech to all participants. No capital investment is needed in order to use this service. Those taking part can join in at the appointed hour on their domestic or workplace telephones. The addition of extra equipment to this basic system increases its potential as follows:

• a loud-speaking telephone, replacing an ordinary handset, lets a small group of people join in at one location, using one line (used at some study centres and regional centres); a low-cost addition;

- a conferencing bridge lets the user (the Open University) activate group calls more flexibly and at lower cost than the use of British Telecom operator-controlled conferences; a medium-cost addition, depending on volume of use;
- graphics or telewriting systems, such as the Cyclops system developed at the Open University, lets visual material be sent and received via telephone lines; in the case of Cyclops this enabled the use of dynamic graphics, an important aspect of science/technology tutorials (McConnell 1984); a high-cost addition.

COSTS

Enhancements to the basic service such as these increase the flexibility and potential of the medium, but also increase costs, sometimes considerably. In general, costs increase as the use of the audioconferencing system moves towards a delivery mode for materials. In the early 1980s, the Open University, seeing a greater potential in the use of audioconferencing for both teaching and administration, put together a proposal for its own dedicated audioconferencing network, but the setting-up and running costs were unfortunately too high to find funding at a time of financial constraint.

Telephone tutoring has been used widely in all thirteen regions since early days in the Open University. There are no figures available for the extent of the use of one-to-one calls since these are not logged unless the university is paying for them, but the volume must be considerable. They take place as a matter of course in students' contact with tutors, and the cost is borne by students. One-to-one tutorials paid for by the university in 1987 ranged from six hours' worth in one region to 880 hours' worth in another (Open University 1988). Overall, their use since 1981 has increased significantly (Robinson 1981, 1988). The costs for calls are the standard charges by British Telecom, who use a band-cost structure based on time of day, distance and duration of call.

Audioconferencing has been used within the Open University for over a decade and has been subject to more chequered fortunes. This is not too surprising since this form is more dependent on the equipment and the technology for its effective functioning, and has been more affected by changes in British Telecom's' price structure after 1987. Conference call charges using the British Telecom Service doubled or tripled in price as a result of these. In 1987, eight out of the thirteen regions used audioconferencing to varying degrees, ranging from five hours in one region to 160 hours in another (Wales). Eleven out of the thirteen regions said that high cost, poor technical quality of calls and old Open University equipment prevented their greater use of it. The remaining two regions saw no need for audioconferencing because of particular demographic or geographic features which allowed other tutoring alternatives (Open University 1988).

Audioconferencing is used for two reasons: to save travel costs and time, and to provide educationally desirable interaction for widely-dispersed groups who would not otherwise be able to meet. Audioconferencing is almost always cheaper than the cost of a face-to-face tutorial when the travel costs of all participants are taken into account. The more usual calculation done compares only the tutor's travel costs (paid for by the University) with the cost of a conference call. On this basis the cost of the conference call may not always be less. Whether or not a conference call is a cheaper way of 'meeting' a group of students depends on the geographical grouping within a particular call and the tutor's particular travel costs for the alternative tutorial. This makes it difficult to generalize about the cost-effectiveness of conference calls. The cost of a conference call is also affected by the use or lack of a conferencing bridge in the Regional Centre: the use of an 'in-house' conferencing bridge has provided much cheaper conference calls than those booked through British Telecom, in some cases 50 per cent less. The average cost of a one hour audioconference call in 1987 was £51; the range of costs was from £12 to £78.

The charges and cost-structure for telephone services vary widely in Europe and, as Horton and Donovan (1987) show, it is difficult for methodological reasons to arrive at meaningful cost comparisons across countries. However, the most recent survey shows that Germany currently has the highest charges for telephone calls, closely followed by Belgium (International Telecom's *Price Survey* 1988). France has recently modernized its telephone services very rapidly; its call charges, both local and long distance, have reduced significantly and continue on a downward trend. The UK has the most expensive local calls in western Europe though comparatively cheaper long distance calls; however, a price restructuring is due in mid-1989, so this may change. The outcome of the European Commission Green Paper on Telecommunications (1988) and subsequent changes in telecommunications policy in European countries are likely to induce some changes in costs, possibly with some rationalization of charging policy between EEC members over the next few years into 1992, and after. The USA continues to provide the cheapest telephone services in the world, which must go part of the way towards explaining why telephone and audioconferencing form a larger component of distance teaching systems in North America than they do in Europe. The cost of use also inevitably affects access for students.

ACCESS

In the Open University, telephone teaching is conducted by means of the now privatized telephone service, British Telecom. Access for students is not a problem since it uses a widely available and familiar domestic technology. No special equipment or connections are needed to enable students to participate. In the United Kingdom population there are 40 telephone lines for each 100 inhabitants. This compares with 45 lines per 100 inhabitants in France and West Germany, 33 per 100 in Italy, and 22.3 per 100 in Ireland (National Utility Services 1988).

With the present rapid growth of existing telecommunications facilities, the development of governmental and inter-governmental information technology policies in western Europe, and the expansion of ISDN (Integrated Services Digital Networks), access is likely to increase. Home access to telephones for Open University students is high. Surveys have shown figures of about 80–86 per cent, though this conceals some regional variation. Where access is lower than this within a region (for example, 60–70 per cent is the estimated figure given by Open University staff in Scotland) it is relatively easy for regional staff to help arrange alternative access. Most telephone teaching is home-based, whether one-to-one or audioconference. A smaller proportion of audioconferences use loud-speaking telephones at study centres.

As well as access to the national telephone network, and the amount of access to use of it permitted by charges and cost structures, access is also restricted or facilitated by the quality of the technology. British Telecom has a programme of modernization of its telephone system, moving from electro-mechanically operated exchanges and analogue signals to electronic switching and digital signals ('System X'). However, the progress on this has been slow and much of the country (often areas with the greatest need) continues with an antiquated system. What this means for telephone teaching is that often the poor quality of the technology prevents effective communication, and the teaching function is hindered. Where the 'old' system is joined on to the 'new' in conference calls, this damages the sound quality of the whole call for all participants, not just for the users living in areas where System X has not yet penetrated. Where the technology is working well, students and tutors rate the effectiveness of telephone teaching more highly and are encouraged to use it more often and more creatively as a teaching medium.

EFFECTIVENESS AND INTERACTIVITY

The telephone, or two-way audio, is an effective communications medium for linking people together for purposes of conversation, for saving time and travel, for quick feedback and resolution of problems, and for humanizing otherwise impersonal systems. It is a flexible medium which complements the use of other media in distance learning; for example, it offers two-way interaction alongside one-way print or radio or video. It allows two-way exchanges which take place in real time and are not attenuated in the way that correspondence exchanges are. It can also play an essential feedback and monitoring role in the learning of modern languages at a distance, a use which is likely to increase.

Research has demonstrated its effectiveness for a variety of cognitive tasks (Williams and Chapanis 1976). In general, tasks involving information transmission, problem solving and generating ideas, giving and receiving information, asking questions and exchanging opinions can be done as effectively by telephone as by face-to-face, and in some cases more effectively than by correspondence.

In terms of its value as a component in a distance learning system, research has shown it to be effective for a variety of cognitive tasks over a range of courses. In an Open University evaluation, telephone teaching was used for individual and group tutorials in arts, social science, education, technology, maths and science courses. The tasks, to name a selection, included clarifying conceptual difficulties in course material, checking through worked answers to mathematics problems, identifying concepts in genetics using diagrammatic aids, evaluating sight-singing on a music course, interpreting sets of data, exchanging interpretations of a thesis, and analysis of argument (Robinson 1984). Some of the success in this use of the medium was attributable to the skill and creativity of the tutors in its use.

Limitations of telephone teaching relate to media effects on the nature of the tasks and to the quality of the technology. The medium is user-friendly in the sense that it is a familiar technology and does not require new equipment and management of it in order for people to participate. However, it does require some adaptation in behaviour in communicating without visual cues. This is particularly so in audioconferences. New users, especially tutors, experience some anxiety at first, but their adaptation to the medium is fairly rapid. A key element in this is the quality of the training provision made. This, together with the experience of the technology used, has major effects on whether tutors and students will continue to use it.

In the Open University experience, poor telephone technology has hampered greater use of telephone teaching. Where digitalized systems are in place, communication is largely trouble-free, and students who have no other forms of contact available to them rate telephone tutoring highly. Where the telephone system is not yet modernized, the difficulties of holding group discussions by telephone interfere with effective communication and learning.

More specific limitations relate to task. Some tasks are difficult to do with an audio-only medium and are more appropriately done by other means.

Telephone tutorials in the Open University context were found to be ineffective for lecturing, constructing a complex diagram from scratch, conveying lengthy and detailed instructions, or for courses needing the exchange or construction of spontaneous or dynamic visual materials (Robinson 1984).

The absence of graphics has been more of a problem on science, mathematics and technology courses, which have all made less use of audioconferencing than arts, social sciences and education courses. The development of new teaching strategies can resolve this problem to some extent, for example, by circulating in advance diagrams, colour-coded worksheets and charts, and many Open University tutors have developed considerable expertise in teaching in this way. However, there is still the need for two-way graphic exchanges in some subject areas. The addition of the Cyclops telewriting and shared-screen facility (McConnell 1984) met this need during its experimental period at the Open University but unfortunately it is now no longer available, because the University was not willing to fund further technical development or the running costs.

In sum, the telephone (or two-way audio) is a highly interactive medium which is effective in helping students to learn. As with other media, effective use of it lies in recognizing its strengths and limitations, and in developing its use in ways complementary to other media. It lacks the glamour of other developing technologies but is a valuable utility with considerable potential, not yet fully exploited.

INTO THE 1990s

The medium of telephones or two-way audio has been used less in European distance teaching systems than in North America or Australasia. Its potential appears to be undervalued. Greater distances involved in these other distance teaching projects do not altogether account for its low level of use in Europe. Other relevant factors seem to be comparatively high user costs, out-dated and inadequate technology, and different cultural attitudes to the use of the telephone and to notions of teaching and learning. The potential of telephone or two-way audio communication is perhaps too often perceived only in terms of a domestic technology with restricted applications.

This limited perspective is likely to change in the light of two recent developments: changes in telecommunications facilities; and policy currently under way in Europe and the attempts to put together Europe-wide projects for 1992 and beyond.

Quality of facilities

The quality of telecommunications services in Europe varies widely from country to country. France has a highly digitalized modern network which guarantees good performance and allows a wide range of services to be provided. Italy, by way of contrast, has an old telecommunications network which functions uncertainly and which is suffering from lower investment in it than is the case in either France or West Germany. The control and organization of telecommunications services differs nationally, as do standards and type of equipment, cost structures and tariffs.

In an attempt to harmonize technical standards, equipment and policies, and in order to open Europe's heavily regulated telecommunications markets to greater competition by 1992, the European Commission put forward a set of proposals in its Green Paper (1988) aimed at more coordinated strategies within Europe by 1992. These are, at the time of writing, the subject of lively debate among member countries.

At present, for reasons of cost and technical constraints, audioconferencing is not much used in distance education within individual countries. The current cost of audioconferencing between member countries of the EEC is even higher and can best be described as prohibitive.

Access to voice and data networks via satellite would resolve some of the problems described. If this is not to be a possibility for use by distance teaching institutions in Europe, then the most promising opportunities for improved facilities via terrestrial networks lie with the development of ISDN. Integrated Services Digital Networks is a world-wide development which has the capability to transmit voice, data, facsimile and slow-motion video simultaneously on a single telephone line. It offers considerable potential for distance teaching. Whether cost and access allow this for educational users remains to be seen.

REFERENCES

Horton, R. and Donovan, J. (1987) 'International comparisons of telecommunication charges', *Telecommunications Policy* 11, 3.

National Utility Services International (1988) *Telecom's Price Survey (1988)*, Croydon, UK, and Ridge Park, N. J., USA: National Utility Services.

McConnell, D. (1984) 'Cyclops shared screen teleconferencing', in A. W. Bates (ed.) *The Role of Technology in Distance Education*, London: Croom Helm.

The Open University (1988) *Delivery Technologies*, Milton Keynes: Open University (Report to Visiting Committee, VCO (88)20).

Parker, L. and Olgren, C. (1984) *The Teleconferencing Resource Book*, Amsterdam: New Holland.

Robinson, B. (1981) 'Telephone tutoring in the Open University: a review', *Teaching at a Distance* 20: 57–65.

Robinson, B. (1984) 'Telephone teaching', in A. W. Bates (ed.) *The Role of Technology in Distance Education*, London: Croom Helm.

Robinson, B. (1988) *Survey of 1987/88 Regional Use of Telephone Tutorials and Audio-teleconferencing in the Open University,* Nottingham: Open University.
Williams, E. and Chapanis, A. (1976) 'A review of psychological research comparing communications media: the status of the telephone in education', in *Proceedings of the 2nd Annual International Conference, on Telecommunications,* Madison, Wisconsin: University of Wisconsin Extension.

16 Multifunction microcomputer enhanced audio teleconferencing: moving into the third generation of distance education

D. Randy Garrison

The purpose of this chapter is to describe a multifunction microcomputer-based enhancement of audio teleconferencing. As a framework for discussion, distance education technologies are structured into three generations – correspondence, teleconferencing, and computer-based. It is argued that microcomputer-enhanced audio teleconferencing represents a move into the third generation (computer-based) of distance education delivery. While audio teleconferencing represents significant advances over correspondence study in terms of its communications capabilities, there does not exist an ability to interact visually in real time or provide continuous support and guidance. As a result of a discussion of common audiographic systems it was concluded that a microcomputer-based system which can support telewriting, computer-assisted learning, computer messaging, and computer graphics represents the most cost-effective multipurpose enhancement of audio teleconferencing available today. The system is designed for the addition of other technology (e.g. videodisc, videotex), thus providing a foundation for future developments and reducing the possibility of technological obsolescence. It is anticipated that the additional communications capabilities of this system will not only improve the quality of audio teleconferencing in general, but will make it possible to deliver courses requiring a visually interactive medium which were not previously possible.

INTRODUCTION

In this chapter a multifunction microcomputer enhancement of audio teleconferencing is described and justified from a theoretical and pragmatic perspective. The chapter begins by providing a conceptual order of communication technologies and a brief discussion about the adoption of distance delivery methods by institutions of higher education. Next, a detailed discussion of audio teleconferencing and a comparison of various enhancements is presented. Finally, the microcomputer-based enhancement and its application within an extensive network is described.

Distance education is currently attracting great interest and is being discovered as a viable and cost-effective means of supporting the learning of individuals across geographic, psychological, and temporal distances. Clearly, the growth of distance education has been largely due to innovations in telecommunications and microprocessor technology making it possible to meet the educational needs of a diverse range of individuals in society. Bates (1984: 223) states that new technology promises 'a wider range of teaching functions and higher quality of learning; lower costs; greater student control; [and] more interaction and feedback for students'.

Although all communication technologies have their unique advantages and symbol systems, a distinction must be made between broadcast (mass) media and technologies capable of interactive and individualized delivery. This distinction separates what Toffler (1980) refers to as Second and Third Wave Societies. He argues that there is currently a process of de-massifying media resulting from new microcomputer-based or -driven technologies that have proliferated and challenged the mass media.

It no longer makes sense to broadcast educational programmes to vast segments of society when messages need to and can be designed and directed to specific target audiences. The demand is for access to personalized and individualized information. From an educational perspective media are be able to support two-way communication, and broadcast (mass) media is by definition a unidirectional delivery system. For this reason it is perhaps not surprising to find that broadcast television and radio are proving to be of less significance in distance education (Bates 1980). What makes distance education possible is the two-way communication technologies it uses to mediate instruction.

DISTANCE EDUCATION TECHNOLOGIES

The separation of teacher and student is the obvious physical characteristic of distance education. On the other hand, the essential process characteristic is the two-way communication between teacher and student which necessitates the use of technology to mediate this interaction. Due to the essential nature of technical media to support two-way communication at a distance, it is particularly important to view this technology from the perspective of distance education characteristics. As a result, three distinct generations of technological delivery as well as various ancillary media have been identified (Garrison 1985). The three generations are correspondence, teleconferencing, and computer-based. Other media are seen as ancillary because of their general inability to support two-way communication (see Table 16.1).

202 *Media in distance education*

Table 16.1 Technology and media in distance education

Distance education technologies (two-way communication)

1 Correspondence (First Generation) Message: Print Delivery Mode: Mail Instructional Method: Individual
2 Teleconferencing (Second Generation) Message: Audio/Video/Computer Delivery Mode: Telecommunications Instructional Method: Group
3 Computer-based (Third Generation) Message: Audio/Video Delivery Mode: Telecommunications/Micro-processor Instructional Method: Individual

Ancillary media in distance education (one-way communication)

1 Print material
2 Audio/Video-cassettes
3 Audiographics*
 – Facsimile
 – Slow-scan television
 – Compressed video
 – Telewriting
 – Videotex
 – Videographics
4 Laser videodisc
5 Satellite broadcast

Note: *May support two-way communication.

In summarizing this classification of distance technology, correspondence education is an individual mode of study which supports interaction between the teacher and student through the printed word and postal system. This method of distance education can be enhanced by a variety of means such as audiotapes and telephone tutorials. Teleconferencing is a group method of distance education and consists of three basic types – audio, video and computer. Audio teleconferencing. the most prevalent and cost-effective method of teleconferencing, often builds on the technology of correspondence by supporting the learning experience with extensive print materials. Although the microcomputer has been with us for over ten years and computer-assisted learning (CAL) for over twenty-five, it has only been in the last few years that efforts have been made to implement computer-based distance education. This is a significant development in distance education because of the computer's potential for making distance learning both interactive and independent. Finally, a number of other media are also available but are generally viewed as enhancements of the three previous technologies because of their inadequacies in supporting two-way interaction.

ADOPTING DISTANCE EDUCATION

The adoption of distance learning methods by institutions of higher learning is the result of an increased realization of the public demand for continuing education beyond the walls of formal institutions. Many institutions are beginning to overcome their agoraphobia and have accepted the responsibility of helping individuals learn in their communities and homes. However, for institutions of higher education one of the greatest barriers to such an innovation is the need to maintain academic standards. Ellis and Chapman (1982: 276) suggest that institutions of higher education must make 'changes in their regulations and ways of dealing with remote adult students before [they] can be accepted as having received an academically equivalent course'. Although academically equivalent programmes and quality instruction are possible with most distance education technologies, for many in institutions of higher learning it is difficult to accept this innovation.

To have a chance of breaking free of the status quo and adopting distance education it is important that administrators and instructors are able to identify with, and understand, distance delivery. The great advantage of audio teleconferencing is that it is a group method of instruction which emphasizes interactiveness among students and instructor. For this reason, an instructor teaches in a manner similar to what might happen in a traditional classroom setting. While special efforts must be made to overcome some of the visual deficiencies, it is still easier for institutions to understand and adopt a form of distance delivery that is group-based and directed by an instructor. The same cannot be said for individual methods of distance delivery such as computer-based study. Since resistance to individual methods of distance education appears to exist in institutions of higher learning, one strategy is to introduce this technology as an enhancement of audio teleconferencing. The additional capabilities would greatly enhance teleconferencing and allow for a gradual acceptance of individual learning through microcomputer technology.

The obvious deficiency of audio teleconferencing is a visual channel of communication which is essential in many teaching situations. In the traditional classroom, the instructor is likely to use media such as a blackboard or overhead projector and have the advantage of visual feedback from the learners. Audio-only teleconferencing can successfully overcome the lack of visual cues from learners by encouraging participation and verbal feedback, but some subjects simply cannot be delivered in a quality manner without real-time visual display of course content (e.g. maths and science). The continued use and growth of audio teleconferencing may well depend upon acquiring an interactive visual channel of communication. As a result, much effort has been devoted to enhancing audio teleconferencing with respect to visual communication.

ENHANCING AUDIO TELECONFERENCING

While audio teleconferencing provides immediate feedback and makes possible interaction among learners, it must rely on aural communication supported by print materials. However, the quality of the educational experience and the motivation of the learner are very much related to the variety and interactivity of the channels of communication. As such, perhaps the greatest limitation in audio teleconferencing is the lack of an interactive visual medium. To overcome this limitation, a number of audiographic enhancements can be integrated into an audio teleconferencing system.

The transmission of visual information over a narrow band telephone line during a teleconference is referred to as an audiographic enhancement. Audiographic enhancements can significantly improve the quality of audio teleconferencing. Some of the more common audiographic systems are facsimile, slow-scan television, compressed video, videotex, and telewriting. Determining which audiographic system(s) should be used to enhance audio teleconferencing will depend on a number of factors such as the purpose of the teleconference, subject matter to be conveyed, ease of use, and cost. Parenthetically, while it is risky to report costs of rapidly changing technology, they are necessary for comparative purposes; however, at the same time it must be realized that costs may vary considerably depending on the manufacturer and the quality of hardware. The currency used here is Canadian dollars.

Facsimile devices transmit an image from hard copy. A fast digital machine can transmit an image in approximately fifteen seconds with a cost of over $10,000 per unit. Although transmission time, resolution, and cost are important considerations, it must be realized that this device does not lend itself well to real-time instruction. Only one copy is made that would have to be shared by all participants at a remote site. More importantly, the teaching process cannot be natural and interactive due to transmission time. If audio communication is to proceed while transmission of the image is taking place, a second line would be required, adding to transmission costs.

A powerful and relatively inexpensive method of transmitting a visual image captured by a television camera is slow scan. The image is displayed on a monitor and is easily observed by participants at a local site. The cost of a low resolution slow-scan unit is approximately $10,000 per site plus $10,000 for a transmitter. Transmission time for an image is roughly thirty-five seconds. Also, a second telephone line is required which would double transmission costs. Notwithstanding the need for two transmission lines, the real limitation in a teaching situation is that it is clumsy and discontinuous when attempting to teach through this visual mode. Since it requires an operator, transmitter, and is slow, it is not practicable to support two-way visual communication (i.e. transmit and receive at a remote site).

At the same time, full motion compressed video systems must be seen as being unrealistic and impractical for most distance education applications. They are unrealistic in terms of the enormous costs, which can be twenty times that of other audiographic systems, and impractical for multi-site, two-way transmission. Compressed video uses a codec (coder/ decoder) to remove redundant information and sends a digital message across special data lines. The cost of a codec is over $100,000. To make use of this technology requires a clearly defined need and a considerable amount of capital. Furthermore, the need for full motion video is questionable in light of the many other cost-effective technologies available to transmit visual images.

Videotex is a generic term which describes an electronic system of accessing computer-based text and graphics to be displayed on a monitor. Telidon is a particular graphics presentation protocol used in North America. Image creation and transmission costs at the original site would be approximately $10,000, while local sites could be equipped for around $3,500. The critical cost, however, is in the ongoing creation of graphics. This is likely to be done by a technician for $5–10 per page depending on the complexity of the graphic. The difficulty of getting graphics produced and budgeting for this expense has seriously impaired the Telidon project at the University of Calgary. The alternative is a video page creation camera which costs approximately $40,000. At present this system is not interactive and without a second telephone line requires an interruption of 10–20 seconds while the graphic is being transmitted.

The most exciting audiographic enhancement of audio teleconferencing has to be telewriting. Telewriting images can be produced by three major systems – light pen, electronic blackboard, and tablet. A light pen can be used to write on a television screen and transmits this image to monitors at the local site. The electronic blackboard looks very much like a typical blackboard where the instructor writes with a piece of ordinary chalk and the image is transmitted to a monitor at the site. Although the blackboard provides a large writing surface, it is not convenient for an instructor in a small studio.

Also, this system requires a second communication line which adds to the transmission costs.

Digital tablet telewriting systems allow real-time interactive exchange of written, graphic and text information. Telewriting is to distance education as a blackboard or overhead projector is to traditional classroom instruction. One system with great promise can transmit information from a digital tablet concurrent with a voice signal. This provides for a very natural and cost-effective means of communication among numerous sites. The cost for a fully interactive microcomputer-based system is approximately $11,000 per site. In addition, the system can create and transmit computer graphics, support CAI/CMI, and provide computer messaging. With some additional hardware, other enhancements such as Telidon and laser disc technology can be easily integrated into the system.

The telewriting tablet system described above is much more practical for a studio-based teleconference set-up in that the instructor can have the tablet on a table along with his/her notes and other reference materials. An electronic blackboard is not only expensive but is inconvenient for a non-classroom situation. The multiple and flexible capabilities of the tablet telewriting system also demonstrate its superiority over a slow-scan video system. It can be used for a variety of purposes, has little overhead cost, is fully interactive, and is naturally integrated into the instructional process. Systems such as slow scan and videotex have limited capabilities compared to the telewriting system while being comparable in cost. With the future impact of computer-based instructional systems, the microcomputer-based telewriting system is one that can be added to and still provide the best form of affordable visual interaction existing today.

A MULTIFUNCTION MICROCOMPUTER-BASED ENHANCEMENT

Telewriting is the crucial component of the microcomputer-based enhancement described here that reduces the inherent limitations of an audio-only teleconference system. Through the addition of telewriting capabilities, courses (e.g. maths, science) that rely on interactive written communication can be offered on a narrow band teleconference network. The telewriting system uses a graphics tablet and keyboard on which the instructor can write or type a message which is transmitted immediately and concurrently with the audio communication along a telephone line. At each of the centres, students will view a handwritten, typed text, or graphic message appearing on a monitor. In addition, each centre will have the capability to alter the message, use a cursor to draw attention to some aspect of the message, or send its own message. These messages are viewed simultaneously in all centres.

The telewriting system proposed here provides a unique opportunity to communicate simultaneously in two modes (aurally and visually). This is accomplished by a special modem that is able to transmit both voice and data down the same telephone line. Instructor(s) and students will have a unique opportunity to discuss and explain their problem both aurally and visually. In addition, the system will support computer messages between teleconference sessions, computer-based learning, and computer graphics. With some additional hardware it will also support videotex (i.e. Telidon) and other ancillary media. As a result, this system provides a link to the next generation of distance education technology – computer-based delivery.

Keeping in mind the importance of two-way mediated communication in distance education, the implementation of this system will provide an opportunity to study the impact of additional channels (visual and computer simulated) of communication from the perspective of both the learner and instructor. Such data will contribute to theoretical considerations of mediated two-way communication which is the quintessence of distance education. Certainly the form and variety of mediated communication have greater potential impact on the success and continuance of distance education than any other characteristic or condition.

The technological innovation described previously will be integrated into an extensive audio teleconference system linking nearly sixty centres across the province of Alberta. The system is made possible by a network of dedicated long distance lines (set monthly rate) funded indirectly through the provincial government. As a result of this system, various educational institutions can afford to deliver more courses to more students in all quadrants of the province without excessive consideration of long-distance costs. Not only is audio teleconferencing educationally viable from the delivering institution's perspective, but it becomes extremely cost-effective with reduced long-distance costs.

CONCLUSION

The quintessential characteristic of distance education is technically mediated two-way communication between teacher and student. For many institutions of higher education, audio teleconferencing (viewed here as the second generation of distance education) is a viable and cost-effective means of reaching out to students at a distance. However, due to the limitations of an audio-only channel of communication, teleconferencing often needs to be enhanced with a visual channel in order to offer a full range of courses and maintain delivery quality. It is argued that one of the most educationally sound and cost-effective enhancements of audio teleconferencing is a multi-function microcomputer-based system capable of providing telewriting graphics, messaging and computer-assisted learning.

One serious concern when designing computer-based delivery is the integration of these capabilities into a unified system. Lampikoski (1982: 296) states that a 'central decision criterion is whether computer functions can be integrated into a single well functioning totality where different functions support each other'. A microcomputer-based enhancement of audio teleconferencing has many distinct and complementary functions. It can support both group and individualized learning methods, aural and visual modes of communication, synchronous and asynchronous communication. This is a well-integrated system capable of supporting additional technological enhancements, it is not likely to be made obsolescent in the short term and it provides an easy transition into the third generation of distance education technology characterized by highly interactive, personalized, and independent forms of learning. The power and flexibility of a micro-computer-based enhanced audio teleconferencing system is capable of delivering quality distance education that is sure to gain greater acceptance and recognition in higher education.

REFERENCES

Bates, A. W. (1980) *The Planning and Management of Audio-visual Media in Distance Learning Institutions*, Paris: International Institute for Educational Planning.

Bates, A. W. (1984) 'Putting it together: now the future', in A. W. Bates (ed.) *The Role of Technology in Distance Education*, London: Croom Helm.

Ellis, G. B. and Chapman, R. S. (1982) 'Academic equivalency of credit courses by teleconferencing', in J. S. Daniel, M. A. Stroud and J. R. Thompson (eds) *Learning at a Distance: a World Perspective*, Edmonton: Athabasca University/International Council for Distance Education, 276–8.

Garrison, D. R. (1985) 'Three generations of technological innovation in distance education', *Distance Education* 6, 2: 235–41.

Lampikoski, K. (1982) 'Towards the integrated use of the computer in distance education', in J. S. Daniel, M. A. Stroud and J. R. Thompson (eds) *Learning at a Distance: a World Perspective*, Edmonton, Athabasca University/International Council for Distance Education, 296–8.

Toffler. A. (1980) *The Third Wave*, New York: Bantam Books, Inc.

17 The coming of the new distance educators in the United States: the telecommunications generation takes off

Becky Duning

INTRODUCTION

Correspondence education in the United States will be one hundred years old in 1992, if one's reckoning takes as its starting-point the University of Chicago's correspondence study department formed by William Rainey Harper. At almost the same moment, little more than one hundred years ago, Alexander Graham Bell was attempting in 1877 to convince Western Union to purchase the patents for his new invention, the telephone (they refused). Considering how very new the field of telecommunications is, it perhaps shouldn't be startling to recognize that a scant twenty years ago the field as we know it today didn't exist at all. As one report puts it, the communications world in 1970 was 'pre-microelectronics and pre-fiber optics, pre-micro-computer and pre-VCR' (US Department of Commerce 1988: 4).

To assert that we are witnessing a telecommunications revolution in higher education and training in the United States is now, finally, indisput-able. This chapter examines one of the video-based aspects of this phenomenon, live videoconferencing, looking at: (a) the forces driving this growth and development phase; (b) some of its early effects; (c) the part schools, colleges, universities, and industry are playing in this emerging scene; (d) the status of these developments at this moment in time; and (e) the likely outcomes in the United States in the next two decades of applying video techniques to all levels of education and training.

This chapter uses the terms videoconferencing and teleconferencing interchangeably to refer to live, interactive one-way video, two-way audio programming. Its title is a play on the now famous 1988 article by Peter F. Drucker, said to be the most requested article in the recent history of the *Harvard Business Review:* 'The coming of the new organization'. Probably the most tightly-argued position to date on the implications of the emerging 'information-based' organization, it predicts profound changes in the struc-ture of the workplace. It can be argued that equally fundamental changes in distance education are approaching with lightning speed, fostered less by the traditional distance education community than by a dazzling array of professionals who equate distance education with telecommunications-delivered training and instruction.

It is well to remind ourselves just how young the 'satellite era' is. Its origins are the stuff of novels, traceable to an article by science fiction writer and scholar Arthur C. Clarke. It was Clarke who conceptualized that a satellite in a circular orbit above Earth at an altitude of 22,300 miles (36,000 kilometres) would have an orbital period of 24 hours (NASA 1988: 2). Thus in synchronization with Earth's own 24-hour revolution, the satellite would appear, if above Earth's equator, to be stationary. Hence the term 'geosynchronous' applied to today's more than 120 communications satellites positioned above the equator. The National Aeronautics and Space Administration (NASA) first tested Clarke's idea successfully on 12 August 1960, followed in 1962 by the first active satellite capable of receiving and relaying radio messages. This 1962 satellite, Relay 1, was the first satellite link between North and South America and Europe. It was not until 19 August 1964, just 26 years ago (and 19 years after Clarke's article) that the first geostationary orbit was accomplished with a communications satellite. It was only 16 years ago, 1974, when the first satellites for educational uses were launched.

Americans have a long-standing affection for change. Often, however, they seem reluctant to tie the knot. American higher education institutions in general, and non-traditional educators and administrators in particular, exhibit little enthusiasm for introducing fundamental change in their way of doing things. The propensity to retain inherited modes of operation, apart from some tinkering, is usually couched in terms of financial expediency and careful weighing of the prospects for a successful outcome. Failed ventures are cited and derided. The risk-taker is not typically described in glowing terms. Indeed, American administrators in the fields of distance education and non-traditional learning in higher education often feel like targets as they carry out their day-to-day tasks. The institution reluctantly cooperates, viewing success with grudging recognition and looking sternly upon failure. For these and other reasons the catalyst for applications of videoconferencing to distance education is not, for the most part, found among the distance education community in American colleges and universities.

FORCES DRIVING GROWTH AND CHANGE

In the early 1980s, the Adult Learning Service (ALS) of the Public Broadcasting Service (PBS) emerged as a force bringing a new degree of cooperation between local public television stations and higher education institutions in the United States. ALS is the first nationally coordinated initiative designed to make college credit courses and other formal learning opportunities available through television to adults. While its early years were devoted to telecourses, ALS helped set the stage for higher education teleconferencing and is now incorporating teleconferences into its programming. Although the embrace has not been universal, nor particularly fond in all instances, the video medium in the service of education under ALS auspices has inspired joint activity among parties that have had little to do with one another previously. A parallel service of PBS, the National Narrowcast Service (NNS), launched in 1987, is designed to deliver video-based education and training, much of it on videotape, directly to the workplace. Like ALS, NNS has begun to blend a handful of live videoconferences into its televised programming.

At the outset, 80 per cent of public television stations agreed to cooperate with the new ALS service; more than 95 per cent have participated at one time or another. Some 400 colleges and universities started with the service in 1981, little more than 13 per cent of all post-secondary institutions in the country. Even at this, the numbers exceeded expectations. To date, about one-third of the country's higher education institutions have participated in ALS programming, with about 600,000 students having enrolled during its first six years. This is, of course, barely a ripple in a higher education population of 12.5 million students.

ALS attributes its progress in part to a second set of forces: the demographics of an ageing society. Forty per cent of all college students in America are over twenty-five years old and more than half attend part-time. By the 1980s, producers of educational programming in the United States had received the message from this emerging public: televised programming that did not make use of the powerful visual dimensions of the medium would not be generally well received. Among those who responded creatively were the Dallas Community College District in Texas, the University of Mid-America, consisting of institutions in seven Midwestern states, the Maricopa Community Colleges in Arizona, and the Southern California Consortium comprised of thirty-seven colleges. Their efforts in video were largely telecourses, not live video programming, but during the 1980s it was these and similar institutions that set new standards and higher expectations for the video medium. There are many indicators that suggest that numerous members of the American Association of Community and Junior Colleges will very soon demonstrate similar energy and creativity in the use of live teleconferences, very likely surpassing the typical level of university attention given to uses of this medium.

The third driving force was an infusion of funding. Telecourse development received a dramatic boost in 1981 when the Annenberg/ CPB Project was announced, funded with $10 million a year for fifteen years by the Annenberg School of Communications. In 1981, ALS had seven telecourses available nationally; by 1986 that number had climbed to 32 courses produced by a multiplicity of entities and funders. These broadcast quality courses have, for the most part, been produced with impressive printed support of the video courseware.

Faculty attitudes toward this programming are still confined to a truncated spectrum, from disregard to disdain. Instructors said to number in the thousands who now teach via television have not significantly influenced colleagues' views. Some administrators share these views. It is safe to say that their awareness of ALS programming is minimal. These attitudes are unlikely to be altered by a fourth force, the onslaught of delivery mechanisms. These include agreements with local cable systems, admittedly fraught at times by cumbersome and costly arrangements and undermined by deregulation that removed earlier obligations placed on cable operators to carry public television channels. Instructional Television Fixed Service (ITFS) technology with its relatively low-cost transmit-and-receive antennae is now common, as is one-way videoconferencing. ITFS is closed-circuit microwave video operating on frequencies awarded by the Federal Communications Commission for primarily educational purposes.

Today some 500 post-secondary institutions, still under 20 per cent of total institutions, are equipped for reception directly via satellite. Among higher education institutions in the United States, 250 are fee-paying members of a satellite-based consortium, the National University Teleconference Network (NUTN). An unlikely consortium, consisting of technical institutes, community colleges, and four-year research universities, the network produces and facilitates programming aimed primarily at professionals employed in business and industry. Established in 1982 by sixty-six campuses and the Smithsonian Institution, NUTN is one of the few survivors of the videoconferencing experiments of the last eight years. This amalgam of producing and receiving campuses is an anomaly in American higher education. Its cooperating institutions would in the past seldom have had any type of communication with each other. It brings together professionals in continuing education and media who have little in common other than their Network activities. Few are drawn from the ranks of distance education.

DETERMINING THE LOCUS OF CHANGE

The question remains: Where *is* the locus of change in telecommunications applications to education and training? Precisely what kind of change is this likely to be? Indicators of the dimensions of the telecommunications transformation in the United States are available from several sources. One of the largest associations of non-traditional education administrators in the United States is the National University Continuing Education Association (NUCEA). It was not until 1978 that its Division of Educational Telecommunications was formed, growing out of earlier committees and a Section of Educational Broadcasting that existed during the 1970s. In 1988, this group printed its first *Directory of Distance Education through Telecommunications*. A total of eighty-three institutions representing thirty-eight states plus the District of Columbia supplied information. Since there are over 3,000 institutions of higher education in the United States, this is not a 'sample' but the responses provide an indicator of trends. As a particularly active group of telecommunications entities, this offers a useful snapshot of telecommunications at some of the universities in the United States.

A typical state with efforts in their infancy has a profile that looks something like this. The State Department of Administration will have an Office of Telecommunications that may be especially centred on voice and data hardware and transmission via microwave. Primary users will be state agencies such as the police and highway departments. Layered with that will be a Commission of Higher Education or a Board of Regents struggling to knit together the interests of higher education. Parallel to this activity, a consortium of community colleges and technical institutes will have acquired some accessing route of their own. They will be trying to use it to send programming in two directions: to businesses and industry, and to elementary and secondary schools for education and in-service teacher training. There will be at least one task force or consortium that has disbanded. The public broadcasting service will be looking to popular programming just as the educational community is becoming insistent that its facilities be used more heavily for educational purposes. For the most part, the premier universities in the state can be expected to be tentative regarding educational telecommunications or, if interested, determined to seize the leadership. Whatever the stance of higher education, these institutions will nevertheless be the recipients of attention by agencies seeking to serve their interests. This 'top down' orientation in planning tends to relegate secondary education to the back seat in many states. Planning efforts are seldom coordinated in states where telecommunications is in its infancy. Whatever *ad hoc* activities are under way tend to be disjointed efforts, duplicative of what is being undertaken elsewhere.

SOME SOURCES OF TELECOMMUNICATIONS INITIATIVES

The most advanced states are not duplicates of each other, but they have all taken some similar decisive steps to reward planning, to inspire cooperation, and in many instances, to reduce dependency on a single major provider of services. Frequently, the potential for dependency on cable companies or on public broadcasting systems has been part of the motivation for states to develop systems that are free of these agencies. Public broadcasting, a cooperating entity in some states, has been regarded as a system to be by-passed in others. There is a distinct preference for live, full-motion video geared to satellite-based programming and supported by various systems of terrestrial delivery, frequently ITFS systems. The orientation to satellites is driving commitments to equip elementary schools, technical institutes, community colleges, and universities with downlinks. It is worth noting that leading states show a greater propensity to equip the lower end of the education spectrum first, or at least simultaneously with the upper end.

Most notably, and with some striking exceptions, in only a few states does a college or university or a higher education system or consortium play a leadership role in teleconferencing developments. If distance education units are exercising strong leadership, that is nowhere apparent in surveys that take a broad brush approach to describing these developments. On the contrary, the major initiative is more typically attributed to the state government apparatus, either the governor's office or the legislature, or to a telecommunications unit within a State Department of Administration or State Budget Office. Much less commonly, strong initiative can be attributed to a State Department of Education, which is oriented to elementary and secondary schools.

As visions of the future go, this is not an especially heartening portrait of educators. One explanation for the overall lack of leadership by educators would cite such factors as traditional animosities between higher education institutions. They are loath to cooperate and reluctant to agree on who will take the leadership, if cooperation were to occur. At the elementary and secondary school end of the educational continuum, cooperation has seldom been a hallmark either. Yet the costs and nature of telecommunications make some form of cooperation mandatory. Another explanation would attribute the general lack of initiative among educators, including distance educators, to the absence of professional rewards and funding. This weary explanation can account for almost all lack of action in almost every arena of life, but it is rarely the entire answer. A deeper explanation must confront the striking absence of attention to telecommunications among educators or administrators, whose mission is distance education. Until very recently, they have not been clamouring about telecommunications as a desirable but unreachable feature of their goals. With very few exceptions, applications of video telecommunications have not been viewed as a vital priority by those who administer traditional post-secondary distance education programmes in this country. If this apparent disinterest persists, there is every likelihood that the new distance education infrastructures may have the same effect on correspondence programmes, as does a super highway on local businesses in the town it bypasses.

EFFECTS OF TELECOMMUNICATIONS ON THE MEANING OF DISTANCE EDUCATION

Already the term 'distance education' is coming to take on a meaning that is tied directly to delivery via telecommunications. Some of the effects of this development are not difficult to predict. There is a distinct possibility that within the traditional distance education areas, correspondence instruction will be relegated to a field separate from 'distance education'. Some will be content with this shoal in the moving river. Others will find it discouraging that their hard-won expertise about distance learning and the learner is bypassed in favour of those who combine that type of knowledge with emerging educational technologies. Embracing the new technologies may seem to some to represent disregard for the strength of traditional correspondence study programmes and thus prevent them from acting decisively.

Distance educators, whose propensity to feel relatively ignored and unappreciated on their campuses is often cited (Duning, 1985: 209 and 1987: 40), will be sorely tested in the next ten years of telecommunications developments. Reluctance to be assertive in adopting the new technologies and to familiarize oneself with the considerable body of research in educational technology will not be rewarded. This generation of distance educators has been unusually fortunate: opportunity is virtually kicking the door in. Administrators who carry on in business-as-usual fashion will risk being bypassed by other areas of the campus. These areas will adopt the language of distance education, assert themselves in the strategic planning process, and come to be seen as the distance educators of the coming decades.

EFFECTS OF TELECOMMUNICATIONS ON FORMS OF DISTANCE EDUCATION

It is well to observe here that, in the instances where states noted their motives for embracing telecommunications in the 1987 survey, the list doesn't entirely have the ring of traditional distance education. They cited a desire to enforce coordination; to act on the need for educational equity (addressing particularly isolated elementary and secondary students rather than adults); to respond to economic needs state-wide, to bring efficiency and economy to education (again looking at the lower end of the educational spectrum); and to exploit the potential opportunity to share educational resources.

While the latter notion envisages sharing within each state's own education community, there will inevitably be sharing regionally and nationally.

One such spawning ground is the federally-funded Star Schools Project. Star Schools programming got under way in 1988. Prior to that, in 1984, live video programming for secondary schools began in concerted fashion in Oklahoma, after the College of Arts and Sciences at Oklahoma State University (OSU) had raised requirements for entering a degree programme. Since this included a foreign language requirement that could be met either by two years of high school study or one year in college, the smaller, rural schools among Oklahoma's 611 school districts, 75 per cent of which averaged daily attendance of under 800 students, clamoured for opportunities to meet the requirement during high school. The result was a college credit course in German by satellite in 1985. This live distance education programming was followed by other advanced language, science and mathematics courses received by high schools in twenty states. Today, one-third of all high schools in Oklahoma receive college credit courses by satellite from OSU.

The Star Schools Project is a grant-funded set of four 'demonstrations' supported by $19 million appropriated by the United States Department of Education and awarded for a two-year cycle of funding beginning in October 1988. The second year of the cycle is funded by $15 million. This project is intended to bring televised education to elementary and secondary schools via satellite, assuring that it is technically in reach of virtually every school in the country. The competitively-awarded funding covers hardware and programming expenditures of consortia formed for the purpose of meeting the needs of rural and inner city elementary and secondary schools and their teachers by sharing resources in mathematics, science, and foreign language. There are some 8,000 rural high schools (grades 9–12 and 10–12) in the United States. The operative language – 'consortia' and 'sharing' – is becoming almost a litany of telecommunications. This language is a further indicator of the power of satellite teleconferencing to induce changes in working relationships among secondary and post-secondary institutions and across formerly almost impenetrable educational boundaries such as state borders and institutional territory. As an indicator of the kind of change we are seeing, Star Schools speaks to the fundamental nature of this change.

Other factors built into the eligibility for Star Schools grants are instructive. A Star Schools consortium had to include a minimum of three partners, at least one being from the private sector and at least one education agency from the local or state level. Programming had to be state-wide and preference was given to multi-state programmes. Fifty per cent of services had to go to disadvantaged children, up to 25 per cent of activity had to be production and delivery-related, and a 25 per cent quantity of matching funds was required. There was no emphasis in the criteria on satellite delivery; that emphasis emerged in the proposals themselves, of which there were sixty-seven, from which four were selected.

The multi-state Midlands Consortium Star Schools Project (MCSSP) provides live, interactive, satellite-based instruction and teacher training in the Star Schools subject of emphasis. Another Star Schools project is the Satellite Educational Resources Consortium (SERC) that brings together the Public Broadcasting System (PBS) and State Departments of Education in fourteen participating states plus cities in two other states. A third project, TI–IN United Star Network, will respond to the needs of students and teachers at 244 Indian and other disadvantaged schools in sixteen states. Finally, the Technical Education Resource Centers (TERC) is an interactive computer-based instructional programme.

BUSINESS-RELATED APPLICATIONS HAVE HAD A CATALYTIC EFFECT

Another outcome of telecommunications opportunities is the National Technological University (NTU). NTU was developed in 1985 in response to engineers seeking to work on advanced degrees in the workplace. This is live via satellite classroom programming utilizing one-way video and two-way audio formats. The growing network now includes twenty-four universities, among them some of the most outstanding engineering campuses in the country. This consortium offers over 300 accredited courses and brings together several thousand dispersed faculty. NTU students receive accredited engineering degrees at the master's level. Administratively, this represents no small feat in a country where territoriality in education has been fiercely guarded in the past. As a benchmark, it represents deep and fundamental change in distance education.

The concentration of effort and resources is probably greatest, to date, in industry and its training programmes as Moore (1988: 2–5) has reported. Business television, as live video training conducted privately by businesses around the country has come to be called, was used by more than 300 corporations as long ago as 1974. Their estimated spending on such programming was then $48.5 million. By 1986 it was estimated that 8,500 corporations were producing video in some form for communications and training. The early users included IBM, with its own in-house system since 1981; Aetna Life and Casualty Corporation, which has since 1981 used teleconferencing to link its offices and for various forms of training; and Hewlett-Packard, which has stayed in contact with its dispersed sales force through live videoconferencing for the last nine years.

A quickening pace and scale that characterizes business use of live videoconferencing for education and training is amply demonstrated by some selected recent statistics. Nearly fifty corporate and government agency networks are now operating in the United States. It is estimated that over

19,300 sites receive business television programming as of 1988, up from 12,000 a year earlier. The Bankers TV Network acts on behalf of financial services professionals, as do the Certified Public Accountant Network and the Institutional Research Network. Most major computer manufacturers have their own networks, including Apple, Amdahl, IBM, Hewlett-Packard, NCR, Tandem, Texas Instruments and Wang Labs. The computer field's programming network is Computer Channel, Inc. The Automative Satellite Television Network, which calls itself the country's largest business network, has over 3,900 sites. Chrysler reported that it anticipates its current expansion to grow to 6,000 sites. Retailers such as J. C. Penney, K-Mart, and Sears also have growing networks. Penney's moved from 200 to over 700 locations, Sears now has 490 and K-Mart grew recently from 5 to 800 sites. That the vitality and drama are in arenas other than traditional distance learning is amply demonstrated. Similarly, by 1987, NUTN's membership had grown almost 80 per cent since its inception. This network's live, talkback video teleconferencing now numbers over 100 programmes annually received by thousands of business participants at numerous locations around the country. Network presentations run the gamut from the 'how-to's of business management to topics such as regulations affecting hazardous materials, new developments in computer programming, social issues of illegal drugs, child welfare, ageing, and the revamping of the nation's workforce. No issue is too large or small for this network's panoply of institutions, some of which can be counted upon to have an audience whatever the topic.

Among the most advanced corporate teleconferencing, IBM's training programmes have recently been augmented by The Interactive Satellite Education Network (ISEN) run entirely by IBM on satellite. Talkback by students to instructors is handled ingeniously by voice and technology that allows the instructor to check comprehension at each site through light boards that register answers to questions in various formats, instantly revealing any lapses in learning. Among other corporations reporting widespread use of live via satellite training are Federal Express, with daily programming to 800 downlinks nationally, and Eastman Kodak, whose two-hour twice weekly training will go international in 1989–90. Tandem Computers reports 72 locations in North America and sites in 11 European countries. Domino's Pizza dispatches its portable uplink to any location that has something to teach the rest of its national workforce. The American Rehabilitation Educational Network (AREN) is received by health care professionals at nearly 100 national sites. Its Management Vision programming was among the first in the country to put management training into a yearly series.

Arizona State University has offered live credit courses via television for thirty-one years. Their remote sites now number thirteen. Overall, their comparative studies of groups taking courses by television and traditionally have revealed no statistically significant differences. Grade distributions indicate that distant students suffer no academic disadvantages that have resulted in grade differentials. For over ten years, California State University at Chico has used interactive televised programming. Chico is in an under-populated area of California with widely dispersed communities. Offering over fifty academic courses annually via television, they describe their programme as both academically and economically sound. While all of these reports have dealt with ITFS delivered instruction rather than satellite, the viewer via satellite would have an identical visual and interactive experience. The viewer would be as unaware of the origin of the video signal as one is unaware of differences among telephone companies in various parts of the country.

INTRIGUING QUESTIONS ON THE HORIZON

We have seen where we stand now and what those interested in new directions might expect in the future. One of the still unanswered questions raised by Johansen and others in 1984, and earlier, is: 'What might the medium allow us to do that we cannot do now?' (Johansen and Bullen 1984: 166). Like others in this field, Johansen is struck by the 'horseless carriage' mentality that persists in videoconferencing, seemingly dictating that we continue to try to recreate traditional classes and meetings rather than allowing the medium to alter the way we communicate, teach, and learn (Johansen 1984: 8). Johansen and his co-workers were wondering back in 1979 whether telecommunications didn't, in fact, require new communication skills.

Those working today on advanced projects known under the catch-all term 'hypermedia' have more reason than ever to assert that a new kind of teaching/learning modality is upon us. Hypermedia, a fluid mixture of voice, video, and computer technologies that allows learners to progress through material in the sequence of their choice with a touch of their finger to a computer screen, heralds much to come. The 'telecomputer' is virtually a reality for those in hypermedia. The 'video dial tone' seems close at hand. With visual, voice, data, and multimedia efforts in the hands of both the instructor and learner, the result is a blend of independent, self-determined learning and high interactivity that was unreachable just a few years ago. This is well beyond anything we have previously dubbed programmed instruction. In fact, what we in distance education have known as programmed instruction looks as unlike hypermedia as illuminated manuscripts look like the first printed texts.

VIDEOCONFERENCING IS CHANGING THE RULES

Comparative studies have sometimes been criticized for examining the wrong factors. Instead of looking at the medium and asking if it matches the results obtained in traditional classrooms, it is argued that the real question is what is good instruction (Whittington 1987: 54). Whether the telecommunications medium has no more effect on instruction than does a highway on how well one drives is an intriguing avenue of inquiry. Some observers of these media are assembling evidence that communication, teaching, and learning via television are influenced by the medium (Johansen 1984: 7). For these observers, the problem is not how to cancel out these influences but how to make better use of their special characteristics.

Some of the early effects of the video conference phenomenon have been salutary indeed. One of the most striking has been cited throughout this chapter: the greater receptivity to consortia and partnerships among otherwise non-cooperating, disparate parties. Another is the surge forward by business and industry, largely independently of higher education. Seizing its own training initiative, one such programme at IBM reports committing $250 million to this undertaking at its inception in the 1980s, estimating that $150–250 million would be saved as a result of cost-effective delivery systems. These training systems now handle an average of 18,000 employees daily. The attention given to redressing the balance of opportunity for less-advantaged primary and secondary students and their teachers has opened up relatively effortless possibilities of electronic networking with students and teachers across education levels. There is also the inherent appeal of speaking easily across state boundaries in what might be termed an emerging regional and soon-to-be national classroom that will ultimately alter traditional relationships among educational levels.

Another effect of videoconferencing has been to underscore that higher education as a whole will, for the most part, only reluctantly take the early lead. It also points up a high potential for a 'haves' and 'have-nots' dichotomy to emerge among states. Unquestionably, the states that have forged ahead have a telecommunications lead that will be easily maintained for the foreseeable future. It would be difficult not to imagine that there will be greater possibilities for economic development in states well-networked for superior communication and with greater capacity via satellite to educate a dispersed and diverse workforce.

At the time of writing, relatively few traditional teaching faculty among the 400,000 in higher education in the United States are aware of the Star Schools Project or of the many impending integrated uses of technology affecting every discipline. But it is inevitable that by the year 2000 virtually every faculty member in the country will be a regular user of some type of advanced technology for teaching and research, in one form or another. Why inevitable? Because anyone engaged in research and teaching will simply be unable to keep up in their field if they shun telecommunications. Telecommunications in the United States nationally and internationally is on the verge of becoming a new medium of exchange so pervasive that, like any valued currency, it will make older currency worthless. With the classroom doors flung open by satellite, as will also inevitably occur, the effects on interactive teaching are also likely to be profound. For example, the additional planning that is incumbent on the televised instructor is well-documented and the mercilessness of the medium when confronted by evasiveness has been demonstrated.

MORE PROSPECTS FOR TELECOMMUNICATIONS, FEW CERTAINTIES FOR DISTANCE EDUCATORS

What is on the minds of those in this country who are thinking about the potential of video and other educational technologies is neatly compressed in a 1987 publication, *Technologies for Learning Outside the Classroom.* Ably summarized in a review by Apps (1988: 90), he notes that in less than a decade

> we have seen what some call a revolution in educational technology, brought on by the personal computer, the popularity of home video players, and the ease with which vast amounts of information can be collected, stored, transmitted, and retrieved.

For a number of the authors in this compendium, the future of educational television lies in integration with other media. Others see the future prospects of telecommunications resting with how well we are able to turn these 'new electronic bridges' to the service of learners' needs. Of the prospects ahead, one contributor writes of

> tying computers with telecommunications and video to make unlimited information available to users virtually anywhere in the world . . . What is impressive about the new information technologies is their capacity to present the learner information resources of many kinds or from many sources and to enable the learner to integrate those various forms of information into learning programs that make sense.
>
> (Apps 1988: 91)

What is foreseen among the potential benefits awaiting learners is more and better access to more and better information sources, greater variety in learning strategies, a boost in learner motivation, and more individualized and cooperative learning. Issues foreseen include concerns about costs limiting the educational equity that these technologies could potentially promote; elusive standards of quality; determination of what information will be made available; obsolescence; developmental costs; human interaction in the use of the new technologies; and training for users. Wider issues such as what becomes of information when it becomes a commodity; how, and whether, technologies impact on more in-depth levels of learning; what the technology will contribute to truly self-directed learning; and the influence of these technologies on definitions of teaching and learning, were alluded to as fertile areas of future analysis and dialogue (Apps, 1988: 91–2). The most intriguing observation was made by Apps (1988: 92):

> Is it possible that our traditional definitions of the role of the instructor and the place for the educational institution might be stood on end, given the potential of the new technology?

There is every indication that where telecommunications technologies are concerned, the future lies with the learner: integration of technologies; interconnectivity, locally, regionally and globally; retrievability on one's own terms and timetable; and the potential for far greater interactivity than is possible in a standard classroom. Among those in America who are writing and talking about the possibilities now being glimpsed, there is considerable excitement. A fascinating future, tantalizingly malleable, looks to be within our grasp, if we can but exercise the wisdom and the will that the new technologies require.

REFERENCES

Apps, J. W. (1988) 'Technologies for learning outside the classroom. Book review', *American Journal of Distance Education* 2, 1: 89–92.
'The best companies in the country use business television' (1989) *Business TV* March/April : 1–2 to 1–7.
Drucker, P. F. (1988) 'The coming of the new organization', *Harvard Business Review* January/February: 45–53.
Duning, B. (1985) 'The independent study image dilemma', *Journal of Continuing Education: Continuum* 49, 3: 209–12.
Duning, B. (1987) 'Independent study in higher education: a captive of legendary resilience?' *American Journal of Distance Education* 1, 1: 37–46.
Johansen, R. and Bullen, C. (1984) 'What to expect from teleconferencing', *Harvard Business Review* 2: 164–74.
Moore, M. (1988) 'Telecommunications, internationalism, and distance education', *American Journal of Distance Education* 2, 1: 1–7.
National Aeronautics and Space Administration (1988) *NASA Educational Briefs for the Classroom*, Washington, D.C. : National Aeronautics and Space Administration.
US Department of Commerce (1988) *NTIA Telecom 2000: Charting the Course for*

a New Century, Washington, D.C. : National Telecommunications and Information Administration Special Publication, 88–21, October.

Whittington, N. (1987) 'Is instructional television educationally effective? A research review', *American Journal of Distance Education* 1, 2: 34–43.

18 IBM distance learning developments using videoconferencing

Barry Scott

INTRODUCTION

IBM, in the UK, France and Germany, is developing two-way video distance learning systems for training internal staff and customers. We are doing this in order to increase instructor productivity, to reduce travel and lodging costs for customers and ourselves, and to make the best use of our specialist instructor skills.

One-way video teaching, via satellite, with an audio return path, is already in widespread use in IBM, in the US, Australia and Japan. In France, IBM is operating a two-way video teaching system, based on 2 Mbit compressed video lines. It has been in use since 1989, with a teaching studio in Paris, and six regional classrooms, in Bordeaux, Lille, Lyon, Marseille, Nantes and Strasbourg. The system is used, mostly, for teaching IBM product courses to customers and internal staff. Because it is based on videoconferencing equipment, as is the Education Television Network (ETVN), the instructor teaches sitting down, using an overhead camera to display teaching visuals to the students. Students are able to respond to multiple-choice questions using keypads, but there are no PS/2s on the students' desks.

In Germany, IBM has commenced operation of a network of one studio and twelve remote classrooms, connected at 140 Mbits, via optic fibre links. The centre of the network is in Herrenburg, with remote classrooms in Berlin, Hamburg, Hannover, Dortmund, Düsseldorf, Cologne, Wiesbaden, Frankfurt, Mainz, Nuremberg, Stuttgart and Munich.

A major difference between the system in Germany and those in France and the UK is that the central site in Germany has students present in the same room as the instructor, in addition to students in the remote sites.

Because of the full bandwidth (140 Mbits) of the communication lines, the German system does not use video compression, and hence the instructor is free to move around, teaching in a manner that is similar to a normal classroom. This necessitates a camera operator, in an adjacent area, to follow the instructor, zooming in on material he/she displays or writes. The students sit around a bank of monitors on which remote students will be displayed if they ask questions. In remote classrooms, the instructor appears on a central bank of monitors. There are no student PS/2s involved in the system for student use. Hence there is no attempt to teach practical classes.

This chapter will concentrate on the development, design, and use of the UK system – Education Television Network (ETVN).

IBM UK's EDUCATION TELEVISION NETWORK

In the UK, we have been developing IBM's ETVN since October 1988. It is based on two-way compressed video over 384 Kbit lines, and has significant IBM PS/2 control technology in its design. A separate 64 Kbit circuit is used for connection of the PS/2s.

At the beginning of the project we defined some major objectives we would evaluate:

- What kind of courses suit this medium?
- What kind of training do instructors need?
- How much conversion is required to take an existing course (with all its visuals) into this medium?
- Is it necessary to have purpose-built classrooms?
- Can a large system be controlled by one person?
- What level of video quality (and hence line speed) is acceptable? And, of course, the most important objective . . .
- Will the result be acceptable to customers and internal students?

ETVN FEATURES

ETVN currently has an instructor's teaching studio in London, and classrooms in London, Portsmouth, Bristol, Croydon, Glasgow and Manchester. Each classroom can accommodate twelve students, with two students sharing one PS/2. Each pair of students also share a microphone and are allocated one of the six classroom cameras. In addition, there is a wide-angle view of the classroom from a seventh camera. The seven cameras are mounted above the two video screens in a cabinet at the end of the classroom.

The main features of the system are as follows.

- The instructor controls the system through an IBM PS/2, using either a mouse or a touch-screen.
- Students indicate they have questions via their keyboards, and the system attaches the location and name of the student, so the instructor knows to whom he's speaking, and can take questions in any order from a computer-managed queue. The student PS/2s are connected by Token Ring to each other and can also access the IBM network for practical courses.

- The seven classroom cameras are selected, as are the microphones, by a local PS/2 which receives commands from the instructor's control PS/2 in response to a question being accepted by the instructor.
- Computer (text) screens can be transmitted in both directions via the system during practical courses, enabling the instructor to demonstrate computer systems attached to IBM's internal network, and to view the students' screens during practical exercises. The transmission is limited to text screens simply because the amount of data involved in a graphics screen would cause the transmission to be unacceptably long.
- Instructors' graphics can be displayed directly on the students' PS/2 screens, as can multiple-choice questions. Graphics, in hard-copy form, can also be displayed on the video screens, via two overhead cameras.
- The instructor is able to transmit the following devices over the video-conferencing lines to the TVs in the classroom:
  - his or her own (live) image
  - videotape
  - PS/2 as a TV image, suitable for simple graphics
  - left and right overhead document cameras
  - a mobile camera, frequently used for showing a second speaker.

There are two TV screens in each classroom – a live screen, and a graphics (still) screen, used like an overhead projector in a regular classroom, and normally used to display a paper-graphic via an overhead camera.

ETVN COURSES

We have now run over 80 courses, with more than 1,600 students being taught remotely. The majority have been technical product courses, delivered both to customer and internal audiences, and to IBM's business partners (agents, dealers, etc.). In addition, we have a growing usage for the system for internal business support, product announcement workshops, etc. The product courses, for example, cover various IBM operating systems, introduction to network concepts, and introduction to relational databases.

We have tried some experiments with more 'syndicate' type workshops, and concluded, so far, that the medium is more suited to 'hard' technically-based product courses. However, the earlier trials of 'syndicate' courses were conducted at a time when the students in various locations were able to hear, but not see, each other. The addition earlier this year of voice-activated switching may enable us to approach this area again. This feature of the system detects who is speaking and automatically switches that person's image to the remote sites. For example, it shows the student asking a question, then shows the instructor answering, and so on. In this way the students are able to see and identify with their fellow students in remote sites.

By far the largest use of the system at present is for training IBM's business partners (agents) in the use of IBM's dial-in services giving product information.

COURSE MATERIALS

Students are given the same hard-copy course materials as for a normal class. A significant problem arises in the area of standard overhead transparencies. A typical one-day technical course may have over 100 transparencies, many of them 'portrait' (i.e. taller than they are wide), not the 'landscape' format of the TV screen. They are very frequently far too detailed to be suitable for TV display, and may be actual eighty-column computer screen displays.

The initial courses run on ETVN required a significant re-design of most graphics material, in order to make it suitable for use with the overhead cameras and TV displays. This has led us to develop the ability to capture the original foil, which is normally produced by a computer package, as a PS/2 bit-map image. This image can be displayed on the students' PS/2 screens, under instructor control. The instructor is also able to use his own mouse to position a pointer on the students' screens to draw their attention to some detail. In order to avoid the lengthy transmission times for graphics images, all such material is previously transmitted to the classroom PS/2 servers over the same network, and simply called up from there during the course.

Another area affecting the design of courses is the need to make frequent use of multiple choice questions, via the students' PS/2s, in order to keep the students involved, and to check on their comprehension level. This is necessary, because, in spite of the two-way video which is very effective in close-up situations, the instructor does not get the same degree of feedback from body language, particularly with a large audience.

ROLE OF THE PS/2s

The PS/2s have several important roles, first, in the studio:

- instructor control interface to the network control and videoconferencing hardware,
- instructor workstation for the transmission of electronic displays, multiple choice questions and practical course screens,
- management of the Token Ring Bridge links to the classrooms;

and second, in the classrooms:

- control of the videoconferencing hardware, e.g. camera selection,
- storage (on a PS/2 server) of pre-transmitted screens and multiple-choice questions,
- student systems, providing student names to the instructor, raising questions, answering multiple-choice questions, receiving display graphics and for doing practicals.

ORGANIZATIONAL IMPLICATION

ETVN has much wider implications than just education. It provides a new communications medium. It enables immediacy of communication (two-way), as well as immediacy of training. For example, on the day of some major product announcement or organizational change it is vital that the key people are informed, trained, and can interact with the presenters. This can be done over ETVN in a way which is not possible for a travelling education course, except at great travelling expense and cost in people's time.

RESULTS AND CONCLUSION

Reaction from students is encouraging, with over 85 per cent of students rating the system 'very good' or 'good' as a means of distance learning. Their comments are interesting. It is a new experience for them, and some of them admit to feeling nervous about being seen on a video screen around the location. This initial nervousness soon wears off, and there is general appreciation of the savings in travel time – plus demand for more widespread availability of the network. There is, of course, some feeling of remoteness, and the inability to speak privately to the instructor. So far we have no control-group comparisons with regular classroom courses, but the normal measurements of meeting objectives are quite satisfactory.

The experiences of instructors are very important. It is quite a novel experience for instructors. They are required to teach sitting-down, like a TV news broadcaster, in order to minimize the motion-blurring effects of video-conferencing equipment. In brief, this is caused by the compression of a full bandwidth video signal into a narrow bandwidth data line. The resultant picture quality is dependent on the line speed (hence costs), and rapid movements cause a blurring of the image.

It is important that the instructor actively promotes interaction with the students, by means of multiple choice questions, and by asking open questions. A key concern in the early design of the system was the likely maximum number of students that an instructor could handle. There are three aspects to this.

1 Ease of use of the control system. The design of the PS/2 touch-screen interface has been a major contributor.
2 The rate of questions.
3 The complexity of practical courses.

The largest number of students taught at one time so far is fifty-nine, out of a maximum seating capacity of seventy-two. The question rate has not approached any kind of limit so far. The best analogy is that teaching over this system is rather like addressing a university lecture-hall. Practical courses are a different matter – a practical for more than the conventional number of students must be very simple and must be very carefully designed (and documented) to minimize the amount of individual support each student needs. The largest number in a simple practical course has been around thirty.

In general, our conclusions relative to the original objectives of the products are as follows.

- What kind of courses suit this medium?
  – Technical, product overviews.
- What kind of training do instructors need?
  – Surprisingly little, mostly due to the simple control interface – which has been the result of a lot of practical experience – combined with ability to re-design the interface quickly and cheaply.
- How much conversion is required to take an existing course (with all its visuals) into this medium?
  – As mentioned earlier this was a major inhibition to the transfer of existing courses. Use of the students' PS/2 as a direct display medium for existing 'electronic' material has almost entirely eliminated that problem.
- Is it necessary to have purpose-built classrooms?
  – No, but it is important to minimize echo problems by adding sound absorbing materials to the classroom walls and reducing background noise as far as possible.
- Can a large system be controlled by one person?
  – Yes, thanks to the simple control system.
- What level of video quality (and hence line speed) is acceptable?
  – With the current videoconferencing technology, our view is that 384 Kbit transmission is acceptable, but we would not operate at lower speeds.

ETVN is now established as an operational system, providing a valuable addition to IBM's means of training its staff, customers and business partners.

Part V
International perspectives

Introduction

The phrase 'international perspectives of distance education' may suggest global dimensions in the form of international cooperation and collaboration. However, practice invariably starts from previous initiatives focused within national boundaries. It is often when practitioners elsewhere come to know about these national or institutional characteristics that the respective peculiarities – in the use of terminology, in administration of courses, in management of institutions – form the basis of a comparative study in the international arena. The chapters in this section reflect such a pattern of treatment in that they present international aspects of the debate on distance education, as well as of current practice within a particular country or region. Also evident in this section is the political ideology which has influenced the rationale responsible for shaping the institutions in some of the countries which feature here.

As far as the national framework is concerned, conflict may arise in the practice of distance education or in the interpretation of terminology in use. This may particularly be true of countries where there is a widespread use of the distance education mode, as in India or in Australia. It is in such situations that a lively debate is likely to ensue which may develop the theoretical bases of the current situation, not necessarily to support, but rather to explain, the *status quo*. Opinions may be formed and positions taken to widen the debate internally, only to find that it develops an international dimension through the interest shown by practitioners outside the national boundaries. It is in this way that refinement of practice and of concepts takes shape.

In countries where distance education practice is in its infancy as an alternative form of delivery, formal recognition is begrudged distance teaching institutions, on the grounds that the method of delivery is considered inferior to the traditional, conventional method. This is a situation prevalent in many developing countries, especially for programmes offered at secondary school level where a greater amount of student support is necessary than is available. At the tertiary education level, particularly in universities, there is general agreement that the educational structures necessary for an effective delivery of distance taught programmes are often in place, thus allowing the delivery method to gain recognition and validity.

The first chapter in this section is by Ram Reddy (Chapter 19). His use of the term 'temple' to refer to distance teaching universities does not appear to have religious implications other than in the context of access. This particular feature of distance teaching universities and their use of modern communications technologies are regarded by Reddy as 'innovative challenges' to the field of education.

The international outlook of this chapter begins with the author's review of the various names by which these 'temples' are known in different parts of the world and, in this regard, how they reflect the historical context and significance that they individually enjoy.

The controversy which exists in the abuse of distance education terminology is introduced by focusing in on the issue as it relates to India. The terms 'correspondence education', 'distance education' and 'external appearance' are explained as they are used in the Indian context. The practice of interchange in the use of terms 'distance education' and 'correspondence education' is seen as the cause of the confusion that has arisen over the use of 'open learning' and 'distance education'. The debate is extended to the international platform by an examination of the terminology as applied in the writing of leading theorists and practitioners in the field of distance education. What subsequently follows addresses the practice in the administration of these 'temples' in several countries.

Perraton's text (Chapter 20) provides an overview of the range of distance education programmes which are in operation in several countries in Africa, particularly those which were once colonies of the British Empire. In appraising the operations at each educational level, he examines the evidence for external influence on these programmes. This implicitly reveals the lack of both expertise and appropriate infrastructure within the African countries to cope with the educational requirement at the various levels. The support from international agencies associated with these programmes is then seen to reflect a variety of outcomes: the dilemma of dependence without strong political commitment from within the country; educational problems associated with distance education provision at certain educational levels; the extent of South–South cooperation in the spread of the use of distance education materials developed for non-formal education by a single agency for use in several countries. The prospect of international cooperation and collaboration on a South–South, and/or North–South, basis, is considered promising, particularly for those international donor agencies which are yet to make an impact in that geographical area.

The next chapter (Chapter 21) provides a national focus on the media and methods of distance education at a particular educational level. In this respect, Yuhui informs us about the role of television and radio in China's distance higher education system, the largest in the world, and the contribution that the radio and television university system has made in the country's development programme. He explains the system in terms of its organizational structure and the hierarchical links between the radio and television universities. He also shows the relationship between state education systems (national, provincial, civic, county and student) and the media, and between the media and the students. The paper describes the kinds of programmes that are offered and the administrative practices that are in place to cope with the large numbers of students provided for.

The final chapter by Inquai (Chapter 22) looks at the issues concerning access of refugees to basic education. The author, however, makes a distinction between those refugees who settle in Western industrial societies and those who are hosted by countries in Africa and Asia, to highlight the difference in opportunities which exist. The chapter concentrates on the refugee situation in the eastern and southern regions of Africa and the role of a European college in providing the expertise that will enable the refugees themselves to deliver some form of education through distance methods.

19 Open universities: the new temples of learning

G. Ram Reddy

Among the few innovations in the field of education, distance education ranks very high. It has been in existence for quite a few decades in one form or another, but thanks to modern communication technologies, its importance is now being realized by educationists and policy makers all over the world. Although distance education is catching up very fast in all countries, developed and developing, socialist and capitalist, Western and non-Western, it is still little known and less studied. As Keegan points out:

> Even a cursory reading of educational literature shows that distance systems are usually ignored. It merits not a paragraph in most volumes of educational philosophy, in guides to administrative practice or in analyses of didactic strategy.
>
> (Keegan 1986: 4)

Its importance is being realized now because of its usefulness and potential not only to provide greater access to education, but also its ability to make available an innovative and flexible system of education. No wonder, as I shall describe later, policy makers all over the world are looking to distance education for solving some of their problems. So, I shall deal with the three following aspects of distance education here.

- What is distance education?
- Why distance education?
- The 'how' of it, i.e. the organizational forms of distance education.

WHAT IS DISTANCE EDUCATION?

There is no one meaning of the term 'distance education'. It is known by a bewildering variety of nomenclature. In Australia, it is known as the 'external' system. This description is not appreciated very much because it bears similarity to the old London University external system which usually provides examinations but not teaching (Jevons 1983: 344). Unofficially, it is also known as 'off-campus study'. In some countries, the term 'correspondence education' is widely used. But it has increasingly been replaced by the term 'independent study' in North America. 'Home study' is sometimes used to describe correspondence programmes of private schools both in North America and Europe. This is also disliked by many because of its association with some of the correspondence institutions, particularly the private ones, which have only a profit motive. No doubt, some of them enjoy a very good reputation, others do not. Further, several correspondence institutions depend only on one medium, namely, printed material. Distance education today lays emphasis not only on the print medium but also on several other media. In fact, the multimedia approach is the corner-stone of the distance education system.

In France, it is known as *télé-enseignement*; in Germany, it is described as *Fernstudium* or *Fernunterricht;* and in Spanish-speaking countries, it is described as *educación a distancia* (Rumble and Keegan 1982: 11). *Extramural* refers to distance education in New Zealand. These terms have come in vogue because of the historical circumstances in various countries. They have peculiar characteristics of their own, most of which are similar to distance education. For instance, separation of the student from the teacher is a common characteristic of all of them.

In India, we have been using three terms: 'external appearance (private appearance)', 'correspondence education', and 'distance education'. In 'external appearance', a university permits a student to take the examination as a private candidate, and if he passes, he is given the degree. The university does not take any responsibility to impart education to the students. The second, 'correspondence education', has been quite popular in this country. Lately, some of the institutes/universities engaged in 'correspondence education' have designated themselves as 'distance education' and 'open university' systems.

In this connection, it will be useful to know about the two terms which are used interchangeably and about which there has been some controversy: 'open learning' and 'distance education'. Implicit in 'open learning' are innovations and reforms. Included are changes that aim at improving such things as the participation of learners, instructional design, methods of transmitting information and support to learners. Similar views are also expressed in a very comprehensive document entitled *Open Learning: Systems and Problems in Post Secondary Education* by Mackenzie, Postgate and Scupham (1975: 11). In the open learning system, restrictions on learning are fewer than those in formal educational institutions. Educational opportunities are planned deliberately so that access to knowledge is available to individuals in spite of barriers such as geographical distance. It is argued by some that while distance education is accommodated by an open learning system, the opposite premise may not be true. As Ruggles and his associates argue: 'Not all the distance education programmes have the characteristics of an open learning system. Some are very rigid and inflexible' (1982: 3). In their view, this term may symbolize a new and emerging philosophy that will become more closely associated with learning at a distance.

But other writers like Rumble and Harry (1982: 12) find the term 'open learning' unsatisfactory. They quote with approval Mackenzie, Postgate and Scupham that the term 'open learning' poses difficulties. 'Open learning' is an imprecise phrase. Today, a range of meanings can be attached. They write:

It eludes definition. But as an inscription to be carried in procession on a banner, gathering adherents and enthusiasm, it has great potential. For its very imprecision enables it to accommodate many different ideas and aims.

The term 'open' generally refers to four aspects:

- people, since it would not debar applicants on account of their lack of educational qualifications;
- place, in the sense that learning would be home-based and not restricted to classrooms or a campus;
- the use of new methods of teaching; and
- ideas (Rumble and Keegan 1982: 12).

In addition, open accountability is another important aspect of the term 'open'. The course material produced by the open universities is open to scrutiny and is criticized if it is not up to the mark. Second, open access is an equally important characteristic of the system. Most of the teaching material is accessible to people who may not be the registered students of an open university, particularly its radio and TV programmes can be taken advantage of by anyone. Even the print material is available to people other than the students of the open university.

Doubtless, there are several similarities between 'open learning' and 'distance education'. However, the term 'open learning' conveys a certain amount of vagueness about it. Moreover, when we look at the open universities and open learning institutions, we find that all that is conveyed by 'openness' is not to be found in quite a few of these institutions. Open learning, therefore, is not always synonymous with open universities or distance education. Several open universities and open learning institutions prescribe certain entry qualifications and debar those who do not fulfil the conditions laid down by them. Therefore, if the idea is to provide educational facilities to a larger number of people scattered all over, i.e. providing greater access to education, the term 'distance education' would be more appropriate. This term basically emphasizes separation of the teacher and the learner, and planning of educational programmes and material by an educational organization and the use of technical media on a large scale.

Distance education has been defined by several writers like Wedemeyer, Holmberg, Moore, Peters and Keegan, each emphasizing certain aspects of the system. It is, however, to the credit of Desmond Keegan that he has attempted a synthesis of most of the definitions. On the basis of this, he finds that distance education has the following important characteristics:

- the quasi-permanent separation of teacher and learner throughout the length of the learning process; this distinguishes it from conventional face-to-face education;
- the influence of an educational organization both in planning and preparation of learning materials and in the provision of student support services; this distinguishes it from private study and teach-yourself programmes;
- the use of technical media – print, audio, video or computer – unites teacher and learner and carries the content of the course;
- the provision of two-way communication so that the student may benefit from or even initiate a dialogue; this distinguishes it from other uses of technology in education;
- the quasi-permanent absence of a learning group throughout the length of the learning process, so that people are usually taught as individuals and not in groups, with the possibility of occasional meetings for both didactic and socialization purposes (Keegan 1986: 49).

In addition, he finds that there are two other socio-cultural determinants which are necessary pre-conditions and necessary consequences of distance education. They are the presence of more industrialized features than in conventional or oral education; and privatization of institutional learning (Keegan 1986: 50).

WHY DISTANCE EDUCATION?

Distance education is being called upon to meet some of the felt-needs in several countries all over the world (Sharma 1986). The nature of felt-needs varies from country to country, depending upon the stage of its development; but the necessity for distance education is being recognized both in developed and developing countries for a variety of reasons, some of which are common to all, while others are specific to particular countries depending on their individual requirements. For instance, in practically all countries, it is felt that equality of opportunities for education should be provided, and that there should be greater access to higher education (Selim 1986). Those who have missed educational opportunities earlier should have a second chance. Further, continuing education is necessary to meet the changing requirements of those people who are in work and for others such as housewives. These two requirements exist in nearly all countries. But in developing countries, there is also a need to meet the shortages of technical manpower which the existing conventional universities are unable to meet. Also in some countries, students who have completed school education and want to go to university are unable to do so and look to distance education to satisfy their expectations. Further, the quality of education often also has to be improved. A system that can meet all these demands has to be innovative and flexible. In view of certain limitations of the formal education, it is increasingly realized that distance education can meet some of the educational needs in all the countries, irrespective of their ideologies or stages of development. No wonder, several countries in the world practise distance education of one type or another (Taylor 1986). Good examples of distance education systems exist in the UK, Spain, the Netherlands, France, Australia, Canada, New Zealand, Japan, China, India, Indonesia, Pakistan, Thailand, Korea, the USSR, Venezuela, and Costa Rica.

DISTANCE EDUCATION – HOW?

When we look at various distance education institutions in the world, we find that they are of different types. But broadly, as Keegan and Rumble (1982: 28) point out, there are two models: (a) mixed or hybrid institutions and (b) autonomous institutions. Although in the mixed model there are several varieties, here we are mainly concerned with distance education programmes run by conventional universities. The best examples of this are the off-campus studies or external programmes run by Australian universities and correspondence courses in India. The advantage of this model is that generally the same courses which are offered to the on-campus students are also offered to the off-campus students. In several cases, the teaching faculty and the examinations taken by the students are also the same, Therefore, the students in such a system have the benefit of a formal system of education. However, in some countries like India, correspondence courses have been facing several problems. They relate to the credibility of the correspondence courses and autonomy of the institutions. It is alleged that the correspondence courses are looked down upon as second-class education. It is a system of education which is just tolerated by the conventional system. Further, the correspondence course institutions have little freedom to formulate their own courses and the rigidities of the conventional system are also applicable to them. The conventional universities, barring a few exceptions, would not like to spend any money on institutes of correspondence courses. The general philosophy which governs correspondence education is that it should be financially self-supporting and 'not incur any loss'; it should not be 'a liability' to the university. On top of this, the correspondence institutions are expected to earn some money for the university concerned.

The second organizational type of distance education is the autonomous model (Keegan and Rumble 1982: 28). In several countries, full-fledged universities have been started to promote and strengthen distance education. These universities, like their conventional counterparts, are free to frame their academic policies, design the courses, teach the students, examine them and award degrees (Ram Reddy 1986). Though the University of South Africa is the first full-fledged distance teaching university, the British Open University (UKOU) is regarded as the leader in this field. Its establishment and its high quality work have inspired many other countries. As a result, today we find that open universities have been set up in many parts of the world. Examples of other open universities exist in West Germany, the Netherlands, Spain, Canada, China, Japan, Thailand, Venezuela, Costa Rica, Sri Lanka, Pakistan, India, Indonesia, and Israel. While the main features of most open universities are similar they are different from each other in several respects. Each has been established taking into account the peculiar conditions of its own country. In other words, each open university has its own national characteristics.

OBJECTIVES OF DISTANCE EDUCATION

Providing a second opportunity to study for those who missed such an opportunity earlier is an objective of almost all the open universities. There are several sections of society who, for a variety of reasons, do not pass through the conventional education system and who would like to have a chance to study. Access to conventional universities is limited in many countries. By establishing an open university, this access is widened to provide equality of opportunities for higher education. There is a shortage of scientific and technical manpower in some countries and the conventional universities are unable to cope with the demand. The open universities are established with a view to meeting such demands. The best example of this is China's Central Radio and Television University (CRTVU).

Improving the quality of education is another objective. This is particularly so in some of the developing countries like Indonesia and India. There is a need to make education relevant to the needs of the country and also to provide lifelong education for working people and housewives. Such a system needs to be innovative and flexible, which is possible only through distance education. Providing educational opportunities to working adults is the objective of Canada's Athabasca University (AU), Japan's University of the Air (UA), Spain's Universidad Nacional de Educación a Distancia (UNED), India's Indira Gandhi National Open University and the Andhra Pradesh Open University (APOU). Continuing education with a view to meeting professional training needs is also an objective common to most of these universities.

Demands from the growing number of secondary school students who wish to take up university places are increasing in some countries, and often, the conventional universities are unable to meet them. Indonesia has established its Universitas Terbuka (UT) with one of its main objectives being to meet this demand. The Indira Gandhi National Open University, which is the latest to be established, has several objectives before it:

- to provide opportunities for higher education to a large segment of the population;
- to promote the educational well-being of the community;
- to encourage the open university and distance education system in the country; and
- to coordinate and determine the standards of distance education in the country.

Open universities are thus established with certain definite objectives in view.

ADMISSIONS

Admissions into courses are open in some universities but in others they are not so open. The criteria for admissions vary from one institution to another. In the UKOU, admission is open to all and the university does not insist on formal entrance qualifications for its degree courses; the admission is based on a first-come-first-served basis. Athabasca University admits anybody who is 18 years of age and over. The FernUniversität (FU), Universitas Terbuka and the Central Radio and Television University admit students only if they have either a formal university entrance qualification or have qualified in the national examinations held. The Indira Gandhi National Open University and the Andhra Pradesh Open University have a dual approach towards admissions into undergraduate programmes. Those who have the formal entry qualifications are eligible to join and those who do not have such qualifications will have to pass the entrance test conducted by the university. In both these universities, admission into BSc courses is restricted only to the first category of students. Thus, we see that the open universities are not totally open and there are varying degrees of restrictions in their openness. They are, however, less closed and restrictive than their conventional counterparts.

CHOICE OF COURSES

Generally, students of open universities have more freedom than their conventional counterparts to choose their courses. For instance, it is possible in the Andhra Pradesh Open University for a student of philosophy to study chemistry at the undergraduate level, if he so chooses – a combination which is normally not permitted in a conventional system in India.

Three types of programmes – degree, diploma and certificate – are generally offered by several open universities. Degree programmes are undergraduate courses, and in some cases, master's and research. A wide variety of diploma and certificate programmes are available in these universities.

A large number of courses is provided by the open universities for study. The CRTVU in China offers about 149 courses. About 130 courses are available in arts, social sciences, mathematics, science and technology, and education at the UKOU. In addition, science and technology courses such as industry and technology (UA), physics, biology, mechanical engineering, electronics, machine designs, basic and digital computers (CRTVU); music, chemistry and electronics (UKOU), food and nutrition, general science, electrical wiring, child care and development (Allama Iqbal Open University – AIOU); and BSc (APOU), are taught. This disproves the general impression that open universities teach only arts and not the science and technology courses. There are examples of excellent science and technology programmes being offered by these universities. In fact, in China, some of the provincial television universities are even contemplating teaching courses in medicine. It is significant to note that quite a few of the courses provided by the open universities are interdisciplinary in nature. There is a variation in the course system. Some, like the APOU, follow the conventional system and courses have to be studied for a whole year by the students. But several open universities follow the credit system which provides for a large amount of flexibility in their study. The number and size of the credits vary from one institution to another. A student at the UKOU is required to complete six credits (eight if honours is taken) for a degree programme. On the other hand, several open universities have a large number of credits for an undergraduate programme; 124 credits have to be earned at the UA in Japan, and at the IGNOU it is 96 credits. The credit of the UKOU is much larger in size than the credits of other universities. It is generally felt that the smaller the size of the credit, the greater is the flexibility in the system.

INSTRUCTIONAL SYSTEM

Almost all open universities follow the multimedia approach to education.

Multimedia includes print material, audio-video material and broadcasts. Tutorials are provided at study centres. Print material is considered to be the most important in most of these universities. This is supported by radio and television broadcasts and/or audio and video tapes. In the UKOU, multimedia support for print material is provided in the form of television and radio programmes produced in partnership with the BBC. These are an integral part of most courses and they take up around 10 per cent of the students' time on average. At the UA, during the 15 weeks in each semester, 2–credit courses are broadcast 15 times (one lecture a week of 45 minutes each) and 4–credit courses are broadcast 30 times (two lectures a week of 45 minutes each). Each course is relayed from either radio or television. In China, the TV transmission time for the programme offered by the CRTVU is 33 hours per week.

In addition to radio and television relays, provision is made for audio- and video-cassettes. In countries like the UK, individual students can afford to have audio-cassettes and, in some cases video-cassettes also, but in some countries like India, these have to be provided at the study centres. Tutorial back-up is an essential ingredient of the open university education system. Where there is a well-developed telephone system, as in the UK and Canada, students can use the telephones to contact their tutors. In addition, there is also provision for face-to-face tutorials. Dependence on the face-to-face tutorials increases in countries like India and Pakistan where teachers and students have little access to telephones.

ENROLMENT

Open universities all over the world have attracted large numbers of students; in some cases the numbers are staggering. In the APOU, there are about 40,000 students; the UKOU has 100,000; the STOU has 400,000; and the CRTVU has a little more than one million and they are aiming at two million by 1990. These numbers are very high by any yardstick and are unthinkable in the conventional university system. Access to such large numbers is made possible mainly because of the distance education system.

Unlike the conventional universities, open universities attract students from diverse backgrounds – working and non-working, young and old, married and unmarried. At the FU, 77 per cent of the students are males and about 23 per cent are females; about 53 per cent of the students are in the age group of 26–35 and about 23 per cent are less than 25 years of age. About 45 per cent of its students are married.

In the CRTVU, the students comprise workers, cadres and teachers, and science and technology personnel. The profile of the typical student at the UNED is: male, 30 years of age, married, perhaps with two children, employed in public administration or the private sector, whose aim is to achieve a degree in order to increase the possibilities of furthering success in his career. In the Korea Air and Correspondence University (KACU), 80 per cent of the students are gainfully employed; the largest number, 36 per cent, are in business, while teachers and government officials each account for approximately 20 per cent. All age groups are to be found in the university, but a majority of them (about 63 per cent) are between 26–40 years of age. Students over 41 years constitute about 7 per cent.

There are instances of students over 70 years of age studying some of the courses of universities. From this, it is clear that diverse age groups enrol themselves in the open universities and the motives for their enrolment also vary.

STUDENT EVALUATION

Evaluation of the work of the student is of two types: continuous evaluation which involves periodic tests or assignments, and the semester-end or year-end final examination. Generally, importance is attached to both, but this varies from one university to another. At the UKOU and the IGNOU, the students' results are declared on the basis of the combined credits. There are no marks or weightage attached to the continuous assessment at the APOU. Only when the students pass guidance by correspondence with their tutors are they permitted to take the examination at the end of the semester by the UA. In this university, the assessment of students is mainly on the basis of an end-of-semester examination.

At the UNED, the evaluation of the students is of two types: (a) at a distance, and (b) twice yearly formal examinations at the study centres.

Deciding the importance to be attached to internal assessment and external examination depends very much on the prevailing educational systems in the countries concerned. The choice of an assessment system is normally heavily constrained by the social and national contexts within which a distance education institution operates (Connors 1981: 175).

Connors argues that there is a very strong case for informal assessment and formal continuous assessment. Some of this assessment should be conducted under controlled conditions if impersonation, etc., is to be guarded against. The results of this assessment should be conflated in such a way as to satisfy both teachers and students (Connors 1981: 175). Since distance education is still suspect in the eyes of many, high standards in the assessment of students become all the more imperative.

GOVERNANCE

Open universities in all countries have the same status as the conventional universities in the educational system of the countries concerned. But the requirements of the open universities and the nature of their work are very different from those of the conventional universities. As has been pointed out earlier, they have academic as well as industrial characteristics. The governance of such universities, therefore, has to be such that it promotes the cause of distance education (Reddy 1986).

In organising the universities, one clearly sees the impact of the conventional universities. This is mainly because the planners are accustomed to conventional universities and in the case of open universities they would not like to make bold and unknown experiments in their organization.

Broadly, there are three types of staff who work in open universities – academic, technical and administrative and supportive staff. The tasks they perform are very different from those performed in conventional universities. As a result, the persons working in the open universities need to be oriented and trained in distance education. These universities have to evolve a culture of their own and anyone working in them must follow that culture.

REGIONAL AND LOCAL CENTRES

In organizing its work, an open university has to maintain a delicate balance between centralization and decentralization. It is said that in a conventional university, it is the teacher who teaches, but in the open universities it is the institution which teaches. The courses are designed, written, produced and distributed by the university. In all these activities, there is a high degree of centralization. These universities, however, need to decentralize their student support services by establishing regional centres and study centres.

Generally, tutorial support and audio-visual media facilities are available at these centres. This is also the place where students have opportunities to meet their fellow students and exchange ideas. Such peer group interaction has great educational value. An interesting feature of the study centres is that they are set up in existing institutions and no separate infrastructure in the form of buildings is created.

COST-EFFECTIVENESS

Educational planners are attracted by the concept of open universities because of their cost-effectiveness. While it is difficult to compare an open university with a conventional university, it is widely believed that the former is less expensive than the latter. Figures are not available for all open universities but here we shall refer to some work that has been done in the UKOU and a few others. The unit cost of the undergraduate programme in the UKOU was £1,800 per student (in the 1983–4 academic year). It is subject to variation between the extremes of £1,400 for arts students and £2,340 for sciences students per year. This compares favourably with the UGC norms of £3,510 per student a year or over £4,700 per year if the student's maintenance grant is included. The student has to pay around 600 to 800 Marks for a full-time course at the FU in West Germany. At the UT, Indonesia, a student pays between Rs 20,000 and Rs 35,000 for a semester depending upon the type of course. The cost per student is $240 a year in the UNED of Spain. In India, a student pays about Rs 500 a year for the undergraduate course at the APOU. At the IGNOU, the fee is Rs 750 for the one-year diploma course in management. In Thailand, calculations show that the average cost per graduate is lower in the STOU than in other universities (Srisa-an 1986: 31) It is 2,341 baht per student at the STOU whereas at Mahidol University, it is 120,700 baht, which is considered to be the highest among conventional universities and 11,463 baht per student at the Thammasat University, whose per capita expenditure is considered to be the lowest. The Evaluation Mission from the UK Overseas Development Administration estimates that:

> taking into account amortization of capital costs, salaries and other recurrent expenditure together with student numbers, the AIOU (Pakistan) would progressively show considerable cost advantages over other conventional universities.

The cost comparison between AIOU and conventional institutions in Pakistan for students in BA would reveal that in the former it is less by about 39 per cent (Srisa-an: 1986). Thus, the general belief that education through open universities is highly cost-effective is fully supported by the empirical data.

To conclude: I have described the concept, the need, and the organizational form of the open university (autonomous model of distance education). The origin of distance education lies basically in the philosophy that the society has a responsibility to provide educational opportunities to those who, for some reason or another, cannot go to the conventional system. In the *Mahabharata*, there is the case of Eklavya who wanted to learn under the guru, Dronacharya, who, as is well known, refused to take him as a student because he was neither a Brahmin nor a Kshatriya.

However, Eklavya was determined to learn, and his will and devotion made the *vidya* he sought from his guru accessible to him even though the guru himself was inaccessible. In those days, a Dronacharya could refuse to take an Eklavya as a student and society would tolerate it. Today's democratic society can neither afford to overlook the interests of the Eklavyas nor tolerate the Dronacharyas. Distance education and the open universities facilitate this; open universities are universities for the modern Eklavyas. Availability of communication technologies make this possible today. It is said that there was a time when, if a student wanted to learn, he had to go to Aristotle. Today, we have the means of bringing Aristotle to the student. It is time that the educational planners took full advantage of the technologies available for extending educational opportunities to all those who want to have access to them. For open universities are veritably the new temples of learning responding to new needs.

REFERENCES

Connors, B. (1981) 'Assessment of the distance education student', in A. Kaye and G. Rumble (eds) *Distance Teaching for Higher and Adult Education*, London: Croom Helm.
Holmberg, B. (1985) *Status and Trends of Distance Education*, Sweden: Lector Publishing.
Jevons, F. R. (1983) 'The role of distance education: towards parity of esteem', in Association of Commonwealth Universities (1984) *Technological Innovation: University Roles*, London: Association of Commonwealth Universities.
Kaye, A. (1981) 'Origins and structures', in A. Kaye and G. Rumble (eds) *Distance Teaching for Higher and Adult Education*, London: Croom Helm.
Keegan, D. (1986) *The Foundations of Distance Education*, London: Croom Helm.
Keegan, D. and Rumble, G. (1982) 'Distance teaching at university level', in G. Rumble and K. Harry (eds), *The Distance Teaching Universities*, London: Croom Helm.
Mackenzie, N., Postgate, R. and Scupham, J., (1975) *Open Learning: Systems and Problems of Post-secondary Education*, Paris: UNESCO.
Perry, W. (1976) *Open University: a Personal Account by the First Vice-Chancellor*, Milton Keynes: Open University Press.
Reddy, G. R. (1982) *Open Education System in India – its Place and Potential*, Hyderabad: Andhra Pradesh Open University.
Reddy, G. R. (1983) 'Perspectives on distance education', *Indian Express*, 8 December.
Reddy, G. R. (1986) 'Planning, management and monitoring of distance education', in Asian Development Bank *Distance Education*, Manila: ABD, 2 vols.
Ruggles, R. H. (1982) *Learning at a Distance and New Technology*, Vancouver: Educational Research Institute of British Columbia.
Rumble, G. and Harry, K. (eds) (1982) *The Distance Teaching Universities*, London: Croom Helm.
Rumble, G. and Keegan, D. (1982) 'Introduction', in G. Rumble and K. Harry (eds) *The Distance Teaching Universities*, London: Croom Helm.
Selim, M. (1986) 'Distance education in Asia and Pacific', in Asian Development Bank *Distance Education*, Manila: ABD, 2 vols.
Sharma, M. (1986) 'Issues in distance education', in Asian Development Bank *Distance Education*, Manila: ABD, 2 vols.

Smith, R. C. (1986) 'Growth and scope of distance education', in Asian Development Bank *Distance Education*, Manila: ABD, 2 vols.

Srisa-an, Wichit (1986) 'Financing and cost effectiveness of distance education', in Asian Development Bank *Distance Education*, Manila: ABD, 2 vols.

Taylor, J. (1986) 'Application of distance education in formal and non-formal education', in Asian Development Bank *Distance Education*, Manila: ABD, 2 vols.

20 National developments and international cooperation in distance education in Commonwealth Africa

Hilary Perraton

Commonwealth Africa now has more than twenty-five years' experience of distance education. Indeed, Martin Kaunda, who worked in adult education in Zambia, took the story further back with his view of the talking drum as its ancestor (Kabwasa and Kaunda 1973: 3). Even in the 1960s Botswana, Kenya, Malawi and Zambia were among the countries where governments decided to use distance education for teacher training and for secondary education. By the mid-1980s there were between 25 and 30 publicly funded distance-teaching institutions in Commonwealth Africa alone. Distance education no longer looks like a short-term expedient; instead it seems to have a permanent place in the armoury of ministries of education. We therefore need both to define that place – to ask what distance education does best – and to see what we can do to raise its effectiveness. British Commonwealth experience gives some pointers.

For convenience I will define distance education as an educational process in which a significant proportion of the teaching is conducted by someone removed in space and/or time from the learner. This definition thus embraces programmes in which some face-to-face education is linked with work at a distance. It also embraces work that uses a variety of different educational media including both print and broadcasting.

It is useful to look separately at experience in non-formal education, for school level education, for teacher training and for higher education. It is particularly appropriate to start with non-formal education.

NON-FORMAL EDUCATION

In Africa, as in other parts of the South, distance education has been used for non-formal education, in areas like health, agriculture, family planning, rural development and political education. Botswana, Tanzania and Zambia have all used radio campaigns for public education on a large scale. Beyond Africa, the radio schools of Latin America have worked outside the state system of education to offer basic education to adults and children outside school. Ministries of agriculture and health have used distance-teaching methods, sometimes labelling them as development support communication. There is a documented record of success and failure (Young *et al.* 1980; Perraton *et al.* 1983; Hornik 1988) which formed the basis for a pan-Commonwealth meeting held in Nairobi earlier this year [1990] to review the potential of distance teaching for non-formal education. In reviewing Commonwealth experience the draft report of the meeting notes the following.

> In east Africa our host institution, the College of Education and External Studies of the University of Nairobi, has long experience as a specialized distance-teaching institution which has worked mainly in formal education but has also moved into non-formal education in training literacy tutors. Two non-government organizations have headquarters in Nairobi. The African Medical and Research Foundation (AMREF), widely known for its flying doctor service, also runs programmes of public education in health, using distance-teaching methods. The Institut Africain pour le Développement Economique et Social-Formation (INADES-formation), whose parent body was established in Côte d'Ivoire by the Roman Catholic bishops of West Africa, uses correspondence courses with group support for education on agriculture and rural development. Tanzania has run radio campaigns, using both government and party structures for their organization, in order to address topics that have included political education, health and forestry. Botswana's agricultural extension service, which is part of the Ministry of Agriculture, uses both conventional extension methods and mass media with the aim of raising agricultural productivity. In Mauritius, the College of the Air, established by an Act of Parliament with a measure of autonomy but with finance from the ministry of education, offers both formal and non-formal distance teaching programmes.

But these are relatively modest developments, stronger as demonstrations than as permanent services of public education. In many countries there remains a contrast between the achievement and recognition awarded to distance education in the formal sector and the much more limited recognition of its value for non-formal education.

SCHOOLING

When we turn to programmes that are something like schools, it is useful to distinguish between three different approaches to distance education. These are:

1   to provide education outside school, usually by means of correspondence courses, for individual students working at home;
2   to use similar materials for groups of students in study centres, offering something like a school but at reduced costs;
3   using distance-teaching methods within conventional schools in order to raise their quality.

The first model has a long but inglorious history. It was the mainstay of the British and South African correspondence colleges which dominated distance education in Africa until ministries of education and universities moved into the field. It has remained part of their work. But the sad evidence is that few independent students, working at home and without support from a study centre, succeed in studying at a distance. Curran and Murphy (1989: 15) found that in two of the countries they surveyed fewer than 5 per cent of enrolled students had sat for the examinations after five years of study and up to three-quarters of the students had stopped studying completely.

Successful distance study appears to demand high motivation, that students have already learned how to learn, that they have access to libraries when they need them, and can get support from family or friends familiar with the educational problems they are tackling. For many learners, working alone, in many parts of the continent, these conditions do not apply.

The difficulties of the isolated student led to the development of the second model. Both Malawi and Zambia developed study centres with much more modest resources than those of a conventional secondary school and in which the burden of instruction was carried by correspondence courses with some radio support. Study centre supervisors helped students as they used their courses (Wolff and Futagami 1982). Other study centre systems have been developed outside Africa. In some parts of Latin America, for example, radio has been more extensively used to support centres of this kind than has generally been the case in Africa (Perraton 1983).

In the third model, distance-teaching methods have been used to raise the quality of secondary schools and to change their curricula. In some cases, broadcasting has been used on a grand scale in the context of a programme of educational reform. The classic example was in Côte d'Ivoire, but television was also used in American Samoa and El Salvador in similar ways. The high costs of television – sometimes ten times the cost of radio – coupled with the practical difficulty of running a rural television service in a country with a low density of population and limited mains electricity proved disastrous:

> Disillusionment with the initial promise of educational media has been most acute in the case of television. Compared to other media, expectations were higher, the flagship projects received more attention, up front

investments in capital were much higher, goals were more comprehensive and collapses were that much more painfully felt. As a result . . . World Bank lending for television projects has fallen off dramatically and . . . worldwide use of television in distance learning institutions is decreasing.

(Nettleton 1991: 15)

There are, however, other approaches to the use of distance-teaching methods to support schools. Zimbabwe has valuable and encouraging experience of the use of distance-teaching materials to support and supplement education within schools. In Mauritius, correspondence courses with broadcast support have been used to introduce new subjects to the school curriculum (Dodds 1982). There has been widespread use mainly at primary level of interactive radio, in which students are required to make frequent active responses to direct radio teaching in a technique which might be adapted at secondary level.

While the three models are contrasting they share one common feature. All rely on careful and thorough preparation of teaching materials at a central institution. As Nielsen (1990: 12) points out:

One of the particular strengths of the IRI (Interactive Radio Instruction) programs . . . was that the materials and systems were based on solid principles of instructional design, geared towards holding student attention and interest.

The development of high quality teaching materials is a necessary condition for the success of distance-education programmes though not a sufficient one.

There is limited data on the effectiveness of all three models. There are always difficulties in examining the effectiveness of out-of-school education as cohorts of students, studying in-school and out, are rarely comparable. Nevertheless the data on independent distance study, the first model discussed above, is so discouraging that the model would seem to be of limited value for ministries of education or for the people they are serving.

Malawi Correspondence College (MCC) provides the best documented example of the second model of using distance education in study centres. In considering its effectiveness we need to remember that those using study centres had performed less well at the primary-leaving examination than those who went to secondary school. A study done ten years ago found that, with a cost per student lower than that for regular students, the cost per successful student compared favourably with boarding schools but unfavourably with day schools (Wolff and Futagami 1982).

Overall pass rates for MCC students on the National Junior Certificate examination have been between 10 and 22 percent over the past few years.

These pass rates are low compared with those of regular secondary schools, but they are satisfactory in the light of the MCC's much lower admissions standards.

(World Bank 1988: 59)

More recently the study centre system has expanded and, while in 1985 the day secondary schools were still producing junior certificate holders more cheaply than the study centres, by 1988, 'the cost of producing Junior Certificate passes was less in the study centre system, K429 as compared with K1249 for day secondary schools' (Murphy 1990: 41–2).

There is data, too, to suggest that distance-teaching methods can be effective in raising the quality of education in schools. A comparison across five countries of the use of interactive radio concluded that

IRI program classes were consistently and significantly higher than the conventional classes in all countries. Besides that, research shows that both students and teachers are positive about the system and that it engages them fully. Because students achieve better under the system and are more engaged in their studies, drop-out and repeating rates have been expected to fall. So far, however, there has been no firm evidence that this has happened. There is, however, evidence from one country, Thailand, that relative achievement is even more positive in rural areas than in urban ones . . . In another comparison, when IRI was examined in relation to other interventions, its impact on achievement was shown to be greater than for either the introduction of textbooks or teacher training.

(Nielsen 1990: 8–9)

In Mauritius the use of correspondence materials and broadcasts in schools appeared to raise the quality of teaching while broadening the curriculum and achieving improved examination pass rates (Dodds 1982: 123).

Costs for the third model have usually been additional to the costs of regular education. (In the first two models costs have been for an alternative to regular school.) In some cases this means that it has been impossible to institutionalize the programmes: add-on recurrent costs for interactive radio have typically been between US$0.25 and $1.00 per student per year (Nielsen 1990: 9), costs which are relatively high against a 1983 average annual cost per primary school student – the level at which most interactive radio projects have been addressed – of $48 (World Bank 1988: 34).

TEACHER EDUCATION

Ministries of education in Africa have used distance education for teacher training at both primary and secondary level in order to expand the teaching force in response to the expansion of primary and secondary schools. Programmes have varied in size and in duration and in their emphasis on general education, on teaching trainees about the subjects they will themselves teach, and on training them in the techniques of teaching. The extent of African experience means that some firm data is available on the effectiveness of distance education for these purposes: Table 20.1 sets out enrolment and completion data on a number of programmes. In order to expand on what is known about this area the Commonwealth Secretariat and the Commonwealth of Learning are jointly undertaking a review of the use of distance education for teacher training in countries of the North and the South.

Table 20.1 African teacher training projects using distance education

	Enrolled No.	Completed course		Completed course and passed exam	
		No.	%	No.	%
Botswana 1968–72[a]	608	539	88	no exam	
Kenya 1968–74[a]	8,433	n/a	n/a	7,632	91
Kenya 1982–85[b]	3,600	3,500	99	n/a	88
Swaziland 1973–76[a]	600	580	97	no exam	
Tanzania 1976–88[c]	45,534	n/a	n/a	37,988	83
Uganda 1967–70[a]	1,000	948	95	876	88
Zimbabwe 1981–88[d]	8,720	n/a	n/a	c.8000	n/a

Notes [a] Young *et al.* 1980: 34; [b] Curran and Murphy 1989: 81; [c] Mählck and Temu 1989: 27; [d] Gatawa 1986: 20 and 24.

Data on the use of distance education for teacher training goes beyond the narrow questions of cost effectiveness. Internal and external assessments, both of them relatively informal, concluded that the Swaziland scheme had been successful in terms of its objectives of changing both curricula and methods (Young *et al.* 1980: 32–3). In Zimbabwe, where the Zimbabwe Integrated Teacher Education Course (ZINTEC) programme was used to produce primary school teachers urgently needed after independence, the ministry of higher education was sufficiently impressed with ZINTEC's results that it is understood to be in the process of introducing a more permanent element of distance education in its programmes of teacher training. In Tanzania, there is evidence from two separate research studies of the success of the teacher training programme in producing more effective teachers (Chale 1983; Mählck and Temu 1989).

Nevertheless, if we consider the adequacy of the programmes, in terms of the need for trained teachers, criticisms remain. In Botswana, for example, the teacher training scheme which ran from the late 1960s to the early 1970s was designed as a once-and-for all crash solution to the problem of untrained teachers. Today, with a much expanded teaching force, there are still some 2,500 untrained teachers in the system (personal communication). Similarly, despite the running of two programmes through the University of Nairobi, Kenya in 1984 had 33,385 untrained teachers, 28 per cent of the total (Curran and Murphy 1989). It may well be that many educational planners have not been convinced of the legitimacy of distance education for teacher training.

TERTIARY EDUCATION

If distance education has become an accepted and legitimate partner in the last quarter century, this is largely the result of the work of the open universities. The British Open University established in 1969 is now the second largest university in the country (after the federal University of London) not just in student numbers but in numbers of annual graduations. Looking at it in crude terms, it is producing one-fifth of the country's graduates for one-ninth of the cost. But it has had another effect which may in the long run be as significant: of bringing distance education out of the dark, away from the image of the unsuccessful studying from yellowed sheets of duplicated notes and into a position where people are proud to be students of the University and both are justifiably proud of the quality of the educational materials. Where that university led the way, some twenty others have followed - in India and Pakistan, Thailand and Indonesia, Spain and Venezuela and others - but not in Africa. One minor consequence of this is that the evidence on the effectiveness of distance teaching in tertiary education comes mainly from outside the continent. It does, however, suggest that in both industrialized and developing countries it is possible to produce graduates at between one-third and two-thirds of the cost of doing so in a conventional institution (Perraton 1982 and Perraton 1987).

Distance education at tertiary level does not demand an open university. There is an alternative tradition which goes back to the University of Queensland in 1911, of establishing a bimodal university which teaches both face-to-face and at a distance. This has become the dominant pattern in the two rich Commonwealth countries with federal constitutions, Australia and Canada. And this model has influenced the thinking of the Universities of Lagos, Nairobi and Zambia, which already have departments of distance education, and the University of Zimbabwe, which is considering establishing one.

INTERNATIONAL COOPERATION

While much of the development of distance education in Africa has been confined within national frontiers, there have been a number of international activities designed to support that process. Botswana, Lesotho and Swaziland began working together through what became the Distance Learning Association in the early 1970s. Government-supported institutions in all three countries have worked together, particularly in sharing information and in staff training. An African Association of Distance Education was set up in 1973. INADES-Formation has found common ground in a number of countries and is no longer restricted to francophone Africa. And, of course, donor aid has supported the establishment and development of distance-teaching institutions in many parts of the continent.

The Commonwealth has played a part in some of these developments. Commonwealth experience from Australia and New Zealand was called upon in setting up some of the first government distance-teaching institutions in the 1960s and 1970s. The Commonwealth Fund for Technical Cooperation provided course writers who produced materials jointly for use in Botswana and Lesotho. More recently the Fund has been involved with the South West African People's Organisation (SWAPO), the African National Congress (ANC) and the Pan African Congress (PAC) in establishing the Namibian Extension Unit, now repatriated, and the South African Extension Unit based here in Tanzania. Commonwealth interest in and support for distance education remains. That interest led, two years ago, to the establishment by Heads of Government of the Commonwealth of Learning whose function is to

> create and widen access to opportunities for learning, by promoting cooperation between universities, colleges and other educational institutions throughout the Commonwealth, making use of the potential offered by distance education and by the application of communication technologies to education (Commonwealth Secretariat 1988: 2).

The Commonwealth Secretariat has been involved in one other move towards cooperation in distance education: a review of its potential within Southern Africa Development Coordination Conference (SADCC). Following a request from the Regional Training Council of SADCC, the Commonwealth Fund for Technical Cooperation commissioned a review which was completed in 1987 and which recommended the creation of an institute for distance education in southern Africa (Jevons *et al.* 1987). It is understood that the recommendation has been accepted in principle by SADCC but it has not yet been implemented. A further study was carried out on behalf of the European Commission (Leibbrandt 1989): both studies agree that there would be great merit in establishing some kind of structure for cooperation between distance-teaching institutions in the subregion. There is one other, relevant, proposal on the table. In its report on Education in Sub-Saharan Africa the World Bank recommends the establishment of one or more regional centres for distance education within Africa (World Bank 1988: 111). Such an institution might be launched as a university, or develop into one.

It was noted above that Africa has not developed an open university and it may be that the continent should lead the world in doing so not on a national but on an international basis. There is one severely practical argument here, although of course there would be practical and political difficulties as well. It has to do with population and money. The quality of the teaching material produced by open universities is made possible because significant resources are committed to course development. In turn, the scale of those resources is justified by the relatively large number of students who are likely to enrol on the courses. In anglophone Africa, however, with the single exception of Nigeria, national populations are smaller than those of most countries which have successfully established open universities. It is therefore difficult for any one country to justify investment in course development at tertiary level at the scale which has led to the success of the existing open universities. Similarly, even where universities decide to establish a distance-education department, they are likely to have serious difficulties in releasing adequate funds for course development. These are among the considerations that led SADCC to consider the possibility of establishing some kind of cooperative structure for distance education: they may lead this meeting to explore ways of taking the idea further. Of course the establishment of an open university, of one kind or another, is not the only way of doing things: it is necessary to stress – as both the SADCC-based reports do – that a cooperative structure is not necessarily a university which enrols its own students but may equally be an institution which serves, and works with, other educational bodies.

WHERE NEXT?

The Commonwealth Secretariat's work with SADCC, in the process of establishing the Commonwealth of Learning, and in its recent meeting about distance teaching for non-formal education, mean that we have taken a preliminary look at some of the issues to be examined at this meeting. That provides one clear starting-point: the earlier part of this chapter has tried to establish that distance education has worked in Africa. It has successes to its credit. The record of success and failure allows us to build on the successes and avoid the failures with a considerable degree of confidence. Five issues look particularly important.

- Can we take forward the idea of one or more regional institutions?
- There is work to be done in information, including advocacy to decision makers – where there is something good to advocate – in providing information about what distance education can best do for those working in ministries of education and universities and in getting information about good practice to practitioners.
- Training: what is already being done and not being done? We would make a plea here to remember the needs of those working in non-formal education, and those working for non-government organizations, as well as those working in the formal and government sectors.
- Research and evaluation: we don't yet know enough about the best way of doing distance education, and don't effectively disseminate what is known.
- Institutional development: the existing institutions provide a framework within which much good education is being done. But many are starved of resources and could do a significantly better job for a marginal increase in resources.

If we can make progress along all, or any, of these paths, the learners of Africa may in the long run benefit from our decision making and planning here in Arusha.

REFERENCES

Chale, E. M. (1983) 'Teaching and training: an evaluation of primary school teachers in Tanzania following preservice training in teachers colleges and through distance teaching', London: London University, Institute of Education (unpublished PhD thesis).

Commonwealth Secretariat (1988) *Memorandum of Understanding on the Commonwealth of Learning*, London: Commonwealth Secretariat.

Curran, C. and Murphy, P. (1989) *Distance Education at Second Level in Six Countries in Africa*, Dublin: HEDCO.

Dodds, T. (1982) 'The Mauritius College of the Air', in Perraton, H. (ed.) (1982) *Alternative Routes to Formal Education: Distance Teaching for School Equivalency*, Baltimore: Johns Hopkins University Press.

Gatawa, B. S. M. (1986) 'The Zimbabwe Integrated National Teacher Education Course (ZINTEC)' in Treffgarne, C. (ed.) *Education in Zimbabwe*, London: University of London Institute of Education, DICE Occasional Paper 9.

Hornik, R. C. (1988) *Development Communication*, New York: Longman.

Jevons, F. R., Northcott, P. H., and Polhemus, J. H. (1987) *Southern Africa Distance Education Project.* Report to Southern Africa Development Coordination Conference, the Government of Swaziland and the Commonwealth Fund for Technical Cooperation, Geelong: Deakin University.

Kabwasa, A. and Kaunda, M. M. (1973) *Correspondence Education in Africa*, London: Routledge and Kegan Paul.

Leibbrandt, G. J. (1989) *An Open University in the SADCC Region*. Report to the Commission of the European Communities, mimeo.

Mählck, L. and Temu, E. B. (1989) *Distance versus College Trained Primary School Teachers: a Case Study from Tanzania*, Paris: IIEP.

Murphy, P. (1990) 'Costs of an alternative form of whole-time second-level education using distance teaching methods in Malawi', Paper presented to World Bank EDI seminar, Harare, May 1990.

Nettleton, G. (1991) 'Uses and costs of educational technology for distance education in developing countries: a review of recent literature', in Lockheed, M. E., Middleton, J. and Nettleton, G. S. (eds) *Educational Technology: Sustainable and Effective Use*, Washington DC: Education and Employment Division, Population and Human Resources Department.

Nielsen, H. D. (1990) 'Using distance education to extend and improve teaching in developing countries', unpublished background paper for World Conference on Education for All, Jomtien.

Perraton, H. (1982) *Alternative Routes to Formal Education; Distance Teaching for School Equivalency*, Baltimore: Johns Hopkins University Press.

Perraton, H. (1983) *Secondary Education at a Distance*, Cambridge: International Extension College.

Perraton, H. (1987) *The Costs of Distance Education*, mimeo. Background paper for Briggs Group. London: Commonwealth Secretariat.

Perraton, H., Jamison, D. T., Jenkins, J., Orivel, F. and Wolff, L. (1983) *Basic Education and Agricultural Extension: Costs, Effects, and Alternatives*, World Bank, Washington DC: World Bank Staff Working Paper 564.

Wolff, L. and Futagami, S. (1982) 'Malawi Correspondence College' in Perraton, H. (1982) *Alternative Routes to Formal Education: Distance Teaching School Equivalency*, Baltimore: Johns Hopkins University Press.

World Bank (1988) *Education in Sub-Saharan Africa*, Washington DC: World Bank.

Young, M., Perraton, H., Jenkins, J. and Dodds, T. (1980) *Distance Teaching for the Third World: the Lion and the Clockwork Mouse*. London: Routledge and Kegan Paul.

21 China: its distance higher-education system

Zhao Yuhui

China's distance higher education is run on a special system, one which uses radio and television as its main media to deliver teaching programmes. The system is formed by radio and television universities at the central and local levels which have made it possible for more than two million people to receive higher education over the past eight years. Radio and television programmes are broadcast nationally by Central China Television (CCTV) via its microwave network and by local radio and television stations all over the country. Television teaching programmes are also transmitted by China Education Television (CETV) via satellite covering China's vast territory of 9.6 million square kilometres. Taking into account the number of students and their geographical distribution, China's radio and television university is not only the largest institute of higher education in China, but also the greatest distance teaching university in the world.

ORIGINS AND DEVELOPMENT

China was one of the first countries to use radio and television for higher education purposes. During the early 1960s, soon after television broadcasting began to develop in China, the first television universities (TVUs) were founded in the capital, Beijing, and other principal cities to meet the demand for adult education. These new types of universities were well received and showed real potential as soon as they came into being. During the period from 1960 to 1966, more than 8,000 students graduated from the Beijing Television University and over 50,000 students finished single course studies through its teaching programmes. Most of them went on to make valuable contributions to industrial and agricultural enterprises or to cultural and educational institutes. The television universities of other places were all equally successful. Unfortunately, this newly emerging initiative was interrupted by the 'Cultural Revolution' (1966–76).

Since 1976, China has entered a new historical period. The socialist modernization project (the modernization of industry, agriculture, national defence and science and technology) calls for a large number of trained people. Although the general level of primary and secondary education in China was higher than in most developing countries, admission of students to higher education institutes was relatively limited. In 1975 the enrolment rate in China's higher education was less than 2 per cent, whereas in ninety-two other developing countries the rate was over 4 per cent. The number of college and university students constituted a mere 0.7 per cent of China's adults above the age of 25. The number of qualified technicians and engineers accounted for only 2.5 per cent of the country's workforce in state-owned enterprises and institutes. By 1990, China's total workforce is expected to reach 105 million, of which 4.7 per cent should be composed of technical and engineering personnel. In the industrial and transportation sphere, at least 2.9 million new technicians and engineers must be trained. By 1990, 4.3 million secondary and vocational schoolteachers will be required to be college or university graduates, which means some 3.5 million new teachers must be trained. Such a huge task of training so many qualified people cannot be fulfilled by relying solely on conventional colleges and universities within a limited time-scale.

Since TVUs need fewer funds and can train more people in a shorter period of time, the State Council approved a report, jointly submitted by the Ministry of Education, the Ministry of Broadcasting and other ministries concerned, on the founding of a national radio and television university in February 1978. After a year's preparation, the Central Radio and Television University (CRTVU) was set up in Beijing. After that, a system of higher education through radio and television was formed by the CRTVU, 28 provincial radio and television universities (PTVUs), 279 prefectural/civic branch schools and 625 district county work stations. PTVUs were established in provinces, municipalities and autonomous regions; branch schools in towns, cities and prefectural areas; and work stations in districts of cities and counties of rural areas. There are two kinds of work stations: those organized by the county and district offices for small work units; and those organized by particular industries (called system work stations) such as the railways and the bureau of light industry. (All industrial concerns are state-run and administered by an appropriate bureau).

The enrolment of these radio and television universities over the last eight years has totalled 1,291,833, and 590,941 students have graduated. The number of registered students in 1986 was 604,437, constituting one-third of the country's higher-education institute students. The achievements have won the radio and television universities a nation-wide reputation and have attracted the attention of the Chinese Government. As a result, the sixth Five-year Plan for National Economic and Social Development (1981–5) stated, 'There will be considerable expansion of higher education through radio, television, correspondence and evening courses. Students taking these courses will number 1.5 million by 1985'. This plan forecast a rapid development for radio and television universities in China.

In the development of China's TVU system, a turning-point came in 1986 during which year three important changes took place in the entrance examination, the target students and the delivery system. From 1979 to 1985 the entrance examination had been held by the CRTVU. As from 1986, TVU applicants had to pass a national entrance examination held by the State Education Commission for all adult higher education institutes including TVUs, correspondence colleges and evening schools attached to conventional colleges and universities. It was in 1986 that TVUs began to enrol fresh secondary-school graduates in addition to in-service adults and young school-leavers. In October of the same year, TVU teaching programmes began to be transmitted by satellite every evening from 4.50 to 11p.m. Forty-nine teaching hours of transmission time was thus added to thirty-three teaching hours per week by the CCTV microwave network. All these changes have provided new opportunities for TVUs to develop and expand.

ORGANIZATIONAL STRUCTURE

Radio and television universities are run at five levels, corresponding to the organization of China's system of national and regional governments. The CRTVU, at the highest level, is under the direct leadership of the State Education Commission (formerly called the Ministry of Education). The PTVUs, at the second level, are under the auspices of provincial governments. Their branch schools, at the third level, come under prefectural/civic governments. Work stations, at the fourth level, are run either by district/county education bureaux or by a particular industry. The teaching and learning classes (usually called television classes), at the lowest level, work directly with TVU students. There are four kinds of television classes:

- classes run by local government bureaux (a bureau, here, means a department of local government with responsibility for education, or industry or similar);
- classes run by large factories and mines;
- classes run jointly by medium-sized or small work units; and
- classes run by local TVUs at various levels to cater for fresh secondary-school graduates or for young school-leavers waiting to be assigned jobs. The kind of television classes for young school-leavers are also run by large state-owned enterprises.

The CRTVU controls unified admission standards, teaching plan, academic

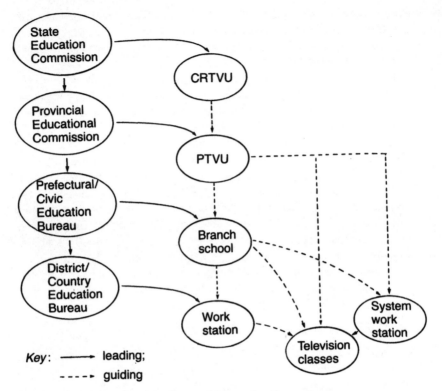

Figure 21.1   Structure of the distance higher-education system

level and examination criteria. It is the national centre of teaching administration, programme production, course delivery and distance-education
research.

Responsibilities shared by TVUs at five levels are as follows.

The CRTVU

The CRTVU:

- makes long-term plans for the development of the TVU system and yearly
  plans for admission;
- guides teaching administration of PTVUs and coordinates academic work
  shared by more than one PTVU;
- makes teaching plans to be carried out nationally and produces programmes to be broadcast nation-wide;

- develops and publishes printed teaching materials, and produces and distributes audio- and video-cassettes for courses offered nationally;
- prepares unified entrance and end-of-semester examination papers and marking standards;
- organizes training for teachers, administrative staff and technicians of the national TVU system; and
- conducts distance-education research and exchanges experiences with similar institutes at home and abroad.

The PTVUs

The PTVUs:

- guide teaching administration of their branch schools, system work stations and television classes directly attached to them;
- organize the implementation of the teaching plans made by the CRTVU, and make teaching plans for courses offered provincially;
- produce and transmit teaching programmes for regional use;
- develop and publish printed teaching materials, and produce and distribute audio- and video-cassettes for courses offered provincially;
- organize entrance and end-of-semester examinations and the marking of examination papers;
- admit students and issue diplomas/certificates;
- train teachers, administrative staff and technicians of regional TVUs; and
- conduct distance-education research and exchange experiences with each other.

Branch schools

Branch schools:

- guide teaching administration of work stations and television classes directly attached to them;
- implement teaching plans made by the CRTVU and PTVU;
- organize the subscription and distribution of teaching materials;
- conduct examinations and tests;
- admit and register students, and keep their study records;
- employ tutors and train them; and
- oversee tutorials, laboratory work and field studies.

Work stations

Work stations:

- organize television classes and guide their management;
- organize tutorials, laboratory work and field studies; and
- distribute teaching materials.

Television classes

Television classes:

- administer teaching and learning classes;
- draw up time-tables for every term;
- organize viewing and listening of teaching programmes, tutoring, laboratory work and field studies;
- encourage students to take part in physical training and recreational activities outside class; and
- maintain contact with work units from which the students come.

China's radio and television universities at five levels share their responsi-

Table 21.1   Evolution of TVU staff numbers

Staff	1979	1980	1981	1982	1983	1984	1985	1986
Full-time teachers	3,871	5,540	6,480	10,101	11,474	11,732	11,229	13,144
Part-time teachers	12,039	14,804	15,521	18,700	25,237	30,285	15,795	21,618

bilities on the basis of balancing centralization and decentralization with the CRTVU as their centre. Along with the development of the TVU system, the number of its staff has been increasing (see Table 21.1).

COURSES OF STUDY AND USE OF MEDIA

The courses presented to registered students are all at undergraduate level. There are other courses for continuing education and secondary vocational education available for short-term training.

In the past eight years of its existence, the CRTVU has offered 150 courses in the subject areas of mathematics, physics, chemistry, biology, mechanical engineering, electronic engineering, chemical engineering, civil engineering, economics, accounting, statistics, finance, banking, industrial management, commercial management, archives management, journalism, law, library science and Chinese language and literature, etc. In addition to courses offered by the CRTVU, PTVUs and their branch schools offer their own courses following an overall pre-established teaching plan to coordinate their outputs at all three levels. Work stations and television classes may organize special courses to suit the needs of work units. In 1987, the total number of courses offered by TVUs at different levels amounted to more than 400 with the possibility of 81 specialities. A TVU student must obtain 60 per cent of higher total credits by courses offered by the CRTVU (Table 21.2).

The TVU courses are multimedia, consisting of radio, television and printed materials. The proportion of television programmes for science and engineering courses is greater than that of other media, whereas radio used to be the main medium for social-science courses. Since the satellite transmission of TVU programmes began in 1986, their social-science courses have increased greatly.

Table 21.2 Number and chronology of subjects offered

Subject	Number of specialties	First offered in:
Mechanical engineering	19	1979
Electronic engineering	14	1979
Chemical engineering	16	1982
Civil engineering	15	1984
Accounting	2	1983
Statistics	1	1983
Banking	2	1983
Finance	1	1983
Management	5	1983
Personnel management	1	1986
Chinese	1	1982
Applied Chinese	2	1985
Basic training for cadres	1	1984
Law	1	1984
Mathematics/Physics	1	1980
Chemistry	1	1979
English	1	1986
Biology	1	1979

Audio- and video-cassettes are also in use in some courses to make up for insufficient transmission time and to provide more convenient access for distance learners. Over one million audio-visual copies of teaching materials are produced and duplicated each year.

Printed teaching materials are available to supplement radio/television programmes for all courses. These materials are divided into three types: course books, reference books and study guides. Most of the course books, introduced or compiled by the CRTVU, are more or less the same as the textbooks used in conventional colleges and universities. Reference books and study guides are compiled by radio/television presenters with the help of TVU teachers at CRTVU and PTVUs. Over the past eight years, more than 400 printed books totalling 40 million copies have been published by the CRTVU Publishing House. These books can be bought at the shops of the national book retailers, New China Bookstores (Xinhua Shu Dian).

At present, radio and television teaching programmes are, to a large extent, a direct transcription of conventional university classroom teaching. Presenters are chosen from key universities all over China. In the initial stage, it is necessary for TVUs to adopt textbooks used in conventional universities and to choose academics with a sound university teaching background as presenters, so that a high standard of tuition can be guaranteed. These two measures have proved to be effective.

Up to 1983, radio and television teaching programmes were produced by the Central People's Radio Station and Central China Television. Since then, more and more audio-visual teaching programmes have been produced by the CRTVU and PTVUs. There are more than forty production centres within the TVU system. Among them, the production centre of the CRTVU is the largest and best equipped as a World Bank loan project. Another nine PTVU production centres in principal cities are better equipped than the rest. The TVU system plans to produce all its radio and television programmes in its own production centres within a few years. The transmission of radio and television teaching programmes is arranged as shown in Table 21.3.

Although radio and television programmes are supplemented with printed teaching materials, face-to-face tuition is also available to students. Tutoring is necessary for two reasons: first, presenters of radio and television programmes cannot answer students' questions directly and there is no immediate feedback for the presenters to adjust their teaching; second, registered students are organized into television classes, listening to and watching programmes together. Television image and radio sound may not be clear for technical or other reasons.

Practical laboratory work used to be done at conventional universities or research institutes during public and school holidays or at other times when the laboratories were not in use. Along with the setting up of TVUs' own laboratories, more and more laboratory work has been done in the TVUs' study centres where there is a laboratory, an audio-visual lab and a small

Table 21.3 Organization of programmes and their transmissions

Broadcasting organization	Media used	Area broadcast to	Time available
CCTV (courses by CRTVU)	Microwave	Nation-wide	33 teaching hours per week[a] (8.30–11.30 am; 1.30–4.10 pm)
CETV (courses offered by CRTVU)	Satellite	Nation-wide	49 teaching hours per week (4.50–11.00 pm)
Provincial and civic radio/television stations (courses offered by CRTVU and PTVUs)	Radio and television	Regionally	Varies locally
Branch schools, Work stations and television classes	Audio-visual equipment, audio- and video-cassettes		

Note: [a] One teaching hour lasts 50 minutes for a radio/television programme.

library. As a World Bank project, eighty-five study centres of this kind have been established. In order to enable students in remote areas to carry out experimental work, physics, chemistry, mechanics and electronics experiment kits have been designed, and some of them have been put to use in large numbers.

For laboratory-based courses, students cannot obtain their credits until they have completed the required practical experiments to their tutors' satisfaction. There is some flexibility in the number of experiments which students are required to carry out, as conditions vary from place to place. Students having access to better-equipped laboratories may perform more experiments than those who have no well-equipped laboratory at their disposal. However, they must complete the required minimum of experiments, without which they cannot graduate or be awarded diplomas.

Engineering majors have to go to factories to gain practical experience during their vacations, and they complete a project before graduation. Social science majors have to conduct field studies, and prepare a report of their findings. Through the above activities, students are expected to cultivate their ability to study by themselves and work independently.

The period of schooling is two or three years for registered full-time students. There are two semesters per year with a total of eighteen teaching weeks in each semester plus two weeks for revision and examinations. A credit system is used based upon one credit for every eighteen hours of teaching and learning. A total of no less than 160 credits are required for a two-year degree diploma, and 240 for a three-year degree diploma. The degrees are equal to those awarded by conventional two or three-year colleges. Students who are successful in the examinations obtain credits. They are then awarded certificates or diplomas according to the credits they have accumulated.

CATEGORIES OF STUDENTS AND MODES OF LEARNING

The TVUs' target students are in-service adults, secondary-school graduates and young school leavers waiting to be assigned jobs. The in-service adults aged about 30 years are enrolled according to training plans drawn up by their respective work units, after which admission is granted to those who pass the national entrance examination held by the State Education Commission for adult higher education. Secondary-school graduates are admitted by national entrance examination for conventional universities and colleges. In this respect, TVUs are regarded as a new type of conventional university. The TVU system began to enrol secondary-school graduates in 1986. Young people waiting for jobs must pass the adult entrance examination before admission. The numbers of this type of student have continued to increase since TVUs were opened to them.

The above-mentioned three types of students are called registered students who enjoy a formal status as students of the TVU. These students are all organized into television classes and are taken care of by a class manager and several tutors. There is still another type of student who does not take the entrance examination and who studies on a self-instructional basis. These students are called 'free viewers and listeners'. These students increased so rapidly in number that it was hard for the TVU system to cater for them. In 1985, the State Education Commission decided to stop receiving free viewers and listeners for a period of time, during which those who had begun learning were registered and organized into study groups. The remaining free viewers and listeners from 1979 to 1985 are allowed to be issued diplomas or single-course certificates if they take and pass the final examinations.

In-service adult students can study full-time, part-time or during their spare time depending on the amount of time they are allowed by the work units from which they come. Secondary school graduates all study full-time,

Table 21.4 Student flows 1979–86

Year	Intake			Graduates			Undergraduates		
	All subjects	One subject	Total	All subjects	One subject	Total	All subjects	One subject	Total
1979	97,746	244,725	342,471	–	–	–	97,502	182,656	280,158
1980	79,377	80,124	159,501	–	92,714	92,714	167,962	156,410	324,372
1981[a]	–	–	–	–	47,590	47,590	170,391	97,635	268,026
1982	184,973	68,083	253,056	92,022	94,566	186,588	258,488	88,679	347,167
1983	235,567	18,728	254,295	67,905	61,286	129,191	414,054	64,704	478,758
1984	205,858	11,992	217,850	17,032	105,185	122,217	599,068	62,249	661,317
1985	273,112	11,446	284,558	165,204	75,386	240,590	673,634	19,986	693,620
1986	215,200	21,861	237,061	248,778	142,015	390,793	604,437	38,978	643,415
Total	1,291,833	456,959[b]	1,748,792	590,941	618,742	1,209,683	2,985,536	711,297	3,696,833

Notes: [a] In 1981, no students were enrolled because of insufficient transmission time;
[b] The total number of one-subject intakes is smaller than that of graduates. This is because all-subject students can become one-subject students if they drop out.

whereas young school leavers can choose their own modes of study. Full-time students must finish their studies in two or three years according to different speciality teaching plans. Part-time students must finish their degree courses in three to six years, and spare-time students are allowed to accumulate credits over ten years.

The number of undergraduate students varies from year to year with the minimum 97,502 and the maximum 673,634, not counting free viewers and listeners, the total number of whom has been estimated at about one million. Over the past eight years, 590,941 students have finished all-subject courses and graduated with diplomas, and 618,742 students have completed one-subject courses and have been awarded certificates.

Students' progress is assessed, in the main, by examinations at the end of each semester. Examinations are set centrally but organized locally, and are held on the same date throughout the country. The standards and conduct of the exams are strictly safeguarded. A drop-out system is adopted for in-service adult students who study full-time. These students must go back to their original work units if they fail two end-of-semester exams in any one semester, or three exams in different semesters. They may go on to become spare-time students taking a single course if this is approved by the leadership of their work unit. The drop-out system is also applicable to other kinds of full-time students who study all subjects.

After graduation, in-service students are recognized as having equivalent status to that of conventional college graduates and, where necessary, they are assigned new jobs in their original work units to suit both their newly acquired speciality and the needs of the unit. They receive the same salary as conventional college graduates. As to the other two categories of students (secondary-school graduates and young school-leavers), they will be found employment according to their study records by the local employment departments. A considerably large number of this kind of TVU graduate become secondary-school teachers after graduation. When they are assigned a new job, they will be treated equally as conventional college graduates.

FINANCIAL RESOURCES AND COST-EFFECTIVENESS

The TVU system's budget comes from a variety of sources. The CRTVU is administered and funded by the State Education Commission with the CCTV and CETV being responsible for television transmission costs. It also receives financial support from ministries which ask the CRTVU to help train personnel needed by them.

PTVUs are under the auspices of provincial governments, and their branch schools under prefectural or civic governments. Funds for TVUs are part of the educational budget of governments at various levels. The amount of budget varies from place to place because of the unbalanced economic development in different parts of the country.

District/county work stations are funded by education bureaux of local governments, and system work stations are financially supported by their respective systems (such as railways, posts and telecommunications, industrial and commercial concerns, etc.). Various kinds of work stations have different budgets because of varied conditions.

Television classes run by work units get financial support from factories, shops, government bureaux, which send students to be trained at TVUs, and television classes run by TVUs at various levels to cater for secondary school graduates are aided by governments at corresponding levels. Each student receives half the amount of money provided by the government for a conventional university student. The other kind of television classes composed of young school leavers can be financially supported by certain work units which will employ graduates from these classes.

In general, TVU students are free from tuition fees except free viewers and listeners who have to pay for registration and examinations. However, all students must pay for their own study expenses, such as printed teaching materials and stationery. It has been estimated that on average one-third of the cost can be saved to produce a TVU graduate who studies full-time and continues to receive full wages; two-thirds can be saved to turn out a part-time graduate. This estimation has been proved true by a cost analysis project done by the Liaoning Provincial Television University in north-eastern China.

The development and cost effectiveness of radio and television university systems have been positively acknowledged by the government leaders.

ACHIEVEMENTS, LIMITATIONS AND NEEDED IMPROVEMENTS

China's radio-and-television university system has made great strides in less than ten years. Courses offered at all levels have been increasing year by year. Enrolled all-subject students have totalled over one million, and all-subject graduates have amounted to more than 500,000. In addition a little less than 500,000 one-subject students are enrolled, and still another 500,000 one-subject graduates have been turned out. The number of TVU undergraduates has helped to increase the ratio of students in China's higher-education institutes from 0.7 per cent in 1975 to 4 per cent in 1987 of adults aged over 25. A large number of TVU graduates have become technicians and engineers who are badly needed in industry, transport and so forth.

Courses specializing in politics, law, economics, management, journalism and library science have helped to improve the irrational curricular arrangement in higher education due to historical reasons. The TVUs have made it possible for more secondary-school graduates to receive higher education, and have provided a second chance for young school-leavers to enter a university. The enrolment ratio of secondary school graduates in Chinese higher education institutes has increased from less than 2 per cent in 1975 to more than 20 per cent in 1987.

The ratio between the first intake and the first graduate is 100 to 69, a drop-out rate of 31 per cent, which has varied from 25 to 35 per cent over the years since then. It has been generally acknowledged by part-time tutors from conventional universities that the level of TVU graduates is about the same as that of conventional college graduates. In-service TVU graduates have made valuable contributions after they returned to their original work units. The other two types of graduates have been welcomed and praised by people from all works of life.

The TVU system has made remarkable advances in the past eight years of its operation. Nevertheless, there are certain educational and administrative problems to be overcome, such as the limited transmission time for television; improper use of media; inconvenient viewing and listening for part-time study, delayed distribution of printed teaching materials, a too large student study load, insufficient provision of experimental work, shortage of qualified staff for research on distance education, and so on. In April 1986, the presidents of the CRTVU and PTVUs held a conference in Hangzhou to sum up experiences of operating TVUs in China and to discuss the new situation confronting the TVU system. They came to the conclusion that China's TVU system had entered a new stage of development and that it had to be reformed in order to meet the needs of China's political and economic reform project. A year later the presidents met again in Beijing for further discussions on how to reform the TVU system. Some ideas concerning proposed improvements were agreed at the conference.

China's radio and television universities were initiated at the beginning of the 1960s, suspended for ten years and resumed at the end of the 1970s. China's TVU system was formed at the beginning of the 1980s and it entered a new stage of development in 1986. In the 1990s two out of five university students will be enrolled in TVUs. The Chinese Government has attached great importance to the development of radio and television universities. Zhao Ziyang, premier of the State Council, said in 1983:

> Television universities are a valuable form of education. Some 92,000 students graduated last year. Those who passed the examinations were awarded diplomas. The levels of graduates are satisfactory. The development of television universities is suitable for China as it is an effective way of training people at lower cost in a shorter period of time . . . . It is very difficult for conventional universities to increase admission by tens

of thousands within one year. But 92,000 students graduated from the television universities last year.

With the progress of China's modernization process and the development of telecommunications and space exploration, the TVU system will have ample opportunity to expand. Looking ahead, China's radio and television universities will play an increasingly greater role in higher education as well as in the national economy and social development.

22 Refugees and distance education

Solomon Inquai

INTRODUCTION

The world is awash with refugees. What was a trickle a few decades back has become a mass outpouring of people across international borders. *The Economist*, in its issue of 23 December 1989, paints a graphic and grim picture of the magnitude of problems facing the world refugee community in general, and those in the Third World in particular. Today there are some fifteen million refugees in the world. Contrary to the myth often held in the West, the vast majority of the refugees are in Asia and Africa and are not seeking greener pastures in the West. Most refugees prefer to return to their countries of origin to settlement elsewhere. But, while waiting for that day when all their woes will end, they encounter many problems.

One of these is the lack of education for their children and themselves. This is true especially with refugees in the Third World, despite the fact that host countries accept the right to education of refugee children. Host countries in the Third World are too poor to provide mass education to refugees. Furthermore, refugee schools, where they exist, are staffed with untrained or under-trained teachers, rendering poor the education provided.

Refugee communities are characterized by a large population of women and children, thus with a large proportion of school-age children. The United Nations High Commissioner for Refugees (UNHCR) started to support primary education in 1966, a decade-and-a-half after the convention was signed.

The crisis in education is even more acute at the secondary and tertiary levels. The UNHCR did not become involved with provision at this level until 1975, when its Executive Committee re-defined refugee rights to education to include access to secondary and tertiary education, and opportunities for vocational and technical education. From that point onward, funds were set aside for the purpose.

The educational needs of refugees in Western countries are met in various ways and rarely pose a problem. Young refugees of school-going age are automatically accepted into local schools. This solves both the agony of waiting and the problems of integration with the local population. Adults are helped with language education and through schemes for further education. Non-governmental Organizations (NGOs) provide scholarships where the state mechanism is not applicable.

But Third World host countries do not have adequate provision for their own nationals, and certainly cannot accommodate large influxes of refugees. When there is the possibility of places in local schools, very often many refugees do not make use of them because of language differences, or differences in educational standards.

The major difference between refugees in the Third World and those entering Western countries is in the way they live. Refugees in the West are quickly integrated into the community. They are usually scattered all over the country, making the burden of providing education manageable for each host community. In the countries of the South, refugees come in such large numbers that they are kept in separate makeshift camps away from the general population. It is only a few, often of urban origin, who settle in cities and towns. But this sporadic settlement is actively discouraged. The large numbers also mean that both the refugees and the host countries agree that integration is not a goal, but that the refugees should maintain their identity and eventually be repatriated. This pattern of settlement and the prevailing wish of refugees to maintain their own national identity means organizing separate education provision.

In addition to the education provided by the host country with funds from the UNHCR and other donors, the charities and the refugees' own organizations also participate in education work among refugees. Their major effort is concentrated on providing primary and some non-formal education. In Africa there is very little provision at the secondary level. The UNHCR scholarship scheme caters for a tiny number. There is the occasional secondary school, like the one in Kassala, Sudan, which is supposed to serve a population of nearly half-a-million refugees. The 600,000 Mozambican refugees in Malawi have no secondary school. The South West African People's Organisation (SWAPO) and the African National Congress (ANC) run their own post-primary schools with the major emphasis being on vocational and technical training.

DISTANCE EDUCATION AS A POSSIBLE SOLUTION

The greatest need is at the secondary and tertiary levels. There is also the problem of poorly trained teachers, and their inadequate number. What can be done? Where do we turn to in our quest to provide meaningful education to the refugee community? These issues have engaged the minds of educators. The International Extension College (IEC) has been in the forefront of promoting distance education as a credible alternative, and an effective and viable approach in tackling the problem of inadequate educational provision. What is more, IEC has expressed the need to treat as a priority, at the emergency stage of any refugee influx, the planning and provision of education to refugees. Experience in expanding access to education shows that distance education as a system of delivery is feasible, especially where financial and other resources are limited.

WHY DISTANCE EDUCATION?

If we are to provide meaningful and effective education through the conventional system, three essential conditions should be met.

There should be qualified teachers in the numbers required at each level. There is a visible shortage of teachers in almost all the refugee camps. Teachers and other professionals in exile are the first to benefit from the opportunity to resettle in one of the industrialized countries in the West, thus depriving refugee communities of essential human resources. There should be adequate physical facilities, such as classrooms, offices and libraries. Finally, we need to have the essential teaching–learning resources. These last two items are not difficult to acquire, provided funds are available. But the cost of building and equipping classrooms is prohibitive. As indicated earlier, the Third World host countries are poor, they do not have the money to build schools for refugees. Aid money is limited and cannot meet all the expenses required. But even if money were not a problem, training teachers in the conventional system takes too long, as do building schools and procuring the essential supplies. In order to join a teacher-training institution, a refugee would need a good academic background. Training takes two or more years under the traditional approach and many teacher training institutions have only a limited capacity. The question is, how do we meet the demand for education for refugees given these constraints? Distance education is used in the training of teachers for primary schools, and in providing both formal and non-formal education.

WHAT IS DISTANCE EDUCATION?

Distance education is an approach that can be implemented quickly. It has the advantage that it benefits from economies of scale. The large numbers of students mean lower unit costs.

The term 'distance education' is relatively new. It encompasses correspondence education, referring to communication through the printed media, and educational broadcasting, which refers to radio and television. Distance teaching implies the separation of the teacher and the learners in time and space. It uses preplanned and prepackaged teaching/learning materials to reach those in need of education and training wherever they are. Students work at a time and place most convenient to them and the style of life they lead. Someone who is unemployed yet could not secure a place in a conventional institution, for whatever reason, can pursue studies at home.

> The term distance education covers the various forms of study at all levels which are not under continuous, immediate supervision of tutors present with their students in lecture rooms or on the same premises, but which, nevertheless, benefit from the planning, guidance and tuition of a tutorial organization.
>
> (Holmberg 1989)

Distance education is an alternative form of education which can help to increase access to and hence, the democratization of education.

Distance education is sometimes referred to as three-way teaching, involving printed material which often is central to the teaching/learning process, broadcast and/or recorded media, and elements of personal contact. The latter could be through letter, telephone or a face-to-face situation. Many distance education institutions provide study centres where learners can meet their tutors and get help with the lessons, and require the learners to attend short residential courses. When a course of study is of a practical nature, students may be required to attend laboratory sessions and/or workshops.

The world has witnessed a phenomenal growth of distance education in the second half of the twentieth century. During this period, country after country, both Third World and industrialized, established their own distance education programmes. During this period there has been a decisive move towards government-sponsored institutions as against the old style commercial colleges. This development has had its effects on privately owned correspondence colleges.

There is no need to build schools specifically for refugees if they are pursuing their education at a distance. The limited tutorial contact required can be organized in existing schools or other facilities after hours. Where no facilities are readily available, makeshift classes shaded by mats and sticks can be organized as happens in the Sudan. As stated earlier, many of the refugee camps suffer from shortages of qualified teachers: in addition, secondary school places and non-formal education are also limited. In all these areas distance education can and does play a useful role in training teachers, and providing secondary and non-formal education.

DISTANCE EDUCATION IN PRACTICE

Teacher training at a distance for refugees is illustrated through work among Palestinian refugees in the Middle East, and Somalia. For secondary level education, work among Namibian and South African refugees and in the Sudan for Ethiopian and Eritrean refugees provide examples.

The first planned use of distance education for refugee education was in the Near East among Palestinian refugees. Following the Arab–Israeli war of 1948, The United Nations Relief and Works Agency (UNRWA) was set up to oversee aid to the Palestinians who were forced out of their homes and became refugees in the neighbouring countries. UNRWA recognized that schools for refugee children should be set up immediately. Entire communities had been exiled and naturally they had teachers among them. The schools were separate from and parallel to those in the host countries because the Palestinians could not be accommodated in the schools of the host countries (Mortensen and Wagner 1980). In setting up these schools, UNRWA was assisted by UNESCO, which provided the professional guidance and direction required. The education offered is comprehensive, covering all levels, including special education. University level education, however, is provided under a scholarship scheme.

The UNRWA/UNESCO in-service teacher training programme began in 1964. At that time only 10 per cent of the teachers were professionally qualified. In addition, 1.4 per cent were in training or had just completed their training, but were not yet certified. Although there had been, since 1950, some on-the-job training for teachers, it was small-scale and unsystematic. It was recognized from the outset that it was unrealistic to train almost 5,000 teachers using the traditional, residential approach. It was thus decided to use distance education for this massive task so as to provide the training in a short time at less cost and with the least disruption of classes. Thus the UNRWA/UNESCO project became the first to use distance education in training refugee teachers.

The basic components of the approach adopted were:

- a series of self-study work assignments supplied on a correspondence course basis;
- direct guidance of the trainees by the school supervisory staff and field representatives;
- summer courses, usually for two weeks, in which instruction is provided by institute staff, subject supervisors and other experts on subject matter and educational theory and practice (Mortensen and Wagner 1980).

A range of training programmes is available under the scheme. These include basic training courses for unqualified elementary and preparatory school (lower secondary) teachers, training for specialist personnel such as head-masters, supervisors, and teacher trainers, and also refresher courses to expose teachers to new ideas and methods and curricula changes.

The duration of these courses varies from two years for the basic training for primary and preparatory school teachers, to three years for preparatory school teachers who have qualified, and shorter periods for the other courses.

The programme has been very successful and Arab states took note of the achievement it registered. The percentage of qualified teachers in the UNRWA schools for Palestinian refugees rose to 94.2 per cent by 1978–9, as compared to only 10 per cent in 1964. What is more, among the qualified teachers in the primary and preparatory schools, 23 per cent were by then holders of university degrees, with more teachers still pursuing their university education. Many Arab countries have since adopted this approach to upgrade their teachers and improve their own educational systems.

The Palestinian experience was the first large-scale application of distance education in a refugee situation. Subsequently, distance education has been used both for similar purposes and for other purposes. Studies have shown there is a great unmet need for education, especially at the post-primary level. Studies also show that teachers teaching in refugee primary schools are either untrained or under-trained, needing upgrading and training. Only a few teachers at a time could be released for conventional training without causing undue disruption in the education of the children. Even when larger numbers can attend, however, the capacity of the teacher training colleges is limited and cannot accommodate them all.

THE INSTITUTE OF IN-SERVICE TEACHER TRAINING IN SOMALIA (IITT)

Somalia has, since the late 1970s, hosted a large influx of refugees from Ethiopia. The refugees in Somalia are largely ethnic Somalis, sprinkled with their kin the Oromos. The vast majority had no language problem and could have been easily integrated into Somali society, as indeed Somalia claims had happened when it estimated the refugee population at 1.5 million. The UNHCR's planning figure for aid purposes was, however, 700,000 people. As is the pattern everywhere in the Third World, they were kept in thirty-five large camps separate from the rest of the population.

Almost from the time of their arrival it was felt necessary to set up schools for the children. However, there were not enough teachers to staff the many makeshift schools that were sprouting up under trees and temporary shelters.

In 1981, IITT was set up 'to provide teachers for camp schools as quickly and as cheaply as possible'. The IITT provides two types of courses. It runs a two-year basic course of in-service training for primary teachers and a four-year upgrading course. Those who complete the first cycle are qualified to teach only in refugee schools. The second cycle enables them to complete their secondary education and be eligible for admission into the national university.

The basic two-year course has the following pattern. Recruits, who have completed at least primary education, receive a 'crash' course in a face-to-face situation, largely on simple classroom management. Once teachers are posted they receive assignments on a weekly basis. Trainees complete 30 assignments per year or a total of 60 assignments for the whole basic course. While they are pursuing their studies, they receive individual training and classroom guidance from the camp-based teacher training supervisors. The supervisors also conduct two-hour weekly seminars for each group of trainees in the schools where they teach. Finally, a three-week residential course is conducted at the end of each year. The final examination is held as part of the course and successful candidates become certified teachers.

Trainees are largely men. Although the number of women trainees has been on the increase, it does not yet exceed 25 per cent of the total. The programme started with an intake of 500 in 1981/2 and by 1988/9 some 3,307 trainees had gone through the programme.

The upgrading course started in 1985. Participation in the programme is voluntary. The course lasts four years and has a heavy academic bias, following the Somali national secondary level syllabus. The major difference between the two courses is that the upgrading course is largely self-study. It uses self-help groups, and once a month tutorial support from a qualified secondary school teacher. The medium of instruction for both courses is the Somali language, and English is taught as a subject in the upgrading course.

Both these courses are popular, and almost all those who complete the basic training go on to take the upgrading course. The upgrading course in its early years had been beset with delays in the production and delivery of study materials, and had difficulty attracting qualified people to work as tutor-markers because of the inadequate pay for marking. Nevertheless it has over the years proven to be successful, in fact too successful, in that those who complete the course tend to leave teaching and join other organizations where the pay is more attractive.

SECONDARY EDUCATION AT A DISTANCE

Access to secondary education is a major problem for the refugees from Eritrea and Ethiopia in the Sudan. The only secondary school, in Kassala, cannot cope with the growing demand for places. Its efforts are supported to a limited extent by a scholarship scheme funded by UNHCR which sends successful candidates to English medium schools such as the Comboni

Colleges in Khartoum and Port Sudan. The World University Service (UK) also operates a scholarship scheme for Ethiopian refugees. These schemes will never entirely meet the need for places in secondary schools.

Unlike refugees in the Horn of Africa, refugees from Namibia residing in Zambia and Angola, together with their counterparts from South Africa in Tanzania, are usually supported by scholarship schemes coordinated by the Commonwealth Secretariat, the UNHCR, and other agencies. Yet not every refugee from Namibia and South Africa can benefit from these special arrangements.

In 1984, the Sudan Open Learning Unit (SOLU) was set up to provide, among other things, secondary level courses to refugees. This has since been extended to include Sudanese nationals, especially those displaced from the war-torn south. The first students were admitted in 1986. SOLU understood from the outset that many of those who would want to benefit from the programme had been away from school education work for too long. They would have forgotten a great deal of their basic knowledge. For this reason SOLU operates a two-stage secondary level course. Stage one, which is aptly called a Refresher Course, is intended to go over the early stages in junior secondary level courses. It lasts one year. Those who complete the refresher course then go on to do two-year senior secondary level courses. SOLU's approach is a combination of heavy reliance on private or individual study, combined with a weekly two-hour tutorial service for each subject. SOLU operates in Khartoum where it has two study centres, and in eastern Sudan, mainly in the towns of Port Sudan, Kassala, Gedaref and Soakin, and in a number of refugee camps. The annual intake, which started at 200 students, is now about 2,000 for the refresher course, and all those who successfully complete the first stage move on to the senior level course. The subjects offered are English, mathematics, biology, chemistry and physics. This limited range of mainly science subjects may explain the high drop-out rate that SOLU has experienced. SOLU is in the process of developing further courses in Arabic, geography, bookkeeping, principles of accounts, economics and commerce. Hopefully this extension into more practical subjects will attract and hold more students. The first batch to complete the senior secondary course will take the General Certificate of Education London examination in 1990. The courses are now being adapted to fit the Sudan School Leaving Certificate syllabus and in the future students will sit for the Sudanese examination and not the London GCE.

SECONDARY EDUCATION FOR NAMIBIANS AND SOUTH AFRICANS

There is a concentration of exiled South Africans and Namibians in the front line countries. The world has expressed a great deal of sympathy for the plight of peoples from southern Africa. There is a great deal of open support for their cause and the provision for their material and intellectual needs. As a result, one finds people from South Africa and Namibia studying under all forms of scholarship in many countries around the globe. However, there are enough adults in the camps who do not benefit from the generosity of the international community that it is necessary to provide alternative forms of education. There are also other factors. Namibians have suffered under the Bantu Education Act, an expression of apartheid. The South West Africa People's Organization (SWAPO) wants to see English become the *lingua franca* of independent Namibia. The schools that movements such as SWAPO, African National Congress and Pan African Congress have set up in the camps do not meet the needs of the young adults who are above school-going age. In any case, there is little provision for secondary education.

It was for these reasons that two separate distance education units were established in Lusaka for Namibians and in Dar-es-Salaam for South Africans. The Namibian Extension Unit (NEU) caters for Namibians, while the South African Extension Unit (SAEU) helps South African refugees, regardless of their political affiliation. Both institutions were the result of commonwealth decisions to help in the education of southern African refugees. They started with basic courses in English, mathematics, health education and agriculture. The target group was those young adults with four years or more of primary education. However, it soon became apparent that there was a need for both junior and senior secondary level courses as well. But the numbers were not enough for the institutions to develop their own courses and they therefore opted to use existing courses developed by other institutions.

They also encouraged their urban-based nationals to enrol with local distance education institutions. The NEU, the older of the two, began using Zambian National Correspondence College materials. It also started to develop its own junior secondary level courses in selected subjects, such as English and mathematics. This was a natural progression from the work at the basic level already done. SAEU, on the other hand, decided to purchase 'O' level courses from a commercial correspondence college in the UK. They both find their arrangements satisfactory for their immediate but limited needs. The NEU, in anticipation of its early return to Namibia, has done a great deal of thinking on the idea of producing its own secondary level courses. Recent developments indicate that it will soon have the chance to translate its ideas into practice as it moves back to Namibia.

Both the NEU and the SAEU follow the same pattern in running their courses. Students study partly on their own and partly in groups. Each group has a trained group leader whose job is to facilitate discussion, and record and transmit queries and problems to the tutor. The tutor visits the group once a month, and conducts both group and individual tutorial work. The topics emanate from the group leader's report and from the tutor's own observation while marking student assignments. The NEU students are in camps in Zambia and Angola and over the years many have benefited from the work of the Unit, especially at the basic level.

CONCLUSIONS

Our experience in using distance education among refugees is limited. However, it is no longer a matter of speculation whether people can learn or not through distance education. The world over, people are getting school education, gaining degrees and diplomas in higher education, and getting training in technical, vocational and professional fields at a distance.

The problem with refugee education is largely political. Refugees in the South are dependent on the generosity of the North. The North dictates what is good for the refugees, and education is not a top priority. Another factor is educational conservatism in poor countries. Education is often seen in terms of classrooms and teachers. People are not aware of ways of reaching more people with the same limited resources. Such lack of awareness on the part of the decision makers inhibits innovation. Very often the money made available for refugee education is limited.

The fact that refugees exist in such large numbers has forced educators to seek an alternative approach, which has been a productive experience, particularly in the training of teachers in Somalia. The number of qualified teachers, despite some turnover, has been growing steadily. The quality of education in the camp schools is better than that available in the national schools. The refugees who have received this training are sought after in the job market, and many are leaving the teaching profession for greener pastures. Among the Namibians many people were able to acquire proficiency in English. As more and more people go through the system, the number with secondary level education available for training has grown.

But only systematic study in the future can determine how effective the system has been. No study has been done on the cost effectiveness of distance education among refugees. The drop-out rate, especially in the Sudan, is worrying. We need to know whether there are any clear reasons for this. Finally, what direction should distance education for refugees follow in the future? This seems to be an open question.

REFERENCES

Boesen, S. W. (1983) *Towards Self-reliance of Afghan Refugees*, Copenhagen: Danish Refugee Council.

Bulcha, M. (1988) *Flight and Integration: Causes of Mass Exodus from Ethiopia and Problems of Integration in the Sudan*, Uppsala: Scandinavian Institute of African Studies.

Christiansen, H. and Scott, W. (1988) *Survey of Social and Economic Conditions of Afghan Refugees in Pakistan*, Geneva: UN Research Institute for Social Development.

Dodds, T. and Inquai, S. (1983) *Education in Exile*, Cambridge: International Extension College.

El Bushra, J. (1985) *Eritrean and Ethiopian Refugees in the Sudan: Case Studies of Educational Needs Among Refugees*, Cambridge: International Extension College.

Fernandez, G. T. *et al.* (1984) *Mexico and Costa Rica: Case Studies of Educational needs among Refugees*, Cambridge: International Extension College.

Gerhart, G. M. (1984) 'Educational assistance to refugees from South Africa and Namibia', *Refugee Issues*, 1, i.

Hamrell, S. (1967) *Refugees in Africa*, Uppsala: Scandinavian Institute for African Studies.

Holmberg, B. (1989) *Theory and Practice of Distance Education*, London: Routledge.

IEC and WUS-UK (1988) *Refugee Education: the Case for International Action*, Cambridge/London: International Extension College, World University Service (UK).

ILO (1983) *Tradition and Dynamism among Afghan Refugees*, Geneva: International Labour Office and UNHCR.

Kibreab, G. (1983) *Reflections on African Refugee Problem: a Critical Analysis of Some Basic Assumptions*, Uppsala: Scandinavian Institute of African Studies.

Mortensen, K. and Wagner, K. W. (1980) *The UNRWA/UNESCO Experience in Refugee Education*, Copenhagen: University of Copenhagen, Institute of Education.

Seshibe, N. R. N. (1979) 'Education planning for South African refugees', University of Massachusetts, unpublished D. Ed thesis.

UNHCR (1988) *UNHCR Assistance to Refugee Education*, Geneva: Technical Support Services, UNHCR.

UNHCR (1988) *Refugee Children: Problems, Policies and Guidelines*, Geneva: UNHCR.

UNRWA (1983) *UNRWA, a Brief History 1950–1982*, United Nations Relief and Works Agency for Palestine Refugees in the Near East.

Part VI
The study of distance education

Introduction

The study of distance education, like that of any other academic field, rests on the twin bases of taught university degrees and the publication to the learned community of the results of debate and research. It is only in the 1990s that distance education has come of age as a field of study.

The subject matter of the study of distance education is the millions of students around the world who study at a distance in the 1990s and the didactic strategies, administrative structures and institutional arrangements that characterize this form of education.

The emergence in the 1990s of taught university degrees in distance education, both face-to-face and at a distance, was the result of a lengthy period of preparation which is reflected in the readings chosen for this section. Four stages in the evolution of the field of study can be distinguished. Clarification of terminology was the work of the 1970s, precision of definition characterized the early 1980s, delineation of the field of study came in the late 1980s, and taught degrees in the 1990s.

Confusion in the terminology that was used to describe the field of study that came to be known as 'distance education' was characteristic of the mid-1970s. In English, the terms included 'home study', 'correspondence study', 'external studies', 'distance teaching', 'learning at a distance' and there may well have been more. About 1978, general agreement was reached that the most suitable term in English was 'distance education'. Since that date, the acceptance of the term has been surprisingly rapid and world-wide. Great benefits to the field of study have flowed from solving the problem of terminology.

Confusion about the definition of distance education reigned until 1980. Little progress in research was possible because of this confusion. Writers did not make it clear whether they were writing about or not writing about 'flexible learning' or 'the use of computers in schools' or 'educational technology' or 'distance education'. Scholars today may disagree on the fine tuning of their definition but there is agreement on what is essential. The volume *Distance Education: International Perspectives* (Sewart, Keegan and Holmberg 1983) reflects this stage of clarification.

By the late 1980s, distance education had developed as a distinct field of study within education but there was still hesitation about the delineation of the field. Books like Garrison's (1989) *Understanding Distance Education* and Holmberg's (1989) *Theory and Practice of Distance Education* lie clearly within the boundaries of a disciplinary field: their authors know clearly when they move beyond the boundaries of this field and into other fields of educational research. But the formal identification of the focus and nature of the field was hardly accomplished before the early 1990s.

The introduction of taught degrees in distance education at a number of universities in the early 1990s resolved a number of issues. In university faculties of education there are many traditional fields of teaching and research: history of education, educational psychology, curriculum theory, comparative education. Some fields, however, like educational administration, educational technology, adult education or distance education are newer or more specialized and may not be found in many universities.

Within the discipline 'education', the new field of distance education can be considered to have affinities to cognate but discrete fields of teaching and research, particularly adult education, educational technology and the study of flexible/open learning.

The fields of teaching and research known as adult education and distance education have a number of distinguishing characteristics of which the most important are the following.

*   Adult education deals with the education of adults; distance education is the study of the education of children and adults at a distance and theoretical positions in this field must be equally valid for children as for adults.
*   Adult group dynamics at the basis of the 'andragogical' approach to adult education would be excluded by definition from distance education.
*   The 70 years history of children's distance education has provided an essential database for distance education research (they do not, for instance, drop out) and the impetus for important innovations (see Vivian, Chapter 13).

The study of flexible open learning differs from distance education in that flexible or open learning systems are rarely at a distance: distance education is often neither open nor flexible. Open learning is a goal or an ideal; distance education is neutral, it can be either open or closed, flexible or inflexible, depending on the course or the system.

Courses on educational technology differ from courses on distance education.

- In distance education face-to-face group-based communication is absent either wholly or substantially; educational technology does not abandon interpersonal communication: it nourishes and supports it.
- Educational technology deals with the use of technology for the education of six hundred million students in the world. Distance education does not.
- Distance education is a form of education in which at least ten million students are enrolled annually in a vast array of subjects and courses with different enrolment criteria and examination structures. Educational technology does not have these characteristics.
- Educational technology is a supplement to the teacher; distance education is a substitute for the teacher.

Progress in the delineation of the nature and focus of this field of study is arguably one of the major developments of the decade covered by this book. The pioneering work carried out in Adelaide to achieve the accreditation of the first degree in distance education, since Mitchell broached for the first time the possibility of a degree in the field at New Delhi in 1978, makes a fittting opening for this section (see Chapter 23). The most ambitious course yet mounted is that of the Télé-université with a dozen conceptually demanding subjects of the type presented here plus a minor thesis and a period of work in a distance education institution (see Chapter 24).

Three consequences can already be seen from the development of distance education as a field of university study. First, there is the prospect of a rapid professionalization of the field – a development already envisaged by Jenkins (see Chapter 25). Then the creation of a pool of postgraduate researchers, professionally trained at Masters level in the theory and practice of distance education, should be able to contribute a new élan and analytical precision which theoretical development in distance education has so far lacked. Finally, the enhanced status of the field should lead more scholars to grapple with the issues outlined by Holmberg (see Chapter 26).

23 Academic education of distance educators

Ian Mitchell

INTRODUCTION

As Head of a Distance Education Department the author had spent several exciting yet exasperating years trying to educate traditional academics into operating in the distance education mode. As some signs of success began to emerge I proposed in 1979 that a formal course of postgraduate tertiary study leading to an award in distance education be developed. The course was to be available to all professional distance educators who wished to broaden the base of their professional knowledge and to improve their performance in delivering their particular academic expertise in the distance education mode. This chapter reports the developments since that time – concentrating in particular on the most recent developments attained in 1991.

The chapter thus covers briefly the introduction of the Graduate Diploma in Distance Education in 1983; its re-accreditation in 1985 and 1990; and the introduction of a further award, the Masters Degree in Distance Education, in 1991. The chapter will cover not only the content of the awards but, equally importantly, the teaching styles and educational values which supported the awards. In themselves, each one of these factors will be cause for debate; and the reader will be aware that different norms apply in different cultures throughout the world.

Overall the awards have been exceptionally well-received and, in no small measure, this is due to the world-wide cooperation we have enjoyed from leading professional distance educators keen to promote scholarship in distance education.

HISTORICAL BACKGROUND: BRIEFLY

Australia has a long tradition in distance education, dating officially from the first decade of the twentieth century. In that decade our first distance education ('correspondence') school and university work commenced, as educational providers grappled with the demands for education from our sparse and scattered population. The early school work was directed to the education of children from isolated families. The early university work was directed to the education of the teachers who served isolated communities.

In the short-term, each State within the Commonwealth of Australia developed its own correspondence school resources and only two of the more remote States developed university resources, since universities were contentedly élite in those times.

In the 1950s, Schools of the Air, that is, regular daily school programmes delivered by radio services, began to prosper. These programmes were possible because Australia had by then developed its Royal Flying Doctor Medical Service, a service whereby anybody, anywhere in remote Australia could call up an aerial medical ambulance by radio and receive emergency medical treatment and, if necessary, rescue and retrieval by aeroplane and transportation to hospital. This radio network provided the basis for the establishment of the radio Schools of the Air – which still function today.

In the 1940s, as military forces were rehabilitated after World War II, massive educational programmes were needed to re-settle the military forces back into civilian life. The demands far exceeded the capacities of buildings, schools, institutes, universities, etc. and distance education ('external studies') was called into service. These new programmes closed the educational gap between the provision of children's-level school programmes and the provision of higher-level university programmes.

In the 1970s, Australia, along with most countries, experienced extensive development of educational services – particularly at the higher education level. Part of this expansion was in distance education, but the rate of expansion in distance education became more frantic as competition for the comparatively few on-campus students became more intense. Quality of educational provision was sometimes neglected, while institutions scrambled for numbers of enrolments to justify their continued existence. Regional institutions, deliberately located in scattered locations away from the capital cities, were forced to supplement their local enrolments with metropolitan distance education students to fulfil enrolment targets.

Then funds began to dry up. Governments began to ask more searching questions about the ways funds were being spent. In the mean while, wild claims of the wonders of new technologies – and what they could achieve for and with distance education – became more pronounced. Rationalization and amalgamation became the order of the day and communication technology was offered as the new 'broadcaster' of distance education services.

So it is that in the 1990s Australia has a much more streamlined distance education service. At the school level, it is much more extensively supported by communication technology; and that same technology means too that many distance education services extend back from isolated families across into the isolated communities identified from the earliest days and to the 'isolates' within the cities as well.

At the technical and further education level, programmes are prepared and shared on a national basis and many programmes are in heavy demand from international sources. Further, the distance education programmes have developed from being mere counterparts of on-campus programmes to be the expression of initiatives in in-house industry training, professional association membership, 'professional development', compulsory courses and more general community 'open learning' courses.

The higher education sector has been heavily rationalized; and the bulk of this level of distance education is provided by eight national Distance Education Centres and various forms of consortia and cooperative activities flourish. But universities have never accepted discipline readily, so many other forms of 'distance education' continue to flourish creatively too and thus provide their contribution to the dynamics which will take us into the twenty-first century.

Australia was amongst the world leaders in distance education at the commencement of the twentieth century. We have no reason to suspect we will not be in a similar position at the commencement of the twenty-first century. Since we lack the technological and financial resources of some leading nations of the world though, we will have to be doubly perceptive in determining our particular contribution to global distance education's future growth. Maybe, the professional development of distance educators is one such contribution.

THE ORIGINAL GRADUATE DIPLOMA IN DISTANCE EDUCATION

In Australian higher education, an accredited award must be offered by an educational institution; it cannot be offered by an individual, a company, a business partnership, etc. So it was not possible for the Australian and South Pacific External Studies Association (ASPESA), the professional association of distance educators in Oceania, to offer the award. I proposed to my institution, The South Australian College of Advanced Education, that we offer to host the award. This was agreed to; we approached ASPESA with this offer and it was accepted. It was agreed by all concerned that no one institution held monopoly on knowledge about distance education so, while one institution would host the award, that institution would go to the best source, world-wide, to gather resources for the award.

While over sixty academics within our institution contributed to the award, a like number from twenty-one other Australian educational institutions also contributed.

The programme has been privileged to enjoy, as well, high international support, typical of which is the highest level of support from the International Council for Distance Education (ICDE) Presidents – no fewer than five of whom made personal contributions to the award. It has been a real point of professional integration when our students have subsequently attended an ICDE conference and said 'Oh! That's Prof . . . Now I can put a face to the voice on tape'. So, the practice of continuing professional growth was advanced.

From the outset the programme attracted international enrolments, without any advertising, and continues to do so.

VALUE POSITIONS

The course consists of the materials and the tutoring relationship

When we have received requests from international sources for copies of the course, we have been discomforted, because our position has always been: 'The course is more than just a box of materials'. We have always regarded as critical the personal tutor relationship we have established with the students. The course is a success when that is a success; and it follows that where that tutorial link has not prospered both the tutor and the student have found the course less than satisfying.

Course materials are triggers to learning – not the last word on a subject

One of the difficulties in graduate studies is that the students are relatively experienced and will bring something of their experience to the course of study. How can a distance education course have its materials ready-prepared for students when they enrol, yet still allow for the course materials to be open-ended to receive the benefit of student experience? One solution is to write materials as though they were introductions to subjects – with enough leads for less experienced or less confident students to feel that they have a substantial introduction into the new subject areas, yet with those very introductions open enough to allow the more confident or more experienced students to bring their wider or more detailed knowledge to the fleshing out of details in areas which hold their interest. This clearly requires the cooperation of a teaching staff who are not preoccupied with 'writing to impress their professional colleagues' or 'writing for promotion'.

The teaching/learning roles are interchangeable

As teaching staff we are dealing with adult professional students. Together we are exploring a field as wide and as comprehensive as distance education. No academic teacher can presume to have the authoritative word on every aspect of distance education; in many aspects it is the student who is the authority. This is one factor which maintains the element of excitement in being a tutor in distance education. Sometimes the tutor is teacher and sometimes the student is teacher. Occasionally it is an outside stimulus which makes us both learners. In some cultures where the teacher is revered as the source of knowledge, the idea of the interchangeability of roles is not accepted easily. This difference of values places special demands and provides special opportunities on cross-cultural tutoring relationships.

Student work is a fertile ground for research data

When we began this award there were no international research journals in distance education, though there was a great need for the conduct of and the benefits from such research. The journal, *Distance Education*, was edited in parallel with the course. This provided opportunity for some of the world's best distance education researchers to publish their work and it also gave impetus for students of the award to aspire to converting assignments and projects into published work. Another avenue for professional development and aspiration had opened up.

This very avenue, though, also created its own discipline and produced a flow-back activity into distance education practice. Students became aware that, if they wished to have their work published, it had to pass an international board of referees. In turn, it meant that, as they were processing data which emerged from in-house professional projects or government-initiated searches, etc., they realized too that these sources of information had to satisfy the requirements of 'an international board of referees'.

Thus the quality of institutional research lifted immeasurably or at least staff were embarrassedly aware of shortcomings. Some of our best students' projects were 'disasters', in that no conclusions could possibly have been drawn from the research project; but some students gained major insights into project design and management, which has stood them in good stead since!

The other aspect of this work too is that all sorts of student networks have been opened up and data is exchanged along all sorts of unofficial channels.

Effective distance education is a cooperatively-run, systems-based enterprise

We required that all our students be practising distance educators. The intent of the course was that all students became more professional in the exercise of their particular strand of distance education and that all students became more efficient and more sympathetic operators within the distance education enterprise. Thus all students had to study an overview of distance education.

For example, the administrator had to experience something of the anguish of a course writer by preparing a piece of teaching materials within administrative deadlines imposed by others. The teacher had to become a communications technologist by preparing some course elements using technology to convert ideas into exhibits. The course writer had to administer a course by producing cash and time budgets.

So all students experienced most major facets of distance education. The net outcome of this exposure was that all students should have become better-informed collaborators within their institutions.

COURSE CONTENT

Choice of course content inevitably presented problems – as every expert had opinions on what should and what should not be in the course. Where some of those experts were appointed to the accrediting body this created particular problems – but that happens on every accrediting body. (Unfortunately this can often create the seductive pressure to design the course to satisfy the accrediting body and allay its criticisms – at the expense of arguing for the acceptance of the course that research has shown will satisfy the needs of students.)

In any case, we were all to be constrained by the amount of time available for study of the course. Furthermore, we were aware that, as soon as we produced the course, it would be outdated. This was nowhere more obvious than in the areas of communication technology and government policy.

Thus we conducted client surveys of what the course content might be and then established broad areas as follows.

- Introduction to distance education
- Programme development in distance education
- Instructional design in distance education
- Communication technology in distance education
- Administration in distance education
- Student support in distance education
- Evaluation in distance education
- Project in distance education.

The extent of the course content was meant to be the equivalent length of one year of full-time graduate study. Being about distance education it was taught only by distance education. This meant that course duration was normally longer than one year.

In addition, students were encouraged to constantly consider their experiences as a distance education student: were the things that were happening to them similar to the things that they believed happened to their students? If they could change the system under which they were presently studying, what things would they change and why? If they couldn't effect changes now, what was hampering them and could any of those restraining factors be moved? In short, we encouraged the students to learn affectively as well as cognitively.

We encouraged them to consider the power relationships that prevail in distance education, with the view to understanding them and making conscious decisions about which ones to work to change and which ones to work to keep.

COURSE WRITING

The writing of the course reflected a series of positions. In the short term, we had been encouraged to use contract writers and this too had been our intent, because we recognized that there was considerable outside expertise upon which we needed to draw. However, over time, we found the management of such writing contracts very tedious; and we realized too that the contracts created considerable strain for writers who were sometimes writing in near-total isolation. It was very hard for them to savour team discussions under those circumstances.

(Remember I am writing about events in 1982; a lot has happened since by way of refinement of technological communication services.)

In the event, we came to develop a core group of writers and gathered around them, as appropriate to the course unit under construction, a team of ancillary experts who contributed their particular skills. Depending on how free they were to commit themselves to the course unit preparation process, some contributed to one section and then departed; others stayed and immersed themselves in the unit development process.

This was not always an easy process, as some writers had their work mercilessly edited, revised and abandoned, etc. Some contributors stayed in the process, murmured that they would never have missed it for the world; and vowed never to get involved in such a process ever again! There was ample opportunity to contribute to, participate in or observe several teams in process. But the pace was hectic, exhilarating and enervating; and the experience illuminating.

While I have used the phrase 'core team', there were in fact several changes to the core team over the writing period of three years; and I think it is important to accept the fact that teams will change over time and thus new value structures will assert themselves. How one determines which are the most important values to preserve amidst the changes is a moot question; there were several instances of downright assertiveness – and maybe they were needed to see the task accomplished.

SUCCESSFUL RE-ACCREDITATION

I will pass fairly quickly over the re-accreditation which occurred in 1985, because it is important now to comment on the 1991 courses which were introduced. They did see several shifts in position from the original proposals which proved so successful.

Normally, after a course has run its accreditation span it is presented again for re-accreditation and this is granted if the course still serves a useful purpose. That is, there is a market for the course. It can be presented economically without excessive demands on staff and resources, etc.

Because our course, first offered in 1983, was so novel, it was initially accredited for only three years. This meant that even before it produced its first graduates it was up again for re-accreditation. Thus we had only the opportunity to conduct but the broadest evaluation of the initial award. Nevertheless it was so obvious that the award was a success that re-accreditation was granted for another five years, with only minor updates to the principles of the award, though there was some update of content and resources.

By 1990, a re-production and extension of the evaluation process confirmed earlier expectations and provided the basis for developing content within the new Graduate Diploma and Masters Degree in Distance Education.

A NEW MASTERS DEGREE AND A RENEWED GRADUATE DIPLOMA IN DISTANCE EDUCATION

By the late 1980s important changes were taking place in the distance education professional field. On the one hand, there had been considerably increased sophistication in the professional practice of distance education. On the other hand there had been a considerable curtailment of indiscriminate expansion. Thus, graduates of our past award were looking for avenues in which to pursue their studies and increase their recognition as professionals. In the mean time, employers of professional staff were going to greater lengths to ensure they acquired staff with qualifications suited to specific tasks to be undertaken.

Amalgamations were put in train by the government and the South Australian College of Advanced Education became the University of South Australia. Distance education at higher education levels became rationalized and collaboration became encouraged. The University of South Australia had an accumulated graduate student body who wished to undertake further study. Deakin University had long ago been granted a charter to mount a Masters degree in distance education at the time when Colleges of Advanced Education were not deemed to be appropriate places for such awards. Deakin had in the meantime been extending its own scholastic base.

It was agreed a joint Masters Degree and a Graduate Diploma in Distance Education would be appropriate. The original model of contributions into an institution was replaced by a model of cooperation between institutions. When the joint proposal was presented to the government it was enthusiastically accepted.

The 'old' South Australian College of Advanced Education was still required to go through the accreditation process before approval would be granted to allow it to offer the Masters Degree. By the time the degree was offered in 1991 the institution had become a University; presumably no re-accreditation process will be required in future.

When we commenced teaching the award in 1983 we anticipated that the student body would consist essentially of Correspondence School and School of the Air teachers, along with various technical and further education, college and university lecturers. In fact, the field was much wider than that.

With the further development of distance education clientele over the last decade, the recruitment field for this award has extended even further. Amongst students today are rural nurse educators, industry training personnel, prison officers, migrant educators, police instructors, etc.

I will attempt now an assessment of the current position in the teaching of the new awards. Since we commenced teaching the award only this semester, readers will understand that I can give no more than a personal perspective – though I have been directly involved in the preparation of two units and directly involved as a contributor and temporary manager of another, while tutoring three others.

PREVIOUS VALUE POSITIONS RE-STATED

The course consists of materials and the tutoring relationship

Again, the course materials have not been prepared as stand-alone packages but as materials to form the basis of the student–tutor interaction. The materials for the first diploma drew upon print, audio-cassettes, video-cassette, tape/colour slides presentations and sample kits of print techniques. The tutor–student interaction was supported by phone and teleconferencing. The video-cassette was the only limited technique in that, though well-presented, it dated so quickly.

Materials this time are in print and audio-cassette only. To phone and teleconferencing we have added electronic mail services and fax.

I suppose, *de facto*, we have come to a stronger position in that the quality of the student–tutor relation is more critical than the adoption of a sophisticated range of presentations. We have proven also that the student–tutor relationship can function world-wide, from our experience with students from many countries.

Course materials are triggers to learning – not the last word on a subject

We have been conscious of some new constraints in this area. When we first proposed a course in distance education so long ago, there was a feeling of dismayed horror amongst our colleagues. Indirectly this was a good thing, because it meant we had to withstand numerous assaults upon our academic integrity, as we moved towards the accreditation process with its external examiners. It was only after we had convinced our colleagues internally that we had a coherent and cogent programme of study to offer that we entered the external debates. By then, we were well-equipped with answers to most questions.

This time – almost ten years later – we did not meet the same internal opposition and we were well-supported by an enthusiastic graduate student-body. We were doubly conscious, however, that we were offering the first Masters Degree in Distance Education in the world. We were much more conscious that our professional colleagues, world-wide, were watching developments – maybe for clues and guidance for their own plans.

Our earlier award attracted its fair share of criticism that it was a 'Masters level' graduate diploma, so keen were we then to be above reproach! I suspect that from some quarters we'll attract a criticism that we now have a 'PhD level' Masters Degree.

It was certainly easier last time to establish a coherent level of expectations about the course in the one institution, than it has been this time operating as we are – across two institutions. This is inevitable, if for no other reason than that the course writing teams are larger and more independent and no attempt has been made to impose a common editorial teaching style across all units.

This leads to comment on another feature of this programme. In one unit, we have used the contributions of all professional tutoring staff in the award.

This has been no mean feat to lay out all those approaches, values and styles side by side in a unit called, *Distance Teaching and Learning 2*. As a reader booklet, we have added several student contributions because we contended that they too are involved in both teaching and learning in their professional and student roles.

In fact, one could argue that many of them are better informed than most of us because many are currently both teachers and learners, while all our teaching is limited to postgraduate adults. It will be interesting to see how this unit is used by students when it is offered for the first time this semester.

The teaching/learning roles are interchangeable

Experience has shown it will be our loss if the roles aren't interchangeable. Yet there is now a subtle pressure on us to assume more the role of the 'august teacher', since our system doesn't allow just 'anybody' to teach at a Masters level. One must have extra qualifications to handle teaching at a Masters level.

Student work is a fertile ground for research data

The very offering of the Masters Degree is itself reinforcement to that value position. Graduate students want avenues whereby they can pursue higher degrees. They want to bring a more demanding discipline to their projects. One course unit is directed towards research; another deals with critical issues; a thesis accounts for one-third of the award.

In addition, students are encouraged to build approved electives into the fabric of their award. The intent is that students will pursue specialist areas of study as they develop their interests or lay the foundations for their thesis exploration.

Access to distance education course units scattered throughout the world is an option that many of them will want to exercise. Conversely, some students undertaking overseas programmes may also want to access certain units of ours for research purposes. That of course will all be a matter of negotiation.

Effective distance education is a cooperatively-run, systems-based enterprise

There is no doubt, operating cooperatively across institutions brings new demands on those who coordinate. We tried the system of sharing the responsibility for supervising the preparation of the units equally across the institutions. If the Chair for one unit rested naturally in one institution, the Deputy-chair of the course team was appointed from the other institution.

Some teams functioned with only two-person membership; others involved multiple membership with more or fewer active members and maybe some other members simply as observer/respondents to proposals.

A common logo was applied across the whole range of resources and this has been effective. It has been criticized by some students, though, as giving too great a recognition to the Masters programme and not enough to the Graduate Diploma. It is unfortunate if a mere logo conveys to some students that they are a lesser breed of student, because the whole programme is seen as integrated with students progressing from one award to the other if they see fit. Nevertheless it illustrates dramatically the importance of a 'mere logo'.

COURSE CONTENT

For the first award, the whole field of distance education was relatively undefined. When we came to determine the content and limits of these current awards, it seemed so much harder when all had hoped it might have been easier. This arose in part because the newly-involved Deakin staff were keen to make their presence felt.

This composite course has the common units of:

- Introduction to distance education
- Management in distance education
- Distance teaching and learning 1
- Distance teaching and learning 2
- Critical issues in distance education.

These units are found in both the Graduate Diploma and the Masters Degree. Graduate Diploma students then go on to add two elective units and a unit called Project in Distance Education. In the mean time, Masters Degree students add two electives, a unit called Research in Distance Education and a thesis.

The Graduate Diploma is again the equivalent of a year-long full-time study programme while the Masters Degree extends to 18 months in total. Studied only by the distance education mode the programme usually takes longer than the full-time equivalent time-span, although students can be full-time distance education students.

COURSE WRITING

It will be more difficult to determine the nature of the course writing process this time. A brief description of how teams operated has been given above. Certainly there was no one person who had an overview of the whole process this time. Each team has functioned to achieve its own deadlines and schedules and in some cases these deadlines were only achieved with great difficulty and after exhausting negotiation. The satisfying thing is that each team did achieve its deadlines.

(During the unit preparation period each one of the University of South Australia staff was away at some time or other on consultancy work conducting staff development programmes contracted because of these awards.)

One of our difficulties has been the reconciliation of the concerns of those who saw themselves as the 'better' writers and the concerns of those who felt they saw students' needs being overlooked. This is a not uncommon problem. A planned evaluation will no doubt throw further light on these concerns.

CONCLUSION

It has been useful to write this chapter because it has provided me with the opportunity to reflect on where we are at present in the stages of our course development. In informal terms, I could describe it as deflated debilitation – all the course units have been prepared and we are all utterly exhausted. But in distance education one doesn't have the time to enjoy a period of recuperation, for enrolment processes began nine months ago and teaching began five months ago, the last two course units have just left the press, and the next lot of students are beginning enquiries about enrolling.

In the formal terms of our course development models, the courses are now being implemented. By next year they will be entering the stabilization phase and meantime evaluation will have begun, so that when the next internal re-accreditation is to hand we will have substantial data. An examination of this data will condition our case for change, adaptation, re-accreditation, etc. Fortunately by now we have some experience in knowing which data yields the most critical information. By then too, there will probably be a bank of students wishing to be supervised towards PhD degrees.

If, in the process, the scholarship of distance education is advanced and aspirations for more professional practice have been achieved for individual distance education practitioners, then these awards will have served a useful purpose.

24 Media and distance education: course description

Louise Sauvé

PRESENTATION

This is the course outline of *Médias – formation à distance* which will be offered to students in the postgraduate degree course in Distance Education (*Diplôme de deuxième cycle en formation à distance*) of the Télé-université. It is available to students who already have an undergraduate scientific or professional background or the equivalent, and who are undertaking – or expect to do so – a career in distance education as an educator, a professional or an administrator. This course could also be offered to graduate students coming from other study programmes who are interested in the use of educational media, or it could be offered to other public or private institutions which want to develop the distance education field.

The description presents the course aims and general objectives, the theoretical orientation and particular approach of the content, a summary of the content, and the pedagogical strategy.

PURPOSE AND GENERAL OBJECTIVES

The purpose of this course is to enable the student to broaden his/her knowledge of the various media used in distance education, their uses in different contexts and their limits.

The general objectives are as follows.

- To understand the role and functions of media in distance education.
- To analyse and to apply, within a theoretical context, the different elements to consider when selecting media to be used in distance education.
- To evaluate the place of media in distance education and to discuss their future use.

THEORETICAL ORIENTATION AND PARTICULAR APPROACH

Can distance education exist without the use of media? Independently of the educational model chosen, the authors (Garrison and Shale 1987; Keegan 1988; Rumble 1989; Barker *et al.* 1989; Holmberg 1989; Keegan 1992) agree that an essential characteristic of distance education is the separation between the teacher and the learner throughout the length of the learning process. This distinctive feature of distance education causes a transformation in the educational act at moments and/or in places requiring *the systematic use of media.*

Excluding the teaching machines created for specific educational outcomes, the media as a whole owe their origin to reasons other than education, even if they have been enabled to transmit, accentuate, distribute, record and reproduce the stimuli which teaching needs to increase its impact. Research on the various media and their contribution to education is old and well established. If we had to assess that research, following the example of Proulx (1991) who has analysed its different trends, we could also conclude:

> In the nineties, research on media keeps on increasing but the results are not necessarily adding up. Since there is no unique theory of media which is unanimously accepted, numerous research projects develop in various directions.
>
> (Proulx 1991: 430)

This established fact brings us to question both the kind of content a course on media in distance education should favour as well as the trends which will be presented in relation to research and practice. As we deal with media used for educational objectives, we will concentrate on the authors whom we find in the educational technology theories field (those interested in the use of media applied to education) and especially on the research that fits in the systems approach as applied to theories of education.

A number of authors have developed the systems approach as applied to education (Stolovitch and La Rocque 1983; Gagné 1987; Dick and Carey 1990; Prégent 1990; Lapointe 1991). This theory of instructional design describes the step by step operations of systematic teaching and specifically the selection of media which, with the teaching/learning strategy, constitutes the heart of instructional design.

Selecting media is an issue which is not the result of research in education alone, other disciplines are interested in it. However, within this course, we will limit ourselves to the studies and research dealing with the educational functions of the media or of a combination of media. These texts will discuss particularly one or more of the following variables:

- the learner's characteristics,
- the knowledge to transmit (from the teacher's point of view),
- the task to achieve (from the learner's point of view),
- the media characteristics: technical attributes, production capacities, distribution modes, conditions of use, costs, legal aspects.

The study of these variables allows us to identify a number of criteria that the students should consider when selecting a medium. We agree with Heidt (1981) and Stolovitch and La Rocque (1983) that using a selection of media is efficient as long as it is within a context, here distance education. We will examine this dimension through the evolution of the various media and their impact on the design modes of the distance courses as well as on the educational functions selected by these different modes. We will also approach the new trends in the use of media.

Two components 'media selection' and 'distance education' are at the heart of the course *Médias en formation à distance*. To study them, the following topics are selected.

- The use of media in distance education: an evaluation.
- Teaching with media.
- Learning with media.
- The individual characteristics of the learner.
- The characteristics of media.
- Taxonomies of media.
- Trends in research on educational media: interactivity and multimedia.

These topics will allow the students to:

- question the place that the different applications (correspondence, multimedia, digitalized information technologies) leave to interactivity, accessibility, dialogue, learning control by the learner, individualization, etc.; the multiple use of media as a vehicle of course content in distance education and the impact of digital information technologies in the organization of teaching and learning in distance education;
- clarify a number of concepts: media, technology, multimedia, hypermedia, interactivity, etc.;
- elaborate a working structure to approach the media selection in a distance education context.

THE SUMMARY OF CONTENT

Whatever the kind of teaching offered in distance education, the educational relation between the teacher and the student cannot exist without the systematic use of one medium or of a combination of media, so let's examine how they have been used in distance education.

The use of media in distance education

First, to discuss this topic, we will study how the evolution of media has marked the development of distance education through the writings of Garrison (1985), Benson and Hirschen (1987), Pittman (1987), Shapiro *et al* (1987), Kaufman (1989), Nipper (1989), Bell (1990), Bates (1991), Gunawardena (1991) and Pelton (1991).

These authors have examined the media by bringing them together in three generations:

- the combined development of the printing techniques and the postal system: the coming of correspondence teaching which expanded rapidly towards the end of the nineteenth century;
- the use of radio, television, audio-cassette, telephone that gave birth in the late 1960s to the multimedia distance teaching concept which integrates more than one medium in appropriate combinations, depending on the learning content to be transmitted and the resources of the institutions.
- the development of digital information technologies (telematics, audio-conferencing, two-way interactive television, etc.) which re-opens the issue of the old methods of course design. New methods of design, namely tele-education and distance open education, are appearing. These tend to fill the lack of first and second generation technologies: the lack of true interactivity in the technological interfaces.

The overview of these three generations of media will highlight different modes of distance education course design still existing today: correspondence teaching, multimedia distance teaching, tele-education, distance open education. We will examine through these methods how the media encourage the learner's control of learning, dialogue, independence, interactivity, accessibility and individualization. We will also see that the digital technologies have challenged the distance education model, where teaching is perceived as a *mediatized product* reaching the student in his/her environment and learning as a result of the reception by the student of the delayed transmission of that teaching material.

Second, this topic will enable students to appraise the use of media in distance education. It will offer the opportunity to consider the advantages and the limits of media in particular contexts of distance education (Western countries versus developing countries) from the learner's point of view (how does one learn with media?) and from the point of view of the course design team (how to select media?). Furthermore, it will also highlight some past mistakes (for example, the use of broadcast television in poor countries for distance education; mediated teaching models introduced in the countries where the accessibility of media is limited, etc.).

Teaching with media

Research has demonstrated that no medium by itself possesses all the essential characteristics to accomplish one or all of the educational functions. Each medium fulfils one or more functions, more or less completely. Considering this fact, this topic will examine how a medium or a combination of media presents the information related to a content or a concept: whether for creating a stimulus, gaining attention, guiding the learning, eliciting performance, providing feedback, enhancing retention and transfer, etc.

Learning with media

This theme will examine how the media can facilitate learning. We will present the different learning conditions which can influence the choice of media, from the contribution of cognitive sciences in relation to this question. We will also examine some authors who were interested in media as a support learning service.

The individual characteristics of learners

In the study of media, it is important to be interested in the learner's individual differences and in the way students react to the media. According to Bates (1981), individuals differ in their preferences as to learning forms and in their competency to learn with different media. Heidt (1981) identifies as individual characteristics the aptitudes, intellectual abilities, cognitive and learning styles, motivation and other individual personality features. Hefzallah (1990) includes in these features the level of literacy which is defined by practices as a whole, behaviour and ability in relation with a medium; the level of experience with a medium will influence the level of literacy.

The characteristics of media

In order to provide better tools to students about media used in distance education, this theme will first illustrate different uses of communication infrastructures and examine Canadian and international media networks useful to distance education. We will describe the voice and data public networks, the multiline interconnection devices or teleconference bridge, the Canadian and American public broadcasting television networks and cable television, satellite and fiber-optic transmission, etc. Finally, we will present some examples of distance courses using radio, audio-cassette tapes, audio-conferencing, two-way interactive television systems, electronic and virtual classrooms.

While providing students with the technical knowledge on media in a specific environment, this topic then offers the opportunity to examine media in relation to constraints other than educational: cost of media, legal aspects of their use, production capacities, distribution modes and conditions of use of media, etc.

Taxonomies of media

Media in education as such do not represent an outcome: they are the tools serving a function or an educative purpose. Since the educators have a large variety of means among which they have to choose the best or the most appropriate, one of their important questions for distance education is as follows: What criteria will enable them to decide what is the best medium or the most appropriate to achieve these objectives?

To answer this question, we will present different classifications or taxonomies on selecting media based upon teaching and learning theories and will take a look at the different criteria about which authors in the field of distance education are arguing.

This analysis of different approaches for classifying the media will enable students to evaluate, to select or to elaborate the model which corresponds to their orientations and to their educational values as well as to their respective environments.

Trends in research on educational media: interactivity and multimedia

Writing on educational media and on distance education is infiltrating into an hypermedia approach focused on the interactive use of technological unities managed by computer. Interactivity and multimedia are concepts at the heart of this research on digital information technologies. The notion of interactivity defined here happens when two individuals or two groups of persons communicate with each other by both image and sound or by one or the other alone, in either real or delayed time (Cartier 1989). Multimedia refers to the capacity to transmit information in many forms (text, data, graphic, video and audio) and to the capacity to access a number of media at the same time. Here are examples of questions which will support this topic:

• Uniqueness, multi-media or integration of media: what will be the status

of distance education in the year 2000? How modified will be the modes of course design and what educational criteria will predominate in the choice of media or of a combination of media in distance education?
- Since current progress and change are the foundation of actual transformations in programmes centred on audio-visual and traditional mass media, what will be the future? Will print always be the medium mostly used? How far will the diversification of media in distance education go? To what point will the digitalized information technologies favour interactivity?
- Does the increasing presence of digitalized information technologies in distance education focus on educational criteria which taxonomies have not considered up to now?

To conclude the study of these topics, we suggest that the students adjust their perceptions on the use of media in distance education by studying the views of practitioners and media specialists, among others D. Keegan, M. G. Moore, A. Stahmer, S. Proulx, T. Bates, N. Mercier, in interviews on audio- or videotape.

PEDAGOGICAL STRATEGY

Learning process approach

The orientation taken in this learning process approach is both theoretical and practical and considers one of the basic objectives of any professional training, that is 'to reach a coordinated theoretical reflexion with practical experience where it is exclusively about technical-professional or other kinds of knowledge.' (Lopez 1988: 43).

The student can approach the seven themes of the course in the order he/she wishes to follow according to his/her learning needs and interests. Different documents will be provided in the course: texts selected in literature or written by the course design team, audio and video documents. Each topic suggests a number of corrected exercises, reading questions, listening or viewing grids allowing one to review the topic treated. The first evaluation work, 'A media selection grid', will enable the students to transfer the knowledge acquired in the topics to a case study. When needed, students will be able to form telephonic work cells or computer teleconferencing to exchange, present and comment on their media selection grids.

Once the topics dealt with and the media selection grid are elaborated, a debate will conclude the course. This activity, joining a maximum of six students, will be done by audioconferencing. The students will present their position in relation to a particular topic: the future use of media in distance education. Prior to this debate, the listening to interviews of media specialists will prepare students to exchange effectively during the discussions. Each student will have to make a brief oral statement on the topic. At the end of the debate, the students will have to produce a second evaluation task. This essay will enable them to evaluate the role and place of media in distance education and to discuss their future use.

Learner support

The teacher and the learning assistant support the students.
Learner support provides:

- individual support carried out by the teacher and the learning assistant with the following means: exchanges by telephone, by mail, by telematics or by fax. A telephonic contact in the first week of the course is also planned.
- group support carried out by telephonic work cells are provided to students in order to exchange their work. An electronic mail telematic service and computer teleconferences are also available to students as an alternative to telephone work cells.

Each student can expect a minimum of fifteen hours of support and consultation for this course.

Choice of media

The media selection used in the course is a reflection of its content. Having to examine the media used in distance education, providing students with examples of this use as well as offering them the opportunity to experiment are fundamental.

- For teaching: audio-visual documents, sound documents, textbooks.
- For learning: student workbook, evaluation guide, computer data book, telephonic work cells and telematics.
- For learner support: telephone, telematics, fax and correspondence.

Here are some further explanations on the selection of visual and audio media in the course. The subject, 'The characteristics of media', requires a support which illustrates the functioning of media and their use in distance education across the world. This support may enable students to thoroughly understand media, while having access to verbal comments which explain their advantages and limits according to learners and course designers. We agree with Bates (1981) and Jacquinot (1985), when they say that the use of video-cassette, besides encouraging an individualized learning, allows the content:

- to synthesize into a coherent whole, a wide range of information which would otherwise require considerable length in print and which would not provide the richness of background material necessary to students in order to understand the functioning of this medium;
- to demonstrate the way in which equipment can be used and its effects;
- to illustrate expensive concrete experiences which the student may not afford to observe;
- to free the students from schedule constraints while giving them control over the development of televised programmes;
- to present televised contents in places where distribution networks are not well organized.

In the last weeks of the course, the students must prepare a debate on the future use of media in distance education. In order to help them, we will offer them recent sources on media which permit the fast update of information. Unlike print material, audio-cassettes introduce to students the views or knowledge of eminent persons who can present in an interview the essential points of an argument or opinion, which otherwise would not have found time to be written (Jacquinot 1985). Furthermore, time and money invested in the design and production of a written text, which will rapidly become obsolete because of the subject presented, is also a point to consider. Finally, audio-cassettes will also ensure a more individualized learning. As to audio-conferencing, it will enable the students to expose their experiences and thoughts in real time and to be challenged by different points of view.

The use of a telematic network composed of interactive information services (electronic mail and computer teleconferencing), while introducing the students to digitalized information technology, offers them an exchange forum, an access to a support and a twenty-four hour learning group as well as control on interaction during learning.

Bibliographical databank services will also be offered; they will enable the students to consult rapidly the specialized references on media and on distance education. These references are necessary to students to realize their course's evaluation works. The selection of this telematic support is essential since it enables regular and inexpensive content reviews and easy access to information.

Learning material

The learning materials for this course include the following.

- A textbook, around 400 pages, describes the seven topics of the course.
- A student workbook, around 100 pages, presents the course general information: learning process approach is suggested to the student,

learner's support, evaluation mode and learning activities. These learning activities are mainly composed of exercises and their key corrections, of reading and analysis questions and visual and listening grids.

- An evaluation guide, around 30 pages, presents the evaluation tasks, detailed instructions and the criteria for assessment.
- Audio-visual documents, about three hours long, relate the views and experiences of media specialists and illustrate communication infrastructures, different uses of media and Canadian and international distance education media networks.
- Documents, about four hours long, present the views and experiences of experts and examples of the uses of radio, audio-cassette and audioconferencing in distance education. They also offer interviews with media specialists on the new trends to consider in the use of media, in distance education.

Students should be able to access the different services such as electronic mail and computer teleconferencing, at home, at work, or in their neighbourhood when necessary. Thus, the student should have a computer with a modem, and communications and word-processing software.

Step by step student's worksheet

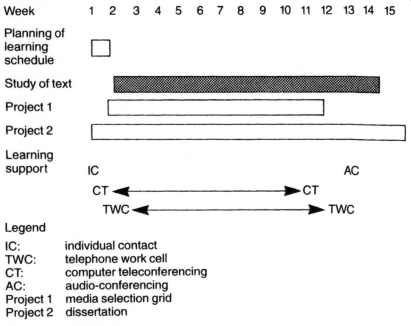

Legend

IC: individual contact
TWC: telephone work cell
CT: computer teleconferencing
AC: audio-conferencing
Project 1 media selection grid
Project 2 dissertation

Figure 24.1   Student's worksheet

EVALUATION

The evaluation of learning is as follows:

• Part 1: From the topics and the analysis of different media selection approaches, the students will have to elaborate and justify a media selection grid in relation to a case study.
• Part 2: Dissertation on the role and place of media in distance education and their future use.

REFERENCES

Barker, B. O., Frisbie, A. G. and Patrick, K. R. (1989) 'Broadening the definition of distance education in light of the new telecommunications technologies', *American Journal of Distance Education* 3, 1: 20–9.

Bates, A. W. (1981) 'Efficacité du message éducatif', *Communications* 33: 25–49.

Bates, A. W. (1991) 'Third generation distance education: the challenge of new technology', *Research in Distance Education* 3, 2: 10–15.

Bell, J. (1990) 'Distance education from correspondence course to CD-ROM and beyond', *Educational Media International* 27, 4: 196–8.

Benson, G. M. and Hirschen, W. (1987) 'Distance learning: new windows for education', *Technological Horizons in Education* 15: 63–7.

Cartier, M. (1989) *Nouvelles Images, Nouveaux Usages: la Navigation à l'Écran dans les Médias Interactifs*, Montréal, septembre.

Dick, W. and Carey, L. (1990) *The Systematic Design of Instruction*, 2nd edn, Glenview: Scott, Foresman.

Gagné, R. E. (1987) *Instructional Design: Principles and Applications*, Englewood Cliffs: Educational Technology Publications.

Garrison, D. R. (1985) 'Three generations of technological innovation in distance education', *Distance Education* 6, 2: 235–41.

Garrison, D. R. and Shale, D. (1987) 'Mapping the boundaries of distance education: problems in defining the field', *American Journal of Distance Education* 1, 1: 4–13.

Gunawardena, C. (1991) 'Current trends in the use of communications technologies for delivering distance education', *International Journal of Instructional Media* 18, 3: 201–13.

Hefzallah, I. M. (1990) *The New Learning and Telecommunications Technologies*, Springfield, Illinois: Charles C. Thomas.

Heidt, E. U. (1981) *Instructional Media and the Individual Learner: a Classification and Systems Appraisal*, London: Kogan Page.

Holmberg, B. (1989) 'Concepts et applications de la formation à distance et de l'apprentissage ouvert' (traduit par C. Marquis), *Innovative Higher Education* 6, 1–2: 24–8.

Jacquinot, G. (1985) 'L'audiovisual, pour une pédagogie spécifique', in F. Henri and A. Kaye (eds) *Le Savoir à Domicile*, Québec: Télé-université et les Presses de l'Université du Québec, 262–301.

Kaufman, D. (1989) 'Third generation course design in distance education', in R. Sweet (ed.) *Post-secondary Distance Education in Canada: Policies, Practices*

316   *The study of distance education*

rt>4ant>(ed.) *La Technologie Educative, d'hier à Demain* (in press).

Lapointe, J. (1991) 'Une méta-vision du processus de la technologie de l'éducation', in *La Technologie Educative à la Croisée des Disciplines*, publié sous la direction de L. Sauvé, Québec: CIPTE et Télé-université.

Lopez, J. S. (1988) 'Langage, contenu et médias', *Actualité de la formation permanente*. Dossier: la formation à distance, Centre INFFO 92, janvier-février: 41–7.

Nipper, S. (1989) 'Third generation distance learning and computer conferencing' in R. Mason and A. Kaye (eds) *Mindweave: Communication, Computers and Distance Education*, Oxford: Pergamon Press.

Pelton, J. (1991) 'Technology and education: friend or foe?' *Research in Distance Education* 3, 2: 2–9.

Pittman, V. V. (1987) 'The persistence of print: correspondence study and the new media', *American Journal of Distance Education* 1, 1: 31–6.

Prégent, R. (1990) *La Préparation d'un Cours*, Montréal: Editions de l'Ecole Polytechnique de Montréal.

Proulx, S. (1991) 'Deux grands courants dans les recherches et théories sur les médias', in *L'État des Médias*, sous la direction de J. M. Charon, Boréal-La Decouverte-Medias Pouvoirs.

Rumble, G. (1989) 'Defining distance education', *American Journal of Distance Education* 3, 2: 8–12.

Shapiro, H., Moller, M., Nilson, N. C. and Nipper, S. (1987) *3rd Generation Distance Education and Computer Conferencing in Denmark*, Guelph: University of Guelph.

Stolovitch, H. D. and La Rocque, G. (1983) *Introduction à la Technologie de l'Instruction*. St-Jean sur Richelieu: Editions Préfontaines inc.

25 Strategies for collaborative staff training in distance education

Janet Jenkins

Training is collaborative when personnel from more than one institution take part in a training activity. This can mean trainers from different institutions teaching together, and it can also mean trainees from different places learning together: sharing of experience is in itself a useful component of training. People from different institutions may also work together to develop training materials. If staff training in distance education is to be taken seriously, then collaboration is essential to develop and sustain local and international training programmes.

Distance education is still a relatively new field of work, and it is becoming widely accepted that those entering the field need specialist training. But newness alone does not make the case for training. We need to look more closely at why training may be needed, who needs training, and what kind of training it should be.

WHY TRAIN?

I had no special training for distance education and I have been trying to analyse what I missed. My first tasks were programme evaluation and editing texts. I lacked specific skills for both these tasks and had to pick them up on the job. I made plenty of mistakes which might have been avoided if I had received training, but these were not serious and I got on reasonably well. Looking back, however, I can see a major shortcoming. I was working without a frame of reference. I had no concept of distance education, and without an organizing framework my work lacked a clear direction and was less effective than it could have been. I would have benefited from an induction course in distance education – although the term had not even been coined then in 1966.

I believe my experience remains relevant. People bring to distance education their existing expertise. To work effectively they need to acquire new skills and understand the context in which old and new expertise is to be applied. Thus training for newcomers needs to include two strands: induction to distance education, and the acquisition of additional technical skills.

It could be argued that both skills and an understanding of distance education could be acquired on the job. From the perspective of the teaching institution, there are two main reasons why this is a poor argument. First, distance education requires its full-time workers to take on multiple roles and depends on a substantial cohort of part-time workers, such as course writers, to complement the full-timers. Discovery learning is time consuming and inappropriate for such a complex educational process. Second, the nature of the distance education process is such that mistakes made at the design stage can only be rectified later at great cost, counted in time and energy as well as money. It is therefore important that those involved in programme design and development are well prepared. Staff training ought to be a priority for new institutions, while an established institution which introduces a new programme will probably recruit new staff for that programme who will also need training.

Training produces and fosters commitment. Many people who enter distance education have been attracted by a sense of its potential; their enthusiasm grows as they understand what to do and why. The benefit to their institutions can be great, with benefits in the longer term to the nation as well. Distance education is only gradually being accepted into the mainstream of education. The professionalization of the workforce will help that process, particularly where initial and further training helps the committed acquire confidence, status and recognition.

WHO SHOULD BE TRAINED? WHAT SHOULD THE TRAINING BE?

All distance educators need training. Who are these people? Distance educators use a confusing range of job titles for different basic functions, while different patterns of work organization mean that in some institutions individuals have multiple roles. It may be helpful simply to offer a list of categories of staff in distance education, using four key functions as a basis for classification:

- administrative staff; ranging from managers and planners to junior administrators
- those concerned with course design and development, including writers, editors, media technicians and producers
- those concerned with course presentation, including tutors and counsellors
- those concerned with research and evaluation.

We can start with an understanding that there is a common training need for everyone when they are first introduced to distance education. Prior to any specific job training, everyone needs a general orientation to distance education. Such training can vary in length and depth, but it has a common core the world over, covering the purposes, potential and methods of distance education. In addition each institution needs to provide its staff with guidance on its own particular aims, role and methods and on its expected student body. A dominant theme of any initial orientation programme should be the student-centred nature of distance education. People need to perceive how every distance education system is constructed round the requirements of learners.

Specifying training needs within each functional area is more difficult. I do not here consider in detail the training agenda for different categories of staff, but in Table 25.1, I provide a training model as an explanatory framework. The table is intended to serve as a framework for planning training, and the entries in each column are intended to be indicative rather than specific and comprehensive.

We can use the case of a tutor to illustrate these stages. When we appoint correspondence tutors we assume that they have subject expertise (Stage 1) and that they are trained teachers (Stage 2). We need, however, to train them to teach by correspondence (Stage 3) and we may need to provide them with additional training in the special requirements of teaching their particular discipline at a distance (Stage 4). And at every stage let us remember that tutors need to be encouraged to relate their new knowledge and skills to their local institutional context and their own learners.

The model identifies four stages of acquisition of expertise:

Stage 1 prerequisites: general education to an appropriate level such as a first degree at university;
Stage 2 basic pre-work training: professional training or experience at the beginning of working life;
Stage 3 basic in-work training: essential training in aspects of distance education related to their role;
Stage 4 further in-work training: advanced training in specialist aspects of distance education.

Entry into distance education comes generally after Stage 2. Occasionally, however, training may be needed in a Stage 2 skill that is essential for distance education and not commonly found among our recruits. For example, those recruited as tutors may lack expertise in techniques of adult education. Stages 3 and 4 are phases of development occurring after beginning work in distance education.

Table 25.1   The training model: functions, skills and training needs for distance education

Personnel functions	Stage 1 Basic expertise	Stage 2 Educational application	Stage 3 Distance education application	Stage 4 Specialized extension
1. Planners managers, administrators	management or administration	educational administration	distance education systems	personal function
2. Course designers a. academics and writers	subject knowledge	curriculum design and materials development	design of self-instructional materials	teaching own subject at a distance
b. editors and instructional designers	copy editing and design	editing and design of educational materials	editing self-instructional materials	specialist text design skills
c. media producers	media production	production of educational programmes	multi-media education	production for subject specialisms
3. Tutors and counsellors	subject knowledge	teacher training and adult education	teaching at a distance	discipline related teaching techniques
4. Researchers	research techniques	research in education	research in distance education	specialist skills

IMPLICATIONS OF THE MODEL

Table 25.1 enables us to tackle a number of questions about training:

- *What expertise should new recruits to distance education be expected to have?* Most new recruits should already have appropriate Stage 1 and Stage 2 skills.
- *What training should the institution expect to provide?* Normally we would expect to cover Stages 3 and 4 in staff development programmes. In some circumstances the institution may arrange Stage 2 training.

- *At what stages in the staff member's career should that training be?* Stage 3 could be immediately after appointment. Stage 4 can be combined with Stage 3 or follow when the staff member has more experience and is better able to benefit.
- *How extensive should it be?* For part-time staff, especially those on short-term contracts, training needs to be brief; for full-time permanent staff it can be longer and phased to encourage the steady consolidation of expertise.
- *What expertise should trainers possess?* Besides the job-related knowledge and skills that they must pass on to trainees, trainers need to be versed in training techniques and need confidence in their capacity to communicate effectively.

The model indicates clearly that training should follow a sequence. Broad educational training (Stage 2) must precede applications in distance education (Stage 3), which in turn must precede specialist applications (Stage 4). For example, training a writer to teach music at a distance must come after training in the preparation of self-instructional materials, which in turn comes after training in musical education and in the subject of music itself.

Given that there are linkages between roles and functions in distance education, we can also consider broader questions, such as what course developers should know about teaching by correspondence. A vertical reading of the columns in the training model suggests how we might proceed. We might conclude that all those who intend to make a career in distance education should in due course study all those items listed as Stage 3. The column reads like an outline syllabus for a diploma in distance education. There are in fact two options for those undergoing Stage 3 training. They may proceed horizontally to Stage 4 in the model, concentrating on developing expertise in their main area of interest, or they may follow, so to speak, a vertical path, covering all the topics in Stage 3. They may then go on to specialist Stage 4 studies. The first approach is appropriate for those who prefer to follow a narrow discipline-related path of career development, while the second is right for those who feel committed to distance education as a permanent career. I should also mention that a diploma based on Stage 3 combined with general orientation to distance education is appropriate pre-service training for those who wish to become distance educators.

We may also use the training model to consider how and when to meet specific training needs:

- Planning and management of distance education institutions
- Instructional design and course development
- Application of new technologies, including computers, in distance education

- Modifications and arrangements for use of course materials from other institutions.

We can immediately see that the first two areas are covered in the training suggestions for the first and second categories of staff. Area 3 is a specialist area of training for certain administrative and production staff, and therefore needs to come at Stage 4 after basic job training in distance education. Area 4 is also a specialist area, of concern in different ways to production and administrative staff.

Sometimes institutions need to recruit people without adequate Stage 2 training. If this occurs, then initial in-service training could combine Stages 2 and 3 and may be interdisciplinary. For example, training in techniques of management may need to be covered along with distance education techniques. Where an interdisciplinary approach occurs, there may be a need for collaboration in training. Later training (Stage 4) is highly specialized, and here again there is likely to be a need for collaboration, as each institution will only have a small number of personnel requiring each specialism, with a consequent need to look outside for training opportunities. Such considerations lead us to consider how and where training may take place, and who will be the trainers.

TRAINING MODES AND STRATEGIES

Training can be arranged in the following ways.

In-house

Informal

- peer attachments: someone new to a job works in partnership with an experienced person doing the same job, who demonstrates and explains what to do
- introductory work experience: a new member of staff spends a short time in every department in order to become familiar with the work of the entire organization. (I am not sure that this is a particularly useful strategy although I have heard it advocated and therefore note it)

Formal

- organised training sessions: seminars, workshops and short courses ranging from a few hours to several weeks
- self-study: using training packages devised or approved for in-house use

- study for professional qualifications provided by the institution (using distance or face-to-face mode of study)

Outside

Informal

- fellowships: time spent in another institution working in partnership with someone doing a similar job. (The reverse of this is an outsider visiting as a consultant and training one-to-one by working with an individual or with several individuals in turn)
- study tours: visits to several institutions to learn how they work, in order to apply that knowledge to one's own work

Formal

- organized training courses: seminars, workshops and short courses ranging from a few days to a few months
- study for professional qualifications through a period of attendance at another institution
- study for professional qualifications offered by another institution through distance study. (Although this last option allows people to be trained without going away, the training is designed, taught and validated by outsiders and cannot therefore be classified as in-house).

These training strategies are not mutually exclusive, and an institution needs to provide a number of different training opportunities for its staff to satisfy the needs outlined in the training model. Courses may be on an occasional or regular basis, with access and strategies varying according to whether staff are part-time and short-term or full-time and permanent. It is desirable for institutions to organize training so that there is a coherent long-term staff development plan.

It may look as though the informal strategies are the least demanding to implement. This is not the case. Informal strategies depend on competent people being willing to give up time. For peer attachments, the experienced staff member must allow double time for his or her work throughout the period of attachment, first to demonstrate an activity, and then to supervise and help the trainee to do it. Inter-institutional fellowships are particularly demanding, as visitors must be accommodated even if pressure of work mounts up unexpectedly, as so often happens in distance education.

Formal strategies all require trainers who not only understand the job of the trainees but are also competent in training techniques. In the absence of in-house trainers, institutions are forced to look outside for training. New institutions inevitably lack in-house training capacity and are therefore likely to send staff out for training or, alternatively, seek trainers who can come to them. Where outsiders are involved in training it is desirable that they work together with in-house personnel, in order that the training may be related to the institutional setting.

The analysis of training needs in the training model suggests that there is a common core of training in every area. This core needs to be complemented by an examination of the local setting and adapted accordingly. Training from outside, including study of a distance course offered by another institution, can lack this localizing element. We may need to consider home-based seminars or assignments to precede or follow up outside training and, for distance study, adapting or extending courses to suit a particular national setting, or using tutors from the home institution to mark and examine trainees' work.

Training that leads to a professional qualification is likely to take one or more years to complete, and is only suitable for those committed to a career in distance education. Such training need not always consist of a single programme of study. It should be possible to gain a qualification by completing a series of training modules which may include both distance and face-to-face study, and which may be offered by different providers but recognized by the award-giving authority.

COLLABORATIVE SETTINGS

Our consideration of training needs, modes and strategies has thrown up a number of potential collaborative settings, which can be used to illustrate how collaboration can be most effective.

Collaborative in-house training

Basic training in distance education

One or more outside trainers works with local partners on short courses providing basic (Stage 3) training in aspects of distance education, such as training course writers. Such assistance is particularly valuable for new institutions which lack training expertise amongst their own staff. It is most effective in circumstances where local partners are trainee trainers, who subsequently run training programmes independently. Continuity is also desirable, with the same institutions and personnel working together until the new institution becomes self-sufficient.

Example International Extension College distance education specialist worked with Indira Gandhi National Open University trainee trainers to provide orientation for new academics.

Training covering distance education and other aspects of education

A specialist trainer in distance education may work together with another specialist who covers Stage 2 skills. For example, a distance educator may train teachers to teach by correspondence alongside a specialist in adult education who trains them in adult education techniques. In many such cases collaboration may be arranged using local resources, but in countries where expertise in certain Stage 2 skills is in short supply, international collaboration may be necessary. For example, outsiders may be needed to train television producers in techniques of making educational programmes, while experts in distance education provide training in how to work in a multimedia setting. A distance teaching institution should not seek to develop an in-house capacity for training its own staff in Stage 2 skills but rather concentrate on training related specifically to distance education (Stages 3 and 4).

Example Namibian teachers writing English language courses needed help from an English language teaching expert to design their units (Stage 2), as well as guidance from a distance education expert in the development of self-instructional materials (Stage 3).

Specialist training

A specialist distance education trainer collaborates with a subject specialist, combining Stage 3 and Stage 4 training. Course writers may be trained on short courses by a combination of a specialist in designing distance education materials and a specialist in teaching a particular subject at a distance; for example, there are special difficulties in teaching science at a distance, and an experienced practitioner may work with a trainer to help new science course writers. This strategy is best reserved for institutions with relatively large groups of writers, or for particularly difficult subjects. It can also be used in the training of tutors, who are often recruited in fairly large numbers. For example, a health education expert may work with a distance education expert to train tutors for a health course. International experience can be particularly valuable when introducing courses in relatively unusual subjects like health.

Example Distance education expert from Ethiopia works with health education expert from AMREF in Kenya to train Namibians as distance tutors on a health course

Collaborative outside training

General basic training

A group of trainees from different institutions come together for training in one or more aspects of distance education as set out for Stage 3. Trainers may also be drawn from different institutions. Such training will normally take place on a national or regional basis, and be for staff of institutions or programmes unable to provide in-house training on a regular basis.

Example Training programmes for course writers run in Kenya on a regular basis, with trainers largely from the University of Nairobi and trainees from a number of Kenyan and other regional institutions involved in distance education.

Specialist training

A group of people with shared interest from several different institutions gather for advanced training. Specialist training (Stage 4) in particular subjects may only be wanted by one or two people in any one institution, hence the need for inter-institutional short courses. An example could be an international workshop on agricultural education at a distance.

Example This appears to be a largely unmet need. I cannot identify a recent example of an inter-institutional advanced course.

Professional training programmes

Individuals committed to a career in distance education may attend extended training programmes, for several months or more, perhaps leading to a professional qualification. Many travel abroad for such programmes. An important element of such training is always the sharing of experience amongst professionals, whether they are teachers or trainees. This could be enhanced by involving more practitioners as teachers on such programmes.

Example University of London/International Extension College training programmes in distance education up to Masters level where a wide range of international experience is always represented.

Collaboration in materials development

Development of training materials

Experts from more than one institution work together to design and develop training materials. This is difficult when the collaborators work from their separate institutions, but costly if they are brought together to work. Potentially it avoids duplication of effort and could result in a higher quality product. Adaptation or extension of existing training materials is another possibility which needs exploring.

Example Current development of Masters programme in distance education, which involves four universities working together on materials development.

Collaboration in informal training

Fellowships and visits

A trainee learns by watching and doing. Training fellowships are best tailor-made, and particularly useful if linked with a training course. Well-planned visits are also useful, and should be open to all (senior staff tend to get more than their fair share). As internships, attachments and visits are individualized, they are rather expensive and probably under-rated and under-used.

Example An administrative officer from the University of Nairobi completes a general course in distance education at London University and then has a month's training fellowship to acquire some basic computing skills and examine computerized systems of student record-keeping in British distance education institutions.

Self-help training

In some cases advanced training needs no specialist training input. Interest groups can meet to share experience and help each other informally to develop expertise. Such meetings are particularly valuable for those involved in new ventures in distance education, such as the training of trainers.

Example An interest group on nurse education at a distance was set up by International Council for Distance Education members; meetings resulted in publication of a book.

THE NEED FOR COLLABORATION

Collaboration in training distance educators is necessary, once institutions give priority to training and particularly once training is considered to be a component of in-house staff development programmes. It is necessary and/or desirable for four reasons:

- there is a lack of trainers; new institutions lack staff with sufficient experience to train, and established small units may lack training capacity
- advanced training is specialized; because it applies to small numbers in most institutions, it often needs to take place in inter-institutional groups or through exchanges
- exchange of experience between institutions is a valuable component of training and could be essential for some categories of staff
- training at a distance or from self-study packages is an important mode of training, to be used as an alternative or complement to other modes of training; since there is a common core of skills and knowledge to be acquired by each category of staff, collaboration in the preparation and use of training materials is desirable.

Barriers to collaboration

An earlier section sketched a number of collaborative settings, with examples. There are a number of constraints which affect all forms of collaboration, and in doing so reinforce a tendency for cooperation to take the form of aid rather than exchange. In many distance education institutions, management lacks commitment to training, an understanding of its benefits, and the resources to initiate a training programme. Many directors acknowledge that training is useful, but do little to introduce a training policy. Perhaps one or two senior staff are allowed to go for training abroad, and the occasional in-house seminar occurs, probably unrelated to the needs of the staff. Conditions of employment may restrict training, such as rules which prevent new staff from travelling abroad, at the very time when they need experience elsewhere. Managers may not see the need to bend the rules. Such a *laissez-faire* approach needs to be replaced by a long-term staff development strategy, which will require resources. With foresight and commitment it may be possible to allocate finance, and designate staff to be trained as trainers if training opportunities at that level are available. Few are at present, so little encourages managers to change their views.

Inter-institutional and international constraints are even greater. If there is to be collaboration and exchange, both partners must be willing; often visitors arriving for training fellowships are seen as a burden, an interruption to work. The attitude needs to change to receptivity. Although people from poorer countries may learn more from working in an environment that resembles their own than from the rich world, movement is often easier between rich and poor countries. Horizontal movement can be impeded by currency and visa restrictions.

Bilateral agencies give added encouragement to North–South movement through their preference for exchange: between their own country and the recipient. They also like to package their support to institutions in the form of a project. This has the advantage of coherence and continuity, especially when the project creates an enduring link between institutions; it has the disadvantage of excluding components which do not match the donor's guidelines, such as regional or third country activities.

Finally, international collaboration on training is, like in-house training, constrained by the shortage of trainers.

Despite these constraints, better use could be made of existing training options. One reason why training opportunities are under-used is that information about them does not reach all those who need them. A second reason is that mechanisms to make collaboration easier need to be put in place. The Commonwealth of Learning can have a role in this.

REQUIREMENTS FOR COLLABORATION

The first requirement for easier collaboration is information. What training opportunities are available? What face-to-face courses and what materials? What are the training needs of staff in distance education? How can they be met? What should be taught and who should teach it? What experience do they need and where can they get it?

A contingent requirement is consultation, needed to collect and disseminate information and discuss and arrange forms of collaboration. Who will collaborate with whom? Who provides training? When and how? Who will be trained?

Collaboration cannot occur without resources. Both finance and personnel are needed, and donor agencies need to be prepared to release funds, to match whatever contributions the recipients of training are able to make. And, if the partners in collaboration include donor agencies as well as teaching institutions and their governments, flexibility is needed. We have seen that effective staff development requires a combination of strategies. Donors need to be flexible in their provision of funding and technical support, while employers of trainees need to allow individuals a suitable sequence of training activities, if necessary by-passing the normal rules.

Finally collaboration requires ease of movement between partners. Mobility is possible only with funds that may be used for travel and, where travel for nationals is restricted, the active support of employing institutions and their governments. That brings us full circle to the need for institutional commitment to training, which is more likely to develop as more training opportunities become available and information about them is widely disseminated.

26 Key issues in distance education: an academic viewpoint

Börje Holmberg

CONCEPTS

A first key issue is the use of concepts in distance education. Most participants in the scholarly debate seem to agree with me that the term 'distance education' covers the various forms of study at all levels which are not under the continuous, immediate supervision of tutors present with their students in lecture rooms or on the same premises, but which nevertheless benefit from the planning, guidance and tuition of a tutorial organisation. Distance study denotes the activity of the students, distance teaching that of the tutorial organization, particularly its authors and tutors (Holmberg 1985a: 1). This working definition implies that, while distance study may well be supplemented by face-to-face sessions, only mediated contact, i.e. non-contiguous communication, is taken to be a characteristic of distance education *per se*.

Normally there are two elements in the distance education process: on the one hand, subject-matter presentation by means of a pre-produced course, i.e. one-way traffic; on the other, communication between students and tutors in writing, on the telephone, by computer and/or other media. One question is whether the offer of a pre-produced course only – without any real two-way traffic – can constitute distance education. While I would not recommend this as an ideal model, I think it must logically be accepted as distance education *if* the pre-produced course resembles a kind of conversation in that the course addresses the student in a personal way, invites him/her to consider and query arguments, attempts to involve the student emotionally by referring to his/her experiences and interests, and generally simulates communication.

The emergence of the concept of open learning makes it necessary to clarify the relations between this and distance education. Contrary to what has been claimed (Lewis and Spencer 1986: 8), distance education can in no way be regarded as a subset of open learning, since the latter must, if the term is to mean anything, be characterized by openness in some respect (open access, open curricula, openness as to periods of study, choice of communication facilities or of approaches of one kind or another). While the British Open University is in at least one respect open, this cannot be said about all distance teaching organizations. Strict entrance requirements, study limited to term time, prescribed pacing, etc., characterize some of these (the West German FernUniversität, for example). The latter apply distance education, but do not cater for open learning in the sense indicated.

In the UK, there is at present a tendency to call all distance education 'open learning' (Thorpe 1987: 56). This is a misnomer from the linguistic point of view, but may represent a trend strong enough gradually to change common usage (as distance education, although nowadays the internationally accepted term, is nowhere a particularly well-liked designation). (See part 1 of Holmberg 1989a.) At the present time the two concepts should be kept clearly apart in the interest of clarity.

A further conceptual matter of relevance is the meaning given to teaching in distance education. This, however, would seem to belong to the next issue to be discussed.

DOES DISTANCE EDUCATION MAINLY CATER FOR CRAMMING AND/OR DOES IT REPRESENT A TRULY EDUCATIONAL ACTIVITY FAVOURING STUDENT AUTONOMY?

The effectiveness of distance education procedures in bringing about learning success cannot be doubted. There has been evidence galore of its excellent results ever since the early studies carried out by Childs, Granholm and others. An important academic concern is to what extent distance education has merely served as a mediator to make students assimilate facts for learning and to what extent it has served more academic purposes. There can be little doubt that in a great number of distance education projects the teaching offered has been little but knowledge transfer 'from one vessel to another' (Fox 1983: 151), but that in others the teaching has offered expert guidance engaging students in individual work and has focused 'attention on the intellectual and emotional development' of the distant student.

> Distance education as a means of imparting knowledge is, in principle, open and not tied to certain aims, purposes or contents. In reality distance education naturally serves the aims of other institutions or society in its widest sense. This is made evident by the fact that distance education would seem to be used mainly in the field of professional training. Content being transmitted in this way will presumably to a large extent – as in all

other educational situations – fit into a framework of professional, scholarly and other conventions. Through the content of their study material the distant students assimilate in a complex manner the conventions of constructivist thinking and its view of the world. Examination results support their conviction that they have acquired a correct view of the world or rather of one facet of the world.

(Lehner 1986: 70)

A self-contained course, which does not cause students to consult other sources of knowledge, may on the one hand be very effective, but on the other hand, it may not engage students in a scrutiny of arguments and develop their thinking. However, such a course can easily become autocratic, telling students not only what to do but what conclusions are the proper ones, thus depriving them of the exercise of their own criticism and judgement. Ways out of this difficulty have been found, but the problem remains a key issue.

The first step on the way towards more academic types of study is to develop courses functioning as study guides to set texts, which consist of papers and extracts from books through which students get into direct contact with authoritative specialist writings. Such texts are usually reproduced in so-called 'readers'. Sometimes, particularly in Australia, where copyright conditions seem to favour distance education (L. Moore 1987: 26), photocopies of new contributions to learned journals are also distributed to students. While this is a practical and, from the students' angle, a time-saving procedure, it evidently limits their choice of literature. Only the use of well-equipped libraries can offer better solutions. Providing library services for distant students is no easy matter; pioneering work here has been done in Australia, e.g. at Deakin University (Winter and Cameron 1983).

Further steps on the same path cause project work of different kinds to be used in distance education. While this type of work demands excellent library services and availability of highly competent supervisors, there is much evidence to show its effectiveness in distance study at the university level (Bynner 1986).

These endeavours to render distance education as 'academic' as conventional university education evidently coincide with attempts to make students as autonomous as possible. Some basic research on student autonomy in distance education that should be mentioned has been done by Moore, who has shown that autonomous persons are particularly attracted to distant methods of learning and teaching, although it has also been found that distant students do not reject guidance (M. Moore 1976).

THE APPLICATION POTENTIALS OF DISTANCE EDUCATION

Traditionally, distance education has addressed individual adults studying in their spare time. Equally traditionally, universities (in the Anglo-Saxon world at least) have tended to teach groups of students, preparing them for simultaneous examinations. When distance education methods have been applied to university teaching and learning, this group thinking has been taken over in a number of cases, particularly in Canada and Australia. This often leads to a type of control of students which is evidently in conflict with endeavours to promote autonomy. A striking example is offered by the work of the Canadian University of Waterloo, described as follows:

> We have fixed starting times for a course, a fixed schedule of assignments, a fixed duration of a course, and a fixed examination schedule. Our approach is to treat students as members of a class, although that class is distributed geographically. Thus our students start a course together at the same time and have to submit assignments and write examinations on a schedule in exactly the same way as a class on campus is required to do.
>
> (Leslie 1979: 36)

In cases like this, distance education merely represents a mode of distribution and is simply a substitute for face-to-face education. A key issue is if this is all that distance education can and should offer.

A different kind of distance education offers students opportunities to study entirely individually what, when and where it suits them, to start and finish when they want to, to submit assignments and communicate with the distance teaching organization at any time, and generally to adapt their study to the conditions of adult life, including job, family and social commitments. In such cases the courses and the tuition address the individual, not a group. The student may have chosen a unique combination of courses and may work at a speed that is quicker or slower than that of any other student.

Most probably the overwhelming majority of distance teaching organizations in the world address individuals rather than groups and, in doing so, to varying degrees safeguard student autonomy. Reporting in 1988 on a comprehensive international research project, I could state:

> Great interest in maintaining and developing student independence is expressed. A clear correlation between success rates and approaches favouring student independence was found. These approaches include individual (free) pacing of the study as to assignment submission, the possibility for students to influence the study content and encouraging querying attitudes among them . . . the majority of the organizations studied do not pace their students but allow them to submit assignments

when it suits their individual timetables. This seems to be a tangible sign of belief in the value of student independence.

(Graff and Holmberg 1988: 90)

Paradoxically enough, the deviations from the individualized type of distance study are mainly found among universities, not among schools offering general education and/or occupational professional training, although the academic endeavours discussed above would seem to go better with the more independent, individual variety of distance education than with the control and pacing caused by the co-ordination required by class or group teaching. The two categories to some extent overlap with the large-scale and small-scale approaches to distance education that I have identified elsewhere (Holmberg 1985a: 8–10).

COMMUNICATION BETWEEN DISTANCE TEACHING ORGANISATIONS AND STUDENTS

Both subject-matter presentation and, on the other hand, tutorial and counselling support are brought about by non-contiguous means. For this, media are required.

It has long been a dream of many educators to create a standard taxonomy ascribing specific functions and applications to individual media so that a natural, logical choice could be made for each individual part of a course of study. Several attempts to develop such a taxonomy have, in fact, been made (Handal 1973).

In distance education, the selection possibilities are often extremely limited. The printed and written word on the one hand and audio-recordings on the other sometimes exhaust the selection opportunities. Suitable combinations of these offer additional choices. It may, for instance, be useful to provide recorded instructions on how to study charts and pictures presented in printed form, a procedure which has proved profitable for target groups with little reading skill. In other cases, however, the choice can be made among several media, for instance, apart from the written and printed word, radio and TV broadcasting, audio- and video-recordings, kits for individual laboratory exercises (in, for example, electronics) and supplementary face-to-face tutorials.

At the present time, when the presentation of text and graphics on a screen instead of on paper is becoming more and more common (videotex, teletext), we should ask ourselves if or to what extent this is a desirable development. It is undoubtedly desirable when urgent, really new information is provided, i.e. information not available in books or articles (the parallel with information about rates of exchange, airplane bookings, etc., is illuminating), but in other cases I am inclined strongly to doubt its value. The same applies to computer print-outs.

For teaching purposes, the presentation of verbal subject-matter in print is in all respects decidedly superior to screen (computer) presentation: it is easier to read, it facilitates leafing and browsing and it is open to all sources available, not only such as have been deemed suitable by decision makers for computer storage or microfiche presentation. There can be no doubt that for all serious study the reading of printed material will remain a prime medium, in distance education often in combination with audio-recordings.

This applies to the one-way traffic concerned with subject-matter presentation. The situation is very different for mediated two-way communication. The great weakness of distance education has in most cases been the slowness of the communication process caused by the corresponding method dominating this kind of education. For a student assignment to be sent by the student, received by the supporting organization, corrected, commented on and returned to the student so that he/she receives it within a week is considered remarkably quick and represents a turnaround time that many distance education institutions (and post offices) seem unable to achieve. Counselling distance students is subject to the same delay. So far, mainly telephone communication has been used to overcome this difficulty, but in most cases where problem-solving in writing, essays and translations are the objects of communications, the telephone is mainly a supplementary teaching medium and remains so even if it is combined with teletransmission of written elements, drawings, etc.

Here modern information technology offers elegant solutions through electronic mail. The principle is that students submit assignments and papers of various kinds by typing the text into their personal computers (or terminals). These communications are tele-transmitted to the computers of the individual tutors or that of the supporting organization, for which a modem is required, and are stored in their mailboxes (teleboxes) where the tutors pick them up to comment on and then return them by telecommunication. By special equipment, called 'printers', both students and tutors can have the complete messages typed out on paper, which is usually necessary. The fact that an international standard for electronic mail has been developed seems to indicate that this technical means of communicating has great potential also in distance education. Evidently a basic condition is the availability of personal computers, modems and printers. Vivian reports on experiments with electronic mail in New South Wales, which among other things show that the 'turnaround time of lessons was dramatically reduced from 2–4 weeks to a matter of days, hours or occasionally even minutes' (Vivian 1986: 246).

What makes this and other possibilities to speed up communication particularly important in distance education is the fact that short turnaround times are very important to students. Empirical evidence shows that while students seem to accept and profit from comments and corrections given within a week after an assignment has been completed, they are usually dissatisfied if the delay is of longer duration. Students expect full comments on their submitted work within as few days as possible. Completion rates have been shown to correlate with turnaround time (and also with encouraging, 'reminding' letters on the occasions when students have been passive for a period) (Rekkedal 1983). Audio- and videoconferencing offer further possibilities (Robertson 1987).

On new media in distance education, Bates (1984) provides an authoritative and a particularly useful presentation. The academic importance of media depends on their potentials for facilitating and speeding up subject-matter presentation and the communication process.

Naturally, the basic concern is what is communicated and how it is done. So far the latter question has barely been touched on in this chapter. Both theoretical considerations and practical experiences have shown that handbook-style and matter-of-fact communication rarely meet students' needs and requirements. A number of studies of course structure as related to communication, language and graphics effective in distance education have been carried out, however (Waller 1977a, Waller 1977b; Macdonald-Ross 1979, Bååth 1980; Doerfert 1980; Rowntree 1986, among others).

A growing concern of academics is the possibility that course development, tutor–student communication and counselling will be guided by considerations of profitability. The following section puts forward the view that this should not be so and that empathy should be taken to be the guiding principle for these activities.

EMPATHY AS A CHARACTERISTIC OF DISTANCE EDUCATION

'Empathy' is usually taken to mean the power of projecting oneself into and understanding someone else's thinking and feeling. A certain amount of empathy in relation to students' work and situation is in my view required of all distance educators.

General theoretical approach

Basically, empathy in our context would seem to denote the capacity and readiness to experience and, as it were, personally to feel students' uncertainty, anxiety and hesitation on the one hand, their confidence, intellectual pleasure and '*eureka*' sensations on the other hand, and share these experiences with them. Empathy in this sense is evidently conducive to counsellor behaviour likely to facilitate mutual understanding and personal contact between students and counsellors. This could, but should not, be interpreted as a hand-holding kind of support, as it were *in loco parentis*.

Distant students are usually mature adults well capable of handling problems and difficulties. Most of them have limited or no experience of what independent study alongside family, social and professional commitments can be like, however, and quite a few seem to be exaggeratedly aware of their own intellectual limitations. Distance education organizations have to pay attention to this in their course development, their tuition and their counselling. Experience fairly generally testifies to practice along these lines as far as the density of information and readability of courses are concerned. It seems more doubtful if the principles of empathy are generally adhered to in subject-matter presentation and tutoring at a distance. This hesitation would seem to apply also to counselling, which – apart from student-centred practice particularly in countries under Anglo-Saxon influence – is too often almost exclusively a pre-study activity.

Empathy in distance education implies more than understanding conducive to helping students to master difficulties. I submit that in serious study most of us feel a need to share discoveries and intellectual experiences with someone else, to exchange views and through this exchange learn confidently to work with the intellectual matter concerned. This evidently implies a need for dialogue. Disregarding the face-to-face elements that in some, but not most, cases supplement distance education, we must find ways to cater non-contiguously for something functioning in the way that dialogue does. This is evidently necessary if we wish to pave the way for the development of empathy.

Distance education theories related to the empathy approach

Thinking along these lines has generated some theory contributions immediately relevant to distance education. These contributions are concerned with both course development and with non-contiguous communication. To the former belong Forsythe's studies of the learning system (Forsythe 1986), Nation's evaluation of 'personal style' (Nation 1985) and others; to the latter, Bååth's and Rekkedal's studies of assignment submission (Bååth 1980; Rekkedal 1983, 1985). While the former underline the importance of dialogue-like course presentation in the form of simulated communication, the latter concentrate on the frequency, speed and personal character of real non-contiguous communication.

THEORY OF DISTANCE EDUCATION

There is evidently some kind of theoretical assumption behind each of the various components and actions involved in distance education. The preceding section will have illuminated this.

Search for an inclusive theory of distance education is a final key issue to be discussed. Keegan comments on this as follows.

A theory is something that eventually can be reduced to a phrase, a sentence or a paragraph and which, while subsuming all the practical research, gives the foundation on which the structures of need, purpose and administration can be erected. A firmly based theory of distance education will be one which can provide the touchstone against which decisions – political, financial, educational, social – when they have to be taken, can be taken with confidence. This would replace the *ad hoc* response to a set of conditions that arises in some 'crisis' situation of problem solving, which normally characterizes this field of education.

(Keegan 1983: 3)

Attempts have been made to meet these tough requirements. As early as 1970, Graff developed a decision model on the basis of a study of the structure and process of distance education, but concluded that the great problems are beyond calculation (Graff 1970: 54).

Perraton (1981, 1987) has ventured other suggestions as steps on the path toward a theory of distance education, and so has the present author in applying hypothetico-deductive methods. Presentations of various theoretical approaches to distance education occur in Keegan (1986) and Holmberg (1985b).

The relation of distance education to a series of well-known theoretical concepts of relevance to general education (among them Skinner's behaviourism, Ausubel's cognitivism, Bruner's discovery learning and Rogers' facilitation of learning) has been analysed by Bååth (1979). In my book (Holmberg 1989a), I present a theory largely based on the empathy approach, which has generated a number of hypotheses testable by refutation attempts in Popper's spirit. Some of them have, in fact, been tested. These hypotheses are of three types: those concerned with distance learning, those with distance teaching and those bearing on organization and administration.

The requirements that the theory is meant to satisfy are those usually expected of educational theories, i.e. that they should

- have internal consistency as logical systems;
- establish functional relationships between the teaching and the outcomes of learning;
- be capable of generating specific hypotheses and predictions;

• be expressed in such a way that research data capable of possibly refuting (falsifying) the theory can be collected.

My theory with its hypotheses in this spirit stresses prediction more than a truly Popperian theory would do (Popper 1980: 61). However, it would seem to have some explanatory power as it implies a consistent view of effective learning and teaching in distance education that identifies a general approach favourable to learning and to the teaching efforts conducive to learning.

Whether and to what extent theoretical approaches like Perraton's or mine will be felt to be fruitful is difficult to foresee. Mine is to be regarded as a modest attempt to suggest guidelines for action while bringing some cohesion into the thinking related to distance education. To me this is a further academic key issue in distance education.

REFERENCES

Bååth, J. A. (1979) *Correspondence Education in the Light of a Number of Contemporary Teaching Models*, Malmö: Liber Hermods.

Bååth, J. A. (1980) *Postal Two-way Communication in Correspondence Education*, Lund: Gleerup.

Bååth, J. A. (1984) 'Pride and prejudice among distance educators', *ICDE Bulletin* 5: 70–3.

Bates, A. W. (ed.) (1984) *The Role of Technology in Distance Education*, London: Croom Helm.

Bradbury, P., Hinds, E., Humm, M. and Robbins, D. (1982) 'Innovations in independent study at North East London Polytechnic', in D. C. B. Teather (ed.) *Towards the Community University: Case Studies of Innovation and Community Service*, London: Kogan Page, 46–8.

Bynner, J. M. (1986) 'Masters teaching in education by distance methods', *Distance Education* 7, 1: 23–37.

Chang, T. M., Crombag, H. F., Van der Drift, K. D. and Moonen, J. M. (1983) *Distance Learning: on the Design of an Open University*, Boston: Kluwer-Nijhoff.

Childs, G. B. (1971) 'Recent research developments in correspondence instruction', in O. Mackenzie and E. Christensen (eds) *The Changing World of Correspondence Study*, University Park: The Pennsylvania State University Press, 229–49.

Coughlan, R. (1980) 'The mentor role in individualized education at Empire State College', *Distance Education* 1, 1: 1–12.

Doerfert, F. (1980) *Zur Wirksamkeit typografischer und grafischer Elemente in gedruckten Fernstudienmaterialien*, Hagen: FernUniversität ZIFF.

Elton, L., Oliver, E. and Wray, M. (1986) 'Academic staff training at a distance – a case study', *Programmed Learning and Educational Technology* 23, 1: 29–40.

Forsythe, K. (1986) *Understanding the Effectiveness of Media in the Learning Process*, paper presented at the World Congress on Education and Technology in Vancouver, May 1986, Victoria, B. C. : Learning Systems, Knowledge Network.

Fox, D. (1983) 'Personal theories of teaching', *Studies in Higher Education* 8, 2: 151–63.

Graff, K. (1970) *Voraussetzungen erfolgreichen Fernstudiums. Dargestellt am Beispiel des schwedischen Fernstudiensystems*, Hamburg: Ludke.

Graff, K. and Holmberg, B. (eds) (1988) *International Study on Distance Education: a Project Report*, Hagen: FernUniversität ZIFF.

Granholm, G. (1971) 'Classroom teaching or home study – a summary of research on relative efficiency', *Epistolodidaktika* 2: 9–14.

Handal, G. (1973) 'On the selection of relevant media/methods for defined educational purposes', in G. Granholm (ed.) *The Selection of Relevant Media/Methods for Defined Educational Purposes within Distance Education*, Oslo: NKI, 1–32.

Hinds, E. (1987) *The School for Independent Study and International Links*, Hagen: FernUniversität (ZIFF Papiere 69).

Holmberg, B. (1983) 'Guided didactic conversation in distance education', in D. Sewart, D. Keegan and B. Holmberg (eds) *Distance Education: International Perspectives*, London: Croom Helm, 114–22.

Holmberg, B. (1985a) *Status and Trends of Distance Education*, 2nd revised edn, Lund: Lector Publishing.

Holmberg, B. (1985b) *The Feasibility of a Theory of Teaching for Distance Education and a Proposed Theory*, Hagen: FernUniversität (ZIFF Papiere 60).

Holmberg, B. (1986) *Growth and Structure of Distance Education*, London: Croom Helm.

Holmberg, B. (1989a) *Theory and Practice of Distance Education*, London: Routledge.

Holmberg, B. (1989b) 'The concepts and applications of distance education and open learning', *International Journal of Innovative Higher Education* 6, 1 and 2.

Holmberg B., Schuemer, R. and Obermeier, A. (1982) *Zur Effizienz des gelenkten didaktischen Gespräches* (with an English summary), Hagen: FernUniversität ZIFF.

Keegan, D. (1983) *Six Distance-education Theorists*, Hagen: FernUniversität ZIFF.

Keegan, D. (1986) *The Foundations of Distance Education*, London: Croom Helm.

Lehner, H. (1986) *Konstruktivismus und Fernstudium*, Hagen: FernUniversität ZIFF.

Leslie, J. D. (1979) 'The University of Waterloo model for distance education', *Canadian Journal of University Continuing Education* 6, 1: 33–42.

Lewis, B. N. (1975) 'Conversational man', *Teaching at a Distance* 2: 68–70.

Lewis, R. and Spencer, D. (1986) *What is Open Learning?* London: Council for Educational Technology.

Macdonald-Ross, M. (1979) 'Language in texts: a review of research relevant to the design of curricular materials', in L. S. Shulman (ed.) *Review of Research in Education*, 6, Itasca, Ill. : Peacock.

Marshall, L. (1984) *Independent Study Contracts: a Guide for Students Considering Applying for Independent Study Contracts and for Staff who Supervise them*, Perth: Murdoch University.

Moore, L. (1987) 'The Australian law of copyright and its application to distance education', *Distance Education* 8, 1: 18–37.

Moore, M. (1976) 'Investigation of the interaction between the cognitive style of field-independence and attitudes to independent study among adult learners who use correspondence independent study and self-directed independent study', unpublished doctoral dissertation, Madison: University of Wisconsin.

Moore, M. (1977) 'A model of independent study', *Epistolodidaktika* 1: 6–40.

Nation, D. with the assistance of Elliott, C. (1985) 'I'm sorry to bother you at home but you said we could ring', paper presented to the Thirteenth World Conference of the International Council for Distance Education, Melbourne, Australia, August 1985, microfiche.

Perraton, H. (1981) 'A theory for distance education', *Prospects* 11, 1: 13–24.

Perraton, H. (1987) 'Theories, generalisation and practice in distance education', *Open Learning* 2, 3: 3–12.

Popper, K. (1980) *The Logic of Scientific Discovery*, London: Hutchinson.

Rekkedal, T. (1983) 'The written assignments in correspondence education: effects of reducing turn-around time. An experimental study', *Distance Education* 4, 2: 231–52. (A translation of: 'Innsendingsoppgavene i brevundervisningen', 1973).

Rekkedal, T. (1985) *Introducing the Personal Tutor/Counsellor in the System of Distance Education. Project Report 2: Final report*, Oslo: NKI.

Robertson, B. (1987) 'Audio teleconferencing: low cost technology for external studies networking', *Distance Education* 8, 1: 121–36.

Rowntree, D. (1986) *Teaching through Self-instruction: a Practical Handbook for Course Developers*, London: Kogan Page.

Thorpe, M. (1987) 'Conference report: Association of European Correspondence Schools (AECS) Autumn Congress 1986 in Munich', *Open Learning* 2, 2: 56.

Tight, M. (1986) 'Defining distance education', *ICDE Bulletin* 18: 56–60.

Vivian, V. (1986) 'Electronic mail in a children's distance course: trial and evaluation', *Distance Education* 7, 2: 237–60.

Waller, R. (1977a) *Three Functions of Text Presentation*, Milton Keynes: Open University Institute of Educational Technology (Notes on transforming 2).

Waller R. (1977b) *Typographic Access Structure for Educational Texts*, Milton Keynes: Open University Institute of Educational Technology.

Winter, A. and Cameron, M. (1983) *External Sudents and their Libraries*, Geelong: Deakin University.

Worth, V. (1982) *Empire State College/State University of New York Center for Distance Learning*, Milton Keynes: Open University (Distance Education Research Group Papers 7).

Index

346 *Index*

Resources Consortium (SERC) 217;
Smithsonian Institution 212;
Southern California Consortium
211; Star Schools Project 216, 220;
Technical Education Resource
Centers 217; TI–IN United Star
Network 217; University of Chicago
209; University of Georgia 143;
University of Mid-America 211;
University of Wisconsin 191
USSR 62, 66, 70, 71, 240

van den Brande, L. 8
Venezuela 240, 241, 256; Universidad
Nacional Abierta 94, 105
Vertecchi, B. 2–3, 112, 126–6
video 98, 99, 100, 101, 105, 159, 174,
311
videocassettes 42, 101, 159, 169, 176,
177, 181–3, 185, 187, 188, 190,
195, 202, 244, 267, 313
videoconferencing 42, 43, 209–23,
224–9, 308–9; videodiscs 97, 176,
185, 188, 189, 200, 202

videographics 202
videotex 157, 158–9, 162, 165–6, 170
200, 202, 204, 205, 206, 334
viewdata 188
Vivian, V. 113, 290, 335

Wagner, L 98, 104
Waller, R. 139, 141, 149, 151, 336
Wedemeyer, C. 10, 13, 239
word processing 163, 168
work-based learning 189
World Bank 173, 253–4, 258, 268–9

Yugoslavia 70

Zambia 73, 250, 252, 283; University
of Zambia 256; Zambian National
Correspondence College 284
Zhao Yuhui 235
Zimbabwe 253, 255; University of
Zimbabwe 256; Zimbabwe
Integrated Teacher Education
Course (ZINTEC) 255